THE ELEMENTS
OF USER
INTERFACE DESIGN

THEO MANDEL, PHD

WILEY COMPUTER PUBLISHING

John Wiley & Sons, Inc.

New York ◆ Chichester ◆ Weinheim ◆ Brisbane ◆ Singapore ◆ Toronto

Executive Publisher: Katherine Schowalter
Editor: Theresa Hudson
Managing Editor: Angela Murphy
Text Design & Composition: North Market Street Graphics

This text is printed on acid-free paper.

Library of Congress Cataloging-in-Publication Data:

Mandel, Theo.
  The elements of user interface design / Theo Mandel.
      p.   cm.
  Includes bibliographical references.
  ISBN 0-471-16267-1 (pbk. : alk. paper)
    1. User interfaces (Computer systems)   I. Title.
  QA76.9.U83M345   1997
  005.1′2— dc20   96-45973

Printed in the United States of America
10 9 8

For confused and frustrated computer users, especially Max Garrett, my father-in-law.

To the continued remembrance of my parents, Dorothy and Siegfried.

And to my wife, Edie, for always being there for me.

Man is one of the best general-purpose computers available and if one designs for man as a moron, one ends up with a system that requires a genius to maintain it. Thus we are not suggesting that we take man out of the system, but we are suggesting that he be properly employed in terms of both his abilities and limitations.

E. Llewellyn Thomas (1965)

ACKNOWLEDGMENTS

I want to thank the following for their support:

- Wendy Francis, Mary Lea Garrett, Judy Underwood, and Doug Brown.
- Terri Hudson and Moriah O'Brien at John Wiley & Sons, Inc.
- David McCreath of Monsterbit Media, for his great graphics work.
- The technical reviewers and copyeditor of the book, whoever they are.
- My professional colleagues throughout the world: Ed Kennedy, Pat Dorazio, Dick Berry, Chuck Schafer, David Schwartz, Christoph Moser, and Andre Geiser.
- My tennis buddies John Collins, Kimm Ketelsen, John Matthews, Mark Olman, Duke Paluch, Peter D'Auray, and Gary Brieden for keeping me in shape.
- Steve Zaslow for providing doubles support in tennis years ago and printing support now.
- Dave Brown and Steve Shipps, my all-time best friends.
- Tracy Leonard, for what we've done together in the past and what we hope to do together in the future.
- Cindy Roosken, whom I forgot to acknowledge in my first book.
- John Rothgeb, for his PC support.
- Kurt Westerfeld of Stardock Systems, Inc., for his ideas and his product, Object Desktop.
- Lauralee Alben, for allowing me to use her material on the ACM/ *interactions* Design Awards '95.

Computers and User Interfaces

- *Do your programs work together intuitively as if they were all one program?*
- *Can you simply drag text, data and graphics from one program and drop them into another?*
- *Is your software intelligent? For instance, can it handle everyday tasks automatically?*
- *Are your programs recognized as the best in their category?*
- *Do your menus, toolbars and other elements look alike and work in the same easy way?*
- *Do your programs have no-charge product support? For how long?*
- *Ultimately, is it worth getting software that doesn't do all these things?*

Software advertisement (1995)

Today's computers utilize a new breed of software that revolutionizes the way people work. The popular belief is that these new systems make people's lives easier and their computing experiences "friendlier." Do they really? If all software products were as well designed as they are advertised to be, all computer users would be very happy in their work and play. Unfortunately, computer software is not as intuitive, easy to learn, easy to use, and as fun as it could be *and should be.*

Why is software *look and feel* so important? What makes a product easy to install, easy to learn, or easy to use? What do tests tell us about the usability of software products? How can you tell what software users want or even need? How about your customers? What types of software and user interfaces do they need? Where are computer user interfaces headed in the future? These are all difficult questions, but one thing is certain—the user interface must be a key element in your software solutions.

Who Is This Book For?

Here are some "typical" attitudes about user interface design from different participants in the software development process.

Executive—"I'll worry about the user interface when someone can demonstrate that it makes a difference in my sales."

Project Manager—"Yes, I'm sure you would love to do some field testing with users, but there's no slack in the schedule or budget."

System Designer—"That's trivial, let them handle it in the user interface."

Software Engineer—"When I'm done they have somebody who comes around and makes the screen look pretty."

Interface Engineer—"Isn't it exciting, I get to design the user interface all by myself!"

Customer—"We require that any software we buy have a GUI, you know, a Generic User Interface."

Bill Curtis and Bill Hefley (1994)

This book is written for a wide range of people involved in software design and development:

- ◆ Software developers
- ◆ Interface designers
- ◆ Information developers and technical writers
- ◆ Help and tutorial developers
- ◆ Usability professionals
- ◆ Project leaders
- ◆ Development managers
- ◆ Students of software design and development

KEY IDEA! *Software design is a team effort—a key theme throughout this book. When I write about developers, I am addressing the members of design and development teams, which include programmers, interface designers, and others. The final outcome of a product is also influenced by other areas—company owners, senior management, marketing, and sales staff members. This book stresses the cooperation between developer and designer. The intent is to foster this cooperation and to avoid an "us versus them" mentality.*

A major theme of this book is "Know thy users, for they are not you!" (See Figure P.1.) Computer users have become extremely consumer oriented and software products must fit how users function in their own environments, or they risk developing an unsuccessful product. You'll learn that the best interface is the one that lets *users* do *what* they want to do, *when* they want to do it, and *how* they want to do it. Successful software design requires the utmost concern for the appropriateness and usability of the interfaces that are presented to users.

This book describes in great detail what a software user interface really is, and its importance for users, designers, and developers. The user interface of any product—especially a computer software program—is probably the most important part, at least to users. You'll find out *why* the user interface is so critical to computer software. The user interface must be designed *for,* and even *with,* users of a product. When users get frustrated and confused using a software product, the problem usually lies in the user interface.

Think about it—if today's operating systems are so easy to use, then why are there *always* new products being developed to make popular programs and their interfaces simpler and easier to use? Even before Microsoft's Windows 95 operating system was an actual product, there were other products, such as Norton Utilities, developed for the beta test release of Windows 95. For the past year or more, I have received a daily e-mail "Tip of the Day" for Windows 95. If these interfaces are so easy, why do users need so many tips to use them effectively? You'll learn why any particular product or user interface can't always be the best for everyone.

An *INFOWORLD* survey (June 12, 1995) summarized the most difficult computing skills to find and hire for major companies in the United States. At the top of the list was client/server technical architects, and second was distributed

Figure P.1   Know thy users, for they are not you.

database experts. Third on the list of difficult skills to find was the *GUI designer,* a skill this book addresses. Further down on the list, at number five, was the GUI programmer.

KEY IDEA! *While being able to program a graphical- and object-oriented user interface is a critical skill,* an even more important skill *is being able to design and analyze user interfaces. You don't have to be a expert programmer to be able to design good user interfaces. In fact, software programming and interface design are separate skills that are* both *needed on a product design team.*

What's in This Book?

The book discusses computer software interfaces in general and focuses on today's graphical user interfaces (GUIs) and newer, more high-powered, object-oriented user interfaces (OOUIs). It also covers emerging computer technologies, such as speech recognition, wizards, social user interfaces, and intelligent software agents.

KEY IDEA! *Throughout the book, important information will be highlighted with the* Key Idea! *sidebar shown here.*

Discussions are supplemented with examples and pictures of interfaces and objects that demonstrate user interface styles and elements. The book details the key user interface design principles and guidelines, and an iterative user interface design process you can follow. You'll learn how human psychology affects how computer hardware and software should be designed.

The history of user interfaces is detailed, from the command line interface of DOS to the GUI and OOUI interfaces you see today. Other key user interface topics are also covered, including usability, help and tutorials, and the merging of PC interfaces with Internet Web browser interfaces.

KEY IDEA! *The examples and guidance provided in this book are based on research, guidelines,* and *practical experience, not just my personal beliefs and ideas about interface design. Whenever possible, historical and expert opinions and guidelines are provided, complete with references.*

How This Book Is Organized

There are four major parts to this book, each with its own roadmap to guide you through it:

- ◆ Part 1: Foundations of User Interface Design (Chapters 1–9)
- ◆ Part 2: Object-Oriented User Interfaces (Chapters 10–11)
- ◆ Part 3: The User Interface Design Process (Chapter 12)
- ◆ Part 4: Advanced User Interface Techniques and Technologies (Chapters 13–16).

Use the four-part pyramid design of the book (see Figure P.2) to build your skills and knowledge and to go directly to a particular part of the book based on your interests and needs.

Part 1 Contents

If you are fairly new to user interface design, start with Part 1, where you will learn the fundamentals—the *whys* and *hows* of good software design. Chapter 1 opens the book with a discussion of quality software design. User interfaces are defined in Chapter 2. Chapter 3 covers user interface models. An overview of the human cognitive and perceptual systems is provided in Chapter 4. I discuss the golden rules (interface design principles) of interface design in Chapter 5. Chapter 6 addresses the role of computer standards and interface guidelines. Software usability is defined, and usability testing goals, objectives, and case studies are found in Chapter 7. Chapter 8 analyzes command-line and menu interfaces, while Chapter 9 covers graphical user interfaces (GUIs).

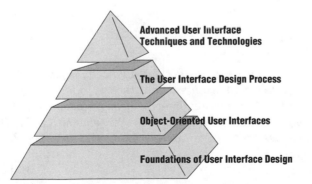

Figure P.2   What's in this book.

Part 2 Contents

To learn about the concepts, examples, and architecture of object-oriented user interfaces, or OOUIs, go to Part 2. Chapter 10 defines OOUIs and discusses objects, views, and core skills needed to use object-oriented interfaces. Chapter 11 shows how to migrate users from GUIs to OOUIs and compares OOUIs to object-oriented programming (OOP).

Part 3 Contents

An iterative user interface design process is defined in Part 3, and a case study is provided. The four-phase design process is based on object-oriented design, but it also works for designing more traditional GUIs. As such, it is fundamental to good user interface design, and Chapter 12 could be read following Part 1.

Part 4 Contents

To read about new and more advanced user interface technologies and techniques, focus on Part 4. This book is designed to give you *practical* guidance in designing software that people can use. Chapter 13 offers a designer's toolkit, full of topics such as graphic excellence, using color, animation, and audio, interface terminology, and international interfaces. Key interface design issues are discussed, along with the top 10 problems with GUIs and OOUIs. Chapter 14 covers help systems, Electronic Performance Support, tutorials, training, wizards, and multimedia in the interface. New interface technologies of agents and social user interfaces are discussed in Chapter 15. Finally, Chapter 16 introduces the new world of Internet interfaces, and covers the merging of PC interfaces and Web-browsing interfaces. Web design guidelines are offered, and we'll look at the future of user interfaces.

From the Author

We need better hardware for the desktop applications part of the market, better software and communications infrastructure, and, perhaps most important, contributions from the solution providers, the people who have provided the consulting and training, who can take these standardized building blocks and put them together in a way that's meaningful for the incredible variety of users out there.

Bill Gates (1996)

These are exciting times in software development and user interface design. The emergence of the Internet and World Wide Web has transformed the face of computing and the look and feel of software is again a hot topic. As with any new technology, users, designers, and developers are jumping head first into uncharted areas. Although user interface design is changing, it is still well-grounded in the history of traditional interface design, which is based on human perception and cognition and commonly accepted design principles and guidelines.

This book is based on my experiences as a user interface architect, designer, and usability professional over the past fifteen years in the computer industry, and is grounded in my training and research as a cognitive psychologist. I have been involved in the planning, design, and usability testing of all aspects of computer hardware and software, from product installation, online and hard-copy publications, and developing product and corporate style guides, to designing and developing software user interfaces and help systems. In my 11 years at IBM, I was part of the Common User Access (CUA) team that developed the Windows and OS/2 style guide and reference and wrote the only industry user interface guide for designing object-oriented user interfaces, *Object-Oriented Interface Design: IBM Common User Access Guidelines.* I also developed technical education courses on user interface design and usability, and performed usability tests on many software products.

This book was written to describe the explosion of new ideas in software user interfaces that have come about since my first book, *The GUI-OOUI War: OS/2 vs. Windows, The Designer's Guide to Human-Computer Interfaces* (published by John Wiley & Sons, Inc., 1994). In addition to drawing from my experiences in user interface architecture design and consulting, I have included examples and materials from my seminars and courses on designing user-oriented and object-oriented interfaces.

User interface design is more than placing controls on the display screen. Cognitive psychologists bring an understanding of how humans *read, learn,* and *think* to help design computers that work within the psychological capabilities and limitations of the people for whom they are designed (Figure P.3).

I've spent hundreds of hours watching people try to use computers in their own work environments and in usability labs. Over the years, users have gradually (and often painfully) migrated from command-line interfaces to graphical user interfaces and are now moving on into the wonderful world of object-oriented user interfaces, with new operating systems like OS/2 Warp and Windows 95. I've seen the confusion and frustration (and only occasionally the joy) that users experience in their work with computers. The insights I've gained regarding this intricate and interesting relationship that has formed between humans and computers should help the reader focus on the

Figure P.3   Computer user interfaces from a psychologist's perspective.

user's perspective and the fact that software must be designed to meet the user's needs, not the designer's or programmer's needs. Designing and building sensible and usable software user interfaces is both an art and a science. This book is designed to enhance your artistic and scientific interface design skills.

CONTENTS

Chapter 8   User Interface Evolution: Command-Lines and Menus   135

Chapter 9   User Interface Evolution: Graphical User Interfaces   157

Theo Mandel is a consultant, author, educator, and industry seminar speaker living in Austin, Texas. He is the founder and principal of Interface Design and Development (IDD).

His first book, *The GUI-OOUI War: Windows vs. OS/2, The Designer's Guide to Human-Computer Interfaces* takes a comprehensive look at past, present, and future software user interfaces and compares graphical and object-oriented interfaces (GUIs and OOUIs). It also offers techniques for interface design and demonstrates the effects of computer interfaces on users. Published by John Wiley & Sons, it was listed by *OS/2 Magazine* as one of the hottest computer books for 1994. One reviewer comments, "This book can be read by anyone who

uses a PC. Read it—it will change the way you think about your computer." The book serves to educate developers on the art and science of interface design. *The Elements of User Interface Design* is Dr. Mandel's second book.

OS/2 Professional wrote: "The GUI-OOUI War is a book that should be forced on every Windows and OS/2 developer working today . . . it will prove invaluable to software developers, and likely intriguing to curious users. If only half the rules in this book were followed, the quality of most programs would increase tenfold. If you want to know what makes an application interface successful or you want to make a good program great, there's no better starting place."

Theo Mandel received his Ph.D. in Cognitive Psychology from the University of Colorado at Boulder. There he conducted research on how people learn, remember, and read. The area of human factors and product usability became critical to the computer industry in the 1980s. Dr. Mandel worked for IBM over 12 years in the areas of software user interface architecture, product interface design, usability testing, consulting, and education. He was a member of the IBM group responsible for the object-oriented CUA user interface architecture. This work was the basis for the successful OS/2 Workplace Shell interface. He has conducted technical education and training in classrooms and on television and satellite education systems, as well as corporate and university-level courses on human factors and user interface design.

Dr. Mandel's consulting, education, and seminars are sought by major corporations, including IBM worldwide, Microsoft, Lotus, NYNEX, USAA Insurance, Swiss Bank Corporation, Canada Gas Consortium, Software 2000, Blockbuster Video, EDS, Day-Timers, University of Texas, and Florida Atlantic University. He completed a video seminar and white paper for Software 2000 with other Object Technology experts titled *Object-Oriented Technology: What Every Manager Needs to Know*. A keynote speaker for Software World USA and OS/2 World conferences, he gave the keynote presentation on "User Interfaces of the Future" at the PC World EXPO in Oslo, Norway. Theo's three-day workshop course, Designing Graphical and Object-Oriented User Interfaces, is offered as a public seminar and as an onsite course for companies.

In addition, Theo is an accomplished tennis player and tennis equipment consultant. He was a member of the Head Racquet Sports Tennis Advisory Staff for over 15 years and is a top-ranked player in Texas in his age group. He coordinates tennis equipment testing for Tennis Magazine. For more information, contact Interface Design and Development at 8001 Two Coves Drive, Austin, Texas, 78730-3125. Telephone/fax: (512)345-2259, E-mail: Theo_Mandel@compuserve.com. Web site: http://www.concentric.net/~tmandel/.

PART ONE

FOUNDATIONS OF USER INTERFACE DESIGN

To make technology that fits human beings, it is necessary to study human beings. But now we tend to study only the technology. As a result, people are required to conform to technology. It is time to reverse this trend, time to make technology conform to people.

Donald Norman (1995)

Roadmap for Part 1: Foundations of User Interface Design

Chapter 1: Designing Quality Software User Interfaces

This chapter sets the tone for readers of this book. It answers the questions, "What is quality design?" and "What are the criteria for effective interface design?"

Chapter 2: What Is a User Interface?

User experiences and expectations are the foundation on which users relate to the rest of the world. This chapter provides some real-world examples and defines software user interfaces.

Chapter 3: User Interface Models

This chapter defines the three models of interface design: users, designers, and developers. Interface metaphors are defined and examples are discussed.

Chapter 4: The Psychology of Humans and Computers

User interface design begins with the study of human cognition and perception. An information-processing model of human memory is discussed, with implications for software design. Human and computer strengths and weaknesses are described.

Chapter 5: The Golden Rules of User Interface Design

This chapter details the "stone tablets" for user interface design. Regardless of the computing environment, basic user interface design principles should be followed to design user- and task-oriented software interfaces.

Chapter 6: Computer Standards and User Interface Guidelines

Industry and corporate standards and guidelines serve to enable designers and developers to build usable interfaces. This chapter describes what guidelines are, where to find them, why one should follow them, and how to produce corporate style guides.

Chapter 7: Software Usability Testing

Usability should be designed into a software product, but how do you know you have achieved usability goals? Usability and usability testing are defined in this chapter. Usability goals and objectives are described and examples are given. Test validity and reliability are defined and compared. Several types of usability tests are discussed and "lessons learned" are offered. A usability test report card is offered to help develop usability test plans and procedures.

Chapter 8: User Interface Evolution: Command-Lines and Menus

The evolution of user interfaces is documented. Definitions, examples, and discussions are presented for command-line user interfaces and menu interfaces. Each interface style is analyzed and summarized with respect to the user's model, user's memory, semantics, and user interaction.

Chapter 9: User Interface Evolution: Graphical User Interfaces

Graphical user interfaces are discussed. Definitions, examples, and discussions are presented from GUI operating systems and programs. GUIs are analyzed and summarized with respect to the user interface architecture, user's model, user's memory, semantics, and user interaction.

CHAPTER ONE

Designing Quality Software User Interfaces

There is a quality about a great design that is difficult to put into words. It's always tempting to focus on just a few aspects of a design, separate from the whole problem. Good looks, good flow, good content—all those things are important, but how do you pin down that feeling of satisfaction you get when you encounter a tool or toy that clicks with you on a deep level?

Marc Rettig (1996)

What Is Quality Design?

Talking about art is like dancing about architecture.

Steve Martin

What defines users' experiences with a product? How do you quantify usability goals like *easy to learn, easy to use,* and *fun to use?* Does a product really do what users expect it to do? Why is it so easy to find examples of poor design and so difficult to find examples of good design? These are some of the problems facing software designers and developers. Alben (1996) describes the problem well:

By "experience" we mean all the aspects of how people use an interactive product: the way it feels in their hands, how well they understand how it works, how they feel about it while they're using it, how well it serves their purposes, and how well it fits into the entire context in which they are using it. If these experiences are successful and engaging, then people value them. We call this "quality of experience."

Quality of Software Products

Quality software takes time, and it certainly costs a little more.

David Wright (1996)

Both software developers and users are now accustomed to using *beta,* or pre-production, software. Beta versions are released for operating system software, development tools, and end-user software. Often, they are sold as products for reduced, *prerelease* prices. It is amazing that software companies charge users for software that is buggy, nontested, and less than production quality. David Wright (1996) wrote in *ComputerWorld,* "The really sad thing about our increasing crop of buggy software is that it has lowered everyone's standard of what constitutes acceptable quality. And the even sadder thing is that it's all fixable—if we really want it to be."

Most software developers are wary of version 1.0 of any software product, never mind beta software. Wright defines quality software as "software that's intuitive, complete, and most important, not broken." Since the user interface is a critical component of software design, the quality issue affects anyone designing user interfaces.

Criteria for Effective Interface Design

Criteria . . . are intended to contribute to the discussion of how interaction design adds value to products and to people's lives. Ideally, designers of interactive products will use the criteria in their work and share them with colleagues and clients; those who teach will present the criteria for discussion and exploration with students.

Lauralee Alben (1996)

While writing this book, I kept thinking about what to say in an opening chapter to point out just how important good design is for *any product,* whether it is a software product, a toy, a tool, items you use where you work, or the things in your home that you use every day. Then I read the May–June 1996 *interactions* journal. This issue was specifically devoted to the ACM/*interactions* Design Awards '95. Not only were the six award finalists presented, but the process of judging the entries was described, and, most interesting to me in writing this book, the criteria used to judge the designs was discussed in great detail. Lauralee Alben showed how important design criteria are for all interface design, not just for this competition.

KEY IDEA! *The entire issue of* interactions *(May–June, 1996) is recommended reading for everyone involved in product design.*

Before you read the rest of this book, read through the design criteria and their descriptions (Figure 1.1 and Table 1.1) to see how your product designs measure up. If you find many areas where the process and the design don't quite measure up, you're not alone. If you are satisfied with how well your designs meet these criteria, then you probably should be writing this book rather than reading it! I included this section to help design teams realize how good their designs can possibly be.

Figure 1.1 shows how the design criteria relate to each other and together form what is called *quality of experience.* Quality of experience can be summed up as follows: "Taken together, the criteria raise one key question: How does effective interaction design provide people with a successful and satisfying experience?" My question to you is—Have you asked yourself and your design team that question lately? Table 1.1 lists each of the design criteria and describes the questions you would ask to evaluate a product's performance in that area.

What Defines *World Class?*

I recently read an article in a wine-growers' magazine, *Decanter,* entitled, "What Defines World Class?" (St. Pierre, 1995). Even though the topic was not software, but wine, the concept of *world class* is something designers should

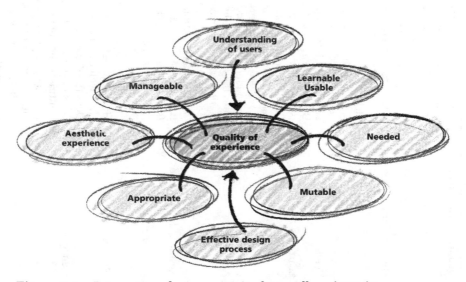

Figure 1.1   Interaction design criteria, from Alben (1996).

TABLE 1.1 Interaction Design Criteria Descriptions, from Alben (1996)

Design Criteria	Description
Quality of Experience	Taken together, the criteria raise one key question: How does effective interaction design provide people with a successful and satisfying experience?
Understanding of Users	How well was the design team grounded in understanding the needs, tasks, and environments of the people for whom the product was designed? How well was that learning reflected in the product?
Effective Design Process	Is the product a result of a well-thought-out and well-executed design process? What were the major design issues that arose during the process and what was the rationale and method for resolving them? How were budgeting, scheduling and other practical issues, such as interpersonal communications, managed to support the goals of the design process?
Needed	What need does the product satisfy? Does it make a significant social, economic, or environmental contribution?
Learnable and Usable	Is the product easy to learn and use? Does the product communicate a sense of its purpose, how to begin, and how to proceed? Is this learning easy to retain over time? Are the product's features self-evident and self-revealing? How well does the product support and allow for the different ways people will approach and use it, considering their various levels of experience, skills, and strategies for problem-solving?
Appropriate	Does the design of the product solve the right problem at the right level? Does the product serve users in efficient and practical ways? How did considering social, cultural, economic, and technical aspects of the problem contribute to an appropriate solution?
Aesthetic Experience	Is using the product an aesthetically pleasing and sensually satisfying one? Is the product cohesively designed, exhibiting continuity and excellence across graphic, interaction, information, and industrial design? Is there a consistency of spirit and style? Does the design perform well within technological constraints? Does it accomplish an integration of software and hardware?
Mutable	Have the designers considered whether mutability is appropriate or not? How well can the product be adapted to suit the particular needs and preferences of individuals and groups? Does the design allow the product to change and evolve for new, perhaps unforeseen, uses?
Manageable	Does the design of the product move beyond understanding "use" merely as functionality and support the entire context of use? For example, does the product account for and help users manage needs such as installation, training, maintenance, costs, and supplies? Have these needs and others been considered in an individual as well as an organizational sense? Does the design of the product take into account issues such as negotiating competition for use and the concept of "ownership," including rights and responsibilities?

have in mind when designing any product. Here are some descriptions of world-class wine that I thought would apply to software interface design:

- ◆ "It must be able to age. Not the ability to last long, but to develop, turning into that pure marvel which is a fully mature wine."
- ◆ "It is made with a combination of intelligence, determination, and skill."
- ◆ "World-class means that it could be appreciated as such by any knowledgeable wine drinker anywhere, without much elaboration."
- ◆ "It must have a definable superiority."
- ◆ "It must have complexity, be interesting, have intensity, depth and richness, and be distinctive. It must have length, in its finish and in our memory, engage our minds, make us think about it."
- ◆ "Essentially, they follow the rules for excellence that all art does; they are important aesthetic experiences. But some standards change, art isn't static. The definition of world-class is not static—wines evolve all the time, and so do the standards."

The goal of this book is to help readers understand what makes up quality software interface design. What are the things that we as designers and developers do and don't do *to* users of our products? What should or shouldn't we be doing *for* them and *with* them? How do you know when you have created a good design? You will learn the correct answers from this book: Ask your users! Design with your users! Conduct usability tests! These are some of the key concepts behind designing usable user interfaces that I share with you throughout this book.

KEY IDEA! *As you read this book, return to this chapter occasionally to remind yourself of the goals and aspirations you should be striving for in interface design. Be known as a designer who works with users to build the best possible user interfaces!*

References

Alben, Lauralee. 1996. Quality of experience: Defining the criteria for effective interaction design. *ACM interactions* (May–June): 11–15.

St. Pierre, Brian. 1995. What defines world class? *Decanter* (November): 76–78.

Wright, David. 1996. Getting back quality software. *ComputerWorld* (July 8): 46.

CHAPTER TWO

What Is a User Interface?

The way a user interacts with a computer is as important as the computation itself; in other words, the human interface, as it has come to be called, is as fundamental to computing as any processor configuration, operating system, or programming environment.

John Anderson (1989)

User Experiences and Expectations

We are surrounded by large numbers of manufactured items, most intended to make our lives easier and more pleasant. In the office we have computers, copying machines, telephone systems, voice mail, and FAX machines. In the home we have television sets, VCRs, automated kitchen appliances, answering machines, and home computers. All these wonderful devices are supposed to help us save time and produce faster, superior results. But wait a minute—if these new devices are so wonderful, why do we need special dedicated staff members ("power users" or "key operators") to make them work? Why do we need manuals or special instructions to use the typical business telephone? Why do so many features go unused? And why do these devices add to the stresses of life rather than reduce them?

Donald Norman (1988)

You probably haven't thought about it in this way, but everything you physically do is a series of interactions with objects that surround you at home, at work, or wherever you are. How you interact with things around you is determined by your *past experiences* with these objects (and other objects like them) and your *expectations* of how things should work when you use them.

For example, when you walk up to a door you just walked through a few minutes earlier, you don't expect to find the door locked when you turn the knob and push (or pull) on the door handle. You base your actions on what you expect to happen, even if you have never interacted with that particular object before (Figure 2.1). As a cognitive psychologist, I study how people deal with the world around them and how they handle complex situations and new experiences.

People try to simplify the world around them and they relate new or unknown things to objects and experiences that they know and are comfortable with. In simple terms, people learn how to act with the things around them and when confronted with things they *don't* understand, they tend to relate them to things they *do* understand. They then react to them in some manner consistent with the way they *think* that type of object behaves. The best way to confuse or scare people, or make them laugh, is to give them a familiar object but change the behavior that normally accompanies that object. This is one of the foundations on which comedy and suspense are based. If you pick up a gun and pull the trigger, you expect it to make a loud noise and shoot a bullet. Imagine your surprise when it turns out to be a cigarette lighter and a small flame comes out of the gun barrel!

Your past experiences and expectations are what film directors plan on when they try to amuse or scare you by changing the behavior of common objects in the film world. This may be amusing to a viewer of a movie or a television show; but when something unexpected happens while you are working on your computer, it may not be amusing at all. It is frustrating, annoying, and can sometimes be dangerous!

Figure 2.1   User interfaces in the real world.

Don Norman wrote a very popular book originally entitled *The Psychology of Everyday Things* (1988). Norman describes many of the everyday situations where something goes wrong with our interactions with poorly designed objects around us. Doors in public buildings are good examples of objects often designed for aesthetic effect rather than for actual use. How many times have you walked up to a door in a building you've never been in and pushed on the door to open it only to find that you should have pulled on the door instead? We often say, "I can't figure out how to use this product. What's wrong with me?"

We tend to blame ourselves before we blame the products we use. As Norman points out, "Humans, I discovered, do not always behave clumsily. Humans do not always err. But they do when the things they use are badly conceived and designed. Nonetheless, we still see human error blamed for all that befalls society." In the product usability tests I've conducted, it is very interesting to see how people tend to blame themselves rather than the products they are using. After all, these software products we use are developed by experienced professionals, right? We try to protect the computer from harm, rather than being concerned that the computer might actually do us (or our information) harm! This tendency is so strongly ingrained that before conducting product usability tests, human factors and usability testing professionals always instruct people that the product is being tested, not the user, and that there is nothing they can do that can harm the computer. And, no matter how many times you tell them you are not testing them, it rarely works. They still blame themselves!

Even Norman himself failed to fully understand the past experiences and expectations of readers and potential readers of his book. Norman's original book was well known and commonly called by the acronym *POET* (from the first letters of *The Psychology of Everyday Things*). However, the paperback edition of the book was retitled *The Design of Everyday Things*. Retitling a book in subsequent editions is a very rare occurrence. In the preface to the new edition, Norman describes how he was surprised to learn that while the word *psychology* in the original title was liked by the academic community, it was widely disliked and misinterpreted by the much larger audience of potential readers, the business community. Norman, a guru of usable product design, had been fooled by his perception of the book's audience. This real-world experience of Norman's shows the importance of designing products that meet user needs based on their experiences and expectations in their different social, cultural, and business environments, rather than based on the product designer's viewpoint. Norman also wrote another book, *Turn Signals Are the Facial Expressions of Automobiles* (1992), that goes further into the "plight of humans confronting the perversity of inanimate objects."

Your *past experiences* with the real world and with computer hardware, operating systems, and programs merge with your expectations of how things should work when you try to do your computing tasks. The process of developing products is really much more of an art than a science, and we need to know much more about who our users really are, what tasks they are trying to do, and how they use their computers.

> **K**EY IDEA! *Everyone carries around his or her past experiences like a set of permanently attached luggage (Figure 2.2). Users interact with computers the way they interact with everything else in the world. Users have some idea of what a computer can do and whether a computer can help them in various aspects of their life.*

Developers don't always realize who their customers are and users don't always know much about computers. If people don't know much about computers, they will attempt to relate to them in ways similar to how they relate to other things in their world. To show you how grounded people are in their own world, and not in the computer world, here's a transcript of an actual customer call to one of the largest PC companies in the United States.

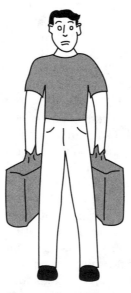

Figure 2.2 Users always carry their experiences with them.

CALLER: "Hello, is this Tech Support?"

TECH REP: "Yes, it is. How may I help you?"

CALLER: "The cup holder on my PC is broken and I am within my warranty period. How do I go about getting that fixed?"

TECH REP: "I'm sorry, but did you say a cup holder?"

CALLER: "Yes, it's attached to the front of my computer."

TECH REP: "Please excuse me if I seem a bit stumped, it's because I am. Did you receive this as part of a promotional, at a trade show, how did you get this cup holder? Does it have any trademark on it?"

CALLER: "It came with my computer, I don't know anything about a promotional. It just has '4X' on it."

As you can figure out, the customer had been using the load drawer of the CD-ROM drive as a cup holder and broke it off! I know my wife won't buy a car that doesn't come with cup holders, but I didn't know that computer users had the same requirements for their new computers!

Here's my favorite example of how real-world cues can actually confuse users. A bar in Boulder, Colorado called the Dark Horse is noted for its unique rest rooms. The men's and women's rest rooms are located side-by-side, with adjacent doors. The doors are marked MEN and WOMEN, giving patrons a strong cue as to which door they should enter. However, each door also has a hand pointing to the other door (see Figure 2.3). Which set of cues should people believe? Should they follow the words MEN or WOMEN on the door, or should they follow the hand pointing to the opposite door? *The two sets of cues are*

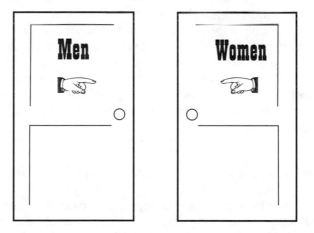

Figure 2.3 Confusing interfaces in the real world.

conflicting. There is usually quite a crowd around the bar near the rest rooms, just waiting for people to walk up to the rest room doors, stop in their tracks, and try to figure out which door to go in. I won't tell you which is the correct rest room door; you'll just have to stop by the Dark Horse bar in Boulder!

KEY IDEA! *Even though this interface was intended to confuse users, it shows how ambiguous and conflicting cues can cause user confusion. Interface cues should give users an idea of the object's* form *and* function *and should allow them to determine their appropriate behavior. In this case, many customers actually wait for someone to come out of one of the rest rooms before they make their decision about which door to enter. They assume that if someone comes out of one of the doors and doesn't look embarrassed, they will be safe following that person's decision.*

What Is a Software User Interface?

Narrowly defined, this interface comprises the input and output devices and the software that services them; broadly defined, the interface includes everything that shapes users' experiences with computers, including documentation, training, and human support.

Baecker et al. (1995)

KEY IDEA! *The term* interface *is one of those words we don't really think much about. The dictionary definition is, "The place at which independent systems meet and act on or communicate with each other." We use the word in a number of ways—both as a noun and as a verb. The doors to the rest rooms are an* interface *to deal with in a bar. People also* interface *with each other, which means they communicate in some way, either in person, on the telephone, or even electronically using computers.*

You perhaps have your own personal definition of the software interface—perhaps "what users see on the screen." I'd like to stretch this definition to encompass the whole experience between the user and the computer. It includes both the computer hardware and software that *presents* information to users and allows users to *interact* with the information and the computer.

The computer's interface includes the *hardware* that makes up the system, such as the keyboard, a pointing device like a mouse, joystick, or trackball, the processing unit, and the display screen itself. The *software* components of the user interface are all the items users see, hear, point to, or touch on the screen to interact with the computer itself, as well as the information with which users work. The interface also includes hardcopy and online information such as manuals, references, help, tutorials, and any other documentation that accompanies the hardware and software. It takes a careful crafting of the hardware and software interface components to allow users to communicate with a computer and allow the computer to present information to users.

The design of a product's user interface is critical to its user acceptance and success. Without a well-designed user interface, even a system with outstanding features will not be successful. Too often, the user interface is used to simply dress up the program's functions. As Norm Cox (1992), a well-known user interface design consultant from Dallas, Texas, says, this effort is much like trying to "put some lipstick on the bulldog." There's only so much a pretty interface can do to dress up a poorly designed product.

This is often the case when you attempt to update older products or programs that were originally developed on a host mainframe (large system) computer. In many cases, you don't want to change the design or implementation of the program. You simply want to put a more usable and more graphic *front end* on the program to make it easier for users. There are many development tools that enable you to build personal computer-based user interfaces to mainframe programs and stored data. All too often the effect isn't optimal and, as Norm Cox says, you end up with an ugly program with a pretty face!

> **KEY IDEA!** *Building a front-end user interface can be effective as long as it doesn't force the user to do things a certain way because the program needs to have the information or actions completed in a certain order. However, in most cases, the best way to give the user a better product interface is to design the software product with the user's beliefs, wants, needs, experiences, and expectations used as the* basis *for product development.*

Take a tip from the entertainment industry regarding interfaces. The Disney company is masterful at designing their theme parks so that users interfacing with the park have an enjoyable experience. They understand who their users are—a mixture of couples and families with children—and how people behave—that people are hungry, thirsty, and tired, and that they don't like to stand around in long lines. Disney's view is that what they are designing is an *experience,* and the design of this experience is an art. They follow a process similar to what I describe in this book, where they first define the experience they want people to have, then develop scripts, then design the experience, and finally test it to see if they need to make adjustments.

References

Cox, Norman. 1992. Not just a pretty interface: Design comes to the computer screen. *IBM Think Magazine* (4): 48.

Norman, Donald A. 1988. *The Design of Everyday Things.* New York: Double-day.

Norman, Donald A. 1992. *Turn Signals Are the Facial Expressions of Automobiles.* White Plains, NY: Addison-Wesley.

CHAPTER THREE

USER INTERFACE MODELS

Luckily, there are now program design teams who realize that the human is a vital component in the interactive system—a component whose complexities should be treated with at least as much respect as those of a laser printer. What causes the human not to be able to play his or her role is no more or less than clumsy program design.

David Hohn (1992)

Users as an Integral Part of the Computer System

Whether a person likes technology or not, his or her economic survival depends on a basic knowledge (or at least an absence of fear) of computers.

Jamie Ray Wright (1993)

Just as you must have the correct cable with the right connections to hook up a printer to your computer, the software interface must be designed to match your needs and wants as a user with the capabilities of the computer (Figure 3.1). Who does this work in designing and developing a computer software product? And more importantly, how well do they do it? This chapter looks at the psychological makeup of the critical human elements in interface design.

User Goals

Why do people use computers or devices that are computerized? It's because they want to complete a task or reach some goal that is more easily and accurately obtained by the use of a computer. Since the computer is really an aid in reaching our goals and performing our tasks, then why do we put up with poor product design? Often we don't have much choice.

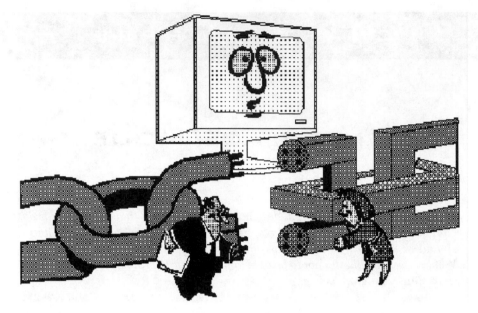

Figure 3.1 Human-computer connections.

You probably haven't thought about it much, but do you know what *your* goals are as a computer user? How about users of programs that you design and develop? Do you understand their goals? User goals might include increased productivity, greater accuracy, higher satisfaction, and more enjoyment with a computer. Children assign a very different priority to their goals when using a computer—fun is definitely at the top of the list!

Today's young computer users will be the corporate computer users of the future. When it comes to technology and computers, they have grown up very differently from the way we grew up. Elliot Soloway, in "How the Nintendo Generation Learns" (1991), discusses the differences that will come about in the computer industry and educational institutions as a result of the way today's children are growing up with current computer technology, entertainment, and television.

Since users have different goals depending on who they are and what they're doing, you'd expect software products to be flexible. Entertainment software is focused on having fun and being "user seductive." The system might be a Nintendo game for a child or a video slot machine for an adult. If the designer's goal is to entertain and keep users putting money in the machine, then the interface must entice people and make it as easy as possible for them to use the machine.

Users probably don't think of fun as a goal when they use the computer for personal productivity or work. In fact, if they're trying to get work done, they want something that is more concerned with ease of learning and ease of use. Developers of business software can learn from the software and interfaces that are geared toward education and entertainment.

People and the Obstacles that Are Put in Their Way

You know how anxious automobile drivers (but not you, of course!) get at a railroad crossing when the train doesn't come after a period of time? Some drivers creep out to see if there really is a train coming and then go around the crossing gate and cross the railroad tracks. The interesting question is, how long do drivers wait before they become too impatient to wait for the train to come? This is a question for psychologists and researchers. Railroad engineers have found that the crossing gates should come down only 20 to 30 seconds before the train approaches the railroad crossing. If the gates are brought down earlier than this, drivers tend to get anxious and go around the gates. If the gates don't come down at least 20 to 30 seconds before the train arrives, there isn't enough time for drivers to be sufficiently warned about the train, which may be traveling at a speed of about 50 to 60 miles an hour.

KEY IDEA! *Understand who users are and where they are trying to go, and figure out how much misdirection and frustration they can stand before they give up and do something else.*

Users Need Multiple User Interface Styles

A computer will do what you tell it to do, but that may be much different from what you had in mind.

Joseph Weizenbaum (1978)

When I began to write my first book, I did my work using a very simple character-based text editor. This work included my proposal to the publisher, rough content outline, more-detailed chapter topics, and most of the text for the first few chapters. Why did I choose this type of program? Because, at that time, I was interested only in getting my thoughts and ideas written down as fast and as easily as I possibly could. Was it a sophisticated program and interface? That is, did it have a visually oriented, graphical user interface? No, but it was the best type of interface to help me *reach the goal I had at that time,* which was just to put words on the screen. Did I continue to write the rest of the book using this simple text editor? No, because it wasn't the best tool or program to help me reach my *new goal,* which had now grown to writing the rest of the book. This included creating and importing the one hundred or so graphics I wanted to use as illustrations and examples.

I also had to format the book according to the publisher's standard page layout, type styles, font sizes, and other aspects of a book that are necessary to get it ready for publication. My simple text editor was no longer a tool that could provide the functional capability or the interface for the tasks I was now required to do to finish the book.

A full-functioned word processing program (such as Microsoft Word, Lotus Word Pro, or, in my case, DeScribe) had the functional capabilities I needed and a user interface that allowed me to do sophisticated word processing and publishing tasks very easily. All these programs have somewhat well-designed graphical user interfaces that let me do what I wanted to do very quickly and easily.

As I began writing with a GUI word processor, I must admit I did fall prey to the seductiveness of trying out different type styles and fonts, page layouts, and other visual effects, rather than writing the book content itself. After all, it had a WYSIWYG interface (*what you see is what you get*), so I could see exactly how the page would look when it was printed! It was much easier, and more fun, to play with what the book was going to *look like* rather than *writing the words themselves.* I found myself thinking, "Hmm, should I center the chapter title on the page, or should I move it flush left or flush right? Should the chapter section titles be in all capitals or not?" This was easier than thinking, "What am I really trying to say in this section about users and their programs?" Ultimately, both tasks had to be completed, but it was easier to procrastinate and do the tasks that are visual and more fun than the tasks that are more work. This is just human nature, I'm afraid to say. As a cognitive psychologist, I realize this, but that doesn't mean I can change my behavior any easier than anyone else!

KEY IDEA! *There will never be only one perfect tool, program, or interface for computer users, since they are constantly changing their goals according to the tasks they are trying to accomplish at any particular time. A basic text editor is no match for a GUI word processor, functionally or visually, but each can be the optimal program for the task users happen to be doing at that time. In fact, a more functional and visually sophisticated program can actually get in the way and distract users from their primary tasks.*

If you don't want people to focus on the visual and graphic aspects of a particular task, then don't give them tools that easily allow them to focus on these aspects. It's like giving a child a big box of 128 different-colored crayons and a coloring book and leaving her alone. An hour later you come back and tell her, "I'm sorry, but you were supposed to use just one colored crayon and you were supposed to draw inside the lines."

Users not only need different user interfaces and programs for different tasks, but their level of expertise can change even *within a task* while using a program. For example, users may use a spreadsheet program for work and may be quite expert on the spreadsheet functions and actions used all the time. For speed and efficiency, there may be certain keystrokes or *macros* that are memorized and can be performed without even thinking about them. However, there may be parts of the task that are done less frequently and users can never quite remember exactly how the commands must be typed, or exactly where the choices are in the menus. Users need support from the program and the interface to help remember how to do the infrequent portions of the task.

KEY IDEA! *Users shouldn't be asked to choose one and only one user interface style to use. There is no one program or interface style that is optimal for users all the time. As a designer, keep an open mind and don't lock in only one interface style. Remember, users have the right to change their mind at any time!*

Different interface techniques are more appropriate for different tasks. If you were asked to sign your name on the computer screen, wouldn't you rather use a mouse than the keyboard arrow keys? On the other hand, if you were asked to draw a rectangle on the screen, using the keyboard arrow keys might be much easier and more accurate than trying to draw a rectangle using a mouse or a pen. Here's another example. I'm left-handed, but I use my right hand with a computer mouse. If I were asked to draw a rectangle on the screen using the mouse, I'd feel comfortable doing it right-handed. However, if I were asked to sign my name on the screen, I couldn't do a good job with my right hand, even though I do all my computer mousing that way. I'd have to use my left hand to do a decent job with my signature.

For these reasons, most operating systems and programs offer more than one type of user interface style. This is much more work for the system and applications designers and developers, but it allows users of different skill levels to use a product in ways they feel comfortable. It also provides users with the appropriate interface style and interaction technique for the task at hand. Most software products, from operating systems to application programs, must be usable by a wide range of users—novices, casual users, power users, and experts.

Models and Metaphors: Transferring World Knowledge

Interface design is a relatively new human endeavor and has benefited much from the application of metaphor in helping interface designers who understand it mainly by virtue of being human: "The metaphor is perhaps one of man's most fruitful potentialities. Its efficacy verges on magic, and it seems a tool for creation which God forgot inside one of His creatures when He made him." (Gasset, 1925)

S. Joy Mountford (1990)

The House-Building Analogy

Why is the user interface so important to users, designers, and developers of software products? Because that is what users view and work with! Differences among developers', designers', and users' experiences, viewpoints, and skills cause many problems in all of our lives, and not just with computer systems. Most books and guidelines on user interface design talk about these viewpoints as different *models* of a user interface. Before I define these models, let's first look at an analogy you'll find familiar.

The people involved in building a custom-built house have very different perspectives on the same product. A house that is designed and built has at least three viewpoints: the architect's, the builder's, and the homeowner's. Each of these people has a very different viewpoint of the same project. Who they are and their role in the house-building project determine the tasks they perform, the goals they desire, the skills they bring to the project, the tools they use, and how they interact with each other. This goes back to *experiences* and *expectations,* discussed in Chapter 2.

The architect studies the lifestyle of the homeowners, their family, and their functional and aesthetic desires for the house. He or she turns all that into the visualization and, ultimately, the design of a house that can be built to meet the homeowners' desires and needs within their budget. The architect acts as the homeowners' representative in designing the plans and specifications and ensuring that the builder follows them.

The builder has the skills and resources to work within the confines of the designs and specifications of the architect to build a house that the homeowners will be pleased with and can live in. These skills include knowing the appropriate materials to use and all of the regulations and codes for building an environmentally and functionally sound structure.

The homeowners will ultimately be the owners and occupants of the final product and are the most important people in this whole project. They're the ones who are paying for the house and have to live in it after it is built. Any homeowner who has had a home designed and built for them knows how complicated and difficult the process of building a house can be. Although we love our beautiful home, my house-building experience with our particular builder was not a very pleasant experience. My wife Edie actually wouldn't marry me until we had finished building the house. As she truthfully put it, "If we can survive building a house together, then I feel we can survive a marriage!" I'm happy to say that we did survive building the house and have been happily married since 1988.

KEY IDEA! *Any project such as building a house or* designing and developing software *involves individuals and groups working together to build something that everyone is trying to make into a successful product. The* architect *represents those responsible for the* product design. *The* builder *represents the groups primarily responsible for the* development of the product. *The* homeowner *represents the customer, client, or* end-user *of the finished product. They all must interact and work together to build a usable product.*

Models and Metaphors

The different roles and viewpoints just described form the three models of a user interface—the user's model, the programmer's model, and the designer's model. These models and their importance are well-described in the IBM Common User Access (CUA) Guidelines (1992) and are pictured in Figure 3.2. A *model* contains the concepts and expectations a person develops through experience. Does this sound familiar? This is just a formal definition of users' experiences and expectations in the world around them.

KEY IDEA! *A* mental model *(or* conceptual model*) is an internal representation of how users understand and interact with a system. Carroll and Olson (1988) describe mental models as "a representation (in the head) of a physical system or software being run on a computer, with some plausible cascade of causal associations connecting the input to the output."*

Figure 3.2   User interface models, from IBM (1992).

People are often not aware of their mental models. IBM (1992) states: "A mental model does not necessarily reflect a situation and its components accurately. Still a mental model helps people predict what will happen next in a given situation, and it serves as a framework for analysis, understanding, and decision-making." People form mental models for a number of reasons. Mayhew (1992) lists why people form mental models:

◆ Models enable users to predict future (or infer invisible) events.

◆ Models allow users to find causes for observed events.

◆ Models allow users to determine appropriate actions to cause desired changes.

◆ Models serve as mnemonic devices for remembering relations and events.

◆ Models are a means of understanding an analogous device.

◆ Models allow people to use strategies to overcome information processing limitations.

Mental models underlie all interaction between users and their computers and thus are the basis for user interface *principles and guidelines.* Why is it so important to discuss these models? Mayhew sums it up well: "Users always have mental models and will always develop and modify them, regardless of the particular design of a system. Our goal as *user interface designers* is to design so as to facilitate the process of developing an effective mental model." Transferring knowledge of the world around them to the world of computers, users rely on models to guide their interactions with computers. This is where the concept of metaphors comes into play.

KEY IDEA! *A* metaphor *(as defined by* Webster's Third New International dictionary*) is "a figure of speech in which a work or phrase denoting one kind of object or action is used in place of another to suggest a likeness or analogy between them." Baecker et al. (1995) describe computer metaphors: "Metaphors aid users in understanding a new* target domain *(e.g., a word processor) by allowing them to comprehend it (up to the point of 'mismatch' . . .) in terms of a* source domain *they already understand (e.g., a typewriter). Metaphors aid designers because adoption of a metaphor allows them to structure aspects of the target system or interface in terms of familiar and commonly understood aspects of the source domain."*

The *desktop metaphor* used in most of today's GUIs and OOUIs is built on the belief that users know their way around an office—they are familiar with the office environment, know how to use objects in that environment (folders, cabinets, a telephone, notepads, etc.), and are comfortable with the idea of an office desktop as a working space. Designers use this metaphor to map the way users do things on the computer to the way users would do them (in an office) if they weren't using the computer.

The User's Mental Model

The reason for discussing models, and in particular the user's mental model, is that software products must be designed to fit in with the way users view the computer system they are working with. Since this is all inside people's heads, it isn't easy to get to and figure out.

The benefits of using computers and graphical user interfaces are many if products are well-designed. GUIs can educate and entertain as well as allow users to do their work. Look at the interface in Figure 3.3. This is one of the rooms in a product called the Playroom, designed by Leslie Grimm and produced by Broderbund Software, Inc. Obviously a child's program, the award-winning product advertises, "Welcome to The Playroom. Where children learn to love learning." The graphical user interface teaches computer and mouse skills, and more importantly, introduces children ages three to six to the valuable basics of reading and math, including:

- ◆ Counting
- ◆ Letter recognition
- ◆ Number recognition
- ◆ Phonics
- ◆ Word recognition
- ◆ Vocabulary
- ◆ Spelling
- ◆ Telling time

Figure 3.3   The user's mental model in the Playroom.

- ◆ Addition and subtraction
- ◆ Strategy and analysis
- ◆ Keyboarding
- ◆ Creativity

The interface follows the metaphor of a child's playroom in a home. Talk about designing a product to match your user's mental model! The interface is full of objects, playmates, and activities. Some of the objects lead to other "rooms" where children play a learning game or activity. To return to the Playroom, there is an icon of a little door in the lower-right corner of the screen. This is a simple, effective way to use a child's knowledge of rooms in a house to allow him or her to navigate through the program.

KEY IDEA! *There are important differences between children's and adults' models. Adults aren't as likely to explore an interface as readily as children. In an interface designed for children, objects and activities are not always made obvious to users, so children are encouraged and taught to explore and click on anything in the interface. Adults aren't as likely to explore an interface without preconceived expectations.*

For example, if you click on the curtains in the window, the curtains will close and Pepper mouse will change into a fire-breathing dragon when the curtains reopen! This approach doesn't work as well with adults. Adults may be more concerned about how to figure out what does what in the interface. This would not be a concern for children, as exploring the Playroom and finding new surprises is all part of the fun and learning goals of the product. Children don't have the years of built-up experiences and expectations to drive their interaction.

Another software product has used a similar home metaphor for its interface. Microsoft Bob was introduced in 1995 and caused quite a debate among the computing world with its *social user interface* and *interactive guides*. Figure 3.4 shows the family room when users enter the program for the first time. Bob's social user interface will be discussed in Chapter 15.

Superstitious User Behaviors

Poor product interface designs often lead users to doubt their interaction strategies and develop strange and superstitious behaviors to account for illogical

Figure 3.4   The user's mental model in Microsoft Bob.

and inconsistent system design (Figure 3.5). Here's a personal example of how a bad experience with computers will impact user behavior in the future. The task I was trying to perform was a simple one, but the system responses led me to establish superstitious behaviors that still occur when I do this task now.

I wanted to discard one file from a list of files using a command-line interface. I know the command name I always use on this system is *discard*. However, when I typed *discard*, the system rejected the command and gave me an error message, saying "unknown command." I know that the *discard* command is correct, yet sometimes the system gets fouled up and doesn't recognize it as a valid command. I don't know why or when this happens, but it does happen once in a while. I know that another command, *erase*, does the same action. (That's *another* whole discussion: Why are there two different commands if they both do the exact same action?) So I typed *erase*, the file was deleted, but I received a confirmation message, "File *discarded* or renamed." Imagine my frustration! Also notice that the confirmation message was obviously serving a dual purpose to be used for both *discarding* and *renaming* files.

Figure 3.5 Superstitious user behaviors.

What was so bothersome about this episode was that if the file was *discarded* correctly, then why didn't the system let me use the correct command in the first place? When this happens, my internal model of how the system works tells me that the computer is a little confused and my superstitious behavior is to restart the computer and it doesn't happen again! I don't know why or how it happens, but I do know that restarting the system seems to cure it.

How do you find out about the user's model, since it's inside someone's head? Because a user's mental model is based on a person's experiences and expectations, the only way to assess and understand a user is to talk with him and watch him work. CUA recommends five ways to gather information from users:

- ◆ Analysis of user tasks
- ◆ Surveys and interviews of actual or potential users
- ◆ Visits to user work sites
- ◆ Feedback from users
- ◆ Usability testing

KEY IDEA! *Gather feedback and input from* users themselves, *not their managers or a company executive. Get information from the people who will be* using the product themselves, *rather than someone who will be managing users or someone who really has only a limited view of what users really do. You get very different input and feedback from the people who make purchasing or management decisions concerning software than from the people who use the products to do their work.*

A separate, yet just as important, issue is that it is difficult to get reliable feedback from users. Users often tell you what they *do*, rather than what they would like to do. I call this phenomenon WYKIWYL (*what you know is what you like*). You must also be very careful about what you do with information you get from users. They aren't system designers and often aren't aware of the technology involved in computer hardware and software (that's your job!). Users tend to rely on their memory of how they *think* they do their work, rather than actually how they do it. Therefore, it is important to also *watch* them as well as *listen* to them.

Whatever users tell you represents their own personal views and preferences on the product you're designing or evaluating. Gather feedback from a large enough sample of users so that you can determine common suggestions and problems in their feedback, rather than individual opinions. You don't want to evaluate or design a system based only on a few users' personal preferences and habits. Remember, there is no such thing as an "average" user. While users may share some common experiences and feelings, you are collecting feedback from a group of individuals with a wide range of personal, professional, and computer experiences.

The Programmer's Model

> *This would be a great job if it weren't for all those damn users.*
>
> Ed Kennedy, programmer

The programmer's model is the easiest to visualize because it is explicit and can be more formally defined. In fact, the programmer's model is most often seen in the form of the functional specifications for a software product. A programmer is a person who actually writes the code that makes up the system or program.

The objects and data that make up the product are of interest to the programmer, not necessarily the way the user will interact with the information. A programmer interfaces with a computer hardware system and, for example, stores and retrieves data as fields or records in a database of information. The user's view of that data should be quite different. The same data might be entries in a software checkbook program, a personal address book, or a business phone book. It should be obvious to the reader by now that a computer user has to be shielded from the programmer's view of the computer system and the system's representation of the user's data.

The programmer's knowledge and expertise (see Figure 3.2) includes the development platform, operating system, development tools, and programming guidelines and specifications necessary to build software programs. However, these skills don't necessarily provide a programmer with the ability to provide users with the most appropriate user interface models and metaphors.

Gould's (1988) quotes (see Figure 3.6) show that some (though obviously not all) programmers are unaware of the user's model of computer systems and programs. Programmers have their own experiences and expectations of how computers work and these experiences guide the way they build their products. Programmers are often more concerned with the program's function than the program's interface. For example, if 24 lines are available in a text window, programmers might use most of those 24 lines regardless of whether the information will be readable to users.

The Designer's Model

Most software is run by confused users acting on incorrect and incomplete information, doing things the designer never expected.

Paul Heckel, 1984

The main purpose of the user interface designer is to act like an architect. Building a software product is like building a house. The *designer* (architect)

Figure 3.6 Programmer's comments on software and users, Gould (1988).

takes the ideas, wishes, desires, and needs of the *user* (homeowner), merges that with the skills and materials available to the *programmer* (builder), and designs a *software product* (house) that can be built and the user can enjoy. Figure 3.7 shows the designer's model as the intermediary between the user's model and the programmer's model. Programmers don't often meet the users of the products they develop. The gap between the user's environment and the programmer's world is bridged by the user interface designer and others on the design team who work directly with product users.

What exactly does a user interface designer do? How does the designer's model map the user's mental model to the programmer's model of the system and its capabilities? The designer's model describes the *objects* the user works with, their *presentation* to the user, and the *interaction* techniques used to manipulate the user's objects.

Figure 3.8 is known as the look-and-feel *iceberg* chart. It is based on the early user interface work done by scientists at the Xerox Palo Alto Research Center (Xerox PARC). The chart is attributed to David Liddle, formerly the head of Metaphor Computer Company. It shows that the interface designer's model is made up of three components: *presentation, interaction,* and *object relationships.*

The look and feel of a product may catch users' attention and interest when they first see a product and try it out. As they use the product further, however, the initial good feelings may wear off if the interface doesn't fit well with expectations of how it should work. The chart is depicted as an iceberg for a good reason. The percentages associated with each of the three areas and their location in the iceberg are very important.

The tip of the iceberg is the *look* element. It's the *presentation* of information to users, and it accounts for only about 10 percent of the substance of the designer's model. This aspect of the product interface includes using color, ani-

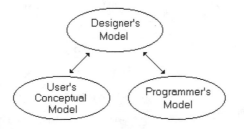

Figure 3.7   The role of the designer's model, from IBM (1992).

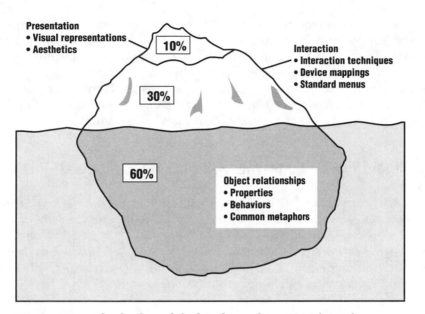

Figure 3.8 The look-and-feel iceberg, from IBM (1992).

mation, sound, shapes, graphics, text, and screen layout to present information to the user. Although it is the most obvious part of a user interface, the presentation aspects aren't the most important part of the interface.

For example, the overuse of color in the interface can initially interest users, but often detracts from the task at hand when the product is used over time. This is called the *Las Vegas effect,* for obvious reasons—there is a lot going on that is only superficially relevant to the tasks at hand. I'll cover the appropriate use of color and other aspects of the presentation of information in Chapter 13. Spicing up the presentation aspects of an interface is like putting icing on the cake, or, as Norm Cox would say, putting lipstick on the bulldog.

The second layer of the iceberg is the *feel* of the interface. This is the *interaction* area, and it accounts for about 30 percent of the designer's model. Here user interaction techniques using the keyboard, function keys, and other input devices such as a mouse, trackball, or joystick, are defined. This also covers how the system gives feedback on user actions. A good example of consistent interaction techniques is how an automobile works. Imagine how confused you would be if your car's stickshift were redesigned so you had to shift through the five gears in reverse order from the way the car works now!

By far the most important part of the iceberg (60 percent) is concerned with the things that are most critical to the user interface—object properties and the relationships between objects. This is where designers determine the appropriate metaphors to match the user's mental model of the system and the tasks they are trying to do. Also note that this part of the iceberg is shown as being submerged and not easily visible. It is not obvious to developers that they need to be concerned with this area of user interface design. However, it is by far the largest layer of the iceberg. It is also the most dangerous because a ship (a software product) can be hit and sunk if attention isn't paid to it.

Why Should You Be Concerned with Interface Models?

> *Architecture and interface design have an important goal in common: to create livable, workable, attractive environments. Corbusier was initially viewed with skepticism when he proposed that a house was a "machine for living," as opposed to the traditional idea that a house was a shelter. He likened a house to a ship or bridge in its function. Likewise, we are only just beginning to conceive of computers as extensions of our functional everyday lives.*
>
> S. Joy Mountford (1990)

This discussion on user interface models is not an academic exercise in the theoretical design of user interfaces. It is very real and describes the failure of many products that may have contained incredible technological and functional elements but were otherwise lacking in their attention to the user interface. These models should be understood by all those who participate in the development and use of software products.

KEY IDEA! *Defining the user interface as* simply the look and feel of a product *is not only inappropriate but is grossly incomplete. This viewpoint is overly naive and does not give user interfaces the credit for the role they play in user satisfaction, perception, and performance. Unfortunately, consumer and user first impressions are based on the look and feel aspects because they are the only visible and tactile parts of the interface initially available. Finding out if the software really works well with a user's model takes much more time and resources (usability testing). This situation leads consumers and users to equate look and feel with product usability.*

A case in point is the Macintosh interface. Mac software is perceived as being much easier to use than DOS products, often because of the familiar colors, buttons, and icons shared among all Macintosh products. But even Mac developers agree that some Mac software products aren't all that well designed or usable once you go underneath the Macintosh look and feel interface veneer. As a whole, most Macintosh software is very well designed, but there are no boundaries to poor user interface design—unfortunately, poor products aren't limited to the DOS, Windows, and OS/2 environment!

KEY IDEA! *Even the Mac interface can be made easier. Apple customer surveys showed that some computer novices needed an even easier, less sophisticated interface than the Mac. Apple designed a simplified interface, called At Ease, that has screen-sized file folders and extra-large icons and buttons to launch applications with a single-click of the mouse. Weinstock (1993) points out that there always will be a large group of computer-naive users: "Although At Ease may make the Mac more accessible to the technologically intimidated and the very young, it serves as a poignant reminder that even the friendliest computers still frighten a large segment of the population."*

As you can see from the iceberg chart and this discussion, the look and feel of the interface are the easy and more obvious parts of a product to focus on and build. As a user interface consultant, I've had customers ask me to help design their screen icons. This is before we've even discussed who the users are, what tasks they will be performing, and what type of interface they need! Presentation aspects of the interface account for only 10 percent of the total design of the product. Yes, icon colors, graphics, and text do need to be designed so that they are recognizable and understandable by users; but that should not be the first or most important design step. The designer's model is best formed from the bottom of the iceberg up. In fact, as the most important aspects, such as defining the objects and metaphors used in the interface, are worked on, the visual and aesthetic aspects of the interface, such as icons, will usually evolve logically and easily.

References

Baecker, Ronald M., Jonathan Gridin, William A. S. Buxton, and Saul Greenberg. 1995. Designing to fit Human capabilities. In Baecker et al. (Eds.), *Readings in Human-Computer Interaction: Toward the year 2000.* San Francisco, CA: Morgan Kaufmann.

Carroll, John and J. Olson. 1988. Mental models in human-computer interaction. In Helander, M. (ed.), *Handbook of Human-Computer Interaction.* Amsterdam, Holland: Elsevier Science Publishers.

Gould, John D. 1988. How to design usable systems. In Helander, M. (Ed.), *Handbook of Human-Computer Interaction.* Amsterdam, Holland: Elsevier Science Publishers, pp. 757–789.

IBM Corporation. 1992. *Object-Oriented Interface Design: IBM Common User Access Guidelines:* New York: QUE.

Mayhew, Deborah. 1992. *Principles and Guidelines in Software User Interface Design.* Englewood Cliffs, NJ: Prentice-Hall.

Soloway, Elliot. 1991. How the Nintendo generation learns. *Communications of the ACM* 34(9): 23.

Weinstock, Neal. 1993. Why make the Macintosh easier to use? *International Design* (March–April): 85.

CHAPTER FOUR

The Psychology of Humans and Computers

People and computers have quite different—often diametrically opposite—capabilities. With a "good" interface, human and computer should augment each other to produce a system that is greater than the sum of its parts. Computer and human share responsibilities, each performing the parts of the task that best fit its capabilities. The computer enhances our cognitive and perceptual strengths, and counteracts our weaknesses. People are responsible for the things the machine cannot or should not do.

Ronald Baecker et al. (1995)

The Psychology of Users

Computers may outthink us one day, but as long as people got feelings we'll be better than they are.

Elvis, in "The World According to Elvis," Jeff Rovin (1992)

Involving the user in interface design is critical. Interface design should be based on a knowledge of the user's experiences and expectations. You should be familiar with the basic physical, perceptual, and cognitive abilities of users.

Cognitive psychology is the study of how our minds work, how we think, how we remember, and how we learn. This is an *information-processing model* of human cognition—a model that says that human cognition is similar enough to a computer that a single theory of computation can be used to guide research and design in psychology and computer science. However, there are other models of cognition and there is more to human cognition than computation and storage.

The information-processing model views learning as a developmental process, incorporating prior experience, knowledge, and expectations. As such, it can be useful when designing software.

In this chapter, I'll cover the basics of human perception, cognition, and memory of interest to software designers. There are many textbooks on these subjects and there is a tremendous amount of published research that covers these areas and how they apply to the human-computer interface. The references listed at the back of this chapter are a good starting point for those interested in further readings in any of these areas.

Human Perception and Attention

Perception can be thought of as having the immediate past and the remote past brought to bear on the present in such a way that the present makes sense.

Robert Bailey (1982)

Until computers work totally by voice recognition and response, users must rely on the computer to present information visually on a computer display. Research on human perceptual abilities is critical even to simple techniques in software design. Here's just one demonstration of how computer systems must work within our human perceptual abilities.

Have you ever had a message flash on your computer screen and then suddenly disappear before you had a chance to read it? Frustrating, isn't it? The human visual system requires a certain small amount of time to react to a stimulus and to move the eyes to where the information is presented. It then takes time to actually read the message on the screen, and you might even need to read the message more than once to understand it. These basic human perceptual and psychological limitations and capabilities must be understood when determining the time period for displaying and removing messages on the screen.

Perception is not simply the act of seeing. It is the combination of information available through our senses (seeing, hearing, tasting, smelling, and touching) with knowledge stored in memory. The process of perception is relating new experiences with old experiences and expectations (Bailey, 1982). Does this sound familiar? The pervasive thread of user experiences and expectations runs through the human-computer relationship.

Here's a simple, yet effective example. In a classic experiment, people were shown either a capital letter (for example, an A) or a two-digit number (for example, 17). Then they are shown 13 (a broken capital B) and are asked what they saw. What would you guess they said? Yes, it does depend on what they saw first. People who saw a letter first tended to say it was a B, while people who saw a number first tended to say it was 13. Mayhew (1992) also shows this same effect in Figure 4.1. Reading across the row, you think the item in the middle is a 13. Yet, reading down the column, you recognize it as a B. It seems trivial, yet this is how humans work. The human perceptual system will attach meaning to information it receives, whether or not the meaning is intended or accurate.

There is so much information around us that our senses are constantly processing information, although we aren't necessarily aware of this process. What attracts our attention are any changes in the environment. Have you ever been in a crowded room talking to someone, when all of a sudden you hear your name mentioned in some other conversation all the way across the room? You didn't think you were paying attention to any other conversations going on in the room, but when your name was barely spoken across the room, you knew it almost immediately! This is called the *cocktail party phenomenon.* It shows that your sensory system is constantly monitoring the world around you. This also shows that you automatically process external information to the point where you can attach meaning to the information without being aware of it.

When there is some physical change in the environment, or even a change in the meaning of information you are processing, then you immediately change your focus and pay attention to that information. Any sudden or significant change in your perceptual system will attract your attention. This may be the result of changes in light, sound, movement, color, novelty, or complexity of the information you are processing. This is why all of the bells and whistles you hear coming from your computer can distract you from what you are trying to do, unless they are being used to tell you something that you should pay attention to.

Human Information Processing: Memory and Cognition

Never let a computer know you're in a hurry.

John Collins (1995)

Computers can't think like humans (at least not yet), but at the same time, humans can't do things that computers do very well. To get a better understand-

<table>
<tr><td></td><td>A</td><td></td></tr>
<tr><td>12</td><td>13</td><td>14</td></tr>
<tr><td></td><td>C</td><td></td></tr>
</table>

Figure 4.1 Human perception example, from Mayhew (1992).

ing of the way computers can and should help us to work and play better, we need to know more about how the human memory and cognitive systems work.

Figure 4.2 shows the components of the human information processing and memory system. These components are sensory storage, short-term memory, and long-term memory. I'll give you some practical examples of how each of these works and how computers and user interfaces can help aid each of these processes.

Sensory Storage

Sensory storage is a set of buffers where all of the automatic processing of information from your senses takes place (for example, the cocktail party phenomenon). We process an incredible amount of information without even knowing it. These *buffers* (auditory, visual, tactile) must be large and hold a very high level of detail to be able to automatically handle all of the information your senses are monitoring.

Think of your sensory processors as your interface sentries or outposts looking for information in the world around you. They don't have to be very smart, but they have to be very *attentive* to all that is happening around them, and they have to be very quick to spot any changes that they see. Because there is so much going on around you, the sensory system can't keep information around very long; it has to keep bringing in new information. Remember, this is all happening without your paying any attention to these processes. When something happens that causes you to pay attention to it, then the information is passed on to the higher memory functions. I discussed this area earlier in the section

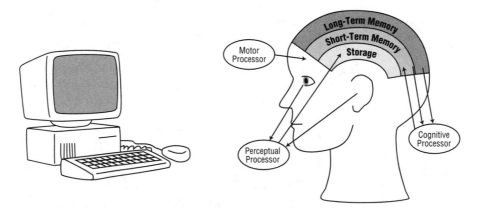

Figure 4.2   The human information processing and memory system.

on perception and attention. When you're watching a movie, you don't realize that you are actually seeing a steady flow of static frames of film. Your sensory system is processing that information, frame by frame, as fast as it can. Your higher-level processes smooth out all of the sensory information so that you perceive the movie as one continuous image. Only when the movie projector breaks down and the frames aren't shown so fast do you notice that you were watching individual frames of film.

KEY IDEA! *Messages must remain on the screen long enough for users not only to realize that the message is there, but to pass the information on to higher functions to read and respond to it. The human sensory system takes in information from everything on the computer screen. An animated screen background program is fun to watch. However, as you work in a window while the animated background is running, your sensory system is doing a lot of unnecessary work. You are processing all of that activity going on in the screen background while you are trying to work in the window. This extra visual processing may even cause eye strain and fatigue.*

Constant or repeated stimulation actually tires the sensory mechanisms and they become less attentive and less able to distinguish changes. This is called *habituation,* and it applies to all sensory information, including information on computer screens and in the physical environment. All factors, including light, temperature, sound, motion, and color affect human senses in this fashion. Thus, all elements of the computer interface are important and must be designed to serve a definite purpose for users.

Short-Term Memory

Short-term memory (STM) is the second stage of information processing. Information that is *recognized* and *perceived* is passed on from sensory storage to be processed further. STM also gets information from your permanent memory (*long-term memory,* or LTM) through the process of *cognition.* STM is the weakest link, or bottleneck, in the whole information processing system. It is a memory buffer that is limited in capacity to about seven plus or minus two items (that is, between five and nine items). Also, new information coming into STM bumps out older information if the buffer is filled. Information can be maintained only for a limited amount of time, at most about 30 seconds, without practice. STM is also called working memory because this is where you do your thinking, or processing of information. If I asked you to multiply 6 times 538 in your head, you would be doing this processing in short-term memory.

It's easy to see how STM works. It is also very important for you to know about people's STM limitations when interacting with computers. For instance, computers have easier access to stored information, while we have to work much harder to get to information we may already know. As an example, let's look at telephone numbers.

The telephone company has all of its phone numbers stored in computers and also printed in phone books. If you need a phone number you don't know or can't remember, you can either look it up in a phone book, if there is one available, or call the phone company. Either way, you have to somehow remember the number you find long enough for you to make your telephone call. What do you usually do when using a phone book? You may write down the phone number, which serves as an external memory aid, so when you go to dial the phone you don't even have to remember the number. You may try to remember the number in your head, which means you have to keep the number in your STM long enough so it is still there when you dial the phone. Just how do you keep the phone number in your head? If you are using the phone book in one corner of the room and have to walk to the other corner of the room to use the phone, you'll have to keep the number from being lost or replaced in memory.

People use various strategies to keep information in short-term memory. These techniques include rehearsal and chunking. We use whichever technique is easiest or most appropriate for the type of information, and they can be combined. A telephone number can be rehearsed simply by saying it aloud or silently to yourself. However, remember that any other new information or distraction may cause you to lose the numbers you're rehearsing. As you're repeating the phone number someone might mention to you "Hey, it's eleven thirty-five already, let's go to lunch!" The numbers you were just rehearsing have probably disappeared from your head and now you're repeating "11:35, 11:35" and wondering what happened to the phone number you were trying to remember.

Chunking is a very important memory strategy. It involves taking many pieces of information and grouping them together by associations, order, and meaning. Chunking is used both in remembering information in STM and in LTM. Remembering the phone number 123-4567 is easy. Seven digits can be chunked into only two "things" to remember—start with the number 1, and then increase each digit by one.

Take a look at the phone numbers that businesses choose. They create telephone numbers that customers can easily remember by chunking to create more meaningful phrases or numbers. For example, 1-800-IBM-SERV is used as the toll-free number for reaching IBM's Service Center. People use chunking to remember other sets of numbers. My bank's automated teller machine (ATM) is called LOGIC and my ATM password can be five digits. So I use the numbers that spell L-O-G-I-C on the ATM and all I have to do is look at my card to remember the scheme I used for my password. Unfortunately, credit card thieves are just as clever and could probably figure out my ATM card password very easily!

Even telephone companies use computers to provide support for our short-term memory limitations. If you call for information, the operator will usually transfer you to an automated system that tells you the telephone number. The system will announce your number twice. Why do they repeat the number? To help with your short-term memory! It is allowing you to make sure you heard the number correctly and it is helping you rehearse the number. The phone company even offers another service to save you time and effort. Instead of remembering the number, hanging up, and then dialing the number, the phone company will call the number for you (for a small fee, of course!). If it is a number that you don't need to remember (place in long-term memory), then for 50 cents you can let the phone company do the work of your short-term memory for you. Just think, ingenious computer developers can make money by understanding about human memory and cognition and counting on people's willingness to let someone else do their mental processing for them!

KEY IDEA! *Be aware of short-term memory characteristics and limitations when designing interfaces. For example, if users try to fill in information on a screen and ask for help on one particular item, don't cover up that item with help information so they can't see what they wanted help for in the first place! This type of help is often called "destructive help" because it covers up what users want to focus on. Users often go back to the help screen two or three times before they get all of the information they need. Don't build a help system or messages that cover up user information.*

It is annoying to be forced to remember information from screen to screen, or even retype information. The computer can easily bring previous information along and have it available on the next screen. I travel all the time and am always on the telephone with travel agents or airline, hotel, and rental car reservation agents. I'm constantly amazed that they often have to ask me for my customer number or other information multiple times because they are on a different screen than when they first asked for the information. They usually apologize for the inconvenience and remark that they don't know why the computer makes them type the information again when it already has the information on another screen. Rather than accept this situation, they should work with the system developers to remedy the situation.

Long-Term Memory

Long-term memory (LTM) is analogous to the phone company's computer database of telephone numbers or the phone book. LTM is a memory storage warehouse of possibly limitless capacity and duration. Computers are also large-capacity, permanent storage devices, but they have different strengths and weaknesses (see Table 4.1). The main problem lies not in the amount of information we can remember or for how long, but *how to access the information.* Finding the correct information in the telephone company's computer or from a phone book might be easier than trying to remember a phone number you once knew, but it isn't perfect. How can you possibly find Jane Smith's phone number in the phone book if you don't know her address? There are too many Smiths in the phone book for you to find her number without any additional information. The information may be there in the computer and in your long-term memory, but you don't have the ability to *retrieve* the information.

How many times have you tried to remember someone's name or the title of a movie and been so close to remembering it, but can't quite get it? This is called TOT, or *tip-of-the-tongue* phenomenon. You are so close to remembering something it almost hurts! You know how it sounds, or what the first letter is, or what the person looks like, but you can't quite make the final connection.

TABLE 4.1   Human and Computer Strengths and Weaknesses, from Mayhew (1992)

	Strengths	Weaknesses
Humans	◆ Pattern recognition ◆ Selective attention ◆ Capacity to learn ◆ Infinite-capacity LTM ◆ Rich, multikeyed LTM	◆ Low-capacity STM ◆ Fast-decaying STM ◆ Slow processing ◆ Error prone ◆ Unreliable access to LTM
Computers	◆ High-capacity memory ◆ Permanent memory ◆ Fast processing ◆ Error-free processing ◆ Reliable memory access	◆ Simple template matching ◆ Limited learning capacity ◆ Limited capacity LTM ◆ Limited data integration

You can remember some, but not all, of the features of the information. The amazing thing is that if you stop trying so hard to remember the information, usually a few seconds later it will just pop into your head. Our LTM storage is extremely complex and information is encoded in a rich network structure. By remembering a few features of the information you have reestablished a few of the links in the network and can usually get to the information given a little time.

As there are strategies for helping keep information in STM, there are also strategies for helping to retrieve information. *Mnemonics* involve attaching meaning to information you are trying to remember. Part of the telephone number you are trying to remember might be the street address of your old house. You then need only think of "your old house" and that will help you remember the number. People have trained themselves to accurately remember amazingly long lists of items by creating internal visual *hooks* on which they can hang each piece of information they are trying to remember. They can then mentally go to each hook and retrieve the item from the list that they hung on that hook. There are waiters and waitresses who can remember the food and drink orders for all the people at a large table by successfully developing memory enhancement strategies such as this.

We also use chunking strategies in LTM with items we always have to remember, like our home and work telephone numbers, Social Security number, ATM codes, computer passwords, and so on. Your Social Security is a nine-digit number, which is a long string of numbers to remember. However, you probably don't think of your Social Security number as nine separate numbers. You think of it as three numbers with three, two, and four digits in each number. You've just taken nine individual numbers with no logical connection and chunked them into three numbers that fit together.

Since long-term memory retrieval is a major problem for users, computer interfaces should be sensitive to this and offer support wherever they can. The two main methods for retrieving information are *recognition* and *recall*. Notice the convenient memory mnemonic aid for remembering this topic: *r*etrieval is *r*ecognition and *r*ecall. Just remember 3 *R*s and you've got it. That's using mnemonics and chunking strategies!

Why force users to have to recall information, even if they do know it? Why not give them a menu or list and let them recognize an item? Recall usually involves trying to retrieve information without any cues. What is the keyboard assignment for pasting text in a document from your favorite word processor? Recognition involves trying to retrieve information with some cues present. Look on the Edit menu on the word processing screen and you can just select the Paste choice and it should also tell you that Shift+Insert on the keyboard will do the same action.

Humans and Computers Working Together

This chapter has been a brief tour of the human information-processing system. This knowledge should be useful as you design user interfaces. Mayhew (1992) provides a good summary of the strengths and weaknesses of humans and computers in Table 4.1.

An understanding of human capabilities and weaknesses helps you know when to lead, when to follow, and when to support users. Don Norman (1990) summarizes the human-computer relationship well:

> People err. That is a fact of life. People are not precision machinery designed for accuracy. In fact, we humans are a different kind of device entirely. Creativity, adaptability, and flexibility are our strengths. Continual alertness and precision in action or memory are our weaknesses . . . We are extremely flexible, robust, creative, and superb at finding explanations and meanings from partial and noisy evidence. The same properties that lead to such robustness and creativity also produce errors.

KEY IDEA! *Design user interfaces based on what is known about people's cognitive and perceptual abilities. One of the most important things an interface can do is to reduce users' reliance on their own memory and use the computer's strengths to support users' weaknesses.*

References

Bailey, Robert W. 1982. *Human Performance Engineering: A Guide for System Designers.* Englewood Cliffs, NJ: Prentice-Hall.

Mayhew, Deborah. 1992. *Principles and Guidelines in Software User Interface Design.* Englewood Cliffs, NJ: Prentice-Hall.

Norman, Donald A. 1990. Human error and the design of computer systems. *Communications of the ACM* 33(1):4–5,7.

CHAPTER FIVE

The Golden Rules of User Interface Design

Make it simple, but no simpler.

Albert Einstein

Before you buy software, make sure it believes in the same things you do. Whether you realize it or not, software comes with a set of beliefs built in. Before you choose software, make sure it shares yours.

PeopleSoft advertisement (1996)

User Interface Design Principles

The golden rule of design: Don't do to others what others have done to you. Remember the things you don't like in software interfaces you use. Then make sure you don't do the same things to users of interfaces you design and develop.

Tracy Leonard (1996)

Why should you need to follow user interface principles? In the past, computer software was designed with little regard for the user, *so the user had to somehow adapt to the system.* This approach to system design is not at all appropriate today—*the system must adapt to the user.* This is why design principles are so important.

Computer users should have successful experiences that allow them to build confidence in themselves and establish a self-assurance about how they work with computers. Their interactions with computer software should be characterized by "success begets success." Each positive experience with a software program allows users to explore outside their area of familiarity and encourages them to expand their knowledge of the interface. Well-designed software interfaces, like good educators and instructional materials, should build a teacher-student relationship that guides users to learn and enjoy what they are doing. Good interfaces can even challenge users to explore beyond their normal boundaries and stretch their understanding of the user interface and the computer. When you see this happen, it is a beautiful experience.

You should have an understanding and awareness of the user's mental model and the physical, physiological, and psychological abilities of users. This information (discussed in Chapters 3 and 4) has been distilled into general *principles* of user interface design, which are agreed upon by most experts in the field. User interface design principles address each of the key components of the look-and-feel iceberg (see Chapter 3): presentation, interaction, and object relationships.

Interface design principles represent high-level concepts and beliefs that should be used to guide software design. You should determine which principles are most important and most applicable for your systems and then use these principles to establish guidelines and determine design decisions.

KEY IDEA! *The trick to using interface design principles is knowing which ones are most important when making design trade-offs. For certain products and specific design situations, these design principles may be in conflict with each other or at odds with product design goals and objectives. Principles are not meant to be followed blindly, rather they are meant as guiding lights for sensible interface design.*

The three areas of user interface design principles are:

◆ Place users in control of the interface.
◆ Reduce users' memory load.
◆ Make the user interface consistent.

Where to Find Interface Design Principles

User interface design principles are not just relevant to today's graphical user interfaces. In fact, they have been around for quite some time. Hansen (1971) proposed the first (and perhaps the shortest) list of design principles in his paper, "User Engineering Principles for Interactive Systems." Hansen's principles were:

- Know the user.
- Minimize memorization.
- Optimize operations.
- Engineer for errors.

A more recent and encompassing list of design principles can be found in *The Human Factor* by Rubenstein and Hersch (1984). This classic book on human-computer interaction presents 93 design principles, ranging from "1. Designers make myths; users make conceptual models" to "93. Videotape real users." I've listed some key books in the reference section at the end of this chapter. These books fall into two categories: books on interface design and software design guides. Some good interface design books (in addition to Rubenstein and Hersch) are Heckel (1984), Mayhew (1992), and Shneiderman (1992).

The major software operating system vendors have all either published or republished their design guidelines and reference materials in the past few years as they introduce new operating systems. These guidelines exemplify and encapsulate their interface design approaches. It is critical to keep up to date with these guides for your design and development environment. These software design guides include Apple Computer, Inc. (Apple, 1992), IBM Corporation (IBM, 1992), Microsoft Corporation (Microsoft, 1995), and UNIX OSF/Motif (Open Software Foundation, 1993). All of these design guides address, at a minimum, the importance of user interface design principles.

KEY IDEA! *The most recent industry guide is* The Windows Interface Guidelines for Software Design *from Microsoft, published in conjunction with the release of the Windows 95 operating system. Most people don't know that the document is also available online as a Windows 95 Help file. It can be found on the Windows 95 Developer's Toolkit CD-ROM (files UIGUIDE.HLP, UIGUIDE.CNT, UIGUIDE.FTS, and UIGUIDE.GID). It can also be found on the Microsoft Web site at http:///www.microsoft.com/win32dev/uiguide/. Those designing Windows applications should have this document close by, both hardcopy and online!*

Readers should use the publications that best address their learning and working environment (including hardware, operating system, and key software products). The interface terminology may differ slightly among the various books, but they all address, at some level, the user interface principles that make up the major categories described here.

Why Should You Care about Interface Design Principles?

The conclusion: interface inconsistency can cost a big company millions of dollars in lost productivity and increased support costs.

Jesse Berst (1993)

These principles are generally thought to be common across all computer hardware and software environments. They also apply across all interface types and styles. They have evolved over time through many years of interface design efforts, research, testing, and user feedback in computing environments from mainframes to the Macintosh and PCs.

These principles should endure as new user interface technologies emerge. Jakob Nielsen (1990) noted, "The principles are so basic that even futuristic dialogue designs such as three-dimensional interfaces with DataGlove input devices, gesture recognition, and live video images will always have to take them into account as long as they are based on the basic paradigm of dialogues and user commands."

KEY IDEA! *The actual implementation of these principles will, of course, vary according to the hardware environment, operating system, user interface capabilities of the system, and interface design goals. Often, business decisions influence the designer's use of the principles and the priorities that may be assigned to them. The user's and designer's models should also determine how the principles are applied to user interface design. At critical points in the interface design process you'll be asking the question, "What happens next?" The answer should be, "Whatever users want to do!" Remember— know thy users, for they are not you.*

An interface design team, in conjunction with managers, team leaders, and workers, should figure out together which principles are the most appropriate for their environment and work tasks. They should then focus on purchasing or developing software products that offer usable and productive interfaces that exemplify those key principles.

Golden Rule #1: Place Users in Control

The first set of principles addresses placing users in control of the interface. A simple analogy is whether to let people drive a car or force them to take a train (Figure 5.1). In a car, users control their own direction, navigation, and final destination. One problem is that drivers need a certain amount of skill and knowledge before they are able to successfully drive a car. Drivers also need to know where they are going! A train forces users to become *passengers* rather than *drivers*. People used to driving their own car to their destination may not enjoy the train ride, where they can't control the schedule or the path a train will take to reach the destination. However, novice or casual users may enjoy the train if they don't know exactly where they are going and they don't mind relying on the train to guide and direct them on their journey. The ultimate decision to drive a car or take the train should be the user's, not someone else's. Users also deserve the right to change their mind and take the car one day and the train the next.

Let's first look at the banking environment, where computer users range from bank presidents to bank tellers. Presidents have more flexibility and authority in the tasks they can do with the computer system. Meanwhile, bank tellers have a much more limited set of tasks they perform. Their tasks are customer-directed and are repeated very often throughout the work day. Tellers should also not be allowed to access the tasks and information that bank presidents work with.

Figure 5.1   Do users want to take a train or drive a car?

The design principles that place users in control should be used appropriately to allow bank presidents systemwide access and control. The tellers, however, should be given an interface that allows them to work within their limited set of tasks. The interface should also give them some degree of control and flexibility to do their tasks quickly, comfortably, and efficiently. In this environment, the interface designer must determine which of these principles are most important when designing the bank's computer system for all of its users.

KEY IDEA! *Wise designers let users do their work for them rather than attempting to figure out what they want. After designing a complex of buildings, an architect was supposed to design the walkways between the buildings. He did not assume that he knew how users would really use the walkways between buildings. So he didn't design the walkways or build them at the same time as the buildings. Rather, he had fields of grass planted between the buildings. It is rumored that he even posted signs saying, "Please walk on the grass." A few months after the buildings were completed, he came back and saw where the most worn paths were where people walked across the grass between buildings. Then he knew where he should put the walkways.*

This is a wonderful, real-life example of a designer letting *users* be in control, observing their behavior, and then building an interface that allows them to go where they want to go and how they want to get there.

TABLE 5.1   Principles that Place Users in Control

1. Use modes judiciously (modeless).
2. Allow users to use either the keyboard or mouse (flexible).
3. Allow users to change focus (interruptible).
4. Display descriptive messages and text (helpful).
5. Provide immediate and reversible actions, and feedback (forgiving).
6. Provide meaningful paths and exits (navigable).
7. Accommodate users with different skill levels (accessible).
8. Make the user interface transparent (facilitative).
9. Allow users to customize the interface (preferences).
10. Allow users to directly manipulate interface objects (interactive).

The principles that allow users to be in control are listed in Table 5.1. After each principle I've listed a key word to help fix it in your mind.

Use Modes Judiciously

Here's a very familiar example of modes from the real world of VCRs. When you press the Fast Forward or Rewind button on your VCR or on the remote control, you don't always get the same response from the VCR. Why? Because the system's response depends on which mode the VCR is in—either the Stop mode or the Play mode. If the VCR is *stopped,* then Fast Forward or Rewind buttons fast forward or rewind the tape very quickly. However, if the VCR is *playing,* then these buttons *search* forward or backward, showing the picture on the TV. The search functions don't move the tape as quickly as the Fast Forward and Rewind functions.

Say you've just finished watching a rented videotape. You want to rewind the tape so you won't be charged a rewinding fee when you return the tape to the video store. You press the Rewind button while you're watching the film credits on the screen and turn off the television. You won't even know that the VCR is really searching backward in the Play mode. This could take a very long time and since the television is turned off, you can't even see that the VCR is still in the Play mode. What you probably wanted to do was to press the Stop button first and *then* press Rewind. This would rewind the tape quickly, taking much less time and placing less strain on your VCR.

This whole episode I just described recently happened at home to my wife. I had bought a new VCR and she wasn't very familiar with its operation yet. She was rewinding a tape with the television off and she commented that it seemed to be taking a long time to rewind the whole tape. I looked at the display on the front of the VCR and sure enough, there was an indicator arrow (➤) showing that the VCR was still in the Play mode. After I explained this to my wife, she said, "That's a stupid way to design a VCR! Why don't you use that as an example in your book?"

Have you ever used a graphical drawing program on your computer? The palette of drawing tools you use is an example of the use of modes. When you select the draw tool, you are in the *draw* mode. Your mouse movement, mouse button presses, and keyboard keystrokes will all produce some type of drawing actions. Then select the text tool, and the same mouse and keyboard actions produce text and text functions. Modes are a necessary part of many software interfaces. You probably can't avoid using modes altogether, but use them only when needed. A common example of a familiar and unavoidable mode can be found in any word processor. When you are typing text, you are *always* in a mode—either *insert* mode or *replace* mode.

It's easy to find interfaces that put users in modes unnecessarily. Any time a message pops up on the computer screen and users can't do anything else in the program or even anywhere else on the screen, they are imprisoned by a *modal* dialog! There are two types of interface modes, and although they may be necessary in some cases, they are not needed or are unnecessarily restrictive most of the time.

The first type is *application* modal. When in an application mode, users are not allowed to work elsewhere in the program, or it places them in a certain mode for the whole program. For example, when you are working with a database of information and choose the view data mode, the program will not allow you to add, delete, or modify the data record. You would have to change to the update data mode to perform these actions. This may be appropriate for users who are only allowed to browse the database. What if users are constantly viewing data and wish to change data when they want to? Why should they be forced to change modes all the time? Why are users forced to either be in view or update mode in the first place? A more user- and task-oriented approach is to let users access the data without being forced to choose a mode beforehand. If they choose to modify data, they should be able to save the data and update the database without being in a particular mode. If they don't make any changes, they can access a new data record or exit the record, without having made any decision about program modes. Perhaps the best method is to display data in a format that is consistent with a user's access. In the case of limited access, display static text; if users have update access, provide entry fields that are updateable.

The second type of mode is *system* modal. This mode should rarely be forced on users. While in a system mode, users are not allowed to work anywhere else on the computer until the mode is ended, or it places them in a certain mode no matter what program they are using. Let's say a document is printing, and a message window pops up stating the printer is out of paper. Users should not have to get up and put paper in the printer immediately, or even remove the message from the screen. They should be able to continue working with a word processing program or do anything else on the computer. Users might even want to keep the message window on the screen as a reminder to add paper later. Programs sometimes take control of the entire system when they present messages on the screen. There is no reason why the "Printer out of paper" message should be a system modal dialog. Watch out for this especially when designing and programming messages and help information. You can see how frustrating system modes can be for users.

When using modes, it is important to follow the principle of immediate visual feedback. Every time users choose a mode there should be some form of visual feedback while they are in that mode. Many programs change the mouse

KEY IDEA! *Modes are not always bad things. Let users choose when they want to go into a particular mode, rather than forcing them into a mode based on where they are in the program or in the interface. The true test of interface modes is if users don't think about being in a mode or if the modes are so natural to them that they feel comfortable using them. Users don't even think about being in* insert *or* replace *(overwrite) mode while using a word processor—it is natural for them to switch between modes whenever they wish.*

pointer or the text selection cursor to show the current mode. This is an example of the interaction between principles.

Allow Users to Use Either the Keyboard or Mouse

Don't assume that since users have a mouse attached to their computer, they will use it all of the time. Although you may design the interface to be optimized for mouse users, provide a way to do most actions and tasks using the keyboard. One of the key Common User Access (CUA) design principles is that users must be able to do any action or task using either the keyboard or the mouse.

KEY IDEA! *Keyboard access means users can perform an action using the keyboard rather than the mouse. It does not mean that it will be easier for users to use the keyboard, just that they don't have to use the mouse if they don't want to, or can't. Toolbars, for example, are fast-path buttons for mouse users. However, users can't get to the toolbar from the keyboard—they must be able to use the menu bar drop-downs to navigate to the action they want to perform.*

Users have very different habits when using keyboards and mice, and they often switch between them during any one task or while using one program. With the push toward mouse-driven, direct-manipulation interfaces, not all of the major design guides follow this philosophy of implementing both a keyboard and mouse interface. There is not a total consensus of agreement on this principle. Many Macintosh products do not provide complete keyboard access.

However, designers may want to follow this principle for the sake of users as they migrate to graphical interfaces and for consistency with other programs that may only have keyboard input. Users with special needs usually require an interface with keyboard access. Some new interface techniques also may need keyboard support to ensure user productivity. As a user whose laptop mouse has been broken or disabled, or who lost the mouse pointer on the screen, or who's been on an airplane with no room to use a mouse, I appreciate being able to access all important actions from the keyboard. Special-purpose software may choose not to follow this principle, but I recommend that all general-purpose software programs offer keyboard access unless there are compelling reasons to do otherwise.

Allow Users to Change Focus

People are always being interrupted—by a telephone, a colleague, a manager, or other things they have to do. Software interfaces should be designed so users are able to interrupt their current actions or tasks and either continue later or save them in the current state. It's easy to forget that users may not want to complete what they themselves started!

A way to allow users to stay in control is to offer guidance through common tasks as an option. Casual users and novices will welcome the guidance, while frequent users will likely go off on their own without guidance.

KEY IDEA! *Don't force users to complete predefined sequences. Give them options—to cancel or to save and return to where they left off. "Wizards" (see Chapter 14) are used more and more to lead users through common tasks. But don't lead with an iron hand. Let users stay in control while the interface guides them rather than forces them through steps in a task.*

Display Descriptive Messages and Text

"The password is too short. It must be at least 26908 bytes long. Type the password again." I recently saw this system message on one of my client's computer screens! Although it may be *descriptive* and accurate (how are we to know?), it certainly isn't *helpful* or appropriate. Do users know how many characters are needed to be at least 26908 bytes long? I don't think so! Maybe the message's creator can translate bytes to number of characters, but users shouldn't have to. The message also violates the principle of making the interface transparent. Users don't need to know that a password is stored as a certain number of bytes (users may not even know what bytes are!), only that they must remember it when they logon to the system. Here's a more helpful version of the message: "Your password must contain 6 to 16 characters. Please type the password again."

KEY IDEA! *Throughout the interface, use terms that users can understand, rather than system or developer terms. Users don't necessarily know about bits and bytes, and they shouldn't have to!*

This principle applies not only to messages, but to all text on the screen, whether it be prompts, instructions, headings, or labels on buttons. Yes, screen space is valuable, but it is important to use language that is easy to read and understand. Messages are key to a program's dialog with users. All textual aspects of the interface should be designed by those with writing skills. All writing is an art, including writing system and program documentation and messages. In many projects I've seen, all text on the screen, including messages, prompts, labels, titles, codes, and all help information, is the responsibility of information developers or technical writers on the design and development team.

KEY IDEA! *It is critical to establish the proper tone of voice in messages and prompts. It is important to assign no blame for errors or problems. Poor message terminology and tone encourages users to blame themselves for problems that occur.*

Provide Immediate and Reversible Actions, and Feedback

Airline crews rarely used to tell passengers when they were experiencing difficulties with an aircraft on the ground or in the air. There were usually no announcements as to what the problem was or how long it might take to fix. Passengers got very restless and impatient without any feedback. Studies found that people are much more forgiving if they are told the truth about what is going on and are given periodic feedback about the status of the situation. Now, airline pilots and crews make a point to periodically announce exactly what the situation is and how much time they expect to take to resolve it.

I recently went to the MGM Studios theme park in Orlando, Florida. The most popular ride is the "Back to the Future" adventure and there are always long lines of people waiting to get in. Signs are posted in front of each ride telling people how long the estimated waiting time is to get into the ride. There was a 45-minute wait for this popular ride when we were there. However, the entry areas for all the rides are designed like a maze, with walkways winding around and around in a very small space, so you are constantly moving and turning in different directions as you make gradual progress toward the ride entrance. Television monitors preview the ride at stations along the way so that everyone standing in line can see and hear what they are about to experience in the ride.

The entry areas and the television monitors were designed specifically to keep people moving at all times, to distract them, and keep them entertained. It is very important that an "illusion of progress" be felt by users, whether it is people standing in line for an amusement park ride or computer users waiting for a program to complete an action or process. The use of feedback and progress indicators is one of the subtle aspects of a user interface that is of tremendous value to the comfort and enjoyment of users.

The lack of feedback present in most software products forces users to double-check to see if their actions have been performed. In a command-line interface, whenever I delete a file using the DEL command, I usually use the DIR command immediately afterward to list the directory to see if the file was actually deleted. There is no feedback after you type the DEL command! This forces users to perform *superstitious behaviors* to comfort themselves since there is little or no feedback from the system interface.

KEY IDEA! *Every product should provide undo actions for users, as well as redo actions. Inform users if an action cannot be undone and allow them to choose alternative actions, if possible. Provide users with some indication that an action has been performed, either by showing them the results of the action, or acknowledging that the action has taken place successfully.*

Provide Meaningful Paths and Exits

Allow users to navigate easily through the interface. Provide ways for them to get to any part of the product they want to. Allow them to move forward or backward, upward or downward through the interface structure. Make them comfortable by providing some *context* of where they are, where they've been, and where they can go next. Figure 5.2 shows the Microsoft Windows 95 taskbar, with the (by now) famous Start button. The main reason for these interface elements is to show users what programs are opened, and to allow quick access to all programs and data via the Start button.

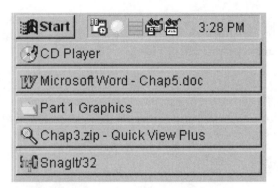

Figure 5.2 Microsoft Windows 95
taskbar and start button.

The many toolbars, launchpads, palettes, dashboards, and taskbars you see in today's operating systems, product suites, and utilities all are designed to help users navigate through the operating system and their hard disk, in search of programs and data. Users want fast paths to files, folders, programs, and common actions, and that's what these interface utilities offer.

System and program wizards and assistants also offer guidance for navigating through a program's functions or tasks. These new interface elements are discussed in Part 4.

KEY IDEA! *Users should be able to relax and enjoy exploring the interface of any software product. Even industrial-strength products shouldn't intimidate users so that they are afraid to press a button or navigate to another screen. The Internet explosion shows that navigation is a simple process to learn—basically, navigation is the main interaction technique on the Internet. If users can figure out how to get to pages on the World Wide Web, they have 80 percent of the interface figured out. People become experienced browsers very quickly.*

Accommodate Users with Different Skill Levels

Users of different skill levels should be able to interact with a program at different levels. Many programs offer customizable interfaces that allow users to choose their interaction level. For example, the menu bar and pull-downs of a program can be set up as *standard* or *advanced,* depending on user preferences and the types of tasks being performed.

Providing both keyboard and mouse interfaces offers users flexibility and allows users at different skill levels or with physical handicaps to use input devices in whatever ways they feel comfortable.

KEY IDEA! *Don't sacrifice expert users for an easy-to-use interface for casual users. You must provide fast paths for experienced users. Nothing drives experienced users crazy like having to go through too many steps to perform an action they use all the time and would like to perform using one step or a macro command.*

Make the User Interface Transparent

The user interface is the mystical, mythical part of a software product. If done well, users aren't even aware of it. If done poorly, users can't get past it to effectively use the product. A goal of the interface is to help users feel like they are reaching right through the computer and directly manipulating the objects they are working with. Now, that's a transparent interface!

The interface can be made transparent by giving users work objects rather than system objects. Trash cans, waste baskets, shredders, and in- and out-baskets all let users focus on the tasks they want to do using these objects, rather than the underlying system functions actually performed by these objects. Make sure these objects work like they do in the real world, rather than in some other way in the computer. Microsoft's Windows 95 interface provides a Recycle Bin, rather than a waste basket or shredder, to remind users that things are not necessarily thrown away immediately.

Other aspects of Windows 95 are not so transparent, however. The Close Program dialog (displayed by keying Ctrl+Alt+Del) not only lists the programs users started and are currently running, but it also displays a long list of other system programs, with names like Explorer, Rscrmtr, Symapudo, Qvp32, and Runner. Users have no idea of what these programs are and where they came from, but they are free to choose any program from this list and, in doing so, inadvertently end that running task. This can be quite dangerous since the system is not well hidden from users.

Allow Users to Customize the Interface

Allow users to customize *information presentation* (colors, fonts, location, arrangement, view types), *interface behavior* (default actions, macros, buttons), and *interaction techniques* (keystrokes, shortcut keys, mnemonics, mouse but-

KEY IDEA! *The secret of a transparent interface is being in synch with the user's mental model. Users should be free to focus on the work they are trying to perform, rather than translating their tasks into the functions that the software program provides. Users should understand simply that their system password must be at least six characters, and should not be concerned with how many bytes of storage that is.*

ton mappings). The rich visual and sensory environment of graphical and multimedia user interfaces requires users to be able to customize the interface. Users feel more comfortable and in control of the interface if they can personalize it with their favorite colors, patterns, fonts, and background graphics for their desktop.

KEY IDEA! *Today's operating systems offer a great deal of customization for interface elements. OS/2's properties views and Windows 95's properties dialogs allow users to set preferences for many operating system features and objects. Windows 95 developers even created an add-on utility called* Tweak UI. *Your products should use operating system properties to remain consistent with other applications. However, all other aspects of the product interface, including menus and buttons, can be customizable at the product level.*

Allow Users to Directly Manipulate Interface Objects

Wherever possible, encourage users to directly interact with things on the screen, rather than using indirect methods, such as typing commands or selecting from menus. While you still must allow for both keyboard and mouse navigation and selection, you should optimize the interface toward users' most natural interaction style.

In addition to the principle of making the interface transparent, users should feel like the interface isn't even there. When determining direct manipulation relationships, work within the interface metaphors and user models. The popular *personal information manager* (PIM), Lotus Organizer, has its own waste basket. Drag an appointment or address book entry to the waste basket and watch what happens—the item bursts into flames! Is this the behavior you expect from a waste basket? I don't think so.

KEY IDEA! *Users begin to question their own beliefs if the results of direct manipulations don't match their own mental model of how things interact in the real world. A simple rule is: Extend a metaphor, but don't break it. Sometimes direct manipulation interfaces fail because users don't know what they can pick up and where they can put it. Your interface objects should shout out to users, "Drag me, drop me, treat me like the object that I am!" If they don't, users won't know what to do. The one problem with direct manipulation is that it isn't visually obvious that things can be picked up and dragged around the screen. Users should feel comfortable picking up objects and exploring dragging and dropping them in the interface to see what might happen. The interface must be* explorable.

At Least Let Users *Think* They're in Control

Users should be given some control of the user interface. In some situations, users should have total control of what they can do within a product or throughout the operating system. In other environments, users should be allowed to access and use only objects and programs needed for their work tasks. It is human nature for people to be frustrated when they want to go somewhere and they can't get there quickly, or they can't take the route they would normally take. Well, there are times when a computer system or program takes a certain amount of time to do some action or process and there is nothing that can speed it up. What do you do to keep users informed of the progress of the action and keep them from getting upset? Is there any way to keep users busy so they won't think that the computer is slow or not working?

Let's learn from the real world how to solve this problem. A maintenance supervisor for a large office building was getting complaints from hurried office workers in the building that the elevators were too slow. The supervisor knew that there was very little he could do to improve the speed of the elevators. He said to himself, "What can I do to take their minds off how slow the elevators are?" In his infinite wisdom, he figured out that if he installed mirrors inside the elevators, that just might keep passengers occupied while the elevators traveled at their normal speed. Guess what? He never got another complaint about the slowness of the elevators after the mirrors were installed. The problem with the speed of the elevators could not be solved, but *users' perception of the problem* could be influenced by the designer. Elevator floor information lights and sounds, both inside elevators and in lobbies, are also designed as visual and auditory progress indicators. Mechanical and electrical engineers know it is a good idea to show the elevator's status or progress, both to inform users and to keep them occupied.

KEY IDEA! *A well-designed interface can comfort and entertain users while the computer system is completing a process. Users don't like to be left just sitting there doing nothing and seeing nothing on the computer screen while the computer is supposed to be doing something. Even if you can't let users be in control, let them think they are! At least entertain and teach them!*

Many product developers (or probably their marketing staff) have realized they have a captive audience while users are installing a new program from numerous diskettes or a CD-ROM. I've seen a number of installation programs that advertise their products on the screen while users are just sitting there waiting for the program installation. Users can't help but read what is presented on the screen. Some products even use this time to teach users about the product so they can become productive with it immediately. That's a good use of the user's time!

Golden Rule #2: Reduce Users' Memory Load

The capabilities and limitations of the human memory system were discussed in Chapter 4. Based on what we know about how people store and remember information, the power of the computer interface should keep users from having to do that work while using the computer. We aren't good at remembering things, so programs should be designed with this in mind. Table 5.2 lists the design principles in this area.

TABLE 5.2 Principles that Reduce Users' Memory Load

1. Relieve short-term memory (remember).
2. Rely on recognition, not recall (recognition).
3. Provide visual cues (inform).
4. Provide defaults, undo, and redo (forgiving).
5. Provide interface shortcuts (frequency).
6. Promote an object-action syntax (intuitive).
7. Use real-world metaphors (transfer).
8. Use progressive disclosure (context).
9. Promote visual clarity (organize).

Relieve Short-Term Memory

As you may recall (and since it was discussed in Chapter 4, I hope it's in your long-term memory by now!), short-term memory helps keep information available so you can retrieve it in a very short period of time. Users usually do many things at once, so computer interfaces shouldn't force them to try to keep information in their own short-term memory while they are switching tasks. This is a design principle that is often violated, causing users to rely on external memory aids, such as sticky pads, calculators, and sheets of paper, to record what they know they will need later in a customer transaction. It is such a simple interface principle, but one that is often neglected.

Program elements such as undo and redo, and clipboard actions like cut, copy, and paste, allow users to manipulate pieces of information needed in multiple places and within a particular task. Even better, programs should automatically save and transfer data when needed at different times and in different places during user tasks.

K**EY IDEA!** *Don't force users to have to remember and repeat what the computer could (and should) be doing for them. For example, when filling in online forms, customer names, addresses, and telephone numbers should be remembered by the system once a user has entered them, or once a customer record has been opened. I've talked with countless airline, hotel, and car rental phone agents who know they need the same information a few screens later. They have to try to remember the information until they get to the later screen, or they have to write down the information while talking to the customer so they have it when they get to the other screen. The system should be able to retrieve the previous information so users don't have to remember and retype the information again.*

Rely on Recognition, Not Recall

User interfaces support long-term memory retrieval by providing users with items for them to *recognize* rather than having to *recall* information. It is easier to browse a list to select an item than to try to remember the correct item to type into a blank entry field.

Take a look at common tasks performed in a popular program such as Quicken. When entering information for a check written from a checking account, a calendar helps users select the appropriate date, a "next check number" selection enters the correct check number, and a list of memorized transactions can fill in the payee and the amount to be paid. Users can complete the task without even typing a word!

Online aids such as messages, tooltips, and context-sensitive help are interface elements that support users in recognizing information rather than trying to remember what they may or may not know.

KEY IDEA! *Provide lists and menus containing selectable items instead of fields where users must type in information without support from the system. Why should users have to remember the two-character abbreviations for each state of the United States when they are filling out an online form? Don't force them to memorize codes for future use. Provide lists of frequently chosen items for selection rather than just giving them a blank entry field.*

Provide Visual Cues

A necessary aspect of any *graphical* user interface (and, of course, an object-oriented user interface) is that users must know *where* they are, *what* they are doing, and *what* they can do next.

Visual cues serve as reminders for users. Figure 5.3 shows what my computer screen looks like as I write this chapter. The many visual indicators tell me what I'm doing. First, the window title bar tells me that I am using Microsoft Word and that the name of the current file is Chap5.doc. This is a *textual* cue. The blinking text cursor tells me where I am in the document when I start typing. The style (Body Text), font (Times New Roman), size (12), emphasis (none), and orientation (flush left) items on the toolbar show the characteristics of the text that is currently selected. The scroll bar shows that I am about halfway into the document. The bottom-left panel of the window tells me I am on page 15. The bottom-middle panel tells me that I am in insert mode or overwrite mode with the OVR indicator (OVR is grayed out in insert mode and is black text in overwrite mode). The page format and the horizontal and vertical rulers tell me exactly where I am on the page. Microsoft Word 7.0 even tells you when you have misspelled (check the figure) a word, or even duplicated a word (check the figure) by showing a subtle red line under the word. The program will even give you a pop-up menu with alternative spellings and choices for the text. There are even more visual cues in the figure that I haven't described. See if you can find other cues to the characteristics of the program and the current document.

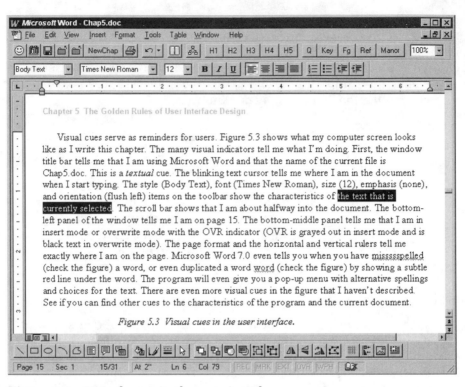

Figure 5.3   Visual cues in the user interface.

KEY IDEA! *Whenever users are in a mode, or are performing actions with the mouse, there should be some visual indication somewhere on the screen that they are in that mode. The mouse pointer may change to show the mode or the current action, or an indicator might toggle on or off. Test a product's visual cues—walk away from the computer in the middle of a task and come back sometime later. Look for cues in the interface that tell you what you are working with, where you are, and what you are doing.*

Provide Defaults, Undo, and Redo

Following the design principles for placing users in control, interfaces allow a wide variety of customizing features. With the power to change the interface, you must also give users the ability to reset choices and preferences to system or program defaults. Otherwise, users will be able to change their system colors, fonts, and properties so much that they may have no idea what the original properties were and how they can get them back.

While editing and manipulating data, such as writing text or creating graphics, undo and redo are very important to users. Undo lets users make changes and go back step by step through the changes that were made. Redo lets users undo the undo, which means that once they go back a few steps, they should be able to move forward through their changes again, step by step. Most programs allow users to undo and redo their last action, or maybe even the last few actions. A few programs can offer what is called "infinite undo." Many word processors actually save every keystroke and action during an entire working session. Users can move forward and backward, step by step or in larger increments, to restore a document to any state it was in during the session. Users can access material from hours before, copy some text that had been deleted, and then return to their current work and paste the text.

> **K**EY IDEA! *Utilize the computer's ability to store and retrieve multiple versions of users' choices and system properties. Allow users to store current properties and possibly to save and name different properties. Provide multiple levels of undo and redo to encourage users to explore programs without fear.*

Provide Interface Shortcuts

In addition to defining both keyboard and mouse techniques for interface actions, determine ways to shorten the number of keystrokes or mouse actions users need to perform common actions. Shortcut key sequences reduce users' memory load and quickly become automatic.

There are two basic ways to provide keyboard shortcuts—mnemonics and accelerator keys. A *mnemonic* (also called an access key) is a single, easy-to-remember alphanumeric character that moves the cursor to a choice and selects the choice. Mnemonics are used in menus (menu bars, pull-down menus, pop-up menus) and in lists to navigate and select an item in the list. Mnemonics must be unique to the current menu or list. A typical window menu bar configuration shows standard mnemonics—F for File, E for Edit, V for View, and H for Help. The next level of menus, pull-downs, each have their own set of mnemonics for items in the menu. For example, the File pull-down has N for New, O for Open, C for Close, and S for Save. Mnemonics speed up navigation and selection using menus and lists. To close the current window, users can key Alt (an accelerator key to navigate to the menu bar), then F (File pull-down), and C (Close action).

An *accelerator* (also called a shortcut key) is a key or combination of keys that users can press to perform an action. In the above example, Alt is a keyboard accelerator to move from within a window to the menu bar. Other common actions have standard accelerators, for example, Ctrl+P for Print.

KEY IDEA! *Once users are familiar with a product, they will look for shortcuts to speed up commonly used actions. Don't overlook the benefit you can provide by defining shortcuts and by following industry standards where they apply.*

Promote an Object-Action Syntax

You don't need to build a fully object-oriented interface to benefit from using the object-oriented interaction syntax. Even an application-oriented program like a word processor follows this syntax. Select a word or some text (an *object*), then browse the menu bar pull-downs or click on the right mouse button to bring up a pop-up menu showing actions that can be performed (valid *actions*).

The object-action syntax was specified by Xerox PARC developers when they built the Star user interface in the late 1970s. The Xerox Star was introduced in 1981. Johnson et al. (1989) described how this worked:

> Applications and system features were to be described in terms of the *objects* that users would manipulate with the software and the *actions* that the software provided for manipulating objects. This "objects and actions" analysis was supposed to occur at a fairly high level, without regard to how the objects would actually be presented or how the actions would actually be invoked by users. A full specification was then written from the "objects and actions" version.

The benefit of the object-action syntax is that users do not have to remember what actions are valid at what time for which objects. First, select an object. Then only those actions that can be performed with that object are available. Unavailable menu bar actions are grayed out if they are not available for the selected object. A pop-up menu lists only available actions for the object.

KEY IDEA! *Consistent implementation of object-action syntax allows users to learn the relationships between objects and actions in the product. Users can explore and browse the interface by selecting objects and seeing what actions are available.*

Use Real-World Metaphors

Real-world metaphors allow users to transfer knowledge about how things should look and work. Today's home computer comes equipped with a fully functional telephone, answering machine, and fax machine. How do users interact with these programs? They shouldn't have to learn anything new, since most users already know how to use these devices.

Figure 5.4 shows the interface for my computer's telephone system. Guess what? It looks like a telephone answering machine! It didn't take me long to figure out how to use the telephone or answering system. I didn't even have to look at the brief documentation that came with the product. The same thing happens when users first see a personal information manager, such as Lotus Organizer. People know how to use organizers and Day-Timers already, so they have the experience and also have certain expectations about how an appointment organizer, address, and phone book should work.

Figure 5.4 Real-world metaphors in the user interface.

Lotus Organizer version 1.0 used an icon of an anchor to represent the Create Link action (see Figure 5.5). This was not a very intuitive icon to use. Next to the anchor icon was an icon of an axe. What action did this button perform? You wouldn't guess—it represented breaking a link! How do the visual icons of an anchor and an axe represent these two related actions? Not very well. For the past few years I have used this example of inconsistent metaphors and poor icon designs. None of my students could figure out what these icons meant. Well, Organizer version 2 fixed this metaphor faux pas by using icons of a chain of links and a broken chain to represent these actions (see Figure 5.6). I'm glad Lotus finally listened to me and (I'm sure) other designers and users about these obtuse icons!

KEY IDEA! *Be careful how you choose and use interface metaphors. Once you have chosen a metaphor, stick with it and follow it consistently. If you find a metaphor doesn't work throughout the interface, go back and reevaluate your choice of metaphors. Remember—extend a metaphor, but don't break it.*

Use Progressive Disclosure

Users should not be overwhelmed by what they can do in a product. You don't need to show users all of the functions the product offers. The best way to teach and guide users is to show them *what* they need, *when* they need it, and *where* they want it. This is the concept of *progressive disclosure.*

Some software programs offer graduated menus for users to choose from. Users can choose *simple menus* that offer only common actions and functions for casual use. After they feel comfortable with the product, or if they need more sophisticated product features, they can use the *advanced menus.* The key is that users are in control and they choose how much of the program and interface they see and work with.

New interface technologies such as wizards and assistants use progressive disclosure to guide users through common tasks. Wizards step users through

Figure 5.5 Lotus Organizer version 1.0 icon metaphors.

Figure 5.6 Lotus Organizer version 2.0 icon metaphors.

tasks in a progressive manner where each step is simple and meaningful for even casual users.

KEY IDEA! *Always provide easy access to common features and frequently used actions. Hide less common features and actions and allow users to navigate to them. Don't try to put every piece of information in one main window. Use secondary windows for information that is not key information.*

Promote Visual Clarity

Apply visual design principles of human perception (discussed in Chapter 4), such as grouping items on a menu or list, numbering items, and using headings and prompt text. Think of information on the screen in the same way as information you would present in any other medium.

The general principles of organization, continuity, gestalt, and so on should be followed. Most programs present too much information at one time on the screen. This results in visual clutter and users don't know where on the screen to look for information. Information should be presented with some priority and order so users can understand how it is organized. Remember the old adage, "Form follows function." Some of these graphic principles are discussed in more detail in Chapter 13.

Avoid arbitrary groupings, distinctions, and other elements that seem to provide organizational information, but really don't. Figure 5.7 shows a window layout with haphazardly organized graphic objects and text, resulting in a "clown's pants" effect (from the Yale C/AIM WWW Style Manual, http://info. med.yale.edu/caim/stylemanual). This visual disorganization impedes usability and legibility, and users cannot browse or search for information in an orderly fashion.

Figure 5.8 shows a similar window layout using a carefully organized grid containing both graphic objects and text. The visual organization improves usability and legibility, allowing users to quickly find what they are looking for, resulting in increased confidence in their ability to use the information effectively.

KEY IDEA! *Graphic artists and book designers are skilled in the art of presenting appropriately designed information using the right medium. This skill should be represented on the user interface design team.*

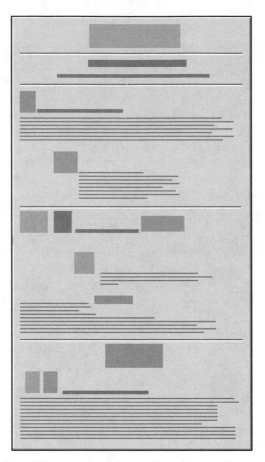

Figure 5.7 Poorly organized window,
from Yale C/AIM WWW Style Manual.

Golden Rule #3: Make the Interface Consistent

Consistency is a key aspect of usable interfaces. It's also a major area of debate. However, just like all principles, consistency might be a lower priority than other factors, so don't follow consistency principles and guidelines if they don't make sense in your environment. One of the major benefits of consistency is that users can transfer their knowledge and learning to a new program if it is consistent with other programs they already use. This is the "brass ring" for computer trainers and educators—train users how to do something once, then

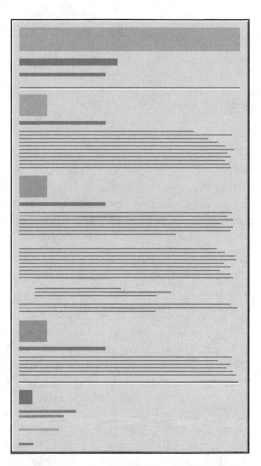

Figure 5.8   Well-organized window,
from Yale C/AIM WWW Style Manual.

they can apply that learning in new situations that are consistent with their mental model of how computers work. Table 5.3 lists the design principles that make up user interface consistency.

Next time you're on a commercial airplane, notice all of the little signs on the walls and doors of the toilets. Each of the signs has an identification number in one corner. This is done to ensure consistency in the signs you see on every airplane. It also simplifies the process of tracking and installing signs for airline workers. This is a good idea for help and message information you may develop for computer software programs.

TABLE 5.3   Principles that Make the Interface Consistent

1. Sustain the context of users' tasks (continuity).
2. Maintain consistency within and across products (experience).
3. Keep interaction results the same (expectations).
4. Provide aesthetic appeal and integrity (attitude).
5. Encourage exploration (predictability).

Once you create an information message, give it a message identification number. Then, everywhere the message is appropriate, use the same message number instead of writing the message again or writing a similar message. This will ensure that users will see the very same messages every time they are in the same situation no matter where they are in the program or in the system. This layer of consistency is very comforting and friendly to users.

Sustain the Context of Users' Tasks

Users should be provided points of reference as they navigate through a product interface. Window titles, navigation maps and trees, and other visual aids give users an immediate, dynamic view of where they are and where they've been. Users should also be able to complete tasks without having to change context or switch between input styles. If users start a task using the keyboard, they should be able to complete the task using the keyboard as the main style of interaction.

Users should also be provided with cues that help them predict the result of an action. When an object is dragged over another object, some visual indicator should be given to users that tells them if the target object can accept the dropped object and what the action might be. Users should be then be able to cancel the drag-and-drop action if they wish.

Context-specific aids, such as help and tips on individual fields, menu items, and buttons, also help users maintain the flow of the tasks they are performing. They shouldn't have to leave a window to find supplemental information needed to complete a task.

Maintain Consistency Within and Across Products

One of the most important aspects of an interface is the way it enables users to learn general concepts about systems and products and then apply what they've learned to new situations in different programs or different parts of the system. This consistency applies at three levels: presentation, behavior, and interaction techniques. Consistency is one of the key issues behind user interface guidelines and standards discussed in the next chapter.

Consistency in *presentation* means that users should see information and objects in the same logical, visual, or physical way throughout the product. If information users can't change (*static text*) is in blue on one screen, then static text on all other screens should also be presented in blue. If a certain type of information is entered using one type of control, then use that same control to capture the same information throughout the product. Don't change presentation styles within your product for no apparent reason.

Consistency in *behavior* means that an object works the same everywhere. The behavior of interface controls such as buttons, lists, and menu items should not change within or between programs. I've seen programs where the menu bar choices immediately performed actions, instead of displaying pulldown menus, as everyone expects. Users should not be surprised by object behaviors in the interface.

Interaction technique consistency is also important. The same shortcut keys should work in similar programs. Mouse techniques should produce the same results anywhere in the interface. Keyboard mnemonics should not change for the same menus from program to program. Users expect the same results when they interact the same way with different objects.

KEY IDEA! *Learning how to use one program should provide* positive transfer *when learning how to use another similar program interface. When things that look like they should work the same in a different situation don't, users experience* negative transfer. *This can inhibit learning and prevents users from having confidence in the consistency of the interface.*

Interface Enhancements and Consistency

Windows 95 and OS/2 Warp are the current popular PC operating systems. Numerous visual enhancements were made to both interfaces. This example points out the power of consistency and the problems of inconsistency. Figure 5.9 shows the window title bar button configuration used in older versions of Windows—the familiar down and up arrows. The rightmost button (Λ) is the Maximize/Restore button and to its left is the Minimize button (V). Users can perform these actions by clicking on the system menu in the left corner of the title bar, and then choosing the window action. This common task involves two mouse clicks, so the window-sizing buttons on the right of the title bar represent quicker one-click ways to size windows. This title bar button configuration should look familiar to PC users, since over 50 million users (according to Microsoft) see this button configuration in their version of Windows. Users have learned to move the mouse to the top right button on the title bar to maximize a window or to restore it to its previous size and location. This is visual and positional consistency found in *every window* on their screen.

To close an opened window, users must click on the system menu and then select Close. A shortcut technique is to double-click on the system menu. Either technique is a two-click process. Windows 95 offered a usability enhancement by providing a one-click button as a way to close a window rather than the two-click methods. That's fine by me, but I don't like the way they did it (see Figure 5.10). The new Close button (with an X as the button icon) is now the rightmost button on the title bar and the size buttons are moved to the right. Instead of adding a *new* button and providing a *new* technique or button location to access that action, Microsoft added a *new* button and *changed* the way users interact with the traditional window-size buttons. It may seem like a minor thing and an inconsequential change, but every time I use the mouse with Windows 95 I have to unlearn behaviors ingrained in my by previous Windows operating systems. I keep going to the rightmost button to maximize the window, and instead the window is closed. In my opinion, the benefit of the new Close button does not outweigh the inconsistent behavior users have to perform in unlearning years of mouse usage.

Take a look at how the same new concept was implemented in OS/2. The OS/2 Warp version 3 operating system uses slightly different graphic icons, but the window-sizing buttons are in the same place as in earlier versions of Windows. A new product, Object Desktop, developed by Kurt Westerfeld at Stardock Systems, provides the new Close button, but it is placed to the left of the window-sizing buttons (see Figure 5.11). If users want to use this new button, they can quickly learn to move the mouse to the new position on the title bar, and *they don't have to change their already learned behavior* when using the window-sizing buttons! Users of both operating systems, such as myself, can transfer our learned behaviors between the two operating systems when common buttons retain their positional consistency across operating systems. I like this implementation of the new interface feature much better than the Windows 95 method.

Object Desktop even added a new button, the Rollup button, to the window title bar (see Figure 5.12). Notice where it is placed on the title bar. The window-size buttons are not changed, and the Rollup button is placed between the Close button and the Minimize button. This arrangement provides both *location* consistency and *position* consistency. The sizing buttons are always in the

 Figure 5.9 Windows 3.1 title bar buttons.

 Figure 5.10 Windows 95 title bar buttons.

Figure 5.11   OS/2 Warp version 3 with Object Desktop Close button.

KEY IDEA! *As both a designer of products and a user of products, be aware of how you use learned behaviors and be careful how you introduce new behaviors. When interface enhancements are made, users should have to learn only a few new behaviors or techniques. They should not be forced to unlearn behaviors they have been using for years. Unlearning trained behavior is much more difficult than learning new behavior.*

same location, providing consistency for common mouse actions. The Close button provides *position* consistency, that is, it is always in the same position with respect to the other buttons in the group, at the left of the group. Position consistency is also important in determining menu bar pull-down choice location, where certain menu bar pull-down choices will always appear in the same position, regardless of the other items in the pull-down list. OS/2 Warp version 4 added the Close button to the window title bar (see Figure 5.13). Notice the graphics are 3-dimensional and embossed, and the Close button is to the left of the Minimize and Maximize buttons, in its new position.

Keep Interaction Results the Same

As mentioned above, consistency in interface behavior is very important. If users experience different results from the same action, they tend to question their own behavior rather than the product's behavior. This leads to users developing *superstitious behavior,* that is, they think they must do things in exactly a certain way for the desired result to happen, otherwise they are not sure of the results.

Sequences of steps and actions should also be consistent throughout a product. I've seen products where users had to logon multiple times to access different parts of the program. This was bad enough, but it was made worse

Figure 5.12   OS/2 Warp version 3 with Object Desktop Close and Rollup buttons.

Figure 5.13   OS/2 Warp version 4 Close button.

because the logon process was different each time. Navigation sequences must also be consistent—don't use Esc to back up one step in one window and then use Exit in another window to do the same action.

Standard interface elements must behave the same way. For example, menu bar choices must always display a drop-down menu when selected. Don't surprise users by performing actions directly from the menu bar. Don't incinerate a discarded object when it is dropped in a waste basket!

KEY IDEA! *If by design results might be different from what users expect, inform them before the action is performed. Give them the option to perform the action, or cancel the operation, or perhaps perform another action.*

Provide Aesthetic Appeal and Integrity

Many of today's products look like they were designed and developed by different people or even different divisions who never talked with each other. Users question the integrity of a product if inconsistent colors, fonts, icons, and window layouts are present throughout the product.

Just as a printed book has a predefined page layout, font, title, and color scheme, users should be able to quickly learn how product interfaces visually fit together. Again, utilize the skills of graphic designers on the design team.

KEY IDEA! *A pretty interface can't cover up for a lack of product functionality. Users don't just want lipstick on the bulldog, they want a visually pleasing interface that allows them to get the job done.*

Encourage Exploration

A goal for most user interface designers has been to produce user-friendly interfaces. A friendly interface encourages users to explore the interface to find out where things are and what happens when they do things, without fear of negative consequences. We are slowly achieving this goal, but users now expect even more from a product interface. They expect guidance, direction, information, and even entertainment while they use a product.

KEY IDEA! *Interfaces today and in the future must be more intuitive, enticing, predictable, and forgiving than the interfaces we've designed to date. The explosion of CD-ROM products and Internet browsers, home pages, and applets have exposed the user interface to a whole new world of computer users. It's time we moved past user-friendly interfaces to user-seductive and fun-to-use product interfaces, even in the business environment.*

References

Apple Computer, Inc. 1992. *Macintosh Human Interface Guidelines.* Reading, MA: Addison-Wesley.

Hansen, W. 1971. User engineering principles for interactive systems. *AFIPS Conference Proceedings* 39, AFIPS Press, pp. 523–532.

Heckel, Paul. 1984. *The Elements of Friendly Software Design.* New York: Warner Books.

IBM Corporation. 1992. *Object-Oriented Interface Design: IBM Common User Access Guidelines.* New York: QUE.

Johnson, Jeff, Teresa Roberts, William Verplank, David Smith, Charles Irby, Marian Beard, and Kevin Mackey. 1989. The Xerox Star: A Retrospective. *IEEE Computer* 22(9): 11–29.

Mayhew, Deborah. 1992. *Principles and Guidelines in Software User Interface Design.* Englewood Cliffs, NJ: Prentice-Hall.

Microsoft Corporation. 1995. *The Windows Interface Guidelines for Software Design.* Redmond, WA: Microsoft Press.

Nielsen, Jakob. 1990. Traditional dialogue design applied to modern user interfaces. *Communications of the ACM* 33(10): 109–118.

Open Software Foundation. 1993. *OSF/Motif Style Guide, Revision 1.2.* Englewood Cliffs, Prentice-Hall.

Rubenstein, R. and H. Hersch. 1984. *The Human Factor: Designing Computer Systems for People.* Newton, MA: Digital Press.

Shneiderman, Ben. 1992. *Designing the User Interface: Strategies for Effective Human-Computer Interaction.* Reading, MA: Addison-Wesley.

CHAPTER SIX

COMPUTER STANDARDS AND USER INTERFACE GUIDELINES

I can't tell you what I want, but I'll know it when I see it.

A computer software user

Computer Standards

The trouble with standards for computers is that you don't want to standardize so much as to stymie further product improvements.

John Karat (1991)

Standards make our lives easier by defining characteristics of objects and systems we use every day. The layout of the telephone keypad, for example, is a standard you depend on every time you make a telephone call. If you're a typist or a computer user, you should feel comfortable using the standard QWERTY keyboard (named for the top-left row of alphabetic keys), even if you use a different typewriter or computer.

There are standards across all industries, including the construction industry. Standards allow the home architect and builder to communicate with everyone involved with home construction. They can transfer their knowledge into the design and building of a home mainly because they all understand the standards involved in the construction business. There are electrical, mechanical, plumbing, and environmental standards that enable everyone to more easily do a better job.

Computer design standards are established by state and national government organizations, and also other national and international groups. Some of the more familiar standards organizations are the U.S. American National Standards Institute (ANSI), Germany's DIN, and the International Standards Organization (ISO).

Hardware standards have been defined for computer displays, keyboards, system units, and even furniture. For example, there are standard cables, connectors, electrical busses, and electronic transmission protocols. To connect a printer to a computer, you will most likely use a parallel printer cable with the standard connectors for the computer and the printer. Most hardware standards address the important ergonomic human-computer interface areas. For example, one international standard states, "The slope of the keyboard shall be between 0 and 25 degrees."

Software standards usually apply to basic user interface characteristics. Gould (1988) tells us why software standards have evolved: "The stated motivations for developing user interface standards are to make information processing equipment easier and safer for people to use through establishing minimum manufacturing requirements and by eliminating unnecessary inconsistencies and variations in the user interfaces. Standards can be seen as a way of insuring that good human factors are incorporated in the system."

There are even standard paper sizes in the United States and internationally. You can see the benefits of this standard in your favorite word processing program. Since there are international page-size standards, they should be offered as choices in the program properties for the page size of your document. I've had to prepare presentations and manuscripts for courses and conferences in Europe and Asia. If the standard page-size formats were not made available to me in my word processing program, I would have no idea what was the appropriate page size to use for my international audience. Designers and Developers should learn from these experiences and provide support for users by giving them standard configurations and properties as choices in the interface. Your users will thank you for this thoughtfulness.

KEY IDEA! *Standards must be continually reviewed and updated. If not, they tend to freeze technology and stifle innovation. Many of today's standards don't take full advantage of current computer hardware and software technologies. They also don't address all of the needs of today's computer users. Many of our major computer hardware manufacturing and software development corporations are directly involved in the international standards organizations. They usually have two goals: to help develop improved current and future standards, and to try to guide standards toward adopting their own product designs.*

User Interface Guidelines

There are increasing numbers of guidelines, reflecting the increasing numbers of people designing and using computer systems. The continuing effort to produce more and better guidelines reflects how difficult it is to design systems from guidelines. Design is a series of tradeoffs, a series of conflicts among good principles, and these concepts are hard to incorporate into guidelines.

John Gould (1988)

Why are interface design guidelines needed? Shouldn't you be able to follow interface design principles to develop usable products? *Unfortunately, interface design principles alone don't guarantee a usable and successful software interface.*

The principles discussed in the previous chapter address all areas of the designer's iceberg chart. Guidelines, however, typically only address the presentation and interaction elements of the iceberg. *Guidelines* are simply rules and interpretations to follow for creating interface elements, their appearance, and their behaviors.

Following interface design guidelines without regard for users will probably result in a mismatched interface. You should not have a cookbook view of interface design, where guidelines are followed without regard to the quality of the ingredients and the way they interact with each other. Blindly following any set of guidelines does not build you a usable or consistent user interface. Gould (1988) said it well; "Most guidelines center on 'knob-ology' and have little to do with cognition and learning." In fact, following interface design guidelines doesn't guarantee a usable product.

Some developers feel that following user interface guidelines stifles their creativity. The group that enforced the IBM Common User Access (CUA) user interface guidelines at one time were unkindly referred to by some developers as the "CUA Cops" or the "Compliance Police." This caused unnecessary and unproductive contention between interface designers and developers and compliance coordinators.

However, most people see guidelines for what they are—industry and corporate aids to help you do your job and enable you to build more consistent and usable interfaces. Guidelines are not meant to stifle interface design creativity. You should build usable and competitive products with interface features that meet interface guidelines.

Guidelines should also allow users to transfer their real-world knowledge to the interface. The interface should be consistent with real-world objects and metaphors. For example, if users see a set of buttons on the screen that look like buttons that set the stations on a radio, then their knowledge of how those buttons work on the radio should allow them to correctly understand how the buttons work in the computer interface.

KEY IDEA! *Interface guidelines address current input and output technologies. They also begin to cover emerging technologies, such as pen, handwriting gestures, and voice input. One problem with developing guidelines for new technologies is that it is difficult to define user interactions with technologies when users haven't interacted with them very much! That is why it takes time to develop good guidelines. They should be based on observations of user behavior over time, and it takes time for users to try out new interface technologies and figure out how best to use them. Don't attempt to define guidelines before you've understood how users work with new technologies.*

What Do Guidelines Look Like?

Be obscure clearly.

An old proverb

Guidelines generally fall into three areas of user interface design: physical, syntactic, and semantic. The *physical* area applies to the hardware portion of the user interface. This includes devices used to input data, such as the keyboard, mouse, trackball, and touch screen. These guidelines address topics such as the location of keys, the layout and design of keys on the keyboard, how the mouse is used, and pen gestures. For example, IBM (1992) guidelines define mouse button 1 as the selection button and mouse button 2 as the direct manipulation button. Microsoft (1995) guidelines define mouse button 1 as selection and default drag and drop, while mouse button 2 is used for nondefault drag and drop.

Syntactic guidelines refer to rules about presenting information on the screen and the sequence and order of user actions. For example, to print a document using direct manipulation, you must first drag the icon for the document and then drop it on the printer icon. This is the correct sequence of actions. Dragging the printer icon and dropping it on the document icon is not a valid action.

The third area covered by guidelines is the *semantic* aspect of user interfaces. This refers to the meaning of elements, objects, and actions that make up a part of the interface. For example, the term *Exit* has a certain meaning to users and it performs a certain action that is expected by users. This is very different from the meaning and expected action for the term *Cancel.* Exit finishes the interaction with a dialog box and usually leaves the program completely. Cancel, meanwhile, usually stops any pending actions and backs up one step from the dialog box.

Guidelines are usually classified by how important or critical they are to the user interface. Figure 6.1 shows a sample page from the IBM (1992) design guide. Each guideline has a "When to Use" and a "How to Use" section. Items with a check mark are *required* (critical) guidelines that must be followed to maintain consistency with the overall design goals and the CUA interface. Items that are not checked are still important to creating consistent interfaces, but are not essential. Designers should follow all of the required

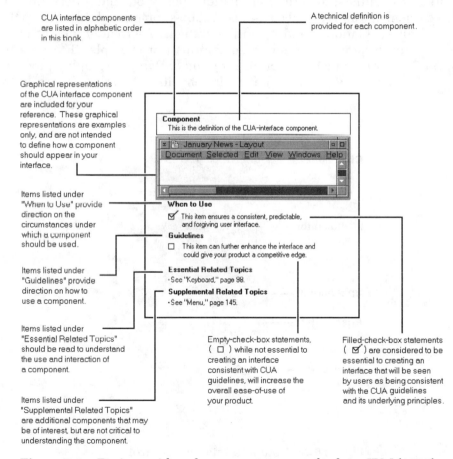

Figure 6.1   Design guide reference entry example, from IBM (1992).

guidelines to establish a basic level of consistency in an interface. Decisions to implement optional guidelines should depend on individual or corporate style interpretations, development schedules, resources, and development budgets.

You may wish to extend an interface beyond the guidelines. You may create a new interface element or you may modify an existing element to improve its usability. The Apple (1992) guidelines offer these suggestions in this area: Build on the existing interface, don't assign new behaviors to existing objects, and create new interface elements cautiously. Also, any deviations from the guidelines should happen only if there are usability test results that justify departing from them.

Guidelines define standard presentation, behavior, and interaction for interface elements and controls. Figure 6.2 shows some standard controls that are used on all platforms and operating systems. Each environment might have slightly different terms for these controls (for example, IBM uses the term *radio button* while Microsoft uses *option button*), the graphic presentation might be slightly different, but their behaviors should be basically the same.

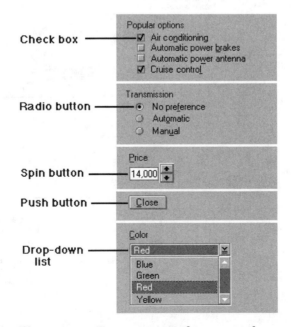

Figure 6.2   Common interface controls, from IBM (1992).

KEY IDEA! *Guidelines for interface elements or controls tell you: (1) When to use them, (2) how to present them, and (3) what techniques should be used (such as keyboard sequences or mouse actions) to interact with the interface elements. A complete set of guidelines covers every object and element of the interface in terms of its presentation on the screen, its behaviors, and the techniques users have available to interact with them.*

The Evolution of Current Interface Guidelines

Software design guides are the main source of interface design guidance for the major computing environments: Apple (Macintosh), IBM (OS/2, DOS), Microsoft (Windows), and UNIX (OSF/Motif). Smith and Mosier (1986) of the MITRE Corporation also publish a very complete set of user interface guidelines for general interface design. Edward Tufte, who helped with the graphic design of the OS/2 interface, has a very good book on the visual display of information (Tufte, 1983).

Apple and IBM have published their guidelines for many years. Apple's guidelines were originally published in 1985 as *Human Interface Guidelines: The Apple Desktop Interface* in the *Inside Macintosh* series. The new guidelines (Apple, 1992), *Macintosh Human Interface Guidelines,* are published in a large-sized, easy-to-read book with more graphics and examples. Guidelines for the OSF/Motif UNIX environment are published by the Open Software Foundation (1993). Recently, a consortium has been formed by Sun, Hewlett-Packard, and IBM, called the Common Desktop Environment (CDE). A style guide and certification checklist has been published and is available from any of the consortium member companies.

KEY IDEA! *Many software products are designed for use on multiple platforms. Since each of these platforms have different operating systems, tools, and interface styles, it is often difficult to design one interface that fits on each platform, or that can even be implemented on each platform. A recent addition to the set of industry design guides was developed by Bellcore (1996).* Design Guide for Multiplatform Graphical User Interfaces *specifically provides descriptions and guidelines for major components of GUI design on IBM CUA, OSF Motif, Microsoft Windows, and the CDE environments.*

IBM (1989) first introduced the concept of the *workplace* environment as an extension to the graphical user interface (GUI) model: "The workplace environment describes the integration of applications into an electronic version of a working environment that simulates a real workplace. For example, an electronic workplace for the office would have mail baskets, file cabinets, telephones, and printers that all applications could share. The separate applications are integrated as objects that appear as icons in the workplace environment." This information was provided by IBM to help designers and developers prepare for the natural evolution of the CUA interface.

The object-oriented workplace environment is fully documented in IBM's *Object-Oriented Interface Design: IBM Common User Access Guidelines* (1992). Microsoft user interface engineers were initially involved in this work but dropped out as Microsoft steered away from OS/2 back to the Windows graphical environment. OS/2 2.0 began the implementation of the CUA workplace environment and OS/2 Warp is the latest version. The evolution of the CUA interface architecture and its implementation in the OS/2 Workplace Shell are covered in depth in two articles in a 1992 *IBM Systems Journal.* Dick Berry (1992), affectionately known as the "Father of CUA," wrote a detailed discussion of the designer's model of the CUA Workplace. Berry and Reeves (1992) discuss the evolution of CUA's interface.

Until 1991, Microsoft and IBM worked closely together on a strategy that positioned Microsoft's Windows operating system as a stepping stone in the migration path to OS/2. While I was a CUA interface architect, Microsoft's interface designers worked closely with us as we defined the CUA 1991 user interface architecture and wrote the CUA guidelines. These guidelines were developed for both the DOS/Windows and the OS/2 environment. Microsoft even shipped the *Advanced Interface Design Guide* (IBM, 1989) as part of the Windows 3.0 Software Development Kit. As the two corporations' software strategies began to drift apart, so did Microsoft's involvement with the CUA effort. Microsoft kept shipping the CUA guidelines with the Windows toolkit until 1992. At that time, however, Microsoft finalized the divorce by publishing their own set of guidelines (Microsoft, 1992).

Windows developers, already using the CUA guidelines shipped with the Windows Development Kit, suddenly had a new set of guidelines to follow. Windows developers couldn't build the CUA 1991 object-oriented interfaces with the Windows interface environment. Microsoft didn't want to continue to use IBM's CUA 1989 guidelines, or use the CUA 1991 application-oriented guidelines while OS/2 2.0 designers and developers migrated to the object-oriented CUA 1991 environment. So they wrote their own set of graphical interface guidelines. In the book's introduction, Microsoft explains this shift in design guides: "These guidelines were developed to be generally compatible with guidelines that may be appropriately applied from the IBM Common User Access (CUA) version 2.0 definition, published in *IBM Common User Access: Advanced Interface Design Guide* (Boca Raton, FL: IBM, 1989); but they are not intended to describe user interface requirements for CUA compliance."

The latest entry in the official software design guide collection is the Microsoft (1995) book, *The Windows Interface Guidelines for Software Design.* This guide covers interface design for the Windows 95 user interface environment. It is a well-written book, by Tandy Trower, director of user interfaces at Microsoft and a former member of the IBM-Microsoft core CUA design team. As mentioned in Chapter 5, the book is also available as a Windows 95 help file on the Windows 95 Developer's Toolkit CD-ROM and at Microsoft's Web site.

Microsoft also helps promote consistency in Windows 95 products by forcing developers to follow a set of programming standards in order to use the Microsoft Windows 95 logo on their product. These programming standards are, among other things, that the product:

- ◆ Is a Win32 executable, compiled with a 32-bit compiler
- ◆ Has a fully automated, graphical installation program
- ◆ Has a fully automated uninstaller
- ◆ Supports long file names
- ◆ Supports Windows NT
- ◆ Registers itself in the Windows Registry
- ◆ Supports program icons, system fonts, and system-sizing metrics
- ◆ Supports OLE 2.0 if it is a file-based product

As part of the Windows 95 logo compliance process, Microsoft recommends that developers follow the guidelines in *The Windows Interface Guidelines for Software Design.* Microsoft does not (and cannot) monitor compliance to the interface guidelines. At IBM, we tried to enforce product conformance to the interface guidelines in the early days of CUA, but found the process to be complicated and contentious, and ultimately, an impossible one.

KEY IDEA! *The goals of design guides are straightforward: Allow users access to their data and information, anywhere in the system, in any form, and provide a user interface that empowers and excites people. A well-designed interface allows users to focus on their tasks and not on the underlying hardware and software system.*

How to Benefit from Guidelines: Corporate Style Guides

In addition to providing guidance on user interface design and implementation, guidelines provide a number of additional benefits, if properly utilized. If you develop more than one software product, or products on multiple platforms, guidelines should not only aid the interface design efforts for a particular product, but should also apply across a range of similar products, and across platforms.

One benefit of guidelines is that a common user interface specification, or *style guide,* can help ensure that similar products and services have similar interfaces. Developing a style guide can also simplify and improve the product development process. Interface elements, controls, and dialog boxes can be reused and shared between programs. Usability testing results on interface elements and techniques can be generalized, and design decisions based on human factors testing can be applied across the range of products. Style guides can also serve to focus efforts to define, test, and implement new key interface technologies and techniques. They can then be applied quickly and consistently in the products covered by the interface style guide.

Style guides not only contain the guidelines critical to common interface design efforts. They should also contain visual presentation styles and interaction techniques that are not necessarily addressed or specified by general guidelines. For example, where does the user's logon dialog box appear on the screen and how should the data entry fields be organized in the dialog box? What is the color and font scheme for static or variable text appearing against a background color in a window? How are the function keys mapped onto user actions? What actions happen when the mouse buttons are pressed? These stylistic and functional attributes must be specified and documented so they can be consistently implemented.

Follow these simple steps to benefit from the years of experience, skill, and testing that have gone into design guidelines (Berst, 1993):

1. Get the appropriate industry guidelines for your software environment.
2. Create a company style guide for your own product interfaces.
3. Pick a target application to follow that uses those guidelines.
4. Follow the guidelines when developing your own applications.
5. Follow the guidelines when shopping for software products.

Figure 6.3 shows how standards, industry design guides, and style guides are built on each other to provide a sturdy foundation for product design. Style

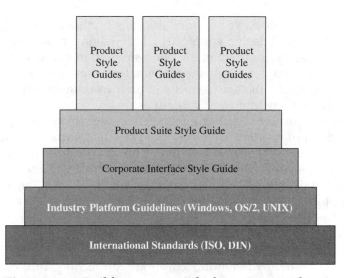

Figure 6.3 Building a pyramid of corporate and product style guides.

guides can be developed at the corporate level, at an product suite level, and at a product level. *Corporate style guides* focus on common presentation, behaviors, and techniques that must be implemented across all products in the company. One goal of corporate style guides is to maintain and reinforce corporate identity—that is, the use of colors, graphics, and icons that present a consistent visual image of the company logo and color scheme throughout product interfaces.

There are two basic ways to develop corporate style guides. You can usually get permission to use the materials from the industry design guides to piece together your own style guide with your own additions and changes. This style guide would then *replace* the industry design guide you use—it would be a standalone document. I don't recommend this method. You end up duplicating most of the original design guide and don't do as complete a job as the original. Designers and developers end up going back to the industry design guide anyway to get more information.

The suggested method is to build your corporate style guide *on top of* an industry design guide. I recently developed a corporate interface style guide for a Swiss bank. We built our style guide as a *delta* to the new Microsoft (1995) Windows 95 design guide—it was specifically designed *not* to be a standalone document. We only included items in our style guide if they fell in one of three categories related to the Windows design guide: supplement, addition, or contradition. A *supplement* entry provided information that enhanced or clarified a topic in the Microsoft design guide. An *addition* entry provided information that was not contained in a topic in the Microsoft design guide. A contradiction contained information for bank developers that was an exception to the Microsoft design guide. In that case, the guide's recommendations should be followed rather than the Microsoft guidelines.

In addition to a corporate style guide, you may wish to define specific *product suite guides* and *product style guides.* A product suite may wish to offer design guidance across a related group of products. Finally, individual products may have a separate design guide. As shown in Figure 6.3, these documents should be based on the underlying standards, design guides, and corporate style guides already developed. Again, rather than duplicating information in these references, it is better to describe deltas to the corporate style guide using the same format of including only supplements, additions, or contradictions. For example, a touch-screen kiosk product will not need to follow the keyboard interaction corporate guidelines, but will probably need to supplement and add guidelines on screen presentation and touch input.

KEY IDEA! *Interface goals and guidelines must be* realistic *and* achievable *with the available skills, computing environment, languages, and tools. Work within the business constraints of your environment. Your interface guidelines and goals must also be* testable. *There is no point in developing a company style guide if you can't test the resulting interfaces to see if product and interface usability goals are met. There must be development support for adhering to the guidelines. Remember, the responsibility for developing a usable and consistent interface belongs to the design and development teams. Take this responsibility seriously and your users will thank you later.*

The Problem with Guidelines: Do They Work?

Designers striving for user interface consistency can resemble Supreme Court justices trying to define pornography: each of us feels we know it when we see it, but people often disagree and a precise definition remains elusive. A close examination suggests that consistency is an unreliable guide and designers would often do better to focus on users' work environments.

Jonathan Grudin (1989)

User interface consistency is one of the main goals for user interface design, yet there are arguments that this is an unobtainable and unreasonable goal (Grudin, 1989). Consistency is very difficult to identify, define, and implement. In addition, interface consistency may not even be an appropriate goal. Grudin proposes that, "When user interface consistency becomes our primary concern, our attention is directed away from its proper focus: users and their work."

KEY IDEA! *System and interface consistency can sometimes conflict with what users expect and want. Don't follow consistency guidelines just for the sake of consistency—design something well first, then apply it consistently throughout your interface.*

There is always a substantial amount of interpretation involved with implementing guidelines in a product interface. No matter how detailed they are, I have yet to see an interface without some element or behavior being different from the way "it was intended it to be" in the style guide. Interface guidelines are not, and never will be, a cookbook for software design.

Researchers have studied how designers use guidelines to design interfaces. One particular study was conducted as a critical part of the development of the IBM (1992) user interface guide and reference books. Tetzlaff and Schwartz (1991) asked designers to build compliant interfaces based on drafts of the CUA interface guidelines. They found that designers missed several critical concepts and details. Designers preferred graphic illustrations and examples rather than text for learning design concepts and wanted to be able to explore the examples interactively. Although their final designs were judged to be largely compliant, there were differences in interpretations of the guidelines. Interface design is like many other areas of our lives—*there isn't always one right answer to a particular question.*

Another study (Thovtrup and Nielsen, 1991) found very similar results. Only 71 percent of their participant's designs were compliant with the design standard they were given. Most of the differences were due to influences from designer's experiences with nonstandard interface designs. They also showed that it is difficult to evaluate interface designs for compliance. When given an interface to evaluate, designers found only an average of 4 out of 12 deviations in the designs. This was especially surprising, since the test participants had expressed an above-average interest in interface usability.

KEY IDEA! *Interface design is more an art than a science. Concrete examples are extremely useful for supporting design guidelines. Tools are necessary for supporting compliant interface design. Education and training are also needed to teach designers how to build interfaces utilizing design principles and guidelines when appropriate.*

Unfortunately, even with all of these guidelines at hand, *there is no guarantee of a usable interface.* One of the worst things that can happen is the belief that because guidelines were followed, the interface is compliant and therefore usable, and the product doesn't need any usability testing!

Even with all these problems, it is still generally agreed that it is better to use accepted interface design principles and guidelines than not to use them. Alan Zeichick (1991) summarized this discussion well; "The moral: follow existing user interface guidelines when developing programming tools and consumer products. Follow them even if you think the guidelines are flawed. Perhaps your design is superior, but ask yourself: will this superior function-key mapping scheme or improved menuing metaphor help my application become a seamless part of the user's working environment? Or will it be a continual annoyance, helping turn my perfect product into shelfware?"

Macro versus Micro Interface Guidelines

When developing user interface guidelines, be sure to address user interface design and usability from two perspectives—the micro level and the macro level. *Micro-level* guidelines usually address individual interface elements (often controls, such as push buttons, check boxes, text boxes, scroll bars, etc.), regarding how they should be presented to users and how users can interact with the interface element. Readers should also be told when to use (or not to use) each particular control. Micro-level guidelines may be described in a reference section, as seen in IBM's (1992) guidelines, or in a separate section, as in Microsoft's (1995) guidelines, titled *Part II: Window Interface Components.* This type of information may in fact be more useful for determining how to program the presentation and behavior (interaction) of interface elements.

Macro-level guidelines address the user interface from a broader perspective. They address higher-level user interface design issues such as window types, window layout, navigation, selection, menu design, and determining objects, models, and metaphors. Macro-level guidelines are usually described up front, as with the *Design Guide* in IBM's (1992) guidelines or the first section in Microsoft's (1995) guidelines, entitled *Part I: Design Principles and Methodology.*

KEY IDEA! *Macro-level interface design represents the* gestalt *of user interface—how the whole product fits together and makes sense as users navigate through and interact with different parts.*

Designing Interfaces for Worldwide Use

The venue of software development and interface design is an international one. Any software product developed today has a potentially large audience of users from different countries, languages, and cultures around the world. This area is called *internationalization,* or *national language support* (NLS). It is a key factor for the worldwide success of software products.

Today's programming and interface tools allow much of what the user sees and interacts with on the screen to be separated (soft-coded) from the rest of the program (hardcoded information). This allows programs to be offered in multiple languages with less effort. By separating all information such as text, symbols, and icons from system code, you ensure easier access for both translators and users.

Many areas of an interface require additional consideration for national language support. Think of all of the different monetary currencies in the world. A few U.S. dollars may be presented on the screen in only a few characters, such as $9.23. This same dollar value may be equal to several million Italian lira, which takes up quite a bit more screen space as L.2,450,000. An entry field for monetary data input must be large enough to accept different national monetary amounts. How much screen space is needed for translating text? Translating text from English to other languages typically requires from 30 percent up to 100 percent *additional* screen space. What about the different date formats around the world? How do you ensure that programs will be usable in different nations and cultures?

Most design guides offer advice for developing interfaces for the international audience. Table 6.1 lists some of the areas that must be addressed for international design. How many of these areas would you have thought of by yourself if you were asked to develop an international version of a software product?

TABLE 6.1   Areas of Concern for International Interfaces

◆ Capitalization	◆ Double-byte character sets
◆ Column headings	◆ Date formats
◆ Descriptive text	◆ Time formats
◆ Field prompts	◆ Measurement formats
◆ First letter cursor navigation	◆ Currency formats
◆ Icon design	◆ Numeric formats
◆ Use of color	◆ Separator formats
◆ User of symbols	◆ Telephone number formats
◆ Length of text	◆ Paper size formats
◆ Shortcut keys	◆ Address formats
◆ Keyboard combinations	◆ Acronyms
◆ Function key assignments	◆ Abbreviations
◆ Sorting information	◆ Humor
◆ Mnemonic selection	◆ Grammatical person and voice
◆ Bidirectional languages	

A true test of a well-designed international product is when users can switch from one language to another and still understand how to use the program. A few years ago, I taught a user interface design course at the IBM Yamato Laboratory in Tokyo, Japan. I normally give students in my course a copy of the IBM CUA user interface guidelines. When I asked the Tokyo course coordination if I should send copies of the books for the students, I was told that the books had already been translated into Japanese and students would be given a copy of those books. Amazingly, the Japanese books were printed in exactly the same format as the English version, so I could still use my own book to point to a particular paragraph or illustration on a page and it was on the same page in their book. How's that for consistent presentation of information across cultures and languages?

The CUA design books at that time included a sample program developed to demonstrate the guidelines. This program was also translated into Japanese. When I got to Tokyo to teach the class, I had to use the Japanese version of the program that was already installed on the classroom computer. I was amazed (and relieved) to find that I could use the demo program to explain interface objects, elements, and interaction techniques *without understanding a word of text on the screen!* Because I knew how the interface looked and worked, I didn't need to be able to read the Japanese text. I couldn't even read the key labels on the Japanese computer keyboard! For example, the Exit choice on the File menu was still in exactly the same place I was used to and it performed exactly the same action. This shows how following physical, syntactic, and semantic guidelines allows users to maintain consistency between a program they are familiar with and a similar program whose content may be unfamiliar or even unreadable.

Guidelines and Software Development Tools

A graphic end-user environment demands a graphic development tool. Object-oriented tools are often recommended because of their natural fit with the visible objects on the graphical-interface screen.

Peter Coffee (1992)

Very few developers today code systems and programs completely in low-level languages. Developers typically use a programming language and, additionally, some type of application generator or interface builder to design and code common user interface elements and objects. These interface objects and "widgets" make up a collection of building blocks from which related products can be built.

As software operating systems and user interface techniques evolve, development tools must keep pace with them. For example, neither you nor your users should accept a user interface for a new product on Windows 95 that was designed according to the outdated Microsoft (1992) Windows 3.x guidelines. Tools that are successful today in the Windows 95 environment are the ones that will allow interfaces to be designed according to the Microsoft (1995) user interface guidelines.

KEY IDEA! *When new interface guidelines are published, tool vendors move quickly to include the elements and techniques from the new interfaces in their tools. New interface technologies are always forcing new and better tools to be developed. Look at the evolution of Internet development tools. Today's product development tools are quickly merging the worlds of client/server, standalone PCs, and the Internet. Users, designers, and developers are always looking for better and easier ways to do their jobs. Over 50 percent of the developers in the Thovtrup and Nielsen (1991) study complained that their programming tools were not sufficient for supporting the user interface requirements established in the guidelines.*

How do you choose the proper development tools for software products? One key factor is a tool's ability to enable or enforce the current user interface guidelines for your software environment. First, does the tool *enable* you to develop a robust user interface? Second, does the tool *enforce* the appropriate interface guidelines during development?

You are probably interested in developing interfaces that follow basic guidelines. However, if you are more concerned about enhancing or evolving interface elements beyond just the standard interface, you will want a tool that does more enabling than enforcing.

If you want to build an interface that is similar to and consistent with other program interfaces on your system, then you may be more interested in tools that will *enforce* the guidelines. These tools will help you build consistent and familiar interfaces. Some tools even allow you to choose the *enforcement mode* you want to work with. In *lenient enforcement* mode, the tool will simply tell you if you build something that deviates from the guidelines. In *strict enforcement* mode, the tool won't let you build an element or technique that deviates from the established guideline.

Development tools cover a wide spectrum of program and interface development, from building graphical front ends to host programs or databases to building totally object-oriented programs and interfaces using the latest object-oriented programming (OOP) technology. Choose the appropriate tool to meet business needs, and to meet customer and user demands.

Take time to seriously research what tools are being used by your business colleagues and competitors. There are many developer symposiums, business shows, training seminars, and consultants available on all of the major software development platforms. Use these resources to help you reach the correct decisions regarding what turns out to be a major part of your development effort—product design and development tools.

Some tools are very easy-to-learn and use and can build sample programs very quickly. They can be used to design interface alternatives and marketing demos, and are also extremely valuable for early testing scenarios. These types of tools are called *prototyping* tools. Their good points are that they are relatively inexpensive and can be used by nonprogrammers to develop quick-and-dirty interfaces. You shouldn't need a team of programmers to build your demos. However, most prototyping tools generate what I call "throwaway" code, since it usually can't be used as part of the final product code. These tools may be used for demos and simple programs but usually won't stand up to heavy use.

The other types of tools are called *development* tools. Their advantage is that they will build industrial-strength systems and programs. However, these tools usually require a significant amount of programming skill and tool-specific training. These tools, usually called *application* or *program generators,* are quite expensive, but virtually necessary for companywide or commercial development projects.

The evolution of prototyping and development tools has swung like a pendulum. In the late 1980s, prototyping tools were the rage, but then seemed to fade out in favor of major development tools in the early 1990s. Now, as object-oriented technologies begin to infiltrate the tools environment, the trend seems to be swinging back toward easier-to-use tools. The major tool vendors are beginning to realize that their customers want tools that are easy to use for both programmers and nonprogrammers. Tools must be capable of building simple programs as well as large-scale projects that require more skill and effort.

Usability Is More than Standards and Guidelines

Developing and following standards and guidelines is just one part of the interface design and development process. In the long run, usability testing should have an equal or stronger vote. If usability testing tells you that a deviation should be made from standard interface guidelines, weigh the usability test results with the benefits of following guidelines. Then make your design decisions.

KEY IDEA! *Standards and guidelines are building blocks on which to base your design and development efforts. However, just because they exist doesn't mean that every house built according to construction standards or city codes is a well-designed, livable home. Nor is every hardware or software product usable or enjoyable because standards and guidelines were followed. Gould (1988) notes, "However, beyond being good starting points, standards provide little help in designing a system." Standards and guidelines are part of the overall design process that includes design principles, a design methodology, usability testing, and a thorough understanding of users.*

References

Apple Computer, Inc. 1992. *Macintosh Human Interface Guidelines.* Reading, MA: Addison-Wesley.

Bellcore. 1996. *Design Guide for Multiplatform Graphical User Interfaces.* LP-R13, Piscataway, NJ: Bellcore (available at http://www.bellcore.com).

Berry, Richard. 1992. The designer's model of the CUA Workplace. *IBM Systems Journal* 31(3): 429–458.

Berry, Richard and Cliff Reeves. 1992. The evolution of the Common User Access Workplace model. *IBM Systems Journal* 31(3): 414–428.

Berst, Jesse. 1993. Consistency: The hobgoblin of little icons. *Information Week* (January 18): 20.

Gould, John D. 1988. How to design usable systems. In Helander, M. (Ed.), *Handbook of Human-Computer Interaction,* pp. 757–789. Amsterdam, Holland: Elsevier Science Publishers.

Grudin, Jonathan. 1989. The case against user interface consistency. *Communications of the ACM* 32(10): 1164–1173.

IBM Corporation. 1989. *Systems Application Architecture: Common User Access: Basic Interface Design Guide.* IBM, SC26-4583.

IBM Corporation. 1992. *Object-Oriented Interface Design: IBM Common User Access Guidelines.* New York: QUE.

Microsoft Corporation. 1992. *The Windows Interface: An Application Design Guide.* Redmond, WA: Microsoft Press.

Microsoft Corporation. 1995. *The Windows Interface Guidelines for Software Design.* Redmond, WA: Microsoft Press.

Open Software Foundation. 1993. *OSF/Motif Style Guide, Revision 1.2.* Englewood Cliffs, NJ: Prentice-Hall.

Smith, Sidney and Jane Mosier. 1986. *Guidelines for Designing User Interface Software.* Report ESD-TR-86-278 MTR-10090. Bedford, MA: MITRE Corporation.

Tetzlaff, Linda and David R. Schwartz. 1991. The use of guidelines in interface design. *Proceedings of ACM CHI '91,* New Orleans, LA: 329–333.

Thovtrup, Henrik and Jakob Nielsen. 1991. Assessing the usability of a user interface standard. *Communications of the ACM* (March): 335–341.

Tufte, Edward. 1983. *The Visual Display of Quantitative Information.* Cheshire, CT: Graphics Press.

Tufte, Edward. 1992. The user interface: The point of competition. *Bulletin of the American Society for Information Science* (June/July): 15–17.

Zeichick, Alan. 1991. Doing it right. *AI Expert* (May): 5.

CHAPTER SEVEN

Software Usability Testing

There is substantial empirical evidence that attention to usability dramatically decreases costs and increases productivity.

Brad Myers (1994)

The lack of usability of software and poor design of programs is the secret shame of the industry.

Mitchell Kapor, founder of Lotus Software (1993)

Defining Product Usability

Instead of running usability tests at the end of your programming cycle, think of optimizing your applications from the get-go. Call it usability design. . . . Tweaking with a bad design isn't going to help any.

Rachel Parker (1994)

Usability is the glue that holds together all of the pieces that (hopefully) fit together to make up any product. Figure 7.1 shows the different pieces of the product puzzle. Most products today are not simply standalone PC products—they are networked, mobile, database-linked, Web-linked, sophisticated programs for users of many skill levels. How do revised *business processes,* new *technologies,* intuitive *interfaces,* and *electronic performance support* all fit together to give users *what* they want, *when* they want, and *how* they want it? Usability must be built into the product and tested during the design and development process. Only usability testing will give you the answers!

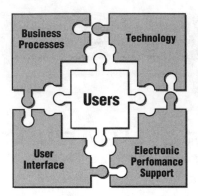

Figure 7.1   Usability: How product pieces fit together.

How do you define user friendliness? How can companies say that their products are easier to use than competitive products? Usability is used too often as a *subjective* notion. The term *user friendly* has no real meaning unless it can be defined in real terms. Usability must be defined so that accurate evaluations can be made. That is, usability must be *operationally defined* (so it can be measured) and then tested. Only then can the *easy-to-use* label mean anything to product consumers and users. Usability testing is based on the process of defining the measures that make up product usability. These measures are then used to evaluate how well products perform when users try to do the tasks they'd like to do with them.

KEY IDEA! *The focus of this book is on good user interface design and usability testing. They are both critical, but you must understand that they go hand in hand—you need to do both to design a good product. Good interface design does not guarantee a usable product, while user testing can never substitute for good design. They are both part of the interface design process called usability engineering.*

Educators and researchers agree that the computer industry tends to employ usability terms very loosely. Anderson and Shapiro (1989) say, " 'User friendly' has become so lacking in content and specificity as to be virtually meaningless." They propose general categories that can be used to get a better definition of usability to be applied to computer software in different user and system environments. Use these categories to better define software usability for you or your business. Also use these categories to develop questionnaires, checklists, or guidelines to evaluate the software products you purchase and use.

The *easy to . . .* categories are as follows:

- ◆ Easy to use
- ◆ Easy to learn (and teach)
- ◆ Easy to relearn
- ◆ Easy to unlearn
- ◆ Easy to avoid harm
- ◆ Easy to support
- ◆ Easy to audit
- ◆ Easy to share within a group
- ◆ Easy to integrate into existing operations

KEY IDEA! *In the past, developers improved software products by adding more function to their products. To sell products, the competitive focus was on the amount of function in a product, with little concern about how users were supposed to use these functions. The focus on program function has changed to today's focus on tasks that users perform. This task-oriented focus should drive all aspects of the user interface, including online and hardcopy help and documentation.*

This chapter looks at usability from many angles. Software usability testing is defined, and product usability goals and objectives are described. Cost benefits of usability testing are also discussed. Finally, a number of famous (and infamous) usability product comparison studies are analyzed for the reader's benefit. Lessons learned from each of these usability studies are presented. After reading this chapter, you should be much more aware about usability, understand the cost benefits it can provide, and become enthusiastic about usability testing your own software products.

Defining Software Usability Testing

Usability lab testing does not produce usable applications any more than functional testing produces quality code. Building successful user-centered applications requires attention throughout the development cycle to users and their tasks.

James Kubie (1996)

Usability laboratories have been around for over fifteen years. Kitsuse (1991) described their history:

> The usability evaluation process was developed by IBM Corporation in the early '80s as a way to make personal computer users more self-sufficient and to cut down on the number of calls to the company's 800-number help-line. The process has since been adopted by most major developers of hardware and software, and over the past two years, has found its way into a growing number of smaller software firms. Large companies that custom-design software for use by their own employees are also experimenting with usability evaluations.

The field of human-computer interaction has been alive since the 1980s. The yearly ACM CHI (Association for Computing Machinery Computer-Human Interaction) conference has been held since 1985. The Usability Professionals Association (UPA) is growing larger since it was founded in 1991. If you are interested in the UPA, call (214) 233-9107, extension 206, or visit the Web site at http://www.UPAssoc.org.

Why is usability testing necessary? At the most basic level, usability testing tells you whether users can use a product. If you believe that a new product enables users to perform their tasks faster, better, and more accurately, how can you be sure these goals are met? Planned user and business benefits and objectives must be validated to see if they have been met. The next section defines product usability goals and objectives and gives examples to follow. Here are a few basic reasons why usability testing is so important:

- Designer's and developer's intuitions about a product aren't always correct.
- Designer's and developer's terminology doesn't always match the user's.
- People differ and therefore there is no "average" user.
- Usability design principles and guidelines aren't sufficient.
- Informal feedback is inadequate for product evaluations.
- Time, money, and resources spent on usability evaluations are worthwhile.
- Products built in pieces will usually have system-level inconsistencies.

- Problems found late in the process are more difficult and more expensive to fix.
- Problems fixed during development will mean reduced support costs later.
- Usability evaluations can provide advantages over competitive products.

KEY IDEA! *What is a usability test? The International Standards Organization (ISO) defines usability as "the effectiveness, efficiency, and satisfaction with which a specified set of users can achieve a specified set of tasks in particular environments." A usability test investigates* users, tasks, *and* environments *to evaluate a product's performance with respect to users'* effectiveness, efficiency, *and* satisfaction.

Usability testing evaluates product designs (paper designs, software prototypes, and final products) to provide feedback to improve product design, to reduce bugs and problems, to compare products and versions, and to validate that products meet predetermined usability goals and objectives.

Usability testing is part of the overall process of *usability engineering* (Chapter 12 covers the iterative design process). You shouldn't just test for usability; you should plan and design for usability. There is a wide range of usability activities that are conducted throughout the design and development process. A good reference is *Developing User Interfaces: Ensuring Usability Through Product and Process* (Hix and Hartson, 1993).

An important part of both software design and testing is building prototypes. Early prototypes may be simple paper-based graphics and designs, while software prototypes range from simple conceptual demonstrations to fully functional programs for functional and software testing, and marketing efforts. Prototypes are discussed in detail in Chapter 12, in the section entitled, *Phase 3: Construct the Interface.* A good reference for developing prototypes is *The Art of Rapid Prototyping,* by Isensee and Rudd (1996).

Some of these usability-oriented activities are part of the interface design methodology I've already discussed, such as following interface design principles and industry standard guidelines (Chapters 5 and 6). Some of the usability testing activities are informal, requiring only pencil and paper, while other usability activities involve using a sophisticated usability test laboratory, complete with user and observation rooms, video cameras and audio equipment, and the hardware and software environments necessary to run the software product being tested. A useful reference for all aspects of usability testing can be found in Rubin's (1994) book, *Handbook of Usability Testing: How to Plan, Design, and Conduct Effective Tests.* The range of usability test techniques includes:

- ◆ Observation
- ◆ Interviews and surveys
- ◆ Contextual inquiries
- ◆ Heuristic evaluations
- ◆ Focus groups
- ◆ Laboratory testing

For example, *heuristic evaluations* are conducted as part of the usability process. User interface designers and experts analyze the user interface by applying checklists, principles, guidelines, and their knowledge of common usability problems. These evaluations are usually done in early phases of design, often with paper designs as well as software prototypes. Heuristic evaluations do not replace usability tests; they are used to find significant usability and interface problems early in product design. A good source of information, case studies, strategies, techniques, and tools is *Usability Inspection Methods* (Nielsen and Mack, 1994).

More formal usability tests are conducted in usability labs where representative users are brought in to use prototypes or versions of the software product. Test subjects are asked to use the system to perform a set of tasks. They are also asked (repeatedly, during the test session) to think aloud while performing test tasks. This helps the test team understand what users are thinking, and it enhances the audio and video data usually collected during the test session.

Recruiting the right users (and enough of them) is an important part of any usability test. Test participants should be representative of the product's actual users. The number of test participants to use is influenced by many factors, including amount of time, resources, money, test design, number and type of tasks tested, and the type of statistical analyses you plan to perform on the test results. If you are looking for major usability problems, four to eight test participants may be enough to find most of them. As you complete each participant's test session, you get a feel for whether the session produced user feedback on new problem areas. If so, continue to run more test participants. If not, you may not need to use more test participants.

The usability measures you choose should be derived from the product goals and objectives (see next section). There are usually two types of measures in a usability test:

◆ *Performance measures* include counts of actions, task completion, task time, errors, and assists. These are also called *quantitative* measures.

◆ *Subjective measures* include oral and written data collected from users regarding their perceptions, opinions, judgments, preferences, and satisfaction regarding the system and their own performance. These are also called *qualitative* measures.

Product Usability Goals and Objectives

To some extent, usability is a narrow concern compared to the larger issue of system acceptability, which basically is the question of whether the system is good enough to satisfy all the needs and requirements of the users and other potential stakeholders.

Jacob Nielsen (1993)

Before product usability testing activities can be planned and conducted, overall product usability goals and objectives should be clearly defined. This is the responsibility of product owners, planners, developers, and designers. As product direction, function, interfaces, and user tasks change over time, usability goals and objectives must be reevaluated before beginning usability activities.

Often, product leaders and developers, when they finally agree that usability tests should be conducted on their product, can't adequately define what the product is supposed to do for users. High-level statements such as "The product should be intuitive and easy to learn" may sound fine, but are not clear enough to serve as usability test objectives.

Booth (1989) defines four factors that make up usability: usefulness, effectiveness, learnability, and attitude. All *operational definitions* of usability should address one or more of these factors. Shackel (1984) also categorizes usability into four similar categories: learnability, effectiveness, flexibility, and user attitude. Table 7.1 shows descriptions and measures for each usability factor.

TABLE 7.1   Factors that Make Up Usability

Usability Factor	Description and Measures
Usefulness	◆ The degree to which a product enables users to achieve their goals. (Can users use the product?) ◆ An assessment of users' motivations for using a product. ◆ Usefulness measures are typically captured by *performance data.*
Effectiveness	◆ How successful a product is in allowing users to perform their work. (How well can users do a task with the product?) ◆ Effectiveness measures are typically captured through *performance data.*
Learnability	◆ Users can use a product to a defined level of competence after a predetermined amount and period of training. (How well trained are users?) ◆ Learnability measures are typically captured through *performance data.*
Attitude	◆ Users' perceptions, feelings, and opinions about learning and using a product. (What are users' thoughts about the usability of a product?) ◆ Attitude measures are typically captured through *satisfaction data* (written and oral feedback).

Usability goals and objectives must be defined for any software product. Usability *goals* are high-level statements of a product's desired benefits in the areas of the usability factors just described. Table 7.2 shows sample usability goals for a new product designed to replace an existing product. Notice that the goals directly relate to the four usability factors.

Usability goals by themselves are not directly measurable—they must further be broken down into usability objectives. Usability *objectives* are refinements of a usability goal that are more specific and detailed, and most importantly, are *measurable.* A single usability goal may generate multiple usability objectives. Objectives should be structured to contain information about *specific performance or actions* relative to *measurable criteria,* given *certain conditions.* Table 7.3 shows how to structure a usability objective.

TABLE 7.2   Example Usability Goals

Usability Factor	Usability Goals
Usefulness	◆ Users will use the new product given the choice between the current product and the new product.
Effectiveness	◆ The product will increase users' productivity.
Learnability	◆ Less training will be needed to prepare users for the new product.
Attitude	◆ Users will be highly satisfied with the new product.

TABLE 7.3   Format of a Usability Objective

Usability Objective	Criteria	Performance	Condition
After 4 hours of training, 90% of the users will complete a customer order within 5 minutes.	◆ 90% of the users ◆ within 5 minutes	◆ complete a customer order	◆ After 4 hours of training

Table 7.4 shows sample objectives for each of the four usability factors.

KEY IDEA! *Usability testing without product goals and objectives is like shooting an arrow in some general direction and then painting a bull's-eye around wherever the arrow landed. You can't tell if you have met product usability goals and objectives unless they have been clearly and* operationally defined *before the product is designed and developed.*

Cost Benefits of Usability Testing

We're talking about designing computer systems for ease of use, exploiting advanced new technology tools and formal methods which impact upon the bottom-line via lower total lifetime costs, higher profits, improved quality and more easily used end-products.

Brian Oakley (1991)

Users want products that are high-tech or new-tech, higher quality, easier to use, and cheaper to develop. The question is, what is the price of usability? However you choose to accomplish these goals, some form of usability evaluations must be a part of the solution. Usability testing isn't done just for the fun of it. It can be an eye-opening experience for you to watch your product being tested.

KEY IDEA! *Every designer and developer should participate or observe usability tests of their products. However, be careful to keep developers from getting too involved in usability tests. Because they are so knowledgeable about how the product works, it is easy for them to cue test participants or steer them toward a solution when they might not find it on their own. Product developers should serve in a support role, rather than as a test monitor who works directly with test participants.*

TABLE 7.4   Usability Objectives for each Usability Factor

Usability Objective	Criteria	Performance	Condition
Usefulness After 5 task scenarios, 90% of the users will successfully complete a task.	◆ 90% of the users ◆ complete the task	◆ successfully complete a task	◆ After 5 task scenarios
Effectiveness After 5 task scenarios, 75% of the users will be able to complete a task within 10 minutes.	◆ 75% of the users ◆ within 10 minutes	◆ successfully complete a task	◆ After 5 task scenarios
Learnability After 4 hours of training, all users will attain a predefined level of product knowledge.	◆ all users ◆ predefined level of product knowledge	◆ successfully attain product knowledge	◆ After 4 hours of training
Attitude After 5 task scenarios, 85% of the users will rate their satisfaction with the product at a level of 5.5 or better (on a 7-point scale).	◆ 85% of the users ◆ satisfaction level of 5.5 on a 7-point scale	◆ satisfaction rating	◆ After 5 task scenarios

Cost-Justifying Usability

The costs associated with an hour of downtime can range from tens of thousands to millions of dollars depending upon the application. And this does not include the intangible damage that can be done to a company's image.

Drew Hannah (1996)

The biggest usability explosion, and one that user interface designers could do a better job of accelerating, will come when businesses are able to account for the real costs of poor user interfaces. Curtis and Hefley (1994) go on to say, "For instance, many companies employ hundreds, perhaps thousands of people who perform repetitive tasks at workstations while interacting with customers. These jobs include telephone operators, sales clerks, and stockbrokers. The benefits of better interfaces for these jobs can range from the hundreds of thousands to millions of dollars for a single company."

Usability testing is an integral part of the iterative product design and development process (see Chapter 12). However, usability testing is often the victim of business and development tradeoffs. Is usability testing worthwhile if the product delivery date is delayed three months? It depends on who you ask—some would say "yes" while others would say "no." Miller and Jeffries (1992) conclude, "As with most things, the more time and money you put into the evaluation process, the more likely you are to get a usable product. Beyond that, you—the person who knows the most about your situation—will have to determine what tradeoffs are acceptable." There are some key questions that must be answered: How can you get the biggest return on your usability test efforts? How do you know when you have done enough testing? How much risk of being off-target with your customer's needs are you willing to take?

KEY IDEA! *Usability testing and evaluations should be budgeted as part of the cost of doing business. Five to 10 percent of a product's total budget should be allocated to usability test activities. As with other business costs, there is a potential return on investment and higher profit due to a better-quality and more usable product. Figuring out how much product savings usability testing can provide is difficult, but there are cost-justification models available that can be used to determine the value of testing. At Ford Motor Company, it was determined that the company's usability program saved them $100,000 on an accounting software system, which more than paid back the company's initial investment of $70,000 in the usability laboratory (Kitsuse, 1991).*

As the field of human factors and usability became mainstream in corporations around the world, executives and managers asked, "What really is the cost of usability and usability testing?" Cost-justifying usability is a necessary skill that user interface designers and human factors/usability professionals have learned over the past few years. If you are interested in reading more about this area, a good reference is *Cost-Justifying Usability* by Randolph Bias and Deborah Mayhew (1994).

Using Cognitive Psychologists and Usability Professionals

Left to our own devices, we will pay more attention to things of less importance to the customer.

Ron Zemke (1992)

A surge in human factors engineering is helping software companies build friendlier programs. If you bring human factors people in at early stages, you can prevent some of these fundamentally dumb decisions.

Jeffrey Tarter (1990)

A better understanding of how humans perceive, store, comprehend, and remember information helps greatly in designing computer user interfaces (see Chapter 4). All aspects of the interface must be designed to meet the basic human physical and mental abilities we all share. Interfaces are general-purpose tools to be used by a wide range of people and thus must also be designed to accommodate natural human diversity. Sounds like a tough assignment for developers, doesn't it? You shouldn't have to take on the additional role of usability professional. Let human factors professionals and cognitive psychologists do their jobs.

KEY IDEA! *The general area of the study of how humans interact with objects around them is called* human factors. *Human factors engineers have been around since World War II when Air Force experts realized that changing the cockpit design of airplanes could reduce the number of flying accidents.* Cognitive psychologists *focus on understanding and researching how people learn, comprehend, and remember information.*

The past fifteen years has seen a tremendous influx of many professionals from academic and other backgrounds into the computer industry. This includes cognitive psychologists, human factors engineers, instructional designers, and information specialists. Why has this happened? Well, the computer industry gradually figured something out: The products people had used with very few complaints were now coming under fire for being poorly designed and unusable. This criticism was coming from "enlightened" users who were slowly realizing that computers were supposed to work for them and not vice versa. An industry publisher, Jeffrey Tarter (Nakamura, 1990) said, "People would put up with anything in the early days, so ease-of-use was less of a priority. The original Aldus Pagemaker was god-awful to use, it was complicated, and it crashed all the time. It just didn't matter because it was so much better than the alternative. But if Aldus came out with a product like that right now, there'd be a rebellion."

The need for expertise in this area is quite universal. Renato Iannella (1992), a university research professor in Queensland, Australia, agrees; "To truly understand the mental process that a typical user has in interacting with a computer system requires the knowledge of a Human Factors specialist. Such a person, trained in some area of behavioral science, has a knowledge of human abilities, limits, and methods to collect analytical data on user interfaces."

Most computer companies have in-house experts in these fields. This effort has been led by industry giants such as Apple, IBM, Hewlett-Packard, and Microsoft. Smaller companies often use consultants rather than hiring a staff of professionals. The study of the human factors and usability of computer products is an interdisciplinary field. For example, cognitive psychologists have greatly helped the computer industry because they have studied the way people read, comprehend, and remember information.

Are Usability Professionals Worth the Cost?

Human interface design arguably represents the most important single discipline in information technology. It is, metaphorically speaking, where the rubber meets the road.

Daniel Gross, 1993

Jeffries et al. (1991) performed a study that showed how critical human factors professionals and cognitive psychologists can be for interface design. A software product was given to four groups for user interface testing. Four human factors specialists were given two weeks to review the product (Group One). A user interface tester observed six test subjects as they used the product interface and then wrote a report (Group Two). Three programmers applied a set of principles (called "guidelines") to the product interface (Group Three). Finally, three more programmers conducted a *cognitive walkthrough* on the product (Group Four).

Their test results were quite interesting. They counted the total number of problems found by each group. They also computed the number of core problems found. Core problems were a set of errors determined by a panel of seven interface design experts. Results showed that Group One, the human factors professionals, found almost four times as many problems (152) as each of the other groups (about 39 each). They also found three times as many core prob-

ity factors. Unfortunately, these marketing promises often don't come true when people actually try to use these products for business or at home. It is at this point, when products don't work the way users expect them to, that people get extremely frustrated and upset.

According to the trade press (*World News Today,* 1992), Microsoft thinks that the value customers place on product usability is a key to sales success. Take a look in any computer magazine. What do you think about software product advertising? Does it make you want to purchase these products because the company advertising says that the product is more usable than its competitor's? How can you be sure of the advertising claims? How can users judge these claims for themselves? PC magazines and journalists help bewildered consumers and users by providing product reviews, tests, and comparisons. Most readers feel better about making purchasing decisions when they have more reliable information than merely that which they get from product advertising.

In a recent "letter to the editor" column in *PC Computing,* magazine editors responded to a query regarding a product's usability test. The defense of their test methodology was:

> All our usability testing is based on a strict, time-tested, replicable scientific methodology. Industry-standard usability studies have demonstrated repeatedly that tests with as few as 4 subjects provide at least 80 percent accuracy. To be safe, our tests normally include 8 or more subjects. . . . The conclusions printed in the story reflect the test results—which measure productivity and satisfaction—rather than anyone's opinions, and we stand behind them.

KEY IDEA! *Microsoft has begun to promote user feedback and customer involvement in their product development. The About Microsoft Works dialog box asks users to send in usability-related comments and "wish lists."* Microsoft Magazine *even asks readers to participate in usability testing of Microsoft products: "We are interested in all types of companies using any type of software, anywhere in the United States. If you'd like to participate in our usability program, please call the Usability Group at. . . ."*

J. D. Powers and Associates conducts periodic polls of computer users on their satisfaction with desktop computer systems. The interesting thing about these surveys is the areas that contribute to a user's definition of customer satisfaction. System ease of use is the top factor, commanding a full 45 percent of users' overall satisfaction. Following that, the other factors contributing to user satisfaction were system capacity, operation, quietness, and repair service. These types of surveys show how users define their satisfaction criteria. You should pay more attention to how users define customer satisfaction, rather than how you define it yourself.

InfoWorld product reviews address all aspects of a product's performance in computing a total score. Usability issues take up between 18 percent (spreadsheets) and 30 percent (word processors) of the product's total score. The weightings are as follows: ease of learning (4–10%), ease of use (8–13%), and documentation quality (5–8%). Error handling, which includes user errors, software bugs, and hardware crashes, makes up another 5 to 8 percent. Usability measures, therefore, can make up about one-third of a product's performance rating, regardless of the function provided by the product.

Marketing Usability and User Interfaces

> *SOLID EDGE is easy to learn and use, so you can spend more time engineering and less time operating a CAD system. . . . With an intuitive interface that emulates a practical and natural mechanical engineering workflow, SOLID EDGE eliminates the command clutter and complicated modeling procedures of traditional CAD systems.*
>
> Intergraph Corporation SOLID EDGE advertisement (1996)

A new CAD (Computer-Aided Design) product, Intergraph's SOLID EDGE, was specifically designed to provide a leading-edge three-dimensional modeling program with a simple and intuitive PC user interface. At $6,000 for the program, it competes directly with other CAD programs in the $20,000 price range that have very complicated user interfaces that only an engineer could love! After a few minutes of practice, I easily created a 3-D rendering of the bottom piece of the mouse for my PC (see Figure 7.2). I could even rotate the finished part around to view it from any angle.

KEY IDEA! *This ($6,000!) user interface is similar to any other Windows program users might purchase for only a few hundred dollars. If they know how to use Microsoft Word or Excel, for example, they've already learned 60 percent of the SOLID EDGE interface. This is an* industrial-strength *example of the consistency and transfer of learning golden rules of interface design.*

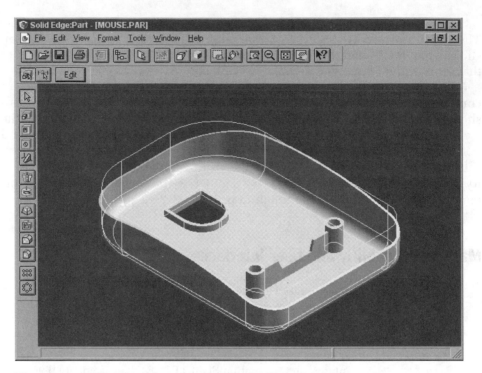

Figure 7.2   User interface for SOLID EDGE 3-D CAD program.

Intergraph uses the new interface style as a marketing tool to promote the product, and rightly so! The interface offers a number of features that highlight the fact that the computer is very good at doing and remembering things that humans don't do as easily. Here are some examples of the product's interface enhancements:

◆ Automatic geometry location dynamically highlights edges, surfaces, and other elements of a model as users move the mouse.

◆ Intelligent sketching automatically highlights key geometric locations (endpoints, midpoints, tangencies) by mouse cursor location.

◆ A FreeSketch tool takes freehand drawings and transforms them into precision geometric elements. For example, when users move the mouse in a circular motion, FreeSketch automatically recognizes the arclike movement and places a precision arc.

- Visual feedback is used to show users their progress through steps of a modeling operation. A SmartStep wizard leads engineers through multiple-step feature modeling tasks. All steps are visualized and the current stage is highlighted. Users can directly access previous steps in the process for flexible modifications (remember the golden rule of user in control!).

- SOLID EDGE extends Microsoft's OLE (Object Linking and Embedding) architecture to add a third dimension for 3-D geometric models that can be used to cut and paste objects the same way users cut and copy objects in documents and spreadsheets.

Intergraph conducted a usability test to compare SOLID EDGE with other PC CAD programs. Users created a 3-D model using each program three times. Average completion times, number of text entries, mouse clicks, and menu interactions were recorded (see Table 7.5). While this study was conducted by a company promoting their product (discussed elsewhere in this chapter), the results are dramatic.

KEY **IDEA!** *This example shows the tremendous power of the user interface, following the golden rules of interface design, and usability testing. Sophisticated and complex programs don't have to provide difficult-to-learn or difficult-to-use interfaces just because the program function is complex.* The difficult part is the designer's job of building simple user interfaces for complex tasks.

The Art of Data Massage: Reliability and Validity

In reality, of course, such company-funded studies are exercises in marketing, not science.

Henry Norr (1995)

TABLE 7.5   Usability Test Results for 3-D CAD programs, from Intergraph (1996)

Product	Completion Time (Minutes)	Text Entries and Mouse Clicks (Number)
SOLID EDGE	7	118
Pro Engineer	15	283
Solid Works	20	159
AutoCAD Designer	14	397

Of course, advertisers want readers to take their test results at face value. I'm not saying that all product usability comparison studies aren't legitimate; I'm saying that users and consumers should look closely at how usability tests are designed and conducted, and how test results are analyzed and presented. The problem is one of test *reliability* versus test *validity*.

KEY IDEA! *Test reliability means that the* same test *can be repeated again and again and will show the* same results. *This is very different from test validity. A test is* valid *if it accurately measures what it was supposed to measure. Product comparison usability tests may be fairly reliable, but don't take their validity at face value. It is easy to design scenarios and tasks that will favor a technique or function in one product over similar aspects of another product. Also, different types of measures used in a test can drastically change test results.*

I once taught an undergraduate college course entitled *Fundamentals of Psychological Research.* One section of it was called "The Art of Data Massage." Here's an example: Let's say we conducted a usability test comparing two products and computed the results shown in Table 7.6. Evaluators of Product A completed a task, on the average, in 44 minutes and they made an average of 6 errors. They gave the product an average score of 7.3 on a user satisfaction questionnaire. Product B evaluators took longer to finish the task—67 minutes—but they made only 3 errors. They gave the product an average 7.2 satisfaction rating. The statistical analyses that generate these numbers are based on the number of test evaluators and their ranges of scores, but I won't go into these here. The scores in the chart are typical of the results you see in product advertisements and brochures.

What conclusions can be made from this test? Which product is more usable? It depends on what the *operational definition of usability* is for the test. If usability is defined as task completion time, Product A is obviously more

TABLE 7.6   Sample Usability Test Results

Product A and Product B Usability Comparison Study			
Product Tested	Completion Time	Errors Made	User Satisfaction on a Scale of 1–10 (10 high)
A	44 minutes	6	7.3
B	67 minutes	3	7.2

usable, since it took only 45 minutes as compared to Product B's 60 minutes. However, if usability is defined as the number of errors made during the task, then Product B is more usable, since an average of only 3 errors were made using the product instead of 6 errors with the other product. Usability might be computed as some combination of completion time and number of errors. Finally, usability might be defined as the evaluators' satisfaction with the product. In that case, there really is no difference in usability for the products, since the difference between the satisfaction scores is minimal.

KEY IDEA! *Be aware of the dangers of presenting usability test results and reports to management and to the general public. Test results scores can be dangerous weapons in the hands of executives or journalists who don't know the background, goals, and design of the usability test, what was measured in the test, and how test results were collected and analyzed.*

You see that each *operational definition* of product usability can result in a totally different conclusion from the test. This is why readers should take test results very lightly, especially when they are found in product advertisements, brochures, and "white papers." The test may be reliable, but you should always question the validity of usability studies when you read their results in the press or marketing materials.

KEY IDEA! *Journalists and users are becoming more sophisticated in their understanding of the usability claims pronounced by software developers. An article in* PC Week *entitled "Let Buyers Beware of the Limits of Usability Testing" (Rossheim, 1993) discusses these issues. Their recommendations were: "First, beware of the gleaming badge of scientific objectivity that vendors pin on the white lapels of their usability testers. Buyers should question assessments of users' work behavior that are made far from the context of their workplace. . . . Second, consider the effects of the observers on the observed. . . . Third, carefully examine claims that software packages have been designed for both optimal ease of learning and maximum ease of use. What's easy to learn may be laborious to use in the long run."*

Usability Testing Interface Styles: CUIs and GUIs

GUI users work faster, better, and have higher productivity than their CUI counterparts.

Temple, Barker & Sloane Study (1990)

This section presents the first of a number of comparative usability tests discussed in this chapter. There are valuable lessons to be learned from these studies.

Over the past few years, a number of studies specifically looked at the benefits of graphical user interfaces (GUIs) over traditional character-based user interfaces (CUIs) for typical user tasks. One well-known usability study is the Wharton Report (1990), *The Value of GUIs.* This report noted the tremendous speed with which American computer users and developers were jumping into the Windows environment. They reported, "U.S. industry observers believe that the speed with which Windows is being adopted could well change the balance of power within the PC software publishing business." This turned out to be quite true, as Windows has become the "GUI for the masses."

The Wharton Report also discussed a (then) new study that addressed how effective graphical user interfaces were compared to character-based user interfaces. This was the Temple, Barker & Sloane study, *The Benefits of the Graphical User Interface.* The study was commissioned by Microsoft and Zenith in 1989, and was completed and published in 1990. The stated goals of the commissioned work were to "develop a research program designed to rigorously validate the benefits of GUI and common user access (CUA) in the white-collar environment."

The study was conducted from November 1989 through April 1990. The CUI environment was represented by IBM-compatible PCs running DOS. The GUI environment was tested with novice and experienced users using a mix of computers running Macintosh and Windows interfaces. The report did not provide specifics on the versions of DOS and Windows, but assuming that they used commercially available versions of the products, they would have used DOS 4.0 (available in 1989) and Windows 2.1 (Windows 3.0 was not announced until May 1990). The GUI user interface guideline followed by Windows at this time was IBM's CUA architecture. CUA 1989 was not published until June 1989. From the dates of the study and the versions of Windows systems used, the Windows GUI interface architecture tested was possibly as old as 1987. This means the study really doesn't tell us much about the GUI environment of Windows 3.1 and doesn't address object-oriented interfaces, since OS/2 2.0 didn't come out until 1992.

The study involved both experienced and novice users performing both word-processing and spreadsheet tasks. Test results were analyzed for speed and accuracy and users rated their subjective experiences both during and after the study. The only information given in the report about the applications used was, "Application software packages available in the CUI and GUI environments are not identical in capabilities. Rather than attempting to assess the quality of competing applications, Temple, Barker & Sloane chose the packages with the greatest market acceptance among white-collar users." I don't know about you, but I'd like to know exactly what products were being used in the study!

The study proposed seven benefits of GUIs over CUIs based on the test results. The benefits were that GUI users:

- Worked faster
- Worked better (completed more tasks)
- Had higher productivity
- Expressed lower frustration
- Perceived lower fatigue
- Were better able to self-teach and explore applications
- Were better able to learn more capabilities of applications

> **KEY IDEA!** *The Temple, Barker & Sloane report deliberately focused on CUIs and GUIs at only a very general level, not even describing the versions of the operating system and not even specifying the names of the applications used in the study. The study may be reliable, but the validity of a study that only addressed the CUI-GUI environments at a very high level is questionable. Readers certainly shouldn't generalize the study's results to today's graphical and object-oriented user interfaces since they are many years ahead of the interfaces investigated in this study.*

Lessons Learned

Computer software and their interfaces must be judged by their support of real users doing real tasks. Otherwise, you are only making a generalization that, of course, GUIs are better than character-based interfaces such as command-lines or menu systems. There are many well-informed and skilled people in the computer industry who don't think that today's GUIs are the be-all and end-all of user interfaces.

Usability Testing New Product Versions:
Windows 3.1 and Windows 95

The early alpha releases of Windows 95 and comments from the company's top developers indicate that Microsoft may be short-changing power users in order to appeal heavily to people who have never before used a computer. The reason is financial. Microsoft's marketing research indicates that something like 90 percent of PC buyers are upgrading from an older computer.

Brian Livingston (1994)

Windows 95 was the most promoted software product of all time. As such, there was tremendous scrutiny of all aspects of the product, especially the new user interface and its usability. Microsoft's stated goals for the design of the Windows 95 user interface were twofold (Sullivan, 1996):

♦ Make Windows easier to *learn* for people just getting started with computers and Windows.

♦ Make Windows easier to *use* for people who already use computers—both the typical Windows 3.1 user and the advanced, or *power* Windows 3.1 user.

Making a product easy-to-learn and easy-to-use are very different, and possibly conflicting, goals. Microsoft had an intriguing problem ushering more than 50 million Windows 3.1 novice and casual users into the new interface style of Windows 95. At the same time, advanced users know how to use the advanced functionality of the operating system. Many rounds of iterative usability testing were conducted during the design of Windows 95. To better understand the skills and problems of Windows 3.1 users, Microsoft gathered market research data and defined Windows 3.1 user's twenty most frequent tasks and twenty most common problems. They also commissioned Usability Sciences, Inc. (1994) to conduct a usability study to compare learning time and productivity for Windows 3.1 and Windows 95. Microsoft first piloted the test in-house to ensure test procedures worked, then turned the test over to an outside vendor so the results could be used in an industry white paper.

Standard performance and preference usability measures were collected. Test results for each measure were as follows. The results were quite positive for Windows 95.

1. Task completion time: Users finished the same tasks in Windows 95 in almost half the time it took them in Windows 3.1.

2. Task success rate: Users completed 94 percent of the tasks with Windows 95 versus 86 percent with Windows 3.1.

3. User satisfaction: Users were more satisfied with Windows 95 in 20 of the 21 categories surveyed.

4. User operating system preferences: Ninety-seven percent of the users said they would migrate to Windows 95.

Lessons Learned

◆ Comparative tests can provide useful information when investigating the usability of current new versions of a software product.

◆ Use common tasks and known problem areas as baseline tasks so accurate comparative measurements can be made between product versions.

◆ Use standard usability measures such as user performance (task completion and success rate) and user satisfaction (satisfaction and preference data).

◆ Use an external, independent vendor to plan and conduct usability tests to reduce corporate and product bias.

Usability Testing Operating Systems: Windows 95, Macintosh, and OS/2 Warp

While the Mac has had a strong reputation for usability, this study establishes Windows 95 as a new productivity benchmark. It's the operating system to choose to get your work done quickly and accurately.

Brad Chase, Microsoft (1995)

Probably the most controversial software usability comparison study of the past few years was the International Data Corp. (IDC) study comparing Windows 95 with Macintosh and OS/2 operating systems. This publicly announced study is worth a closer look from the usability testing perspective. Microsoft commissioned and funded the study, while IDC conducted the study. The November, 1995 press announcement reported the following overall results:

1. Task completion time:

◆ Windows 95 users finished the overall test in an average of 58 minutes.

- ◆ Macintosh users finished the overall test in an average of 72 minutes (19 percent slower than Windows 95 users).
- ◆ OS/2 users finished the overall test in an average of 116 minutes (50 percent slower than Windows 95 users).

2. Task success rate:

- ◆ Seventy-six percent of Windows 95 users completed 8 or more of the 10 task groups successfully.
- ◆ Fifty-eight percent of Macintosh users completed 8 or more of the 10 task groups successfully.
- ◆ Thirty-one percent of OS/2 users completed 8 or more of the 10 task groups successfully.

3. Productivity:

- ◆ Windows 95 users who completed 8 or more of the 10 task groups did so in 22 percent less time than Macintosh users and 51 percent less time than OS/2 users.
- ◆ Eighty-five percent of that group of Windows 95 users completed the test in less than one hour, compared to 47 percent of the Macintosh users.

The Apple and IBM Responses

That's the headline I expect you to hear when the study is released. What they won't tell you is that the methodology of the tests is severely flawed and appears to contain some serious biases. You should insist on reading their full report very carefully.

Mac Platform Marketing, Apple Computer, Inc. (1995)

It seems clear that Microsoft carefully crafted this study to portray Windows in the best light. We believe, as Apple has stated, that the study is flawed and unfair. The tests performed have been biased toward a Microsoft user and therefore would result in an improved performance for their operating system.

Walter W. Casey, IBM (1995)

Needless to say, Microsoft's press announcement and the dramatic results prompted quite a bit of news coverage in the media and, as expected, direct responses from both Apple and IBM concerning the *validity* of the study.

What strikes readers first are the huge differences in performance across the three operating systems. While the results may be extremely encouraging for users of the new Windows 95 interface and operating system, readers also must begin to wonder (as I do) how differences in performance can be so great between these similar PC operating systems.

How can Windows 95 users perform the same tasks *twice as fast* as OS/2 users? If this is true, why are millions of people buying the OS/2 operating system? Before you believe the results of this and any marketing-driven comparative usability study, dig a little deeper to get a better understanding of *how* the study was designed, and *who* were the users and *what* were their tasks. Apple questioned the usability study in a number of ways:

1. *The user sample was biased.* At least 20 percent of the Macintosh users were selected from a list provided by Microsoft.

2. *The tests are biased in favor of Windows.* Tests were suggested by Microsoft that unfairly highlighted Windows 95 features.

3. *The tests are biased against Macintosh users.* Test task terminology and Network protocols and services were not consistent with standard Macintosh interfaces and configurations.

4. *The tests are biased in what they* don't *cover.* The tests covered only a limited number of operating system operations, representing only a fraction of what is involved in defining overall personal computer productivity. The tests did *not* include many common system-level functions in which Macintosh excels but that Windows 95 cannot handle well. The tests don't cover many important areas that can be the real driving factors in user productivity.

IBM also responded to the study, replying, "The study raises more questions than it answers." IBM's concerns covered these questions:

◆ Windows 95 users outperformed users of OS/2 doing what?

◆ How was the study conducted?

◆ Who were the test subjects?

Some of the study design and procedures should make readers take notice. Windows 95 machines were configured with 16MB of RAM—8MB *more* than the operating system's minimum recommended memory. The Apple 8100 Macintosh systems were configured with 16MB of RAM—the system's *minimum* recommended configuration. At one point test participants were instructed to change the screen resolution of their PCs, but were warned not to change the number of colors, because changing the colors would force a restart of Windows 95 but not of the Macintosh. These are items you won't see in the press release for a comparative usability study!

If you are interested in reading more about this study and the surrounding debate, most of the information is available on the Internet at the following locations:

♦ The Microsoft press release (available at http://www.microsoft.com/windows/pr/nov2295.htm)

♦ Apple's response to the Microsoft/IDC study (available at http://www2.apple.com/whymac/idcresp.html)

♦ IBM's response to the Microsoft/IDC study (available at http://www.austin.ibm.com/pspinfo/msstudy.html)

♦ IDC's response to concerns regarding the IDC Special Report (available at http://www.microsoft.com/windows/pr/idc.htm)

Lessons Learned

♦ Be wary of comparative usability studies conducted or sponsored by a software vendor whose product is included in the usability test.

♦ Even though Microsoft turned the study over to an independent vendor, they were still involved in designing, planning, and conducting the usability test.

♦ Computer system configurations and networks can impact performance measurements such as task completion time and user satisfaction measures of perceived system performance.

♦ Task selection is critical to any usability test. Tasks should be representative of the user environment and not biased by the functionality or performance of the tested software systems.

♦ Test measures, criteria, and analyses can greatly affect test results. Are these elements determined before the test is performed, or later, during test data analyses? For example, successful task completion might be defined as *finishing a task within one hour*. If users finish a task in 58 minutes on average using System A, and in 62 minutes using System B, then using the criteria, the task was successfully completed using System A but not System B, even though there were only a few minutes' difference in completion times.

♦ Test support procedures can be biased by the level of support offered to test participants and the experience of the test support personnel. The test and support teams may have different knowledge and experience with the different hardware and software platforms, operating systems, and software products used in the comparison test.

A Usability Challenge: Windows versus Macintosh

At the 1996 Software Publishers Association (SPA) meeting, Apple evangelist Guy Kawasaki challenged Microsoft to a live, onstage, head-to-head contest. Guy had a ten-year-old assistant, while Jim Louderback, editor-in-chief of *Windows Sources,* had an adult assistant. The contest consisted of the following timed tasks:

◆ Installing and setting up the systems, right out of the box.

◆ Installing an Iomega Corporation Zip drive.

◆ Installing a modem.

◆ Connecting a printer.

◆ Connecting to the Internet or an online service.

◆ Setting up and connecting to a network.

◆ Creating a file, saving it, then making a shortcut or alias of an application.

◆ Deinstalling an application.

As Don Crabb (1996) reported in *MacWeek,* "Not surprisingly, Team Mac won. Not at every task, but overall the Mac clearly dusted Windows 95 in these user-friendly tests. The tests showed that despite big gains in Windows 95 installation routines and the plug-and-play hardware standards, it's still no match for the Mac."

Here we have a public contest that refutes the Microsoft IDC study results. As you see, this type of usability study can show very different results that can support either product. Crabb also notes, "While the SPA tests make for good public relations, especially in front of a roomful of developers, the results are not likely to convince anyone to buy a Mac, nor prevent anyone else from migrating to Windows 95 from the Mac. Why? Because you could run the same kind of challenge and pick tasks that Windows excels at to make the counterpoint."

KEY IDEA! *Usability tests and test results should be designed to improve product interfaces and user productivity, and not necessarily to compare and contrast operating systems, products, or user interfaces. This study and the accompanying responses from Apple and IBM are a case study in how to (or how not to) design usability tests and can be used as an exercise in reverse engineering, a usability study to determine users, tasks, measures, and other characteristics of usability studies that designers and usability professionals must be aware of. Try it yourself! Use the Usability Test Report Card at the end of this chapter to reverse engineer this or any other usability study.*

The ultimate conclusion is that comparison usability tests shouldn't be banned, they should be done right! From the studies discussed here, you see that comparison tests can provide valuable information regarding versions of a product, competitive software programs, and even competitive software operating systems. Things just get a little crazy when companies conduct comparison tests with the intent to use the results to promote their products.

The Usability Test Report Card

A tremendous amount of effort, skill, and time goes into designing and conducting usability tests, and analyzing and reporting test results. Project managers and developers may agree that usability and human factors efforts are nice to have and would benefit their product, but many don't fully understand the depth of commitment (in terms of process, time, resources, skills, and money) that is required to achieve the full cost benefits of usability engineering.

To summarize this chapter, a Usability Test Report Card (Table 7.7) lists key topics that must be addressed by any usability test. You must also be prepared to discuss and defend these topics regarding any usability study you may conduct. Use this chart to help design your own usability tests and to evaluate usability studies you read in advertisements, reports, and journals. Please draw your own conclusions regarding whether test results really are valid, rather than relying on the test report or advertisement itself.

Software Usability Testing—Just Do It!

It takes almost a religious zeal to fight for usability testing on software products and to incorporate usability feedback into the product design. Don't give up and go along with project leaders who say, "Oh, we'll add those recommendations in the next version." The more users are subjected to unusable design, the more difficult it is to change the design. Remember the WYKIWYL phenomenon—what you know is what you like. Users can adapt to ill-suited designs, but they shouldn't have to.

KEY IDEA! *Heed Don Norman's final words in* The Design of Everyday Things *(1988)—"Now you are on your own. If you are a designer, help fight the battle for usability. If you are a user, then join your voice with those who cry for usable products. Write to manufacturers. Boycott unusable designs. Support good designs by purchasing them, even if it means going out of your way, even if it means spend-*

ing a bit more. . . . And enjoy yourself. Walk around the world exam-
ining the details of design. . . . Realize that even details matter, that
the designers may have had to fight to include something helpful."

TABLE 7.7 The Usability Test Report Card

Usability Test Topics	Ask These Questions
Test Sponsor/Test Conductor	◆ Who sponsored the usability test?
	◆ Who actually conducted the usability test?
Test Goals and Objectives	◆ Are test goals described?
	◆ Are test objectives described?
	◆ Are test objectives operationally defined (can they be measured)?
Test Design and Procedures	◆ Is the test design appropriate given the test goals and objectives?
	◆ Does the test follow valid experimental design methodology (within-between subjects, random-ized task order, etc.)?
	◆ What are the test procedures (introduction, train-ing, tasks, questionnaires, debriefing, etc.)?
Software Products and Hardware Platform	◆ Are the appropriate products tested?
	◆ Are the appropriate hardware platforms used?
	◆ Are the computers configured appropriately and similarly (processor speed, memory, storage, etc.)?
Test Participants	◆ Who are the test participants?
	◆ What are their demographics (age, sex, etc.)?
	◆ What are their computing skills?
	◆ What applications and operating systems have they used?
	◆ Where and how are test participants chosen?
	◆ What methods and criteria are used to categorize test participants (beginner, intermediate, advanced, etc.)?
	◆ How are test participants assigned to groups?
	◆ Are test participants paid for their cooperation?
Tasks	◆ What are the test tasks?
	◆ Are task scenarios unclear or leading the partici-pant?
	◆ Is actual or test data used in the test?
	◆ Do tasks match test goals and objectives?
	◆ Are tasks performed by all participants?
	◆ Are tasks performed on all machines?
	◆ Are tasks biased toward a particular product?

TABLE 7.7 *(Continued)*

Usability Test Topics	Ask These Questions
Test Assistance and Support	◆ Are test participants trained before the test? How? ◆ Is assistance provided to participants during the test? ◆ Who provides assistance to participants? ◆ Is technical support (hardware and software) available during the test?
Test Measures	◆ What test measures are collected (performance, preference, and observation measures)? ◆ Do the test measures match with test goals and objectives? ◆ How are test measures collected (self-scored, timed, videotaped, etc.)?
Test Criteria	◆ What are the criteria for each measure? ◆ What defines successful task completion? ◆ What defines an assist? ◆ What defines a participant error?
Test Analyses, Results, and Conclusions	◆ Is the original test data available? ◆ Are test analyses defined and described? ◆ Are appropriate and valid statistical tests conducted on test results? ◆ Are test results statistically significant? ◆ Are test conclusions based on test results? ◆ Can summary remarks be generalized from the test design and test results? ◆ Are test conclusions matched back to test goals and objectives?
Reliability versus Validity	◆ Is the usability test reliable (can the results be replicated)? ◆ Is the usability test valid (does the test and the results really measure what the test is supposed to measure)? ◆ What are outside responses to the usability test design and results (regarding reliability and validity)?
Research Ethics	◆ Are participants told about test tasks, measures, and procedures (consent forms, video taping, observers, etc.)? ◆ Are participants allowed to quit the test if they feel they do not want to participate? ◆ Are participants encouraged or discouraged to use certain functions or perform certain tasks? ◆ Are participants encouraged or discouraged to take their time or to complete tasks as quickly as possible?

References

Anderson, Robert H. and Norman Shapiro. 1989. Beyond user friendly: Easy to. . . . *EDUCOM Review* (Fall 1989): 50–54.

Baecker, Ronald M., Jonathan Grudin, William A. S. Buxton, and Saul Greenberg. 1995. Designing to fit human capabilities. In Baecker et al. (Eds), *Readings in Human-Computer Interaction: Toward the year 2000*. San Francisco, CA: Morgan Kaufmann.

Bias, Randolph G. and Deborah J. Mayhew (Eds.). 1994. *Cost-Justifying Usability.* Boston: Academic Press.

Booth, Paul. 1989. *An Introduction to Human-Computer Interaction.* London: Lawrence Erlbaum Associates.

Crabb, Don. 1996. Mac clobbers Windows 95 in SPA demo, but so what? *MacWEEK* (March 18): 27.

Curtis, Bill and Bill Hefley. 1994. A WIMP no more: The maturing of user interface engineering. *ACM interactions* (January): 22–34.

Hix, Deborah and H. Rex Hartson. 1993. *Developing User Interfaces: Ensuring Usability Through Product and Process.* New York: Wiley.

Iannella, Renato. 1992. Designing "safe" user interfaces. *The Australian Computer Journal* 24(3): 92–97.

Isensee, Scott and Jim Rudd. 1996. *The Art of Rapid Prototyping.* New York: International Thomson.

Jeffries, Robin, James Miller, Cathleen Warton, and Kathy Uyeda. 1991. User interface evaluation in the real world: A comparison of four techniques. *Proceedings of CHI'91,* pp. 119–124. Reading, MA: Addison-Wesley.

Kitsuse, Alicia. 1991. Why aren't computers. . . . *Across the Board* (October): 44–48.

Miller, James and Robin Jeffries. 1992. Usability evaluation: Science of trade-offs. *IEEE Software* (September): 97–102.

Nakamura, Roxanna Li. 1990. The X factor. *InfoWorld* (November 19): 51.

Nielsen, Jakob and Robert Mack (Eds.). 1994. *Usability Inspection Methods.* New York: Wiley.

Norman, Donald A. 1988. *The Design of Everyday Things.* New York: Doubleday.

Remich, Norman C. Jr. 1992. Simpler but better. *Appliance Manufacturer:* 650–667.

Rossheim, John. 1993. Let buyers beware of the limits of usability testing. *PC Week* (April 19): 87.

Rubin, Jeffrey. 1994. *Handbook of Usability Testing: How to Plan, Design, and Conduct Effective Tests.* New York: Wiley.

Seltzer, Larry. 1993. Workplace Shell finds friends and enemies. *PC Week* (May 24): S/20.

Seymour, Jim. 1992. The corporate manager: No doubt about it, 1992 was the year of usability. *PC Week* (December 21): 65.

Shackel, B. 1984. The concept of usability. In Bennett, J., D. Case, J. Sandelin, and M. Smith (Eds.), *Visual Display Terminals: Usability Issues and Health Concerns.* New York: Prentice-Hall, pp. 45–88.

Sullivan, Kent. 1996. The Windows user interface: A case study in usability engineering. *Proceedings of the ACM CHI'96.*

Temple, Barker & Sloane, Inc. 1990. *The Benefits of the Graphical User Interface.* Lexington, MA: Temple, Barker & Sloane, Inc.

Usability Sciences, Inc. 1994. *Windows 3.1 versus Windows 95: Quantification of Learning Time and Productivity.* Technical Report (available from http://www.microsoft.com/windows/product/usability.htm).

Wharton Report. 1990. *The Value of GUIs.* Middlesex, England: Wharton Report No. 146.

CHAPTER EIGHT

User Interface Evolution: Command-Lines and Menus

How can you tell where you're going if you don't know where you've been?

Popular folksong

User Interfaces and Operating Systems

The next two chapters detail the history of the development and evolution of computer software user interfaces, from the command-language interface all the way to menus and graphical user interfaces, leading the way to object-oriented user interfaces. The development of user interface styles and technologies parallels the evolution of the personal computer operating systems, as user interfaces for software programs are based on the interface style and technology afforded by the hardware and the operating system.

Today's operating systems have expanded significantly beyond software designed solely for control of user input and computer output. In addition to the basic control of the computer hardware, operating systems offer networking services, object management facilities, multimedia device support, electronic mail, and even hardware optimization, such as disk compression.

One of the single most important benefits an operating system provides today is the user interface style that it supports and promotes for product development. An operating system is itself a software product and thus has interface styles of its own. These interface styles are the most obvious trademark of an operating system. Apple's Macintosh is the prime example. The Mac computer is almost exclusively advertised and promoted by the (supposed) superiority and ease-of-use of the Mac interface. Newer versions of Microsoft Windows and OS/2's Workplace Shell also embody the graphical user interface (GUI) and represent significant steps toward an object-oriented user interface (OOUI) style.

The operating system interface really defines the user interface paradigm for the computer software. A paradigm is, by definition, "an outstandingly clear or typical example or archetype." New interface technologies sometimes enable major steps forward, or *paradigm shifts* in the evolution of user interfaces.

There are a number of factors I'll discuss for each type of user interface. It is important to understand how each interface supports the interface design principles and guidelines discussed in this book. These factors are:

1. How the interface supports the user's model
2. How the interface supports user's memory capabilities
3. The semantics of the interface style
4. How users interact with the interface style

The Command-Line User Interface (CUI)

> *Rule number one for command-line interface users: "Know What You Are About to Do, for There Is No Undo."*
>
> An experienced DOS user

In the Beginning, There Was DOS

> *Welcome to DOS, the most widely used operating system for personal computers.*
>
> IBM DOS version 5.0 User's Guide and Reference (IBM, 1991)

The personal computer became a commercial reality when IBM developed the personal computer (PC) in 1981. The first operating system for the IBM Personal Computer was PC-DOS version 1.0, where DOS stands for Disk Operating System. It is now over fifteen years later, and some 50 to 100 million users later. Although its momentum is on the downturn, DOS is still among the most popular operating systems for PCs.

Even though DOS is being slowly taken over by newer, more powerful operating systems such as Windows and OS/2, DOS hasn't stood still technologically. This evolution is described in DOS *Getting Started* (IBM, 1991): "New ideas, designs, and technologies in computer science evolve almost every day.

New versions of DOS must support this technology. With each version of DOS, new or enhanced features and commands are introduced."

None of the early DOS versions included any enhancements to the original user interface, only new functions and their associated commands. DOS 4.0 offered the first enhancement to the DOS command-line interface, the DOS Shell. While I use DOS as an example of a command-line interface in this chapter, remember that DOS does offer the DOS Shell as a more usable interface alternative. Although I focus on the newer Windows and OS/2 operating systems, the DOS graphical shell does include some of the other interface styles I will discuss as we move through the evolution of user interface styles.

Command-Line Interfaces

The command-line interface is the original human-computer interaction style. Users type in requests or actions using a predetermined, formal language that has its own unique vocabulary, meanings, and syntax. In DOS, this language is a set of *commands* users type that are basic instructions to the DOS operating system. Similarly, any program can implement a command-line interface for its own product that allows users to type product-specific commands to run the program.

In the traditional DOS command-line interface, the only information on the screen that is provided to prompt and instruct users is the well-known *ready prompt* or *C prompt*. To direct DOS to perform a task, you type a command and then press the Enter key on the computer keyboard. Users can typically enter commands at any time and commands can often be strung together in one request. Figure 8.1 shows the typical DOS command-line interface. As you can see, this interface style doesn't provide much information to users, to say the least!

Command-Line Interfaces and the User's Model

KEY IDEA! *The command-line interface is the least effective interface style to help support the user's mental model of how the computer system and its programs work. How poorly does a command-line interface support the user's model? Look at the screen in Figure 8.1. If you were not an experienced DOS user, would you have any idea of what you could possibly do with your computer system? How are you to know what features you have on your system, such as the available printers? What programs are installed that you can use? And what are the DOS commands you have to know to use the system?*

Figure 8.1   The DOS command-line interface.

One of the key problems with the command-line interface is that it does not shield any of the operating system or program from users. To use the interface, users need to know how a computer works and where their programs and data reside. The model embodied in the command-line interface is the programmer's model, not the user's model.

Look at the DOS commands listed in Table 8.1. There are 84 commands listed here, and that's not even all of the possible DOS commands. In addition, many

TABLE 8.1   Some DOS Commands

APPEND	EXE2BIN	PAUSE
ASSIGN	EXIT	PRINT
ATTRIB	EXPAND	PROMPT
BACKUP	FASTOPEN	QBASIC
BREAK	FC	RD
CALL	FDISK	RECOVER
CD	FIND	REM
CHCP	FOR	REN
CHDIR	FORMAT	RENAME
CHKDSK	GOTO	REPLACE
CLS	GRAFTABL	RESTORE
COMMAND	GRAPHICS	RMDIR
COMP	HELP	SET
COPY	IF	SETVER
CTTY	JOIN	SHARE
DATE	KEYB	SHIFT
DEBUG	LABEL	SORT
DEL	LH	SUBST
DIR	LOADFIX	SYS
DISKCOMP	LOADHIGH	TIME
DISKCOPY	MD	TREE
DOSKEY	MEM	TYPE
DOSSHELL	MIRROR	UNDELETE
ECHO	MKDIR	UNFORMAT
EDIT	MODE	VER
EDLIN	MORE	VERIFY
EMM386	NLSFUNC	VOL
ERASE	PATH	XCOPY

of these commands have multiple options and parameters that can modify the command. These commands are familiar to users only if users are familiar with the way a computer works.

KEY IDEA! *For most people, learning to use a command-line interface is like trying to learn a foreign language. If you're talking to someone who can only speak a foreign language that you don't understand, then you're going to have a very difficult time trying to communicate. However, if the person you're trying to communicate with can speak your language, although they can speak another language more fluently, then you are going to have an easier time communicating. Computer software and hardware have their own language that developers know, but computers shouldn't force users to speak their language when computers have the ability to speak the user's language.*

Today's computer software systems have the power and capability to present information and communicate in ways that are familiar to users, rather than ways that assume users have a complete understanding of how the computer works. Command-line interfaces don't do very well in this respect, but there are advantages to them, as you'll see.

Look at the sequence of commands in Figure 8.2. All I was trying to do here was delete the HELP.TXT file in my TEMP directory. The commands in lower-case letters are the commands I typed. The DIR command tells me what files are in the current directory, assuming that I was already in the directory I was looking for. I had to type the DIR command first because I didn't know what files were in the directory. There is no indication of what's in a directory when you get there.

After a command is entered, the system usually responds with just the ready prompt. This lack of feedback leads users to distrust the system and to confirm the results of their actions on their own. (See the discussion in Chapter 3, where I describe my superstitious behavior.) In the example in Figure 8.2, I typed DIR again to make sure the file had been deleted. If there had been a simple one-line message, "File(s) deleted," this superstitious behavior would be discouraged.

Look at the language spoken by DOS during our conversation. DOS required me to know where my files were stored on the computer and which commands to use to delete files. Also look at the extraneous information that DOS provided. What do I care about *The volume label in drive C?* Screen space is valu-

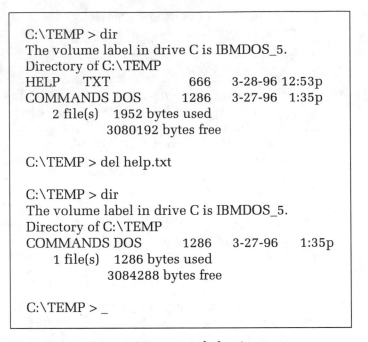

```
C:\TEMP > dir
The volume label in drive C is IBMDOS_5.
Directory of C:\TEMP
HELP     TXT              666     3-28-96 12:53p
COMMANDS DOS            1286     3-27-96  1:35p
       2 file(s)   1952 bytes used
                 3080192 bytes free

C:\TEMP > del help.txt

C:\TEMP > dir
The volume label in drive C is IBMDOS_5.
Directory of C:\TEMP
COMMANDS DOS            1286     3-27-96     1:35p
       1 file(s)   1286 bytes used
                 3084288 bytes free

C:\TEMP > _
```

Figure 8.2   Superstitious user behavior.

able real estate, so don't waste it. The "File deleted" response is much more valuable information to users than stating the volume label of the drive. Whose model is this user interface following? You guessed it: the programmer's model.

On the other hand, the command-line interface is very powerful, flexible, and is totally user-controlled. However, this is an advantage mostly for those experienced users who fit the programmer's model rather than the user's model. For example, the use of wildcards allows users to perform the same task for a group of objects. The one command, DIR THEO?.* /S, will list all of the files that are named THEO_ (with any one character in the fifth position) with any extension name (the * wildcard) in the current directory and all subdirectories of the current directory (the /S option).

I like to watch people use a command-line interface for either an operating system like DOS, or for a particular program. I see how people use the DOS commands quite differently and I always learn some new commands or some new parameter for a command that I didn't know about. One tends to bestow honor and respect on those expert users who can zip through the command-line interface with the skill and mastery of a surgeon.

If users are programmers or expert users of the program or operating system, then the command-line interface can be very powerful. This is because the interface is built on the programmer's model. It takes longer to learn the interface, but can be much faster for end use. What we have is a trade-off between ease of learning and ease of use for certain users and certain tasks.

Command-Line Interfaces and Users' Memory Load

The command-line interface provides little support for the user interface design principles that reduce the user's memory load. As a DOS user, how many of the DOS commands could you recall from memory, without any cues, if you were asked? Never mind recalling them, how many commands do you even recognize in Table 8.1? How many of these commands do you really know and use? Casual and infrequent use of a command-line interface leads users to forget commands they have learned and that have already become familiar.

Command-line interfaces force users to remember commands by making them recall them from memory without any cues from the system. Studies (Furnas, 1985) have shown that users can guess the names of commands chosen by designers only about 10 to 15 percent of the time. This is why most command-line interface users have a user's guide and reference handy while they work. They also have the phone number of someone down the hall who is the well-known command-line interface guru. (There really are a few people who know every one of the DOS commands and how to use them!) Command-line interfaces are much more difficult to learn than other interface styles. Even once commands are learned, time away from the interface and lack of practice make memory retention poor for commands.

Because command-line interfaces don't provide cues for command retrieval, good help systems are critical for operating systems and programs. As software systems have evolved, online help systems have also become more sophisticated and useful. Figure 8.3 shows the help information for the DIR command, which is a very simple command that lists the contents of a directory. User's guides, reference manuals, and online help systems serve as *external memory* for users, because it is difficult for humans to remember things like command names unless the commands are familiar and have some meaning to them. Look at the syntax statement and the parameter list for the DIR command. Can you make sense of the command syntax and the options even if you read it over and over again? And this is one of the simplest DOS commands!

The Semantics of Command-Line Interfaces

As command-line interfaces are designed, effort must be made to ensure that the command language is understood and functionally appropriate for users and their tasks at hand. Designers must determine the functions they will build into the interface and the commands for users to access those functions. Can

```
C:\> DIR /?

Use the DIR command to list the files and subdirectories.

SYNTAX: DIR [drive:][filename]  [/A[adshr]] [/B] [/F]
             [/L] [/N] [/O[nedsg]] [/P] [/S] [/W] [/R]
Where:
 [drive:] [filename] Specifies the directories and files to list.
 /A[adshr]  Displays only specified attributes.
 /B         Displays only filename and extension.
 /F         Displays only fully-qualified files and directories.
 /L         Displays directory information in lower case letters.
 /N         Displays the listing in the new OS/2 format.
 /O[nedsg]  Orders the display by specified fields.
 /P         Pauses after each screen of information.
 /S         Displays all subdirectories.
 /W         Displays the directory listing horizontally.
 /R         Displays .LONGNAME extended attributes.

C:\> _
```

Figure 8.3   Onscreen help for the DIR command.

you understand the relationship between DOS commands and their associated functions? Don't some commands seem ambiguous or too similar to other commands?

A major problem with command-line interfaces is that the meanings of commands are not well understood. Sometimes different commands have very close or even the same meaning. Take the DEL and ERASE commands in DOS, for example. Not only do they *seem* to be very similar, they actually perform the same function. This is not a good thing to do to users. If users see two commands, they expect them to do different things. Here's the help text for both the DEL and ERASE commands (Figure 8.4). They provide the same function, have the same help text, yet have different command names. No wonder users are confused by command-line interfaces!

One final point about the semantics of command-line interfaces. A good interface allows users to be somewhat flexible with their actions, as long as their intentions are correct. A poor interface punishes users for straying from

```
C:\> DEL /?

Use the ERASE or DEL command to delete one or more files.

SYNTAX: ERASE [drive:][path][filename]  [/P]
        DEL   [drive:][path]filename [/P]

Where:
 [drive:][path]filename Specifies the file to delete. The global file name
               characters * and ? can be used in the file name specified.
 /P                 Prompts for confirmation before deleting each file.

C:\> ERASE / ?

Use the ERASE or DEL command to delete one or more files.

SYNTAX: ERASE [drive:][path]filename [/P]
        DEL   [drive:][path]filename [/P]
```

Figure 8.4   The confusing DEL and Erase commands.

the exact form of the command, even if their actions are appropriate. For example, the help text for the DEL command (Figure 8.3) states that the definition of the command is to "delete one or more files." Obviously the command was named DEL as an abbreviation of the word *delete*. Users should be able to remember the appropriate command by remembering the function it performs (delete) and the command name (delete). However, due to some DOS system programmer's inconsiderate and inflexible programming style, if users type DELETE, it is not accepted as a valid command. This inflexibility leads users to call DOS an unfriendly user interface!

How Do Users Interact with Command-Line Interfaces?

First of all, a command-line interface style assumes that users have a keyboard to input commands. There are some modern-day, voice-driven command interfaces, but they basically have the same advantages and disadvantages as keyboard-driven command-line styles. If you're a mouse user, you won't need it when you are using a command-line interface.

User interaction with command-line interfaces most often involves a command syntax style that is *action-object* oriented. Most commands are verbs or actions that users would like to perform. Users first type the action (for example, PRINT) then the object or file (for example, MANDEL.DOC) on which they wish to perform the action. Figure 8.3 shows the syntax for the DIR command. DIR is the action, a particular *drive* or *filename* is the object, and there are multiple options for the command.

This command syntax allows for powerful interaction, yet also produces very high error rates. Commands must be typed exactly as defined, so typing skill is very important and is directly related to error rates. Consistently is critical in defining command-line interaction syntax for commands. For example, the COPY command seems straightforward. The definition for the COPY command is that it "Copies one or more files to another location." The command syntax is COPY the *source* object to the *target* location. Seems simple enough, right? However, things are more complicated than they seem. The target object can be a drive, a directory, a file, or some combination.

Any typing errors can be dangerous. I want to copy the file SOURCE.TXT to the directory, ABCD. If I type it correctly as I do first in Figure 8.5, the correct action takes place and I'm told one file is copied. I double-check the ABCD directory and the file has been successfully copied. However, if I type the directory name incorrectly as ABDC, the target name is now assumed to be a new *file* name, rather than the *directory* name I had wanted (see Figure 8.6). This results in a new file that is created in the same directory instead of copying the file to a different directory. Yet I am given the same feedback that a file has been copied. Only after typing DIR to see what is in the current directory do I see that a new file has been created. These types of errors are very common in command-line interfaces. Sometimes these errors are merely annoying, but they can easily be harmful to users who don't even know they have made an error.

Also notice the inconsistent user feedback from DOS in my examples. Earlier I complained that there was no feedback when I deleted files using the DEL command, so I usually check again to see if files actually were deleted. However, with the COPY command, there is *feedback* that "1 file(s) copied." The provision of similar feedback for the rest of the one hundred DOS commands would be greatly appreciated by the one hundred million DOS users.

The command-line interaction syntax can be improved with prompting to make the conversation more interactive. For example, users could first type the command name. The interface would then prompt for the appropriate location and object(s) for which to apply the action. This interaction style is more work for the programmer, but may be more useful for novice or casual users in certain circumstances.

```
C:\> dir
The volume label in drive C is IBMDOS_5.
The Volume Serial Number is 177B:5811
Directory of C:\

ABCD        <DIR>              3-31-96 8:00p
SOURCE    TXT    1286      3-27-96 1:35p
      2 file(s)     1286 bytes used
                  3078144 bytes free

C:\> copy source.txt abcd
        1 file(s) copied.

C:\> dir abcd
The volume label in drive C is IBMDOS_5.
The Volume Serial Number is 177B:5811
Directory of C:\abcd

.        <DIR>              3-31-63 8:00p
..       <DIR>              3-31-63 8:00p
SOURCE    TXT    1286      3-27-93 1:35p
      3 file(s)     1286 bytes used
                  3079430 bytes free

C:\> _
```

Figure 8.5   The COPY command problem, part 1.

Command-Line Interface Summary

KEY IDEA! *Although DOS still is the most widely used operating system in the world, a command-line interface is best suited to experienced and expert users rather than novice users. The command-line interface was the only available interface for early users to communicate with their computers. These users were typically computer hobbyists and electronics enthusiasts who were both skilled and motivated to use computers. Today's users are motivated to perform their tasks as quickly and as easily as possible, and are not necessarily even happy about using a computer!*

```
C:\> dir
Directory of C:\

ABCD        <DIR>          3-31-96 8:00p
SOURCE   TXT   1286      3-27-96 1:35p
      2 file(s)     1286 bytes used
                    3078144 bytes free

C:\> copy source.txt abdc
      1 file(s) copied.

C:\> dir abcd
Directory of C:\abcd

.        <DIR>                3-31-96 8:00p
..       <DIR>                3-31-96 8:00p
      2 file(s)        0 bytes used
                    3079430 bytes free

C:\> dir
Directory of C:\
ABCD        <DIR>          3-31-96 8:00p
SOURCE   TXT   1286      3-27-96 1:35p
ABDC              1286      3-27-96 1:35p
      3 file(s)     2572 bytes used
                    3079430 bytes free
C:\>_
```

Figure 8.6   The COPY command problem,
part 2.

The interface test results are many and very consistent in their conclusions:
Command-line interfaces are faster and better for experienced users, but worse
for novice and casual users. Don't take my word for it; look at any user interface
guide, textbook, or research report. At any rate, a command-line interface is not
typically your most user-friendly interface. Because of the limited presentation
and interaction technology and techniques, it is difficult to follow the basic
design principles.

Table 8.2 summarizes the advantages and disadvantages of designing and using command-line user interfaces. The conclusion I've reached is as follows: Don't design *only* a command-line interface unless you have *only* experienced users and that is the *only* interface they want. A much better approach is to design other interface styles for your product and then *later* come back and design a command-line interface and its syntax for your experienced users. *But do this only after you've built a more user-friendly interface for novice and casual users.*

Menu Interfaces: Are You Being Served?

Everyone is familiar with menus, but not necessarily as a computer user interface style. We use menus almost daily, especially those of us who eat out a lot! If computer interface designers want to draw on users' everyday experiences in their environment, then computer menus should be very similar to the menus

TABLE 8.2   Advantages and Disadvantages of a Command-Line Interface

Advantages

◆ Quick and powerful form of interaction for experienced users
◆ Flexible interface, easy to combine commands and parameters
◆ User-controlled interaction
◆ Uses minimal screen space
◆ Fast and efficient interface for knowledgeable users
◆ Allows abbreviated command names
◆ Minimal amount of typing required
◆ Can be used in conjunction with other user interfaces

Disadvantages

◆ Little or no prompting and instructions on-screen
◆ Interface enhancements are not visible or known
◆ Usually requires use of hardcopy or online memory aids
◆ Requires user's knowledge of system, programs, and data
◆ Usually provides no feedback or task status
◆ Assumes typing skills
◆ Relies on recall of commands and syntax
◆ Difficult to learn
◆ Command names are not meaningful to users
◆ Command syntax is often difficult to understand
◆ Command syntax must be followed exactly (error-prone)
◆ Commands and syntax are usually not user-customizable

we are already familiar with. This allows users to transfer their real-world knowledge into the software interface arena. A *menu* is simply a list of options that are displayed on the screen or in a window on the screen for users to select their desired choice. Figure 8.7 shows a full-screen menu interface for a popular older word processing application, IBM's Writing Assistant.

Menus are used for two purposes. They allow users to *navigate* within a system by presenting *routings* from one place to another in the system or from one menu to another. They also allow users to *select* items or choices from a list. These choices are usually *properties* or *actions* users wish to perform on selected objects.

KEY IDEA! *Menus are a very important user interface style and are an integral aspect of both graphical and object-oriented user interfaces. The current focus on GUIs and OOUIs has not left menus behind in the dust. Although completely menu-driven programs are not seen much today, menus are critical to any user interface style, and they will continue to evolve.*

Menu interface styles evolved as the personal computer became more of an end-user tool rather than just a programmer's black box or a computer enthusiast's toy. Over the past ten years, menus have perhaps become the most popular interface style, especially for new or casual users. All of the key commercial

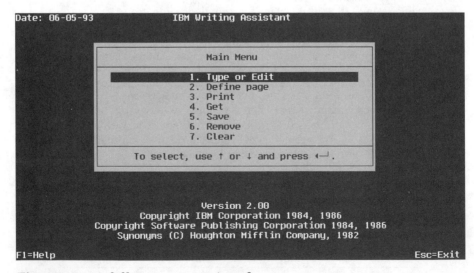

Figure 8.7   A full-screen menu interface.

software packages use menus in some form. Menus are the primary interface style for some of these products, and even the most recent graphical or object-oriented software programs use menus extensively. Remember, all of these interface styles are not mutually exclusive and users should be allowed to use whatever interaction style suits them at any particular time.

Full-Screen Menus

First let's look at the different types of menus. They come in various shapes, sizes, and styles. The earliest type of menu interface was the full-screen, application-driven program interface shown in Figure 8.7. The functions or tasks available to users at any point in time are represented as a list of choices on the screen. The main defining characteristic of most full-screen menu interfaces is that they are hierarchically structured. That is, users must travel through a treelike structure of menus to accomplish their task.

The Writing Assistant program allowed users to navigate to the different sections of the program from this first screen, the Main Menu. There are both good and bad points to a rigidly structured menu interface. I'll discuss them when I talk about menu interaction techniques.

Menu Bars and Palettes

Most of the graphical programs used today have a form of *menu bar,* or action bar, across the top of the screen or window. This menu style provides ready access to menus while users are working within program screens or windows. A menu bar is usually a dynamic list of major sets of actions or choices that route users to other choices presented in individually displayed *drop-down menus.* Figure 8.8 shows a menu bar and drop-down menu in a graphical interface (Microsoft Word 7.0). The menu bar is across the top of the window with the items File, Edit, View, and so on. The Edit drop-down menu is shown.

Menus may also be extended onto additional levels using cascading. Figure 8.9 shows the Windows 95 Start button Programs cascade menu. As you can see, these menus can get quite large!

Menu bars are an integral part of all major graphical user interfaces—Macintosh, Windows, and OS/2—and of all of the programs designed for these operating systems. Consistent design of menu bars provides a stable, familiar presentation and interaction environment for users both within and across programs they use on their computers.

A key feature of menus is that they have the capability of dynamically changing. This provides users with only the valid choices and routings appropriate for their current tasks or for specific objects they have selected. Menu choices can also be grayed out to show that certain actions are not currently available.

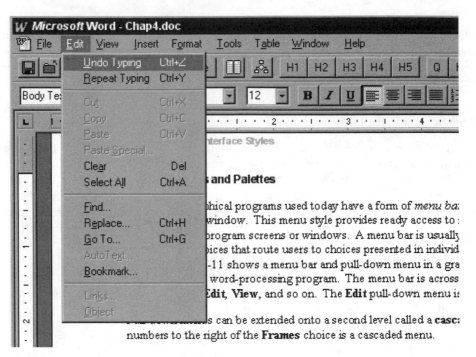

Figure 8.8   GUI menu bar and drop-down menu.

The Cut, Copy, and Paste options on the Edit drop-down in Figure 8.8 are not available, as nothing is selected in the window to be edited. This helps users to easily see what actions, routings, and choices are available to them at any time.

KEY IDEA! *Menu choices are often text items, but they certainly are not limited to text. Menu items may be text, icons, patterns, colors, or symbols. The visual representation of choices should be whatever is appropriate for the interface environment and the tasks users are trying to perform. For example, a graphics program provides menus of the various colors and patterns available. However, it doesn't make sense to use a menu to merely list the names of the colors (red, green, blue, and so on). A graphical menu can show the menu choices as the actual colors as they will appear on the screen. The same applies to the patterns menu. Show users actual items rather than text information describing the choices.*

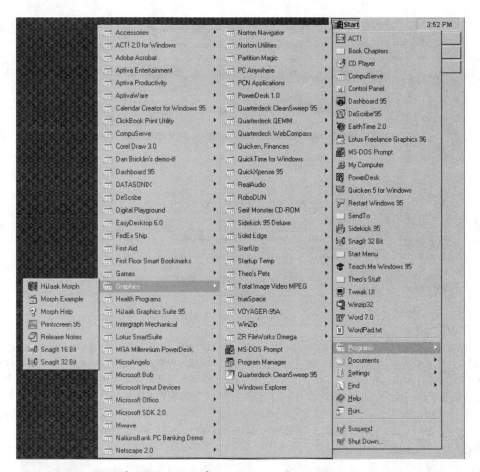

Figure 8.9   Windows 95 start button cascade menus.

There are a few new twists on menus these days. Menus can be detached, moved, and sized to be placed where users want them in relationship to the data they are working with. Users can choose a menu that they use often during a task, such as the Edit drop-down menu they need while creating a graphic illustration, and keep it open anywhere on the screen. This saves the step of selecting the Edit menu bar item each time they wish to select a choice from that drop-down menu.

Other types of menu commonly seen are toolbars or palettes. A toolbar is a graphical menu of program actions, tools, and options users can place around the computer screen. Figure 8.10 shows the Microsoft Word standard toolbar,

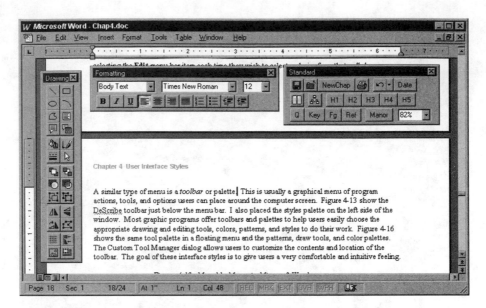

Figure 8.10   Detachable toolbar menus in Microsoft Word.

formatting toolbar, and drawing toolbar detached from the window frame (Figure 8.8 shows the toolbars on the window frame), sized, and placed around the data within the window. Most graphic programs offer toolbars and palettes to help users easily choose the appropriate drawing and editing tools, colors, patterns, and styles to do their work.

Pop-Up Menus

The most recent menu style to have evolved in today's user interface environment is the *pop-up menu.* It is also called a *context menu,* because the contents of the menu depends on the context of the users' tasks at hand. Pop-up menus are appropriate in any type of application, whether it is a full-screen or graphical interface. They are called pop-up menus because they appear to pop up on the screen next to an item when users press the appropriate key or mouse button. Figure 8.11 shows a pop-up menu for a drive object in Windows 95.

Pop-up menus contain only those choices that are appropriate to the current or selected item. These are incredibly powerful interfaces for users, as pop-ups can be designed for any element of the interface. Every icon, menu choice, window element, or interface control (a scroll bar, for example) that is selectable by users can have a pop-up menu. Pop-up menus usually contain a small set of frequently used actions that are also available from the system or program menu bar, if one is implemented.

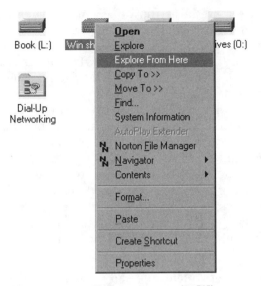

Figure 8.11   Pop-up menu in Windows 95.

That's a brief description of the basic types of menus in today's user interfaces. I'm sure you'll agree that they seem more helpful than the command-line interface. Let's now look at how the menu interface styles support the user's model and memory capabilities, the semantics of menus, and menu interface interaction techniques.

Menu Interfaces and the User's Model

Menus are a very powerful means of translating the developer's view of the system into something that users can see, understand, and use. Menus provide a visual representation of the structure of the underlying system or application and the selections users can make at any time.

The key success factor in the design of menus is how skillfully the underlying computer concepts and functions are translated into a coherent set of user options. Again, it is the designer's job to work with the programmer's model and build a user interface that is appropriate for user tasks and is consistent with the user's model.

Menus should provide users with the *routings* and *choices* that fit their model. With a command-line interface, users have no idea where to go in an operating system (routings) to find programs and files (choices) to perform their work. Menu utilities provide menus listing the places to go (routings) and menus showing the contents (choices) of directories and folders.

Well-designed menu interfaces allow users to easily learn the interface. Even if users don't fully understand the underlying system, menus can make the task of learning the system routings and choices more visible and explicit. Therefore, menus can be very useful for interfaces where users don't need (or are not allowed) to control the system, and where they don't need to understand the system to do their tasks.

As part of the learning process, many systems and products offer users a choice of menu styles they wish to work with. Many popular programs such as spreadsheets and word processors provide both simple and complex menus, calling them *novice* and *standard* menus. Simple menus present only a minimal set of actions that novices or new learners would use. Complex menus provide the complete set of program actions and choices. Users just learning the product or doing very simple tasks would choose the simple menus so they wouldn't have to even see the complexity of the rest of the program functions. Experienced users would probably choose the complex menus.

Menu Interfaces and Users' Memory Load

Menus are easy to learn and easy to remember. Users don't have to memorize complex command names and syntax as they do for a command-line interface. Menus rely on users' recognition rather than recall of information from memory. Users don't have to worry about hidden or new functions. If their system is upgraded and new features or options are available, they should see changes or additions to the menus on the screen.

Menus do, however, take up valuable space on the screen. Full-screen menu interfaces like the one shown in Figure 8.7 use the entire screen to present each menu with its choices. Other menu types use screen space more carefully, mainly because they are usually part of graphical interfaces, where screen real estate is of prime importance.

To help users' short-term memory, menus should not require users to remember information from a previous menu or screen in order to make a selection on the current menu. If that information is needed, the system should present the information wherever it is needed, not just on the original screen. (See Chapter 4.)

The number of items that are placed in a menu should also be influenced by human short-term memory limitations. The capacity of short-term memory is known to be around seven plus-or-minus two items. Users won't be able to remember what is in a menu as they navigate throughout the menu hierarchy if each menu has too many items. In order to maximize screen space and provide all the information to users, many menu interfaces violate this design principle. Long menu lists can usually be grouped into smaller logical groups to chunk items for users to remember more easily. One of the problems with today's dynamic menus is that they often expand beyond the point where they can be reasonably used. Figure 8.9 shows one of the prime examples of this situation. If users install Windows 95 on top of an existing Windows 3.X system, the Start . . . Programs menu contains every group that users had in their Windows 3.X Program Manager. My Programs menu shown here contains 63 items in the cascade menu and requires two columns to display them all. This many items in a menu makes it hard for users to scan and find the item they are looking for.

Menus can also help aid long-term memory retrieval. Menu interfaces should be designed to present items in logical groupings rather than simply in alphabetical or random order. The screen layout and organization of menus allow users to assign meanings to the groupings and make both the menus and the individual choices more memorable. Taking this even further, today's menu interfaces often allow users to customize menu organization and layout to more closely fit the way they use the system and how they remember menus and menu choices. Many word processors allow users to customize the menu bars and drop-downs for the program. Users can customize the menu bar in Microsoft Word by using the Tools . . . Customize option and changing the toolbar icons. Customizing their menus enables users to feel more comfortable using a program the way they like to work. This all goes back to a key interface design principle: *Place users in control!*

The Semantics of Menu Interfaces

Menu terminology can cause user confusion, regardless of how well structured and laid out the menus may be. At times, there are commands that seem very similar and yet have very different meanings. How about menu choices such as Exit, Quit, Escape, Close, Return, Forward, Back, Enter, Accept, Up, and Down? I've seen some of these choices in menus simultaneously and they can be very confusing to users. They all have something to do with navigating within a menu interface! Different developers may define these terms and their actions very differently, so there is often no consistency among menus even within the same program, and definitely a lack of consistency across programs. In the end, unknowing and unassuming users interpret these terms based on their own experiences and make their selections accordingly. Will their expectations of a menu choice match the developer's implementation of that action? Let's hope so!

Summary of Menu Interfaces

Well-structured menu interfaces, such as full-screen menus, are great for novice and casual users. Menu components, such as menu bars, drop-down menus, cascaded menus, toolbars, palettes, and pop-up menus are all interface elements that should be used in combination with other elements in today's graphical and object-oriented programs.

TABLE 8.3   Advantages and Disadvantages of a Menu Interface

Advantages

- ◆ Users don't have to memorize complex commands
- ◆ Reduces keyboard entry errors
- ◆ Structured navigation benefits novices and casual users
- ◆ Can shorten user learning time and effort
- ◆ Easy to track correct responses and errors
- ◆ Minimal amount of typing required
- ◆ Can be used in conjunction with other user interfaces
- ◆ Menu items and layout may be user-customizable
- ◆ Flexible selection techniques (mnemonics, mouse)
- ◆ Supports recognition memory vs. recall

Disadvantages

- ◆ May not be appropriate or efficient for some users and tasks
- ◆ Fast-path navigation and selection techniques are also needed
- ◆ Doesn't necessarily or automatically make an interface easier to use
- ◆ Uses lots of screen space
- ◆ Can force user through many levels of menus
- ◆ Requires quick screen display and refresh rates
- ◆ Relies on users understanding menu groupings and hierarchy
- ◆ Requires some knowledge of underlying system
- ◆ Users may get lost in menu hierarchies
- ◆ Menu terms and names may not be meaningful to users
- ◆ Menu structure follows the action-object syntax
- ◆ Menu syntax must be followed exactly
- ◆ Use of modes forces users to follow the system's path

Table 8.3 presents a summary of the general advantages and disadvantages of using menus. Remember that menus are mainly used in conjunction with the other interface styles. The advantages and disadvantages of any interface style must be weighed against the characteristics of the other interface styles when they are used together.

References

Furnas, George. 1985. Experience with an adaptive indexing scheme. *Proceedings of the ACM CHI'85* (April), pp. 131–136.

IBM Corporation. 1991. *Disk Operating System: Getting Started, Version 5.00.* IBM, 84F9683.

CHAPTER NINE

User Interface Evolution: Graphical User Interfaces

When everything in a computer system is visible on the screen, the display becomes reality. Objects and actions can be understood purely in terms of their effects upon the display. This vastly simplifies understanding and reduces learning time.

Xerox Star designer

On the Road to GUIs: Picking Apples in the PARC

The Apple Macintosh is commonly thought of as the product that brought the graphical user interface (GUI) to life as a commercially successful personal computer desktop. While this may be true, the history of GUIs goes back much further than that. There is a rich and complicated path that leads to the interfaces users see on their PCs today.

It is widely believed that the grandfather of the GUI was the Sketchpad program developed in 1962 by Ivan Sutherland at the Massachusetts Institute of Technology. The program allowed users to draw lines, circles, and points on a computer's cathode ray tube (CRT) display using a light pen. While these tasks are simple with today's computer software and interfaces, thirty years ago this was a revolutionary effort that required immense computing power. Sutherland's program was the first windowing software that assigned characteristics to graphic objects and built relationships between objects. Users could move, copy, scale, zoom, and rotate objects, and save object characteristics. Although this research never was commercially developed, most software engineers credit Sutherland's Sketchpad research and designs as the first step in the evolution of graphical user interface.

The mouse, now the main instrument of input preferred by GUI users, was developed in the late 1960s. Douglas Engelbart began his work in 1964 on a hand-held pointing device at SRI International in Menlo Park, California and carried on with his experimental designs at the famous Xerox Palo Alto Research Center, known as Xerox PARC. The culmination of this work was the first patent for the wheel mouse in 1970.

Continued research and design on the mouse led to the patent for the ball mouse in 1974 by Xerox. The idea came suddenly to Ron Rider: "I suggested that they turn a trackball upside down, make it small, and use it as a mouse instead. Easiest patent I ever got. It took me five minutes to think of, half an hour to describe to the attorney, and I was done" (Pake, 1985). Apple Computer, Incorporated redesigned the mouse in 1979, using a rubber ball rather than a metal one. Variations on the ball mouse are what GUI users mostly mouse with today.

The first computer system designed around the GUI was a Xerox in-house computer system called the Alto in the early 1970s. It had overlapping windows and pop-up menus, and used the mouse. Around 1976, icons were added to the onscreen desktop. The research and design of the Alto system led to the first commercial GUI product, the Xerox Star, in 1981. The Star offered both tiled and overlapping windows and a menu bar for each window, and, of course, the mouse. Xerox designers had a motto: "The best way to predict the future is to invent it." And they did!

KEY IDEA! *The Xerox Star was the first computer to follow the idea of the desktop metaphor. The desktop is still the guiding metaphor for interfaces of the 1990s. The use of metaphors in computer interfaces is an attempt to match the computer system to users' models.*

An early article (Smith et al., 1982) about the Xerox Star said, "Every user's initial view of Star is the Desktop, which resembles the top of an office desk, together with surrounding furniture and equipment. It represents a working environment, where current projects and accessible resources reside. On the screen are displayed pictures of familiar office objects, such as documents, folders, file drawers, in-baskets, and out-baskets. These objects are displayed as small pictures, or icons." This is the beginning of the "messy desk" metaphor that now applies to computer screens across the world.

The engineers at Xerox PARC were great at research and technology, though unsuccessful at commercial product development. The Xerox Star was never a success, even though over 30 years of work went into the product. The development of the first successful GUI computer systems was left up to Apple. The transition of research and technology to product development from Xerox to Apple was both a friendly and a profitable one, as Xerox held 800,000 shares of Apple stock when it went public in December 1980.

Steven Jobs, a founder of Apple, visited Xerox PARC, got his team of designers at Apple excited about GUIs, and the rest is history. The Apple Lisa, the precursor to the Macintosh, came out in 1983 but was a false start. Like the Xerox Star, it did not succeed in the marketplace. It took the introduction of the Apple Macintosh computer in 1984, with a revolutionary advertising approach, to bring GUIs to the computer market successfully. Both the Lisa and the Macintosh had a menu bar for the entire screen and the first pull-down menus in a graphical interface. An Apple designer received a patent for pull-down menus in 1984.

Apple's success with the graphical user interface is legendary and still remains the most familiar example of GUIs. As I try to explain what GUIs are to the uninitiated, I often have to say, "You know, it's like the Apple Mac." After Apple's immense success with GUI development on the Macintosh, an operating system revolution was upon us, and both IBM and Microsoft went to work on PC-based GUIs of their own, along with a number of other software developers.

Microsoft, IBM, and others have had a lot of catching up to do and have had to do it on a hardware platform very different from the Apple Macintosh. One key advantage that Apple has is that they built the whole computer themselves as an integrated system. Their product design philosophy followed the Xerox PARC design methodology. Mike Jones (1992) describes how the Xerox Star was built. "Star began by defining a conceptual model of how users would relate to the system. The interface was completed before the computer hardware had been built on which to run it, and two years before a single line of product software code had been written." What a concept! What a way to design a product! Why aren't more products built this way today?

The PC software development world doesn't have the luxury of the hardware and software environment at Xerox PARC and Apple. Personal computer hardware is independently developed by hardware manufacturers. Then software operating system and program developers build their systems to run on the various flavors and configurations of PC hardware systems. This is why users often wonder if PC hardware and software developers ever talk to each other. Users don't get the same feeling of seamless integration of hardware and software from PCs as they do from Apple Macintosh systems.

Basics of Graphical User Interfaces

And then we need to connect them [users] to their work so easily that using a computer is as natural as picking up a pen or a pencil.

                                                                Bill Gates (1990)

The basic characteristic of a graphical user interface is the integration of a number of elements that bring the tasks and work we do on the computer to life. In simple terms, a GUI is the *graphical representation of, and interaction with, programs, data, and objects on the computer screen.* But it goes way beyond that. GUIs try to provide users with the tools and applications to do a task rather than a list of functions that the computer can perform. *PC Magazine* product reviewers asked Microsoft Corporation for their definition of a GUI. I've combined their list with other GUI features I've collected to come up with the characteristics of a GUI software product or interface (Table 9.1).

Many GUIs today, including Windows, don't fully support all of these GUI criteria as well as they could, as critics are quick to point out. There is a wide range of "GUI-ness" on which an interface may implement many of the items on this list. In the end, users must choose the appropriate graphical interface for the operating system and programs they use, based on how products rate on users' own prioritized list of GUI criteria.

A more humorous description of the WIMP interface is the DOS user's cry, "*W*here *is m*y (Command) *p*rompt?" or "*W*here *is m*y *p*assword?" Another acronym associated with GUIs is WYSIWYG (*w*hat *y*ou *s*ee *is w*hat *y*ou *g*et). In the (not so) old days, you would work with a word processing program or a

TABLE 9.1   Features that Define a Graphical User Interface

1. It has a bitmapped, high-resolution computer display.
2. It has a pointing device, typically a mouse.
3. It promotes interface consistency between programs.
4. Users can see graphics and text on their screen as it looks in print.
5. It follows object-action interaction paradigm.
6. It allows transfer of information between programs.
7. There can be direct manipulation of onscreen information and objects.
8. It provides standard interface elements such as menus and dialogs.
9. There is visual display of information and objects (icons and windows).
10. It provides visual feedback for user actions and tasks.
11. There is visual display of user/system actions and modes (menus, palettes).
12. There is use of graphical controls ("widgets") for user selection and input.
13. It allows users to customize/personalize interface and interactions.
14. It allows flexibility between keyboard or other input devices.

KEY IDEA! *What really makes up a graphical user interface? A good definition that characterizes a GUI is the phrase "GUIs are WIMPs." WIMPs means that GUIs are made of these elements: windows, icons, menus, and pointers. If users are looking at a computer that has these elements on the screen and has a mouse attached, chances are they're looking at a GUI.*

---

graphics program and you'd have to print out your work to see what it really looked like in final form. Then you'd go back to the program to modify your document a little more and then print it again to see what it looked like. The computer screen just wasn't capable of presenting your information on the screen the way it would finally look on paper. Computer displays couldn't handle the text typeface fonts and point sizes. It also couldn't handle the colors, patterns, and complex graphics for a drawing program.

Today's computer display technology allows software programs to show users exactly (or almost exactly) how their objects and information will look in final form if they were to print the document. By itself, WYSIWYG display and software technology doesn't require a graphical software product interface. However, a key aspect of GUIs is that users can see what their objects really look like, right on the screen. Therefore, WYSIWYG displays are an integral part of the whole GUI package.

KEY IDEA! *WYSIWYG has become such a common phrase that even the media plays on this theme. An advertisement for Quest, a Windows multimedia authoring tool, states: "WYSIWYG. You hear many claims from authoring systems saying what you see is indeed what you get. Fact is, only one authoring system, Quest 5.0 for Windows, allows you to create frames in a true visual environment." Quest says its competitors are WYSINWYGBAIRVTWYGE (what you see is not what you get but an icon relating vaguely to what you get eventually).*

An important feature of GUIs is the ability for users to directly manipulate objects and information on the screen. An interface that just presents information graphically to users is not necessarily a GUI. I've seen many software advertisements proclaiming, "GUI Tool Depicts Real Time Data!" One product stated that "when linked to particular applications, the graphical user interface can be used to display the status of data as it changes in real-time mode." I would say that this product provides users with a *graphical representation* of their data, but does not necessarily provide a graphical user interface unless it contains other GUI features. An icon may be used to represent an object, but users must be able to do something with that object other than just look at it. Although there is a wide range of implementation of direct manipulation in interfaces today, this remains a key aspect of GUIs.

Core User Skills Needed for GUIs

I think, therefore Icon.

Jerry Zeidenberg (1990)

Something happens when DOS command-line or menu-interface users sit down and use a graphical user interface for the first time. User interface experts and journalists call it the infamous user interface *paradigm shift.* However, to many character-based interface users, seeing a GUI and using a mouse for the first time is like going up over a hill in a car and all of a sudden running into a brick wall that they never knew was there. The simple truth is that there is a learning curve associated with moving into a GUI software environment. Let's look at what's involved in learning how to use a GUI. There is a basic set of skills and knowledge needed for users to conceptually deal with graphical user interfaces.

K**EY IDEA!** *In preparation for conducting comparison usability tests during the development of Windows 95, a large number of common user tasks were identified from field usability research and market research (see Table 9.2). The goal with Windows 95 was to make these common tasks easy for the novice, intermediate, and advanced user. Some tasks, such as "launch a program," "close program," "open a file," and "save a file" are critical tasks that users of all levels do often, practically from day one. Other tasks, while common among intermediate and advanced users, are often unfamiliar to novice users.*

The following sections discuss a number of key concepts and skills users must have (or learn) to use today's operating system and product user interfaces.

TABLE 9.2   The Microsoft Common User Tasks

- Launch a program.
- Get help on file management topic.
- Open a file (from default directory using common dialog).
- Save a file (from some other directory than default using common dialog).
- Copy file to floppy.
- Change desktop color (or some other system setting).
- Find a file (user knows location).
- Find a file (user does not know location).
- Start second application without closing first and then switch back to first.
- Delete file/folder.
- Rename file/folder.
- Select different printer (using common dialog).
- Create folder.
- View printer queue.
- Place document on server (network drive is already mapped).
- Close a program.
- Undelete/Recover a file.
- Check system resources (memory or hard disk).

Users Must Know the Underlying System Organization

First, users must still have some knowledge of their computer system hardware and software configuration. The Windows 95 operating system and newer user interface do make it somewhat easier for users to work with their hardware and software. However, since there are still elements of DOS under the covers, it is very difficult to hide the underlying system, directory, and file organization from users. The IBM Windows Guide (IBM, 1989) states:

> From the Windows environment you can easily access all Windows and non-Windows applications, files, directories, and disks, and control all DOS-related tasks such as directory or file management and formatting disks. . . . You also should be familiar with basic Disk Operating System (DOS) concepts, such as the role of files and directories.

Figure 9.1 shows the Windows 95 graphical My Computer view of the folders found on the C: drive and the MS-DOS prompt window showing the same items as DOS directories on the C: drive. Users must still understand how drives and directories work, even if they stay within the GUI interface. If files or directories are shuffled around on the hard disk, GUI icons (see shortcuts in Figure 9.2) may loose their link to the program they represent, and users are without a clue as to why the program won't run. To use these icons effectively, users must understand the concepts of hierarchical directories in computer storage and the differences between different types of files, such as programs and data files.

Users Must Understand Icons and Applications

Users must know what graphical objects on their screen represent and must know how to interact with them. Icons graphically represent different types of objects in the user interface. They may be folders, disk drives, printers, programs, or data. What happens if users copy, move, or delete these icons? If the icon is the data file, program, tool, or folder itself, users are performing the action on the object itself. However, if the icon is a *shortcut* to the original object, then the action is performed only on the shortcut, not on the original

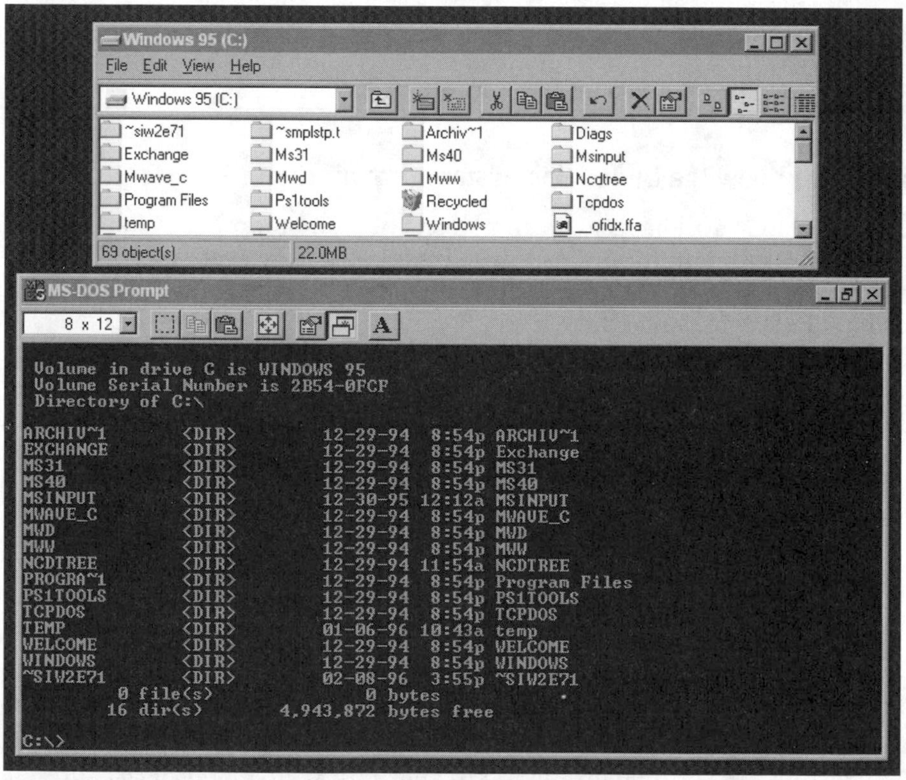

Figure 9.1   Windows 95 folders and the underlying DOS directory structure.

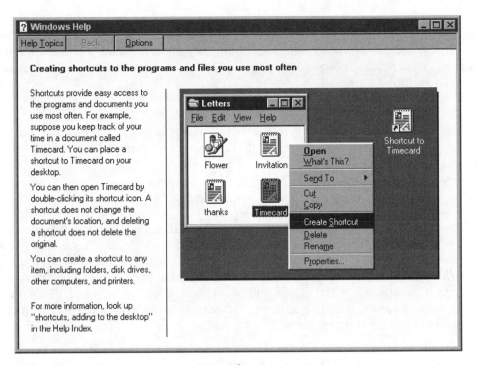

Figure 9.2   Help topic on creating shortcut icons.

object. This can get very confusing, even for experienced users. Figure 9.2 shows the Help topic on creating shortcut icons.

Different results will occur for actions on different types of icons. If users double-click on a program icon, that program is run. If users double-click on a data file, the file is opened by the program associated with that particular file or file type. If users double-click on a folder icon, that folder is opened to show its contents. If users double-click on a tool icon, such as a printer or the keyboard object, the default action for that object is performed. For a printer, it opens up the contents view of the printer. For the Keyboard icon, the Properties dialog is opened.

Users Must Understand the Basic Elements of a Window

Users must understand the basic elements of a window to be able to manipulate windows themselves and the information contained in the window. A window is made up of a window border or frame, a title bar, a control menu and menu bar, window-sizing buttons, and scroll bars. More advanced window elements include the status bar, message bar, and control bars such as ribbons, rulers, toolboxes, and palettes. All of these window elements are defined in the Microsoft and IBM design guides. Users must learn about these elements through experience or by reading product online tutorials and help information or the product documentation.

Basically, users can perform the following actions on a window either from the keyboard or with the mouse: move, size, minimize, maximize, and restore. Since the main purpose of a window is to present information to users, many windows display scroll bars and toolbars for users to manipulate their view of the data within the window.

Users Must Understand How to Use GUI Controls

There are many graphical interface controls that users must understand in order to navigate among windows, make selections, and enter data. Table 9.3 lists many of these GUI controls. These controls should be designed to be intuitive for users as to what they represent and how users can interact with them using either the keyboard or the mouse. The window elements I discussed, such as menu bars, scroll bars, and window-sizing buttons, are also graphical controls that users must understand.

Users Must Understand How to Use a Mouse

Children have no trouble learning how to use a mouse on a computer. Most kids have finely tuned motor skills and hand-eye coordination developed from years of arcade and video games, such as Nintendo. Adults on the other hand, usually require some instruction and take some time learning how to use the mouse. For many adults, using a mouse is a very strange concept. I've even

TABLE 9.3   Interface Controls Used in GUIs and OOUIs

Entry field	Value set
Menu bar	Tear-off menu
Toolbar	Check box
List box	Container
Pull-down menu	Scroll bar
Spin button	Notebook (Tabbed dialogs)
Cascaded menu	Slider
Push button	Drop-down list
Pop-up menu	Combination entry field/list box
Radio button	Drop-down combination box
Tool palette	

heard stories of customers telephoning technical support centers and asking, "What do I do with this foot pedal?"

Users must understand that the mouse moves the pointer on the screen and whatever buttons they press on the mouse will perform some action depending on the location of the pointer on the screen. The mouse is used to manipulate icons, windows, and data on the screen by pointing, clicking, dragging, and even double- or triple-clicking with the mouse buttons. I'll cover mouse inter-action techniques in detail later, in the section How Users Interact with GUIs.

The User Interface Architecture Behind GUIs

A Key to GUI Interaction: The Object-Action Style

KEY IDEA! *The* object-action *style of user interaction is a new concept embodied in GUIs. Users first select an* object *and then select an* action *to perform on that object. This applies to all objects in the interface, including icons, windows, and items within windows. When designers consistently support an object-action approach to user interaction, the user's mental model of the interface is constantly reinforced. The alternative is the action-object approach, which has been used by most command-line interfaces and many menu-driven interfaces.*

The action-object interface style is (unfortunately) still found in many GUI programs. For example, bank tellers may browse a customer profile to view information, but if they need to change a customer's telephone number or address in the profile, they must exit Browse mode and select Edit customer profile. Then they can change customer information. From the database per-spective, this is an easier way of determining when to lock and unlock records in a database. If users are only viewing information, they only need to see what is in the database record, and the record can be accessed or changed by other users. If users want to edit a database record, it must be locked so they can change the data without multiple users trying to edit the same database record at the same time.

Users—bank tellers in this case—should not have to decide up front what actions they might want to perform on the information. If a customer says, "Can you please tell me what telephone number you have for me?" the bank teller should not have to decide whether to browse or edit the customer profile. Users should be able to open an object first, and then choose what actions they wish to perform. In this case, tellers should open the customer profile, and then either view and confirm a customer's telephone number or change it if necessary.

In the GUI arena, objects are the main focus of the users' attention. Most objects that users work with can also be composed of subobjects. For example, a spreadsheet is an object that users can edit, copy, and print. A spreadsheet is also composed of individual cells that can also be edited, copied, and printed. The object-action approach allows users to use consistent and familiar techniques for all levels of objects. Once the objects and subobjects have been determined for a product, actions can modify or manipulate the properties and properties for objects. Each type of object has appropriate actions that can be applied to each object of that type. For example, most window objects can be manipulated by the sizing and moving actions, while a spreadsheet object can be saved, copied, and printed.

How do users follow an object-action sequence? For example, to size a particular window on the screen, users select an object (the window) simply by clicking the mouse anywhere on the window or inside the window. Once the window is selected, the frame is sized directly by dragging the frame with the mouse, or by selecting one of the window-sizing actions from the control menu.

The object-action process sequence has numerous advantages. An object, or objects, in a window can be selected, and then the menu bar actions and routings can be browsed to see which choices apply to the selected objects. Users can perform a series of actions on the same object without having to repeatedly select the object. This object-action sequence can be performed with the mouse via both direct manipulation and the use of menus. The object-action sequence can also be followed from the keyboard by using menus.

A Drawback to GUIs: Application Orientation

One of the drawbacks, or limitations, of the graphical user interface environment and the products developed on the Windows platform is their application orientation. Software development today is somewhere in between the GUI application-oriented world and the OOUI object-oriented world (see Chapter 10).

One of the advantages of GUIs is that users see their information on the screen. Users may also get the idea that they are really working with objects. However, in most GUI environments, users focus primarily on applications. They select an application they want to run and then specify the data file they wish to use. Users also organize applications and data on their computer in the form of graphical tree structures using drives and directories (Windows Explorer). Icons are simply graphical representations of applications, data, and minimized windows. Users must still understand how applications work and must know where files and data that are needed by the application are stored in their computer system.

Let's look closer at the application-oriented approach. First, users must start an application before doing most of their work with files. No other task-specific actions can be performed on the contents of a file unless an application is started and the file is brought into the application.

KEY IDEA! *How can you tell if the products you are working with are application oriented? First, double-click the left mouse button on an icon and see if it opens into a window. If the main part of the window (the "client area" in programming terms) is blank and you have to select File and Open . . . from the menu bar and drop-down menu, then you have an application-oriented product. To avoid this empty-window phenomenon, Windows and other GUIs allow users to associate different types of data files with specific applications. Then users may double-click on a data file icon and the system will automatically invoke the application and bring the data file directly into the application window when it is opened. Users may bypass the File and Open . . . menu bar technique if they have direct access to the data file icons in the File Manager window.*

Another way to tell if users are working with an application is to look at the title bar of an opened window. The title bar provides information about where the window came from and what is contained in it. The title bar of an application window shows a small icon for the application, the name of the application, and the name of the object or file. When users change files, the name in the title bar changes.

If users have to explicitly save the changes to their data, they've got an application-oriented product. If users have to close the product window once they've finished with data files, they've got an application-oriented product. If users have to work the way the product requires them to, rather than the way they would rather do it, the application is in control, not the user! Finally, if users have to be trained on a specific product to learn how to work with their data using that product, they've got an application-oriented product.

Most of what users see in the Windows environment are mainly application-oriented interfaces. However, some object-oriented techniques are being implemented by the applications themselves that are developed on the Windows platform. For example, most word processors now enable users to select a piece of text and then drag it to another location in a document using the mouse. This embodies both the object-action process and an object-oriented approach to working with text objects within a document file. These products also allow users to work with different types of data other than text, such as tables, spread-sheets, graphics, and images, within a document.

The Application-Oriented Menu Bar

Users work with applications in windows that have a menu bar. The menu bar contains routing choices that display drop-down menus when selected. The drop-down menus contain action and routing choices that relate to objects in the window or the application that is represented by the window itself. The main groupings on application menu bars are File, Edit, View, and Help. The CUA guidelines (IBM, 1992) and Microsoft (1995) guidelines offer standard menus to ensure that users are given a common and consistent menu structure across applications.

The File drop-down menu is used for applications that use data files. The menu choices provide the commands users need to manipulate objects as a whole. The standard actions allow users to open, create, print, and save files. The Exit action is also in this menu, and is always placed at the bottom posi-tion of the drop-down.

The Edit menu provides actions to manipulate or reorganize information in the window. Standard choices include Undo, Cut, Copy, Paste, Clear, and Delete. These actions apply to many types of information and objects. Any applications that support the manipulation of data, text, or graphics should use these standard Edit actions.

The View menu allows users to select different ways to look at information or objects in the window. These actions only change views: they do not change the actual data. Items in a View drop-down might offer draft, WYSIWYG, or outline views of text. Tool and color bars and palettes might also be displayed or hid-den with selections in the View menu. Sorting actions such as include, sort, and refresh would also appear in the View menu.

The final menu grouping on the menu bar is the Help choice. This drop-down allows users access to various forms of help information. Typical choices include a help index, general help, help for help, a tutorial (if provided), and product information (About "Product Name").

KEY IDEA! *These menu groupings are defined by interface guides because they are common actions and routings that apply across many applications. Standard menu conventions allow users to trans-fer their knowledge of menus from one application to others, even if the applications and data are very different. This supports the inter-face design principles described in Chapter 5.*

Applications may also implement graphical icon bars, commonly called toolbars, to provide quick and convenient access to application actions and options. Microsoft categorizes these controls as control bars in their design guide. Most of the popular GUI word-processing applications and graphics packages use toolbars extensively. The toolbar is usually located directly under the window menu bar, although it can be located anywhere in the window or in a separate window.

GUIs and the User's Model

> GUIs have made machines more people-literate rather than forcing end-users to become more computer-literate. What does this mean to you? More user-friendly!
>
> Jeff Tash and Richard Finkelstein (1993)

Graphical user interfaces have the capability of bringing user's mental models to life on the computer screen if products are well thought out and well designed. As I discussed earlier, GUIs can also educate and entertain as well as help users do their work. Look at Broderbund's Playroom interface in Figure 9.3. The Playroom is a graphical environment for a variety of objects and applications. The Playroom defines the metaphor that all of the applications will follow and allows users to build a consistent mental model that should be followed by all applications. Does Windows or your GUI do as good a job of building a real-world metaphor for you? Does Windows or your GUI allow you to build a consistent and usable mental model that works for all of the applications you use?

Do GUIs Hide the System from Users?

KEY IDEA! *Since operating systems handle the tasks of managing a computer and the programs and data stored on it, there is little of the system that can be hidden from users. Also, it is difficult to stray too far from a computer metaphor, because of the nature of the tasks done at the operating system level. Individual programs have the freedom to develop more appropriate models and metaphors for their particular users and tasks.*

The Playroom, for example, is a graphical program that doesn't have to worry about any computer system concepts. Its developers built the entire program

Figure 9.3   The Playroom graphical environment.

around a familiar and friendly real-world metaphor and have hidden all of the complexities of the computer from their users. This applies in some respects to more industrial-strength business applications that can build their own metaphors, but also must rely on the user's knowledge of computer concepts of programs and files.

Windows system management applications, like Explorer and My Computer, provide a graphical interface to somehow handle the complex computer tasks that may not be intuitive or familiar to users. As such, they are often the cause of user frustration and a target for software competition. Peter Lewis (1993) says, "Windows makes software easier to use, at least in contrast to the clunky DOS programs that tens of millions of PC owners still use. But Windows is no beauty. Its methods of handling and maintaining files are relatively awkward." There are software products and online e-mail services that provide Windows "Tip-of-the-Day" information. There is even a magazine called *Windows Tips & Tricks.* The popularity of Windows and the GUI environment has provided fertile ground for a growing number of products that are specifically designed to improve the functionality and user interface for elements of Windows itself. Michael Elgan (1993) began his monthly column with, "You may have already found out the hard way how to make Windows play dead. But you can also train Windows to do useful tricks." Not surprisingly, vendors have been happy to build a variety of interface replacements and enhancements that do a variety of things better, faster, or easier.

GUIs and Real-World Metaphors

Let's take a look at how GUI products can build interfaces that match user's mental models for the tasks they want to perform. One of the hot software product areas these days is the personal information manager (PIM). PIMs typically provide integrated services such as an onscreen calendar, to-do list, planner, phone and address book, appointments, and other organizer functions. One popular PIM is Lotus Organizer. Lotus needed to get a PIM to market quickly, so they bought a good product from another company, improved it, and began to market it extensively. Organizer is now one of the most popular Windows PIMs on the market today. The model used by almost all of the PIMs is the one we are all familiar with—the hardcopy organizer and appointment book. By closely following the real-world metaphor, these products can offer users easy-to-learn and easy-to-use interfaces that can make using an onscreen organizer worth the effort. Figure 9.4 shows one view of the Lotus Organizer product. Notice the extensive use of the icon toolbars, both horizontally under the menu bar and along the left side. Can you figure out what each of these icon buttons represents?

One of the secrets of a PIM's success is its use of the power of the computer to keep track of information in multiple places for multiple purposes. For example, my wife Edie's birthday is July 16. I need to type this information only once, in the anniversary section of the organizer. The product automatically places that information in the calendar section on the page for July 16 for every year in the calendar. This feature shows how to utilize the strengths of the computer to help in areas where we have weaknesses, such as remembering birthdays and anniversaries. I'll admit I forgot my mother's birthday while I was deep in the throes of writing my first book. Had I been using a PIM, I might not have forgotten to send her a card and a present. Remember the chart of human and computer strengths and weaknesses described at the end of Chapter 4 (Table 4.1)? This is one example where the chart was used to enhance a software interface.

Even though Lotus Organizer successfully follows a metaphor that is consistent with users' models of their world, a metaphor can be taken too far. Just because you can flip to the inside back cover of your regular organizer doesn't mean that users need to be able to do that on the computer. It may seem realistic, and even cute, but there is nothing that users can do on this page, so why even allow it in the software product? This and other features have caused some reviewers to comment that the product imitates the real-world metaphor of the organizer too closely.

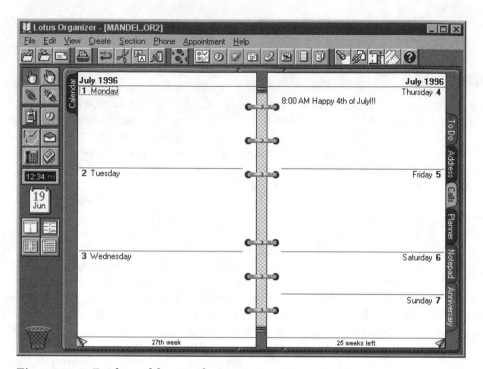

Figure 9.4   Real-world metaphor in Lotus Organizer.

By the way, you should know that usability and usability testing is not just in the minds and hearts of IBM and Microsoft. Many other companies, large and small, have usability labs and usability professionals on staff. For example, Lotus Corporation has a usability lab (and one in Europe) and several usability organizations. They even employ a cognitive psychologist to study cooperative work.

KEY IDEA! *Don't follow a metaphor just for the sake of consistency. Use metaphors where they work and allow users to perform actions and tasks easily on the computer. If there are faster or better ways to present information to users or to allow them to interact with a program, don't tie them too closely to the metaphor. Don't let the metaphor slow users down or force them to do tasks in unnatural ways.*

One final note on using real-world metaphors. If you use a metaphor, don't bend it too far or break it. The Organizer has an icon of a wastebasket in the lower-left-hand corner of the screen. As I mentioned earlier, when you drag an entry to the wastebasket, you see a bright red burst of flames as your entry is incinerated. Do you think you can retrieve that entry? According to the model of what happens to a real piece of paper when it is burned to a crisp, you wouldn't think you could. However, computers have the wonderful capability of undoing previous user actions, if so programmed, so Organizer allows you to undo the drag-to-the-wastebasket action. The flaming wastebasket icon contradicts the tasks users can perform, so the visual cuteness and feedback ends up backfiring and causing user confusion regarding the interface.

Here's another reminder: Even though a product like Lotus Organizer offers a good metaphor for users to work within, it is still an application-oriented product. When Organizer is opened, a blank window lets users know that they have to select an Organizer file to open to do their tasks. Here the Organizer metaphor doesn't quite fit. Users must keep separate files for different organizers. They can't combine, say, two different sets of anniversary dates in the same organizer. Remember, most GUI products are still application oriented. (Unfortunately, users aren't application oriented the way computers are!)

GUIs and Graphical Controls

Graphical controls allow users to make choices, set values, initiate actions, and navigate within a product. Controls range from buttons, check boxes, and entry fields for individual selections, to containers and notebooks or tabbed dialogs that serve to organize objects and information for users. These controls must be designed and used to fit the user's model and the particular metaphor with which users are working. The usage of these controls must also be consistent across programs and GUI environments. Users will get confused if a button does one action in one program and does something very different in another application.

Controls are basically designed after real-world, physical devices you use every day. Take a look at your television, stereo system, and VCR and you will see the interface controls that GUI controls are based on. Table 9.3 lists the controls that are now fairly standard across the different GUI and OOUI environments. Note that menus can be categorized as graphical interface controls. You'll see most of these controls shown in the illustrations presented throughout the book. Well-designed and well-implemented graphical controls foster consistency with the controls users are familiar with in their noncomputer environment.

Tool vendors provide these controls for developers on the various GUI platforms if they are not already available in the GUI developer toolkits. To foster consistent interface development and to help migration efforts from earlier GUIs, vendors offer common controls that can be used in multiple development environments (Windows, OS/2, Unix, Macintosh). Standard file and font dialogs containing multiple controls are also provided to allow developers to build standard dialogs for user interaction.

To see how strongly interface controls can support the user's model and the product metaphors, look again at Lotus Organizer in Figure 9.4. The entire product is built around the appointment book metaphor, which is implemented on the screen using a type of notebook control. Users should have little trouble figuring out how to use the tabs on the Organizer notebook, since they already know how to use tabs in a hardcopy spiral or three-ring binder. This one interface control establishes the product metaphor and enables users to learn and use the product interface quickly and easily.

Customizing GUIs

I've stressed that user customizing is one of the key interface design principles. For a graphical environment like Windows, there are many elements that users can change, such as background and window colors and fonts, mouse and keyboard properties, and even system sounds. The question is, where do users make these system changes?

In an application-oriented environment, users must figure out where these system customizing properties are hidden. For example, do you know how to change the system time and date with Windows 95? You must first find the Control Panel. Open the Control Panel and you'll see the Date/Time icon. Double-click this icon to open the window and finally you can change the time and date. Within an application-oriented environment, users must know how the interface organizes functions and tasks and they must know where to go to find the application that does these tasks.

Can you change the time directly with the clock icon on the Windows taskbar? Figure 9.5 shows how users can right-click on the time (a status indicator) in the taskbar, and select Adjust Date/Time from the pop-up menu, which brings up the Date/Time Properties window, where the time and date can easily be changed. This technique shows how menus and object orientation are critical to helping users easily perform routine tasks.

GUIs and the Multiple Document Interface

Many Windows products still follow the multiple document interface (MDI) model, where an application manages multiple applications or windows within that application. The MDI model allows users to manage multiple objects, or multiple views of the same object, within the main application window. This automatically provides task management for users. Figure 9.6 shows an example of the MDI window model used in Microsoft Word.

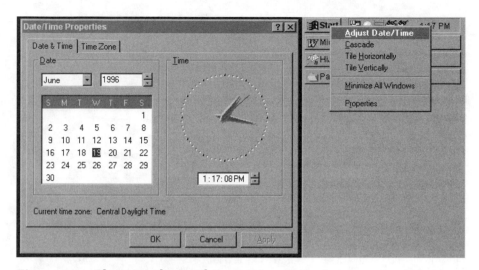

Figure 9.5   Changing date and time properties using a pop-up menu.

Open windows and objects in the main application window share the menu bar and also must appear within the borders of the main window. Contained windows cannot be moved or sized outside of the main window and are clipped if the main window is reduced. Although this method allows some degree of task organization, it is rigidly structured by the application and forces users to work with a number of windows within a very small piece of real estate on the computer screen. An object-oriented interface can provide task organization without the restrictions of the MDI model. I discuss this in the next section on designing object-oriented user interfaces.

GUIs and the Iceberg Chart

A usable GUI product is more than just a bunch of windows, buttons, and colors on the computer screen. There is a great difference between a *graphical* interface and a *human* interface! Many products have "gone GUI," but few have gone all the way to building a usable and familiar human interface for their products.

This goes back to the discussion of the iceberg chart in Chapter 3. A basic GUI gives you little more than the *look* (only 10 percent) and the *feel* (only 30 percent) of the designer's model. The key to a successful GUI (or OOUI) is how well it addresses the human aspect of the interface. This is the more important layer of the iceberg (60 percent) that addresses how the design of a product and its metaphors relate to users and their mental models.

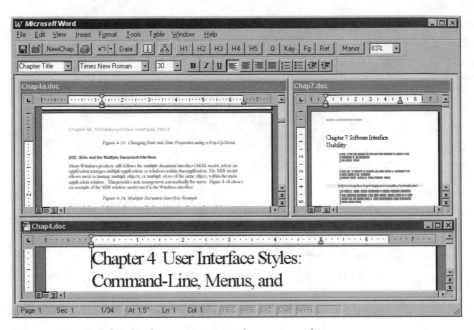

Figure 9.6   Multiple document interface example.

GUIs and Users' Memory Load

Any well-designed software user interface should reinforce the design principles that reduce the users' memory load. Graphical user interfaces have the additional advantage of being able to provide very visual cues and information that use the computer's information storage and retrieval strengths to offset human memory limitations. Do you remember all of the DOS commands discussed earlier? Should you have to remember these commands in a GUI environment? The answer to both questions is an emphatic *no!*

Menus as GUI Memory Aids

The extensive use of menus is critical to the success of GUIs. I discussed the advantages of menus and mentioned that they would play a key role in GUI interfaces. Even though there may be a wide range of graphical interfaces available to you as a computer user, menus are probably one of the main elements implemented in all of them. Graphical menus should be provided for numerous areas of GUIs, including windows and icons.

The menu bar, with its drop-down menus and cascaded menus, provides a consistent and familiar place for users to browse through all of the actions and routings available in an open window. The menu bar allows users to recognize actions rather than having to recall the appropriate actions from memory.

The power of the menu bar is tied to the object-action process. Users first learn the sequence of selecting an object, or objects, in the window and then selecting an available choice from the menu bar. The menu bar additionally provides contextual information by changing dynamically depending on the current contents and selections in the window. Choices in drop-down menus are grayed out (called *unavailable emphasis*) if they are currently unavailable, based on selected items in the window. Choices that are never available to users, based on their job function or access level, should not be shown in the menu bar.

KEY IDEA! *Many products don't take full advantage of the bene-fits of the menu bar. Dynamically showing appropriate choices and emphasizing currently available choices for selections allows users to explore a product interface. The menu bar visually highlights the relationships among objects, selections, and actions in the win-dow. It is important to show choices that may be appropriate, yet are currently unavailable.*

There are two reasons for showing currently unavailable menu choices: first, for consistency, so users know, for example, that the Save as . . . choice is always listed in the File drop-down on the menu bar. Second, it allows users to get help on a menu item even though it may not be currently available.

Menus also help users' memory by chunking actions and menu choices into logical and meaningful groups within the menu bar. Once users are familiar with the menu bar in one application window, they can transfer their under-standing of where common actions are in the menu bar to another application window, even if the applications are very different. This reinforces the princi-ple of making the user interface consistent and provides users with the conti-nuity of menu bar groupings across applications. This is why the IBM, Microsoft, and Apple design guides define standard menu bar groupings such as File, Edit, View, and Help. A standard menu bar structure provides a mem-ory aid to users that reduces the need to remember where to go to find the actions and choices needed to do a task.

Interface Controls as GUI Memory Aids

Graphical controls allow users to make choices and properties and initiate actions at the interface. One of the most important and creative aspects of interface design is deciding what controls to use in the interface to best allow users to do their work. Many of the graphical controls provide information in the form of lists or choices to reduce the amount of information users must recall. Other controls, such as the entry field, force users to remember information and correctly type it.

For example, when asking users to set information as simple as the time, don't force them to type in *a.m.* or *p.m.,* when you can provide radio buttons with the two choices. When users are filling out forms, don't force them to type in information where the computer already knows the list of valid entries. If a data field requires the abbreviation for a state in the United States, allow users to type in *TX* for Texas if they already know the abbreviation. In addition, provide a scrollable drop-down list that displays all of the state abbreviations so users don't have to even try to remember them. This same strategy applies to any set of choices, such as fonts, point sizes, colors, patterns, and so on.

Visual Feedback as GUI Memory Aids

The strengths of high-resolution displays and graphical interfaces should be used to provide memory aids to users during their work tasks. Status areas and information areas have been defined as window elements and should be made to keep users informed of activity within a window.

A status area should be used to provide information regarding the state of the application or the information within the window. For example, if information in the window has been sorted or filtered, some feedback like "Showing 140 of 268 matching items at 10:15 A.M. on Monday, August 21, 1996" should be displayed in the status area. The information area can be designed to guide users or provide information about an item in the window or on a menu. For example, if the keyboard cursor or mouse pointer is on the File Open . . . menu bar choice or on the Open icon on the toolbar, the information area might state "Opens a document." This type of information reinforces learning of the interface and allows users to rely on the system to provide helpful reminders about appropriate actions rather than having to remember what every menu item or icon in the interface is for.

Some GUI operating systems and programs have taken the information area concept and made it more dynamic. In many GUI products, when the mouse is moved over an item (or stays there for a short delay) a small text description is displayed. This is often called *balloon help.*

There are many other visual techniques that serve to remind users of modes they are in or the current state of the system. For example, the mouse pointer should change dynamically to show the actions available or currently in use, or the status of an application or system process. The mouse pointer can show window-sizing information, object manipulation information, text entry locations, a do-not-drop indicator, and a wait pointer to show that a lengthy process is underway. All of these visual indicators are subtle, yet important, reminders to users of the context of their actions. If users are distracted and look away or leave their computer for a time, there should be some visual indicators on the screen when users get back to let them know where they were when they left their task.

There's one more area where interfaces should do a better job of informing users and relieving their memory. Operating systems and programs have been notoriously bad about letting users know what step they were at in a lengthy process such as installing or updating the system of programs. Many GUI products used to have a very non-GUI installation interface, where users had little idea of where they were in the process and what was expected of them next.

Many GUI programs have finally improved their installation interfaces to show the steps in the install sequence, such as "Now installing Disk 1 of 3." They are also using graphic controls to illustrate that something is actually happening and that everything is running smoothly. I installed a program last week and suddenly realized halfway through the install process that I had selected the wrong drive as the target for the program installation. The only way I realized this was that while it was installing, the interface let me know where in the computer it was installing the program. I had forgotten which drive I had chosen and I wouldn't have noticed I had made a mistake unless the program had reminded me. That's the kind of interface design that makes users feel comfortable using a computer.

Progress indicators may be graphical, animated, or even textual, as long as they show progress in terms users find meaningful and informative. Progress information may be shown as percentage completion, time completion, or number of items already installed and how many are left to install. Be sure to let users cancel the process underway if they decide not to continue it for whatever reason.

The Semantics of GUIs

Some of what is best about graphical interfaces ends up also being what is most dangerous about them. Every control, every icon, each color, all emphasis, all screen animation, and every sound should have some meaning to users and should serve some purpose in support of users performing tasks with an operating system or program interface. Semantic feedback is a reminder to users that an object has some meaningful characteristic or that a meaningful action is being performed.

Careful use of metaphors allows users to build meanings and expectations based on visual and graphical elements of the user interface. Things that look like each other on the screen should behave like each other. Icons that look like folders should behave like folders. Things that are highlighted in the same color should have some relationship to each other. Doesn't this make sense? Sure it does, but that doesn't mean designers think enough about the meanings that will be associated with the interface elements they design and build.

It may seem minor, but (as with the case of the flaming wastebasket) semantic mismatches among interface elements and their expected and actual behaviors undermine the comfort users feel with the interface and may lessen the confidence they have in their ability to understand and use a product.

Drag and Drop: What Does It Mean to Users?

Because GUIs promote directly manipulating objects and other interface elements, semantic feedback is often combined with syntactic feedback (discussed in the next section). For example, users can drag an object such as a text document to a printer or to a wastebasket. The different meanings associated with the same direct manipulation *technique* cause very different actions to take place. Let me explain. There's a lot happening at the interface level for every seemingly simple drop-and-drag action.

When users drag an object, they should get some visual feedback that the object has been grabbed and they are doing something with it. This is called *source emphasis.* Also, when users grab an object and drag it, some default action is assumed. In most interfaces, the default action is the *move* action. In some graphical operating systems, such as Windows and OS/2, the mouse pointer actually can reflect the meaning of the drag operation. When the document is dragged over the wastebasket icon, there should be some visual feedback that this object accepts the dragged object. This is called *target emphasis.* After the document is released on the wastebasket, the action is complete. Look on the screen where the document was originally. Is it still there? It shouldn't be, since it was just thrown away in the wastebasket.

Halfway through this scenario, let's say the user decides to print the document instead of throwing it in the trash. The same mouse action technique is used, but instead of dropping the document on the wastebasket icon, the user decides to drop it on the printer icon. No problem, you say; that is a valid action. But printing a document is very different from deleting a document. Deleting an object means the object is *moved* from its original location to some other location, in this case, the wastebasket. The *meaning* of the action is different when an object is dragged to the printer. The original object is not being moved or deleted, it is actually being *copied* to the printer. That means the object should remain where it was on the screen after it is dropped on the printer. The copy is now being printed and all is well in the interface.

The subtle, yet important, difference in the meanings of these two similar direct manipulations should be communicated to the users. Both Windows 95 and OS/2 Warp change the mouse pointer from the *move pointer* to the *copy pointer* when an object is dragged over a device object like the printer, which won't accept the move action, only the copy action. A similar situation applies when an object is dragged to a different disk drive, which by default performs a copy action rather than a move.

Both Windows and IBM's CUA user interface design guides recommend that a way to override the default interpretation of the drag operation be provided by using modifier keys in conjunction with dragging with the mouse. However, the Windows guide recommends only that the mouse pointer be changed during the drag operation to reflect the action, while CUA requires that the copy and move pointers be used to reflect the drag operation, stating that this is essential to creating an interface that will be seen by users as being consistent with the CUA guidelines and its underlying principles. You need to decide for yourself and your products how important this area is for your product interface.

How Users Interact with GUIs

A GUI should entice users to grab the mouse, trackball, or any other pointing device and jump right in to interact with everything they see on the screen. GUI interaction techniques involve both keyboard and pointing devices to navigate, select, and directly manipulate information in the interface. As I've discussed, GUIs typically combine the three basic interface styles (command-line, menus, and direct manipulation) on the screen. A well-designed interface should allow users to choose the appropriate interface style depending on the tasks they are performing and their own personal interaction style preferences. The difficult part is providing a consistent, intuitive interaction style so users don't feel like they have to, as Peter Coffee (1992) comments, "point, click, and pray!"

To Keyboard or To Mouse, That Is the GUI Question

Writing this chapter, I am using the keyboard almost exclusively, since I'm obviously typing lots of words. Any actions I want to do, including copying and moving text, I should be able to do without taking my hands off the keyboard. Yes, it may be easier and quicker to select some text and copy or move it elsewhere in this chapter using the mouse, but while I am doing lots of typing on the keyboard, I want to do these actions without reaching for the mouse. A well-designed product user interface should let me do all of the actions on the keyboard that I could do using the mouse.

However, I find that I do some actions, like copying and moving text, using the mouse even when I'm mostly working on the keyboard. It should be my choice whether I want to use the keyboard or the mouse at any particular time.

I remember many frustrating GUI products that forced users to go to the keyboard to perform certain actions when they were doing everything else using the mouse. Lately, I've also seen the interaction pendulum swing the other way to the point where GUI products get so wrapped up in direct manipulation techniques that users aren't allowed to perform some of the actions using the keyboard. Sometimes the keyboard technique is so convoluted that there's no way users can remember the keystrokes.

Don't forget a product's keyboard users. Make sure that the interface is still keyboard-usable! Don't forget that menu bars and most other menus must have mnemonics and shortcut keys to allow fast keyboard interaction. Also, remember that whether using the mouse or the keyboard, users should be able to choose only currently available menu options.

KEY IDEA! *There must be a happy medium somewhere between the keyboard and mouse extremes. Who determines on which interaction styles and techniques products should place their emphasis? Yes—users should determine how they would like to interact with products. Unfortunately, there is no average user out there, and different users will describe very different personal interaction style preferences. To make it even more difficult, users change their own interaction styles to suit the different tasks they do. Don't just design for different user types; design for the different tasks that users do at different times.*

Using a Mouse with a GUI

Let's take a look at how users interact with GUIs using a mouse or other point-ing device. When IBM and Microsoft were working together on the IBM CUA user interface guidelines, there was a difference of opinion over mouse interaction techniques. Microsoft designed Windows to use only mouse button 1 (usually the left mouse button) most of the time. This means that selecting items and directly manipulating them are both done with the same mouse button. This may be comfortable for most Windows users, but they don't realize that they lose the ability to do some extended selection techniques because only one button is used to both select and directly manipulate objects.

Microsoft would not support the IBM mouse button model. In the Windows interface, mouse button 2 (right mouse button) was used only to bring up context-specific menus. IBM was looking forward to the object-oriented world where selecting and directly manipulating objects are related but separate techniques. The IBM CUA architecture opted to clearly split these techniques. OS/2 uses mouse button 1 for selection and mouse button 2 for direct manipulation. Windows 3.x applications used the right mouse button only sparingly, but that changed drastically with Windows 95. Windows 95 direct manipulation straddles both worlds—the left-button Windows technique and the OS/2 right-button technique. The left button performs the default drag action, while the right button drag allows users to choose an action when the object is dropped.

Mousing Through Menus

It's important to study how the mouse is used to navigate through menus and to make selections. Most GUIs support two styles of mouse interaction with menus: *press, drag, and release* and *point and click*. Again, personal preferences determine how users weave their way through an interface with a mouse.

Press and drag means that users may start anywhere in a visible menu by *pressing down* the mouse button over a menu choice. If the mouse pointer is on an item in the menu bar, the drop-down menu appears. Still holding down the mouse button, users can move through all of the drop-down menus by *dragging* the mouse pointer across the items in the menu bar. Moving down a drop-down menu will highlight a choice and will even open a cascade menu if there are any. *No choice is selected or action begun until the mouse button is released.* This technique allows users to easily explore all of the menu bar groups and choices just by moving the mouse pointer through the menus while holding down the mouse button. To select a menu choice, users simply *release* the mouse button when the mouse pointer is over the choice they want. If users don't want to make a selection, all they have to do is move the mouse pointer out of the menu anywhere in the window and then release the mouse button.

The other technique, point and click, allows users to make selections and then move the mouse quickly to another selection. Users don't have to worry about moving the mouse while holding down the mouse button. They just *point* to a menu choice by moving the mouse pointer over the choice. *Clicking* the mouse means pressing and releasing the mouse button without moving the mouse. Clicking on a menu bar item displays a drop-down menu. The drop-down stays displayed until users point and click somewhere else in the menu bar to display another drop-down, until they point and click on a drop-down choice, or if they click anywhere else in the window.

Mousing with Pop-Up Menus

Pop-up menus, or *context* menus as they are also called, are a newer menu style that are now available in both GUI and OOUI interfaces. Pop-up menus are simpler and more task-related than the menus available through the menu bar. A mouse button 2 click on an item is the technique to display a pop-up menu in both the Windows and OS/2 interfaces. Pop-ups are displayed next to the item they describe. Applications should use pop-up menus to display frequently used actions and menu choices that are available for the item in its current state. Figure 8.11 shows a pop-up menu for a disk drive object.

Pop-up menus are a more dynamic and context-sensitive subset of the whole range of choices that would be available in the menu bar. Users can learn about objects and items in the interface by exploring with mouse button 2 and seeing if they have pop-up menus and, if so, noticing what choices they offer.

The only setback I have found is that users must first learn what pop-up menus are and which objects have them. Then they also need to remember to check for them when working with objects in the interface. Because they are designed to pop up at users, they are hidden to begin with and there is no visual indication that they even exist in the interface. Both the Windows and CUA interface design guides spend considerable time discussing and offering guidelines for designing pop-up menus. If pop-up menus are well-designed and consistently implemented, they can easily enhance user productivity.

The GUI Editing Model

How do users perform editing tasks within the Windows environment? Windows uses the *clipboard model* for editing and manipulating data within and between applications. Cut, Copy, and Paste are the basic editing operations users can perform on their data. The clipboard is a common data buffer that *holds only one piece of information at a time.* Information on the clipboard is available to other applications. This model should apply across all types of data and across all applications. The clipboard even works to transfer data among DOS, Windows, and OS/2 products running under OS/2 and between DOS and Windows programs running under Windows 95.

When users *cut* a paragraph of text from a document within a word processing application, it is deleted from the document and placed on the clipboard. The same thing should happen when users cut a graphic element out of a presentation they are developing within a graphics application. *Copy* places a duplicate of the selected information on the clipboard without removing the original. *Paste* copies the contents of the clipboard to the target location and the information still remains on the clipboard.

One nice feature of the clipboard is that users don't have to think about how to edit in each specific application they work with. A well-designed application should allow users to select an object and select Edit, then Cut, from the menu bar. They can then go to another application, select a target location and choose Edit, then Paste, from the menu bar. If correctly implemented, the clipboard model for editing objects reinforces numerous interface design principles I've discussed. The clipboard model provides consistent interaction techniques for different types of data. Most importantly, it makes the user interface consistent within and across applications.

KEY IDEA! *Users must understand the clipboard model when they do editing tasks. The metaphor is very simple, but it is not a visual one. The clipboard is not visible during its use, and that can be dangerous.* Users must remember whether they have data on the clipboard. *Since it holds only one item, as soon as another object is cut or copied, the new object automatically replaces whatever was on the clipboard. For this reason, a* clipboard viewer *is a utility that lets users see the contents of the clipboard, and also manipulate the data. It is difficult for people to remember what they've got on the clipboard if there is no visual indication of the clipboard itself, much less its contents.*

For example, I had to be very careful when writing this book. Each chapter was contained in a separate file. While writing, I wanted to cut and paste material from one place to another, both within chapters and from one chapter to another. I'd cut a paragraph, intending to paste it somewhere else in that chapter or perhaps in another chapter. However, if I didn't go and paste the information somewhere fairly quickly, I'd forget that I had cut out the material and placed it on the clipboard. I'd continue writing and sometime later cut or copy some other material and end up losing the information I had on the clipboard without even realizing it. This is not a good thing to do to users.

KEY IDEA! *It would be nice for programs (or the operating system) to provide some visual feedback to users that there is something on the clipboard. For example, an information line message, an icon in an application window, or a change to the mouse cursor, could be used to let users know that the clipboard contained some information. This thoughtful and simple design point would go a long way in reinforcing the principles of providing feedback to users and reducing their need to remember whether there was information on the clipboard.*

The clipboard model is very important in most GUIs today because most user interaction with data is still through the use of the keyboard and menus, which is what I would call *indirect* manipulation. As GUIs move toward more pervasive direct manipulation techniques for editing data, the clipboard model will become less important. With direct manipulation, there is no need for a temporary data storage buffer such as the clipboard. Users choose the action by virtue of the type of manipulation they are performing.

Composite Documents in GUIs: OLE

One of the powerful attributes of graphical interfaces is the ability to present different types of data to users and also allow them to interact with these multiple data types in a consistent fashion. A composite, or compound document is an object or document that contains other objects, usually of a different type. In an application-oriented GUI environment, a composite document is a powerful tool. The Windows design guide states (Microsoft, 1995): "The compound document provides the framework for housing different components and for invoking their respective applications."

The technologies behind the compound document strategy are evolving slowly. Now, users are acutely aware that they are working with different types of data and are using different applications to do their tasks, even within one document. Progress is being made to provide better interfaces for users in this area. The Windows design guide also points out:

> In an ideal implementation of compound documents, the user is unaware that different source applications are being invoked. The process of browsing, selecting, and editing information is seamless; users can manipulate various types of information within the body of a single document without the inconvenience of switching from one application to another.

The evolution of application integration technology and graphical user interfaces has led to the development of an architecture called object linking and embedding (OLE). This allows users to create not just compound documents, but *living* documents. That is, *objects* within a document can link or embed other information from the document or even another source. *Linking* provides the ability to keep the original information or object somewhere and to keep a representation of that information in the document. The link serves to get the original information when needed, for example, when the original information is changed or when the display is updated.

Embedding involves inserting a new or existing object, or piece of information, into a document. All of the information contained in this object is now within the document container. This allows users to store all of the components of a compound document in one file, rather than having separate files for each of the different objects contained in the document. However, if these objects are copies of other objects, and those other objects are changed, no changes will be made in the embedded object. There are no links to an original object if an object is embedded rather than linked.

Making OLE concepts and metaphors understandable to users will be a difficult and ongoing challenge. Users should not have to understand the complexities of OLE to do their tasks while working with compound objects. For example, do OLE objects behave the same way as other objects behave for drag and drop? Let's hope so. *Windows* magazine (Heller, 1993) discussed this issue regarding OLE 2.0: "The new drag-and-drop functions should prove convenient for users and programmers alike. . . . From a user's perspective, that means properly written OLE 2.0 applications will automatically 'do the right thing' when you want to drag objects to, from and within them." OLE is a part of Microsoft's evolving Common Object Model (COM) specification.

What's Next for GUIs?

GUIs will probably remain the PC user interface "for the masses" for a few more years as users continue to migrate from the DOS environment. User-oriented enhancements should continue to improve GUI operating systems and programs as competition increases among software vendors. Furthermore, interfaces that go beyond simply graphical to object-oriented should also competitively drive GUIs to become more sophisticated and as usable as they are advertised to be.

KEY IDEA! *Bill Gates' (1990) famous keynote address at Fall Comdex, entitled "Information at your Fingertips" (IAYF), is a memorable event in PC history. Microsoft has since attempted to bring this concept to life with its Windows products. Unfortunately, they aren't there yet. Richard Dalton (1993) says, "My real disagreement with Microsoft's IAYF, however, is that, at best, it's misleading. At worst, it's an exercise in glossy hubris that can't serve Microsoft well in the long run."*

Dalton's main point, and one with which I heartily agree, is that while information at your fingertips is an admirable goal, unfortunately, we're only at the point of *data* at your fingertips. Today's computer technologies and interfaces can dump tons of raw data on the screens of inquisitive users. However, we're a long way from turning those mounds of data into intelligently filtered, organized, meaningful, and useful information for users to deal with. The Internet has brought even more data to the fingertips and eyes of computer users. Ambitious Internet products try to filter and sort through the available data to provide users with useful information.

Bill Buxton, a computer scientist and worldwide interface consultant, fears the widespread adoption of GUIs may slow the development of more powerful user interfaces. He states (Grantham, 1991): "The differences among GUIs are trivial compared to the differences between GUIs and what I know we are capable of doing in user interfaces." With that thought firmly in mind, the next chapter discusses another step forward in the evolution of user interfaces, the *object-oriented user interface* (OOUI).

References

Dalton, Richard. 1993. Industry watch. *Windows Magazine* (April): 49–52.

Gates, Bill. 1990. *Information at Your Fingertips.* Fall COMDEX Keynote Address, Las Vegas. Microsoft Corporation (098-19953).

Grantham. 1991. Painting broad GUI landscapes. *Canadian Datasystems* (April): 18–47.

Heller, Martin. 1993. Strengthening the ties that bind. *Windows Magazine* (March): 129–34.

IBM Corporation. 1989. *Guide to Microsoft Windows.* IBM, 69F9074.

IBM Corporation. 1992. *Object-Oriented Interface Design: IBM Common User Access Guidelines.* New York: QUE.

Jones, Mike. 1992. Apple interface. *Design* (July): 64.

Lewis, Peter. 1993. The executive computer. *Boulder Daily Camera* (March 23): 27.

Microsoft Corporation. 1995. *The Windows Interface Guidelines for Software Design.* Redmond WA: Microsoft Press.

Pake, G. 1985. Research at Xerox PARC: A Founder's perspective. *IEEE Spectrum* 22(10): 54–61.

Smith, D., C. Irby, R. Kimball, W. Verplank, and E. Harslem. 1982. The Star user interface: An overview. AFIPS National Computer Conference (June), pp. 515–528.

Object-Oriented User Interfaces

Object technology offers much deeper approaches to integrating information within the workplace, transcending traditional application boundaries and matching processing power more closely to users' tasks.

Steve Cook (1992)

Roadmap for Part 2: Object-Oriented User Interfaces

Chapter 10: Object-Oriented User Interfaces: The New World

Object-oriented user interfaces are examined. Definitions, examples, and discussions of interface objects, views, and core skills users need for OOUIs are presented. OOUI operating systems and programs are showcased. The user interface architecture underlying OOUIs is detailed.

Chapter 11: Object-Oriented User Interfaces: Meeting User Needs

This chapter continues the discussion of object-oriented user interfaces. OOUIs and user models are examined. How do you migrate users from GUIs to OOUIs? Finally, OOUIs and object-oriented programming (OOP) are compared and contrasted.

CHAPTER TEN

Object-Oriented
User Interfaces:
The New World

Object interface or objects in your face?

Larry Constantine (1993)

In the Beginning . . .

The user interface work at Xerox PARC led to the design of the Apple Macintosh graphical user interface, which later influenced the interface design of both Microsoft's Windows and IBM's OS/2. In fact, after rereading some of the early Xerox research, I am amazed at how many of the concepts of not only the graphical user interface were described, but also the concepts of the object-oriented user interface (OOUI). Concepts such as interface objects, the desktop metaphor, the object-action syntax, and object properties were all defined and discussed back in the 1970s.

Current PC user interfaces, as reflected by the Windows and OS/2 operating systems we use today, give us a snapshot of how OOUIs have evolved and where they are going. IBM and Microsoft began their intertwined operating system development efforts over ten years ago with DOS. Originally designed as a stepping stone to OS/2, Microsoft's work on Windows grew exponentially to the point where Windows rather than OS/2 became the main focus of the company's PC operating system strategy.

The road to OS/2 began in 1985, when IBM and Microsoft signed a joint development agreement to work on an operating system that would go beyond the capabilities of DOS. Under the agreement, both companies would jointly design, develop, and own the final product. Why did these two largest hardware (IBM) and software (Microsoft) companies decide to do this work together? Deitel and Kogan (1992) summed up the simple and obvious strategy that began this phase of the IBM-Microsoft relationship:

> Both companies realized that, if two different advanced DOS systems were developed, the software market would be confused about which was the "right" one. So it made sense for IBM and Microsoft to combine efforts, and to create a single industry-standard operating system that was endorsed by the two leading companies in the PC market.

KEY IDEA! *As it turns out, both Microsoft and IBM stuck by the initial strategy, which was the basis of their joint development efforts. The problem lies in each company's definition of "a single industry-standard operating system." The original intent was for OS/2 to be the mutual goal for this strategy. However, as development of OS/2 progressed slowly, and the development (and popularity) of Microsoft's own Windows product progressed rapidly, Microsoft changed their interpretation of the strategy to replace OS/2 with Windows as the single industry-standard operating system. This strategy switch brought the PC operating system evolution to the GUI-OOUI war between Windows and OS/2.*

All of this repositioning between Microsoft and IBM set the stage for the war between Windows and OS/2 at the user interface. The Windows 3.0 interface rode the GUI wave to success and popularity. Meanwhile, OS/2 1.3 was a stable product with a graphical interface, yet it did not enjoy the same commercial success that Windows had received. This pattern has continued with the new versions of both operating systems, Windows 95 and OS/2 Warp.

IBM, however, was preparing to make a leap, both functionally and at the interface level, with the OS/2 2.0 product. As early as October 1990, press clippings were hinting at IBM's plans for an object-oriented user interface for OS/2 2.0. An article in *PC Week* (Pallatto, 1990) was entitled "IBM to Jazz Up OS/2 PM With Task-Oriented Icons." Cliff Reeves of the IBM Common User Access Interface group in Cary, North Carolina was quoted as saying, "During 1991, we are going to move to a more object-oriented style of dealing with the operating system. CUA 3 is sort of a generic term that we have applied to the next generation of the user interface model." Although OS/2 2.0 did not arrive on schedule in 1991, its ultimate arrival in April 1992 heralded the first product to implement the CUA object-oriented user interface architecture.

What is an object-oriented user interface? How is it different from the Windows-type GUI? The computer industry is slowly embracing object-oriented programming (OOP) technology and also object-oriented interfaces, even though they are very different.

The organization of the next two chapters follows the same organization I used to discuss GUIs in the previous chapter. This should allow the reader to easily flip back and forth to better understand the differences between GUIs and OOUIs.

Changing Gears: More Power for the User Interface

KEY IDEA! *Today's graphical user interfaces (GUIs) and object-oriented user interfaces (OOUIs) are very different from the user interfaces of the past. While they are touted for their ease of use, there is a learning effort required for users to move upward in the evolutionary software user interface chain. There is also a major increase in the programming skills needed to effectively build the sophisticated, event-driven, user-friendly programs that users demand today. GUIs and OOUIs may be popular for their usability benefits, but they are more of a problem for traditional developers. The process of designing and creating graphical and object-oriented user interfaces requires a much steeper learning curve as well as some amount of training to embrace the different programming and user interface environment.*

The type of computer interface chosen determines where the computer hardware will use its processing power. In the past, when user interfaces were not so sophisticated, computing power was used mainly to perform software functions as quickly as possible. Today's powerful computers are using most of their processing power to make the programs you run easier to use at the software interface.

Bud Tribble, vice president of software engineering for NeXT Incorporated, said, "On the desktop today, 80 percent of computing power is going toward ease-of-use, such as menus, windows, and pop-ups. Only 20 percent is actually going towards doing the job, such as calculating your spreadsheet" (Seymour, 1992). However, this is not a bad thing, as most of you appreciate these efforts to make computers easier to use. Tribble continues, "The one thing worth devoting computer power to is the interface. But there's a paradox: The simpler the interface, the more CPU cycles you use up. Interfaces are all about fostering 'appropriate illusions,' and the more realistic the illusion, the more demanding it is in terms of power." Our hope for the future of computing is that the power of computer hardware keeps growing at its current tremendous rate so that this power can be used to make computer software easier to learn and easier to use in the years ahead.

Basics of OOUIs: Beyond GUIs to Objects

KEY IDEA! *What is an* object? *The dictionary definition covers the range of things we think of when we work with real-world objects: "Something that is or is capable of being seen, touched, or otherwise sensed. Something physical or mental of which a subject is cognitively aware."*

Object-oriented user interfaces aren't just a different flavor of graphical interfaces. OOUIs really are a means of taking the graphical interface environment beyond the simple representation of applications and files as icons on the computer screen.

John Tibbetts (1991), an OO software consultant, discusses this difference:

GUIs are the state-of-the-practice interfaces. We see them everywhere we look, but in some senses they are just multiplexing traditional interfaces, not really presenting objects. In a GUI, a window is a viewer into an application. An icon is just a shrunken window; a double-click on an icon means to run the underlying application.

Tibbetts goes on to describe OOUIs:

An OOUI, on the other hand, invites the user to explicitly recognize and manipulate the objects on the glass. In effect, it extends the world of objects all the way out to the user. An OOUI appears to be a simulation, not a representation, of reality. In an OOUI, an icon is an object. Windows are simply viewers into the object. A double-click tells the object to open itself. Note that there don't seem to be identifiable applications in an OOUI; there is merely a constellation of objects that a user can consider and manipulate. In a very real sense, the user is the application.

KEY IDEA! *The basic components of an object-oriented user interface include all of the features of graphical user interfaces described in the last chapter. It is often very difficult to tell the difference between a GUI and an OOUI without actually using the interface. Much of the "look and feel" of GUIs and OOUIs may seem the same on the surface, but the main differences lie in the models underlying the interface. A key characteristic of OOUIs is that they strive to remove the main drawback to GUIs—their application orientation.*

It is critical to understand the differences between application-oriented GUIs and OOUIs. Table 10.1 lists the main differences between the two interface styles.

TABLE 10.1   Application-Oriented vs. Object-Oriented User Interfaces

Application-Oriented User Interfaces	Object-Oriented User Interfaces
◆ Application consists of an icon, primary window, and secondary windows	◆ Product consists of a collection of cooperating objects and views of objects
◆ Icons represent applications or opened windows	◆ Icons represent objects that may be directly manipulated
◆ Users must start application before working with objects	◆ Users open objects into views on the desktop
◆ Containment is mainly shown using text list boxes	◆ Folders and Notebooks are visual containers
◆ Provide users with function needed to perform a task	◆ Provide users with supplies needed to perform a task
◆ Focus on the main task as determined by the application	◆ Focus on inputs and outputs for objects and tasks
◆ Related tasks supported by other applications	◆ Related tasks supported by use of other objects
◆ Rigid structure—by function	◆ Flexible structure—by object
◆ Users can get trapped in a task	◆ Users should not get trapped in a task
◆ Training is centered on the application and its function	◆ Training should focus on common paradigms, look and feel
◆ Users must follow structure of the application	◆ Users may perform task in their own way or innovate
◆ Many applications required—one per task	◆ Few objects—more reuse of the same objects in many tasks

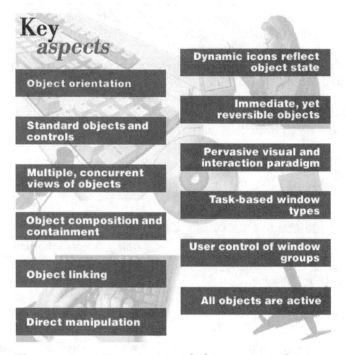

Figure 10.1   Key aspects of object-oriented interfaces, from IBM (1996).

Software developers are moving away from the traditional application-oriented design. Lotus Development Corporation enhanced Freelance Graphics for OS/2 release 2.0 to better coordinate user interaction between Freelance and Lotus 1-2-3. In a review for *PC Week,* Sullivan (1993) notes, "Freelance 2.0 takes much better advantage of OS/2's Workplace Shell than the previous OS/2 version, allowing users to concentrate more on their work than on the interfaces between OS/2 2.0 and earlier OS/2 or Windows user interface conventions."

On its new Human-Computer Interface (HCI) Web site (http://www.ibm.com/ibm/hci/designer/uiarch), IBM describes the key aspects that characterize object-oriented user interfaces. Figure 10.1 lists these key aspects, which are each described in detail. I recommend you browse this material on the Web.

An OOUI Example

Figure 10.2 shows a mix of objects and applications that users might work with on a PC desktop. Objects on the desktop include a clock, a calendar, and a wastebasket. Lotus Organizer is an application running in a window.

Notice that there are two wastebaskets on the screen—one on the desktop and one in the Lotus Organizer window. At first, users wouldn't know that one is a generic, system-level wastebasket (the one on the desktop), while the other is an application-specific (Lotus Organizer) wastebasket. Any icon in a folder or on the desktop can be dragged to the desktop wastebasket to be discarded. Try dragging a desktop object to the Organizer wastebasket—it won't work! The application wastebasket works only for objects in the Organizer application. Users quickly learn that applications and objects don't always mix.

KEY IDEA! *GUIs take a step toward user-friendliness with graphical and visual representations of computer systems, applications, and data files. OOUIs go beyond the look-and-feel aspects of the iceberg chart and focus on building user models that carry over from the real world to the computer environment. The goals of an object-oriented interface are to allow users to concentrate on their tasks and business processes rather than having to focus on how their computer system is set up or how to use the applications and files needed to accomplish their goals.*

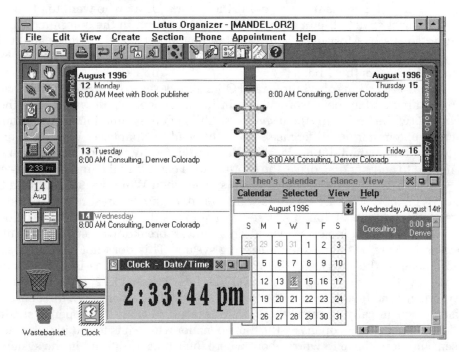

Figure 10.2 Objects and applications on the desktop.

Core Skills Needed for OOUIs

Suddenly the user is dealing with objects he can touch and grab and manipulate.

Jeff Moad (1992)

Object-oriented user interfaces require users to have the same basic understanding of the core set of GUI skills (described in Chapter 9), plus some understanding of object behaviors—that is, which objects to use and how to use them. There are lots of books discussing object-oriented *programming,* but hardly any books discussing object-oriented *user interfaces.* The basic object-oriented interface concepts, metaphors, and techniques are discussed in great depth in *Object-Oriented Interface Design: IBM Common User Access Guidelines* (IBM, 1992). I'll cover the main highlights of the core set of OOUI concepts that go beyond what I already covered for GUIs.

How OOUIs Hide the Underlying System from Users

One main goal of an OOUI is to hide the underlying system organization from users so they can concentrate on doing their work. Users who want to put a particular object or data file in a certain physical location in the computer system can do so easily. Most users, most of the time, don't want to worry about the way the system organizes their information. However, most operating systems don't allow users this luxury.

The newer versions of Windows and OS/2 allow users to create and place icons representing system objects anywhere in the interface. Windows 95 calls them *shortcuts* while OS/2 calls them *shadows.* Although they function quite similarly, there is one important difference. As I mentioned in Chapter 9, Windows shortcuts aren't that smart. If the object or file represented by the icon on the desktop is moved to another disk drive, the shortcut icon can't find the underlying object.

Figure 10.3 shows the message that displays when Windows 95 can't find the underlying object—it asks if users want to link to the "nearest match, based on size, date, and type." I don't think so—I want to use the exact file that I was looking for, not one that is a close match! This shows a breakdown between the interface users work with and the underlying system. This does not enhance users' confidence in the interface. The Windows graphical interface is not as tightly coupled with the operating system as OS/2's interface. In OS/2, if the underlying object is moved (even if it is done from a command-line window), the operating system dynamically changes the link. The result is that users open a shadow object and the system opens up the file, no matter where it is found in the system. Users shouldn't have to worry about where their files are stored in the system if they can see them on their desktop.

Both Windows 95 and OS/2 present the underlying computer system to users as objects that they can interact with in the same way they interact with any other objects on the computer screen. Disk drives and directories are represented as folder objects that offer user actions (move, copy, delete, etc.) and appropriate system actions (format, check disk, etc.). Figure 10.4 shows the Windows 95 Control Panel and opened windows for Power, Mouse, and Printers. As you can see, the objects representing the system are displayed as individual icons that can be worked with however users want. The Windows 3.1 Control Panel was not so object oriented and easy to use. Users could not open more than one item with the Control Panel at a time.

Users Must Understand Objects and Applications

Since OOUIs are a new interface style for the evolving PC environment, users will still be working with applications at the same time as they work with objects. As major applications migrate toward object-oriented interfaces, users will begin to see their favorite applications evolve into integrated sets of sophisticated objects rather than a single complex application. In the meantime, users will be faced with a combination of both application-oriented products and object-oriented products (see Figure 10.2).

KEY IDEA! Using GUIs and OOUIs side by side should allow users to make the best possible comparisons and allow them to personally evaluate application-oriented and object-oriented interfaces and interaction techniques. Users should then demand that developers migrate their GUI products as quickly as possible to the object-oriented environment, assuming that OOUIs work best for them.

Standard objects should be familiar to users in their environment. For example, without ever having used the computer wastebasket object, wouldn't users already have a good idea how it works? At least they would know how the

Figure 10.3   Windows 95 Problem with Shortcut message.

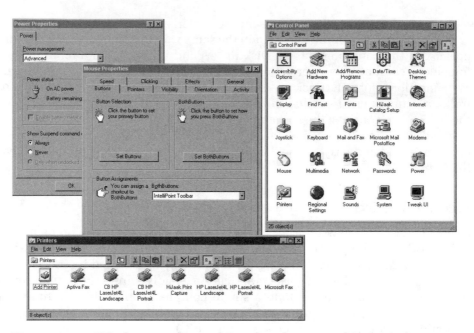

Figure 10.4   Windows 95 Control Panel and system object windows.

object should work, according to their experiences with similar objects in the real world. This is the true test of an interface: Does it match user expectations and experiences?

Users Must Understand Windows and Object Views

In the GUI environment, a window is simply a running application. In an object-oriented interface, objects present themselves and the information they contain as *views* to users. A view is a representation of information about an object. A view might show what is contained in the object. It might be the object's properties. It might be what the object will look like when printed, as in a WYSIWYG view.

KEY IDEA! *Views of objects are presented to users in windows. In an OOUI environment, users can work with multiple views of the same object at the same time, either multiple different views or the same view. Multiple views are a very powerful feature of object-oriented interfaces.*

Figure 10.5 shows the clock and shredder objects in their *default views*—the clock's Date/Time view and the shredder's Properties view. Also opened on the desktop is the clock's Properties view. These views are dynamic—as a change is made in the properties of an object, the change is also shown in any other opened view of the object. For example, if the time is changed in the clock's properties view, it is immediately shown in the Date/Time view.

Note the titles in the title bar of the windows in Figures 10.5 and 10.2. The clock object shows the name of the *object* and the name of the *view* presented in the window, for example, Clock—Date/Time and Clock—Properties. This is a quick way to tell the difference between application windows and object windows. Application title bars typically show the name of the *application* followed by the name of the *data file.* For example, the title bar for the Lotus Organizer application (Figure 10.2) reads Lotus Organizer—[MANDEL.OR2]. MANDEL.OR2 is a data file stored somewhere in the system that can be used only by the Lotus Organizer application.

Users Must Understand Graphical Controls

OOUIs use similar graphical controls that are commonly found in most GUI products, such as radio buttons, push buttons, check boxes, and so on. As new interface controls are developed in one operating system or tool, vendors quickly try to develop a market for those controls in other operating systems and for other tools. As new controls such as a slider and notebook were developed by IBM for the OS/2 2.0 environment, they were also packaged and made available for GUI developers on the Windows platform. Users migrating from GUIs to OOUIs should have no trouble recognizing and using the graphical controls. Users migrating from character-based interfaces will have to learn how to use graphical controls in either environment.

There are a few differences when using some controls and windows in the OOUI environment. OS/2 gives users the capability of making changes immediately, rather than having to perform any explicit actions to commit their changes. This is called an *immediate* commit model. For example, users may change the colors and fonts for objects immediately, by dragging a color or font onto an object, rather than choosing a particular color or font and then selecting an Apply push button. When finished, users only need to close the window; they don't need to press an OK push button to complete the action.

KEY IDEA! *Some controls have specific uses and characteristics in the user interface. The notebook and tab control are all-purpose controls used to present organized sets of information to users.*

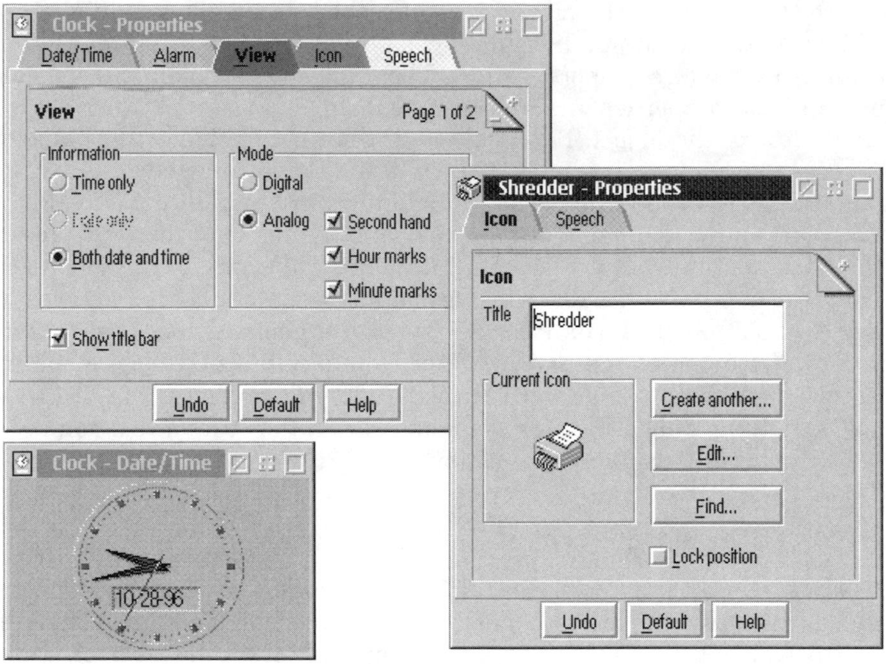

Figure 10.5   Multiple views of objects.

In OS/2, the notebook is used to present properties views of objects, while Windows 95 uses the tab control to present object properties. Figure 10.5 shows the notebook control in the properties view for the clock and the shredder. Figure 10.6 shows the tab control in a properties window in Windows 95.

Users Must Understand Direct Manipulation (Drag and Drop)

OOUIs rely heavily on allowing users to work directly with objects to perform even basic actions, rather than interacting with menus. Context-specific and product-specific actions and processes can also be performed using direct manipulation. Direct manipulation is usually done using the mouse. There are many games that are designed to help users learn to use the mouse. In fact, the Windows Solitaire game has won industry awards for teaching computer users mousing skills.

KEY IDEA! *Users must understand that direct manipulation is pervasive in OOUIs. They must be aware of this because there is one drawback to direct manipulation—users can't see any indication on the screen of the possible actions they can perform directly on objects. Keyboard actions and choices are listed in menu bars and context menus, but there is no way to visually show what direct manipulation may be available to users.*

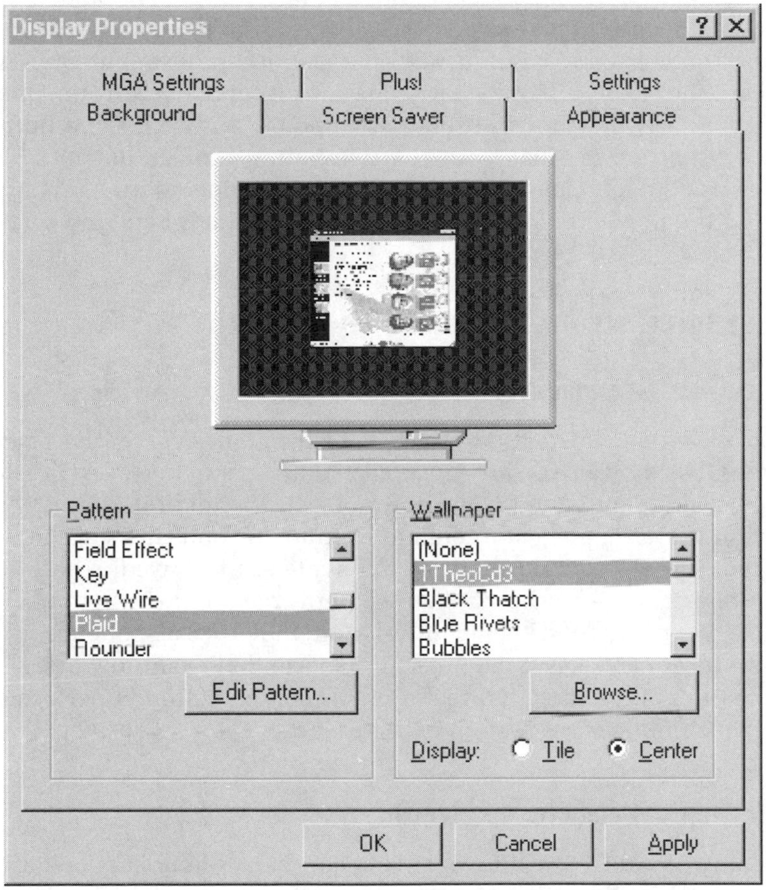

Figure 10.6   The tab control in properties views in Windows 95.

Users must learn to use the right mouse button to pop up the context menu showing a list of possible actions for the object. It is also not obvious as to which objects can interact with other objects. Therefore, it is very important to build objects that are as intuitive as possible. Users must learn which objects interact with each other and how they should interact with objects.

For example, in an object-oriented office environment, users should be able to drag the icon representing a customer and drop it on a telephone object. This action should dial the customer's phone number or prompt users if there are multiple telephone numbers associated with that customer. The same action also applies to dropping the customer object on a fax object. This action should transfer the fax phone number for the customer to the fax object, and allow users to type or select the information to be faxed to the customer.

GUI users are already familiar with the use of a mouse, but DOS users and even GUI users from different hardware and interface environments use the mouse differently. Macintosh users use a mouse with only one button. Most Windows users are familiar with the two-button mouse, but most Windows interfaces use the left mouse button for both selection and direct manipulation. I'll discuss the new use of the mouse in OOUIs in the interaction section.

The User Interface Architecture Behind OOUIs

The Object-Action Sequence

The pervasive user interaction style for OOUI interfaces is the object-action sequence. GUIs may also follow the object-action sequence (see Chapter 9), but it is an even more important concept for object-oriented interfaces. Many GUIs still rely on the action-object interaction syntax in some areas of the user interface. When the object-action interaction syntax is followed, regardless of the action to be performed or how it is to be performed, either via the keyboard or the mouse, via menus or direct manipulation, the process sequence is the same. Users first locate and select the object or objects they want to work with, using any navigation and interaction technique. Then an action is performed, using whatever technique users prefer.

Object Menu Bars and Pop-up Menus

As you know, most GUI windows have menu bars. Menu bars contain choices that display drop-down menus when selected. Drop-down menus contain actions and routing choices that relate to objects in the window or the object that is represented by the window itself. The GUI application-oriented menu bar is nicknamed the FEVH menu bar, where FEVH is based on the first-letter mnemonics for the standard choices in the menu bar (File, Edit, View, and Help). Let's now take a look at menu bars in the object-oriented interface.

The past few years have revealed some problems with the standard GUI menu bar, especially the File menu item and drop-down. On one hand, users are familiar with File as the first choice on the menu bar in almost all applications. However, many products now do not work with files in the traditional application-data relationship, so the File menu choice may seem inappropriate. Most developers are afraid to remove it as a menu bar choice because users are so used to seeing it as the first menu bar choice. The Windows design guide offers no advice in this area. The answer, as discussed below, is that as products move beyond the application-data format to object windows, the File menu bar controversy simply goes away!

The migration from GUIs to OOUIs has brought a change to menu bar, since windows are now *object* windows rather than *application* windows. IBM (1992) states, "The menu bar choices and contents defined in this version of the CUA guidelines provide an evolutionary step towards an object-oriented menu scheme." The change in the menu bar was occasioned by the change from data files opened within applications to objects opened within other objects. Figure 10.7 shows an object-oriented menu bar for a calendar object window. This new menu bar style is called WOSH, which stands for the four areas the menu bar addresses: the *w*indow itself, the *o*bject being viewed in the window, objects *s*elected within the view, and, of course, *h*elp.

Users manipulate the window itself by using the System menu drop-down. This contains choices that change the visual characteristics of the windows and other operating system-specific choices. This menu is the same for both application-oriented windows and object-oriented windows, and is the same as the Application icon in the Windows environment.

The File menu bar choice and drop-down menu from the application-oriented window are changed to provide choices for the *object* represented by the window, since there is no longer the concept of files. The menu bar choice label is now the class name or specific name of the underlying object. For example, if the object is a folder, an open window for that object will display the class name, Folder, as the first menu bar choice. All choices in the drop-down menu act on the *object itself,* not the information or objects contained in the window. The calendar in Figure 10.7 shows Calendar as the first menu bar choice. The drop-down menu offers actions on the calendar object as a whole, such as opening different views and properties, and printing the calendar.

The second menu bar choice is labeled Selected, and is used for container and data objects where objects within the window can be selected and actions applied to them. All choices in the drop-down menu will be applied to whatever

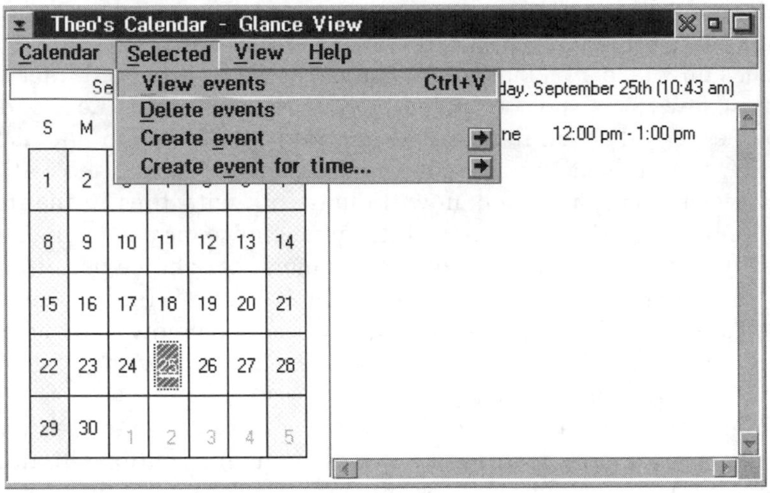

Figure 10.7   Menu bar choices for object windows.

objects are selected in the window. This menu changes dynamically for each type of object selected. For example, with a folder object that contains other folders, when a folder is selected in the window, the Selected menu choices would be the same as in the Folder drop-down menu—the same actions can be applied to the opened folder and the folders it contains. Figure 10.7 shows the Selected menu when a date on the calendar is highlighted. The actions listed in the drop-down menu apply to the selected date—September 25, 1996. This menu bar item is new for object-oriented interfaces. A key benefit is that users don't have to open an object they see in a window to perform actions on it.

The other menu bar choices and associated drop-down menus are much the same for object windows as they were for application windows. The Edit menu provides data manipulation actions on selected objects in the window. The View menu changes the type of view or aspects of the view (such as include or sort) within the window. Help is still a very important menu bar choice in the object-oriented world.

KEY IDEA! *When should (or shouldn't) a window have a menu bar? This is one of the most frequently asked user interface design questions. The IBM (1992) guidelines say, "Provide a menu bar when a window will provide more than six action choices or routing choices. Also provide a menu bar if you provide the functions available in the File, Selected, Edit, or View menus."*

That's why you don't see menu bars on many of the OS/2 standard object windows. They are very simple, general-purpose objects that have only a small set of possible actions. Product-specific objects will most likely have many more possible actions and routings, and thus will require menu bars for their windows.

Pop-up menus are context-sensitive menus that display actions and routings that are currently available for objects. Figure 10.8 shows a pop-up menu for a folder object in Windows 95. Options in pop-up menus should be frequently used choices for that object. Pop-up menus should be organized into groups of choices, such as views, data transfer, utilities, and convenience choices. These groupings are designed to help users remember what types of choices are available in pop-ups.

KEY IDEA! *As seen in usability testing and everyday use, users tend to use pop-up menus and direct manipulation more frequently in OOUIs than in GUIs, where they are more likely to use menu bars. Menu bars are a transitional interface element as products move from applications to objects in the interface. OOUI users are quick to learn that they can get a pop-up menu just by clicking mouse button 2 on any object on the screen.*

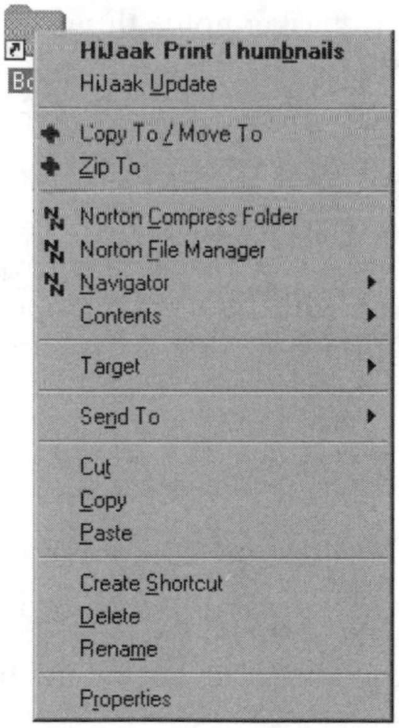

HiJaak Print Thumbnails
HiJaak Update

Copy To / Move To
Zip To

Norton Compress Folder
Norton File Manager
Navigator
Contents

Target

Send To

Cut
Copy
Paste

Create Shortcut
Delete
Rename

Properties

Figure 10.8   Pop-up menu for objects in Windows 95.

Users See Objects Rather than Applications

Objects are anything that users need to work with to perform their tasks. They are things that can be manipulated as individual units, or they may be composite objects made up of other objects that have some relationship to each other. Objects, rather than applications, are the focus of users' work in an object-oriented interface.

KEY IDEA! *When do you know if you have designed or created an object that works for users? If you can't describe the function of an object in a single short sentence, then you don't have an object that will resonate with users, especially if the sentence is as long and convoluted as this one. If users can't tell you what all the important objects are when you talk to them a couple of days later, with no prompting, then you don't have a good set of objects.*

There are several basic types of interface objects. These types make up the fundamental classes of all system-provided objects users see in both Windows and OS/2. They are also the basis for objects developed by others for product-specific user needs and for users to create their own objects. The three basic types of objects are: *data* objects, *container* objects, and *device* objects.

Many objects have characteristics of more than one object class. This follows how objects work in the real world. For example, an in-basket holds things, so it has some features of a container. Its main purpose, however, is to perform some task, such as sending the objects it contains to some person or destination. This behavior classifies the in-basket as a device object. It is important to understand interface object classes and their behaviors. Objects must be implemented so that users' expectations of the behaviors of objects will be met. That is, *an object defines what views can display and modify it.* Objects that have container behaviors should provide views consistent with other containers. Objects that are devices should provide views appropriate for that device and consistent with other devices.

Data Objects

Data objects provide information to users. They may be any type of information users may work with, such as text, spreadsheets, images, graphics, music, recorded speech, video, animation, or any combination of them. Because data objects are usually product-specific, design guides do not define specific data objects. This is a task for product designers.

Data objects may also be composite objects, that is, they may contain other objects. Newsletters, memos, spreadsheets, and presentations are examples of composite data objects. In addition to providing behaviors common to data objects, they may also provide behaviors of container objects, such as a list of their contents.

Container Objects

Containers are powerful tools for users to organize their work objects and tasks on the interface. Containers may store and group any objects together, including other containers. Container objects allow users to present their contents in different ways, to move and copy objects to and from containers, and to arrange or sort their contents in a particular order. Typical containers include folders, portfolios, in-baskets and out-baskets for mail, and so on. In OS/2, even the users' entire screen, called the *workplace,* or *desktop,* is a container and has all of the properties associated with containers. OS/2 provides three basic types of containers for organizing users' tasks: the workplace, folders, and workareas.

The *workplace* is the highest level container users work with. It holds all of the objects in users' computer screens. In many environments, this is called the user's desktop. As a container, it has properties that users can modify in the same ways they work with other types of containers.

Folders are general-purpose containers for storing objects. *Workareas* are special types of folders that provide more task organization than just simple storage. These concepts were designed to follow the ways users work in the real world. Users might store receipts and memos in a general folder, not expecting or needing to use them together to perform a task.

Workareas allow users to group things that they might use during the course of doing their work tasks. For example, you might have two separate projects you are working on at the same time. Instead of having objects on the desktop for both projects, workareas allow you to group together the objects you might use for each project. One project might require a special printer, a calculator, and a special spreadsheet object in another folder. The other project might include your business invoices, billing objects, tools, other folders, and a printer setup for your billing. The advantage of workareas is that you can open up your objects, folders, and tools for a project and then close them up simply by closing up the workarea associated with the project. When you open the workarea for a project the next time, the opened objects and folders will automatically open up just where you left them on the screen when you closed the workarea.

Containers may correspond to directories and subdirectories on users' computer systems, *but only if users want them to.* Most users will create container objects as storage places on the desktop, where they don't need any knowledge of the physical location of the objects themselves. This is a powerful way of shielding the complexities of the underlying system organization and file maintenance from users. System directories are also represented as folders, thus causing some confusion when users might attempt to delete or move folders.

Device Objects

Device objects often represent physical objects in the real world. In the office environment, any of the physical objects users work with can be represented in the user interface as device objects. These may be objects that are not necessarily computer related, such as telephones and fax machines. Computer-related objects include printers, electronic mail in-baskets and out-baskets, and all of the objects that make up the computer system. Figure 10.9 shows some OS/2 system device objects.

The primary purpose of device objects is to provide ways for users to communicate and interact with objects associated with their computers. For example, users currently might follow these steps to send a fax of a memo to a colleague. First, users would write the memo on the computer and print it on a printer attached to the computer. Then they would look up the fax telephone number of the colleague, either on the computer or in a regular phone directory or address book. They would finally go to the fax machine and send the memo to the intended person.

In an object-oriented interface, users might instead create a new memo or a fax object. After typing the information in the memo, users might drag the

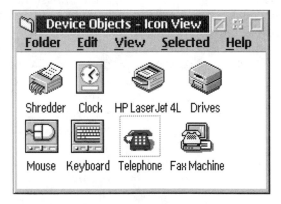

Figure 10.9   Device objects on OS/2 desktop.

memo object to the fax object on the desktop interface. If the fax number was already contained in the memo, that is all that needs to be done. If a fax phone number is needed, users are prompted by the fax object. Users could either type in the fax number or drag an object representing the colleague to the fax object. The colleague's object might be part of an address book or phone book object that contains telephone and fax phone numbers. The fax object and the address book object would know what information is transferable between the two objects.

Device objects may also have characteristics of other types of objects. For example, a printer, fax, and wastebasket contain objects. The printer has a print queue associated with it, a fax contains jobs and pages, and a wastebasket should allow users to open it up and see what objects are contained within. The type of object characteristics and behaviors for any particular object will determine what views are appropriate for that object.

Views of Objects

I already mentioned that users must understand windows and views of objects. *Views* are simply different ways of looking at an object and the information within it. Different views present information about objects in different forms, the way we look at objects in the real world. Designing OOUIs requires you think about how users want to work with objects—then give them views that allow them to do their work.

Aaron Marcus (1990) discusses the importance of using multiple views to improve communication in the interface. He talks about views of all information and data, not just interface objects. Marcus shows how multiple views are used to provide:

- ◆ Multiple forms of representation
- ◆ Multiple levels of abstraction
- ◆ Simultaneous alternative views
- ◆ Links and cross references
- ◆ Metadata, metatext, and metagraphics

There are four basic types of object views: composed, contents, properties, and help. Views are presented to users in windows. What appears in the window and how users can interact with that information are determined, in part, by the type of view of the object. Users may interact with objects via direct manipulation, but they may also interact with objects, and the objects they contain, using views displayed in windows.

KEY IDEA! *The power of object views lies in users' ability to open multiple views on the same object at the same time. For example, users can display the time and date in one view of the clock and at the same time change the clock's properties and characteristics in another window containing the clock's properties view. More sophisticated and product-specific views can give users dynamic interrelated views of objects.*

The view types described here are defined for standard objects. You should start with these basic views and build product-specific views for your objects.

Composed views present information and objects contained in an object, showing their order and relationships to other components of the object. Composed views are often the primary view associated with data objects. For example, for this book, each chapter I wrote is a data object that I created as a composed view. The order of text and graphics in each chapter is important and determines the meaning of the chapter. If I changed the location of a paragraph, the meaning of the information also changed. I also created a master document object, containing all of the individual chapter objects. Of course, the order of chapters in the master document is important, so I also worked with the master document in a composed view.

Composed views are very specific to the products and tasks users work with. For example, a car is an object. An artist creating drawings of the car for a brochure might use or create front, side, back, and interior views of the car object. A car salesperson, however, might work with a general information, or sticker price list, composed view of the car, and also views of the options and packages available for a car. Figure 10.10 shows a composed view of a car object used by a salesperson.

Contents views display the components or contents of objects. Contents views are standard for container objects. The order of contents views is not necessarily important and does not change the meaning of the object itself when the contents are rearranged. Three standard layouts are provided for contents views in OS/2: icon, details, and tree. Windows 95 provides icon, list, and details views for opened folders. These contents views are shown in Figure 10.11.

Any object having container properties might have a contents view. Printer objects have a contents view in addition to the properties view of the printer. Data objects may also have contents views listing their components, but since the relationships among components of a data object are important, their order in a contents view does have some meaning.

Properties views allow users to view and change information or properties of objects. All OS/2 properties views are presented using the notebook control. Figures 10.4 and 10.5 show properties views in OS/2 and Windows 95. These views should be provided for all types of objects. In application-oriented programs, options and properties are usually presented in dialog boxes within the application. In an object-oriented interface, users should be able to change all aspects of an object in a properties view, including colors, fonts, names, and so on.

The notebook and tab control can be broadly applied to many types of objects. As I showed with Lotus Organizer, the notebook concept is central to the real-world metaphor built by the product designers. Any type of address book, phone book, or information container object might be represented in a type of properties view, where users can view, organize, and store information about people, appointments, dates, and important events.

KEY IDEA! *Views of objects should be dynamic and tightly interrelated. As users make changes to an object that affect other views, these changes should be reflected immediately, or as quickly as possible. Using multiple views allows users to see the immediate visible effects of any changes they make. For example, in OS/2, users can open the icon contents view of a folder, then open the properties view of the same folder. Any changes made in the properties view that affect the contents view are immediately made visible.*

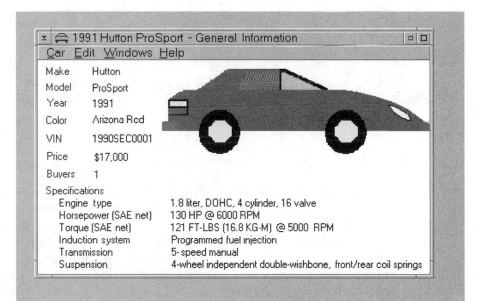

Figure 10.10   Composed view of a car object.

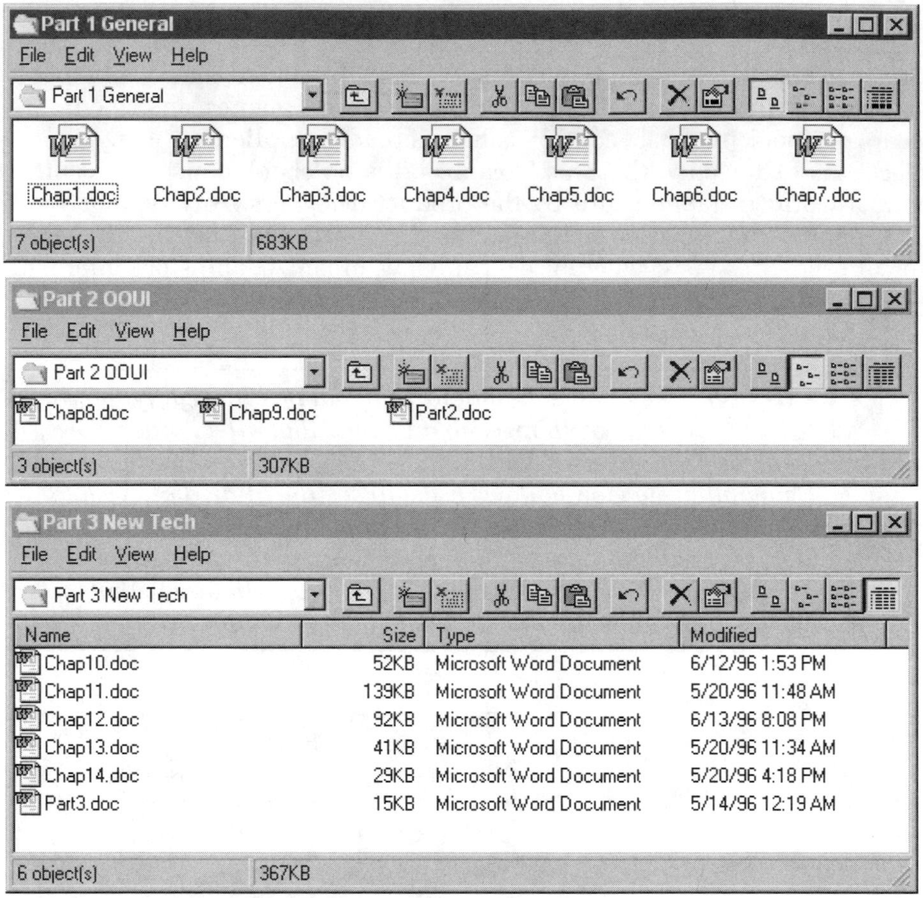

Figure 10.11   Contents views of folders.

The final type of view, and definitely not the least important, is the Help view. Information is presented in help views to assist users as they work with objects. From the designer's perspective, help is a view of the object, but users typically access help information from the help choices in the menu bar or from pop-up menus. Help may be provided at the object level, and also at the individual element level, for example, for an entry field. This is called *contextual* help, and can be accessed by pressing the F1 key, if contextual help is available.

KEY IDEA! *Help should be provided for users in whatever form they desire or require. Help is a view of an object, and as such, it is made up of information. This information may take any form, as help is a data object. Traditionally, help has been largely textual information. Much research and the advantages of multimedia technology available in computer systems have enabled designers to provide help in a multitude of forms, including text, graphics, audio, animation, and video. Find out what type of help users would like. Help is part of the user interface, and is just as important as the design of information on the screen, such as icons and objects. Advanced help techniques are covered in Chapter 14.*

The object type descriptions (data, container, and device) are technical terms and users should see only object names or class names, such as document, folder, and printer. *Composed view* is a technical term that should be given a user name, such as WYSIWYG view for a document. *Contents views* are presented to users as the name of the type of contents view (icon, tree, details, or product-specific layout). *Properties view* is both a technical term and a user term, and is displayed just as Properties. Object and view names are displayed most often in menus and window titles. Each open window has the object name and the view name in the title bar. For example, a folder container opened into a details contents view might have Project Edie—Details View in the window title bar.

KEY IDEA! *Defining a product's objects and views is perhaps the most difficult part of the user interface design process. The distinctions between different object and view types can be blurry, so don't be too concerned about the exact categories into which you place objects and views. View types should not necessarily be surfaced to users—they care more about view names than whether an object is a container or data.*

Users should see meaningful and usable names of objects and views for the objects they work with and the tasks they perform. That's where the design focus must be. Carefully design object and view names. Be sure to conduct usability testing with customers and users to make sure they are comfortable with names of objects and views.

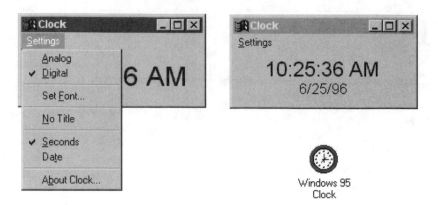

Figure 10.12   GUI clock application.

Examples of Objects and Views

Let's look at a familiar object—a clock. I have seen many GUI clock applications in the Windows environment. Figure 10.12 shows the new clock in Windows 95 PowerToys (developed by Microsoft). Although this is a Windows 95 product, it is still a GUI. There is no concept of objects and views. The clock face is presented in the window client area as the application's information. Users change aspects of the clock by using the Properties drop-down on the menu bar,

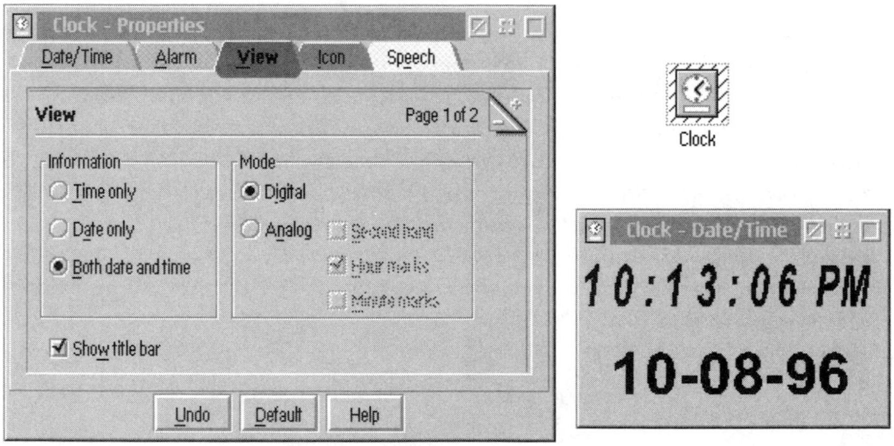

Figure 10.13   OOUI clock views.

as they would with any other application. Everything happens from within the primary window of the application.

Figure 10.13 shows the OS/2 system clock, which has an object-oriented user interface. The clock icon, when double-clicked to open, opens into the *default view,* Date/Time. Users may open another view of the clock, the Properties view, which uses a notebook to show the different properties available for the clock object. These two windows represent two views of the same object opened at the same time. If something is changed in one view that affects the other view, it dynamically changes the other view. For example, if I selected the *Both date and time* radio button, the Date/Time view will immediately change to show both the date and the time.

One of my favorite software programs on Windows 95 is Quick View Plus from Inso Corporation. This product allows users to peek into files without opening the application used to create the file or extracting the file into its component pieces. Quick View Plus works with dozens of data formats for all types of files, including document, spreadsheet, database, graphics, presentation,

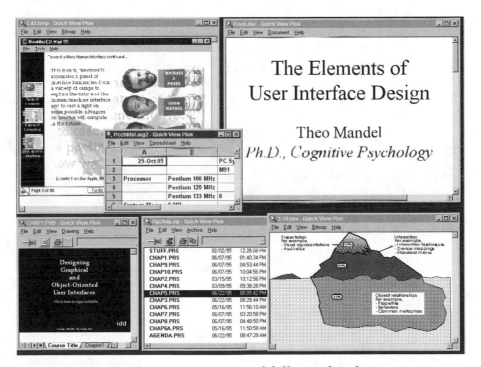

Figure 10.14   Quick View Plus views of different data formats.

compressed, collection formats, and even executable files. This means that users can view, copy and paste, and print data without even having the original applications. Documents and spreadsheets are fully formatted, and even ZIP files can be viewed and manipulated.

Figure 10.14 shows a few of the types of files Quick View Plus can work with. From top left, clockwise, there is a bitmap file, Word document, an encapsulated postscript (EPS) graphic, a ZIP file, a Lotus Freelance Graphics presentation, and in the center, a Lotus 1-2-3 spreadsheet. All of these different types of files can be viewed and manipulated, and *none of the applications are opened!* This wonderful tool illustrates the power of views of information.

References

Deitel, Harvey and Michael Kogan. 1992. *The Design of OS/2.* Reading, MA: Addison-Wesley.

IBM Corporation. 1992. *Object-Oriented Interface Design: IBM Common User Access Guidelines.* New York: QUE.

Marcus, Aaron. 1990. Principles of effective visual communication for graphical user interface design. *UnixWorld* (October): 135–138.

Pallatto, John. 1990. IBM to jazz up OS/2 PM with task-oriented icons. *PC Week* (October 29): 1.

Seymour, Jim. 1992. Opinion: A high "UQ" is what spells business success. *PC Week* (October 5): 63.

Sullivan, Eamonn. 1993. Freelance boosts OS/2's ease-of-use. *PC Week* (February 22): 1.

Tibbetts, John. 1991. *Object-Orientation and Transaction Processing: Where Do They Meet?* Keynote Address, OOPSLA 1991.

CHAPTER ELEVEN

OBJECT-ORIENTED USER INTERFACES: MEETING USER NEEDS

As designers, we must exceed user expectations whenever he or she sits down to work with a computer.

General Walker, USAA Insurance (1996)

OOUIs and the User's Model

Using a more object-oriented interface, a user would be able to concentrate on the business process itself, rather than the applications or files needed to accomplish it.

Jeff Moad (1992)

An OOUI should provide an environment that contains things that are familiar to users. The interface is designed to provide such an environment by presenting familiar work and office objects for users. They can focus directly on business tasks and processes rather than having to translate how applications and system functions help them accomplish their tasks.

OOUIs and Real-World Metaphors

Objects should work like they look and look like they work.

Steve Shipps (1996)

The key to defining interface objects is to build them from objects in the real world. The figures in Chapter 10 and in this one represent familiar objects in an office and/or on a desktop—clocks, wastebaskets, shredders, and calendars. One of the most bothersome things about working with computers is that users can't understand the names of things they see on the computer because they have weird names like ZINST.EXE. It's like learning a foreign language—users shouldn't have to learn a whole new language to be able to communicate with computers.

Look at the Windows 95 and OS/2 interfaces in the figures in this chapter and Chapter 10. Notice that text labels below the object icons look more like regular names, not computer file names. Both OS/2 and Windows 95 allow object names up to 256 characters in length, including spaces and uppercase and low-ercase characters. Text labels may also flow across multiple lines.

Users are no longer arbitrarily restricted to naming things on the computer interface using strange and cryptic titles based on the DOS naming conventions of a maximum of eight characters with a three-character extension. This seemingly simple feature is actually quite complicated under the covers, but it goes a long way in helping users maintain a model of their work as they use a computer. Users had to define terse names that somehow provided information about the contents or purpose of the file or object. Users had to build elaborately coded file names such as THEOLTR6.DOC. The ability to give objects text labels helps users maintain real-world models. It also helps users remember what objects are, and long names can be used to provide additional information of value. Long filenames, in addition to objects on the interface, reinforce the real-world metaphor designers attempt to create.

KEY IDEA! *Personal information managers (PIMs) are popular graphical and object-oriented software products. Most people use some kind of paper-based organizer for work or personal use, thus they have a strong mental model of the objects they work with, such as calendars, to-do lists, appointments, notes, and addresses and telephone numbers. It is often easier to develop interfaces for software products when there are already strong user models and metaphors.*

Real-World Containers

Generic containers go a long way toward allowing users to organize their work on the computer in ways that fit their models. The OS/2 and Windows 95 desktops, for example, are designed to be a user's main working environment. Some people have lots of folders, workareas, and objects sitting on the desktop. This follows the messy-desk metaphor. Others like to keep only a few folders on the desktop and have all their objects stored somewhere in those folders. *There is no one right way for users to set up their desktop!* My physical desks at home and at work definitely follow the messy-desk metaphor, and on the computer I follow the same metaphor, since I like to have lots of objects and containers on my computer desktop. It has been said that a messy desk is the sign of an organized mind!

KEY IDEA! *Common objects such as folders and workareas can be enhanced to build powerful product-specific containers. For example, a library folder could be created that could maintain a record of who has checked out each object from it and the dates of when objects are checked out and returned. This library folder could also determine from user profiles whether users are allowed to check out certain objects and could then restrict them from accessing objects that they are not permitted to use.*

Real-World Access to Objects

Another aspect of OOUIs is the ability to have objects represented in multiple places. In the real world, there are things we have access to, no matter where we are. For example, most people have a telephone answering machine at their office and possibly one at home. Obviously, you can get your phone messages when you are at the location of the machine, but most phone answering systems also allow you to play back your messages remotely from a telephone at any location. This real-world concept is carried onto the computer interface by the ability to create shortcuts (Windows 95) and shadows (OS/2) of any object in the interface.

Shadows and *shortcuts* are icons that look and act just like the object they represent, but are actually just links to that object. For example, users may want to have the same printer and a few charts and documents in multiple project folders. There is no need to copy objects to have them in multiple places. In fact, copying objects can cause problems, since changes made to the original object will not be reflected in the copy. However, any changes made to an object, be it the data that makes up the object or the properties for the object, are automatically reflected in all shadows of the object.

Shadows and shortcuts are often used for objects that may not even be in users' local environment. Remote objects and resources may be available to users, even though these objects may not physically be in users' own locations.

In that case, users may work with a shadow of a printer or other device that is remote yet still available to them. The concept of shadows seems to work well for users in this environment, as they already know that they are working with an object that is not really there, but that represents an object somewhere else that they can still work with. Working with remote objects is the same as working with local objects that are also on the desktop.

It may be difficult to see the visual distinction between the original object and its shadows. Windows uses a shortcut graphic added to the icon and modifies the text label to read "Shortcut to. . . ." In OS/2, text labels for shadows are a different color than the text for objects. These visual distinctions are intentionally subtle, because in users' minds they really are working with the original object when they use a shadow object.

When users open a shortcut, the same thing happens as if they opened the original object. In OS/2, a visual cue that a window is open on an object is displayed on both the object and each of its shortcuts. Changes made to an object are immediately reflected in all of its shortcuts, and changes made to a shortcut are immediately reflected in the object and any other shortcuts of the same object. This means that if the original object is deleted, all reflections of that object are also deleted. However, if users delete one shortcut, other shadows and the original object are not necessarily deleted.

Real-World Sticky Pads

Another real-world metaphor that is extremely useful in an object-oriented user interface is the template. *Template* is the term for what you know as Post-it notes or the yellow sticky pads that everyone uses at home and at the office. The concept is the same on the computer; just drag from a template object and drop it anywhere, and a new object is created. The template is a powerful tool in the object-oriented interface. Any object of any type (data, container, or device) can potentially be made into a template object.

OS/2 provides a folder of templates for all of the system objects. Other products that provide templates may add their templates to the OS/2 templates folder. Users may create templates of any objects they work with and they may keep templates anywhere they like. Creating new system objects such as printers is as easy as dragging a printer icon from the printer template and then defining the appropriate printer driver and output port in the Create Printer dialog box. Users can create as many different system or product objects as they desire and may store them on the desktop or in any containers.

The power of templates is that the original object may contain any type of data, including time-dependent or variable data. For example, invoices, a standard memo, and a form letter all may have variable data that creates data in a new object created from a template. An invoice template might contain an invoice number and the time and date of creation. As users drag an invoice from the template invoice, a new invoice is created containing a new invoice number and the current time and date. Figure 11.1 shows system object templates in the templates folder and a newly created objects in a folder called New Folder.

There is an important difference between shadows or shortcuts and copies of objects or objects created from templates. Shadows are *links to an original object,* so there are no copies or newly created objects, just the original object. A copy of an object is just that; *a new object that is an exact replica of an existing object.* Once copied, the new object is not linked or related in any way to the object it was copied from. Changes to one object now do not affect the other object.

Any object may be copied, including templates. Copying a template is different from creating an object from the template. A copy of a template is

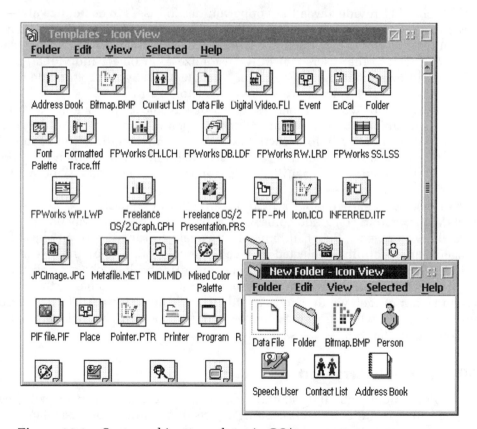

Figure 11.1   System object templates in OS/2.

another template with *exactly* the same characteristics and data. The variable data is still variable data; the invoice number is still a variable, not a new invoice number. Using the real-world sticky-pad analogy, a copy of a sticky pad is a new sticky pad with whatever information that is associated with the sticky pad.

Creating something from a template is like dragging off the top sheet of a sticky pad. You don't get a template like you would if the template is copied. You get an instance of the object with all of the variable data, such as invoice numbers and dates, filled in for the new object. The OS/2 Workplace Shell offers users the templates in the template folder so they can quickly and easily create new containers and objects to customize their desktop environments.

Customizing OOUIs

OOUIs should provide a wealth of opportunities for users to customize almost any aspect of the interface, including the desktop and user objects, the behaviors of objects, and the interaction techniques users prefer. One of the key features of OOUI is that users can fully customize each object individually, in addition to personalizing the system as a whole. GUIs typically provide only system- or application-level properties and customization.

Windows 95 provides properties views of all object types. For example, users can customize how they want folders to open when selected. Folders can either replace the current folder window or open a new window. Microsoft has even developed a set of user interface tools called PowerToys, which includes Tweak UI (see Figure 11.2), a utility for customizing aspects of the Windows 95 desktop.

As I discussed earlier, OS/2 provides a unique way to customize colors and fonts with the font, color, and color scheme palettes. The same way users work directly with objects, they can immediately change properties of an object by dragging and dropping a selected font, color, or color scheme on the object.

Using these techniques, users can customize individual objects and windows, or apply changes systemwide. For example, users can change the background color of each window individually to any color they like. They can also hold the Alt key while dragging a font or color to an object. This will change all the objects of that type in the same way.

OOUIs and the Iceberg Chart

If OOUIs are done right, they should exemplify the designer's iceberg chart (see Figure 3.8). The difficult part is creating objects that follow common metaphors, objects that relate to other objects, and objects that have properties and behaviors users expect from objects.

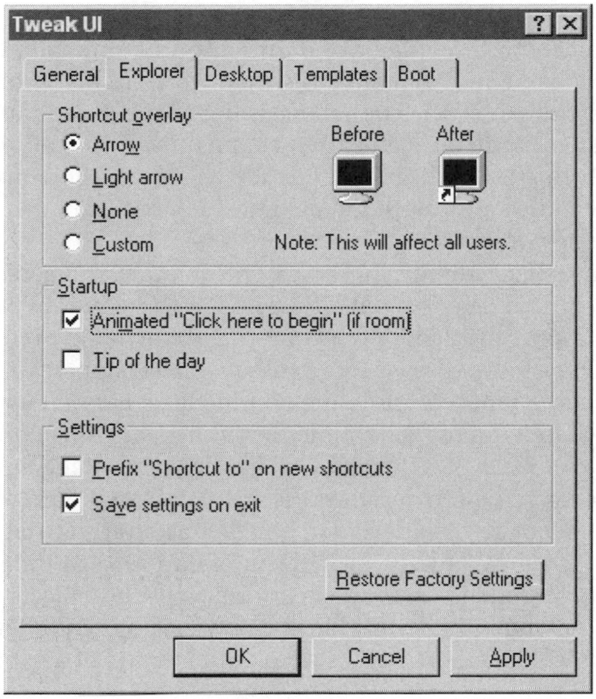

Figure 11.2   The Tweak UI utility in Windows 95.

This is exactly what object-oriented user interface design is all about. GUIs typically focus on the presentation and interaction aspects of the iceberg, while OOUIs' strength is that they follow the object relationships layer of the iceberg. If this is done well, the upper layers of the iceberg—presentation and interaction—become more obvious and should be easier to create.

OOUIs and Users' Memory Load

One of the primary goals of OOUIs, like GUIs, is to reinforce the design principles that reduce users' memory load. Similar to GUIs, OS/2 provides visual choices, lists of items, and graphic controls to allow users to recognize items and make selections rather than having to recall information and type information and commands.

I've already discussed the memory benefits of the different types of help, menus, status bars, and information areas. I'd like to present some of the additional benefits OOUIs provide as memory aids.

Long filenames help users recognize, rather than remember, what all those things are on the screen. People have a difficult time remembering names. We don't remember the names of people to whom we were just introduced, unless we really paid close attention. The same applies to the computer user interface. We are better at recognizing names for commands, applications, and objects than we are at trying to recall them. I already asked you how many of the DOS commands you could recall without any cues. I'm sure you can't remember all one hundred or so commands.

Window names also provide important information to users. GUI windows show the application name and data file name in the window title bar as memory aids. OOUIs show the name of the object and the name of the view, such as Project Theo—Icon View. Since users can have objects open in multiple views at the same time, the information in the window title bar helps users remember what object they are working with and what views they have opened.

Icons represent objects in GUIs and OOUIs. They act as memory aids in addition to object names. Graphic design skills are usually required to develop icons that are useful memory aids rather than cute but arbitrary visual symbols. Icons can be used as memory aids to provide information regarding object names, types, functions, or actions users may perform with the objects they represent. Often, usability testing is done early during interface design to let users evaluate sets of icons. Typical icon usability tests look at a number of attributes, including:

◆ Object meaning (which icon best represents an object)

◆ Object identification (which icon in a group represents which object)

◆ Icon effectiveness (to what degree an icon accurately represents an object)

◆ Icon groupings (which sets of icons are more appealing to users)

Visual containers, such as folders, also aid the memory. In Chapter 4, I discussed how people remember things better by organizing and grouping them into chunks. Container objects organize and group objects in ways that have meaning to users, especially since users organize the containers on the desktop themselves. The workarea container not only allows users to group objects together, it provides task management by opening and closing all related objects within a workarea as the workarea is opened and closed. This task-oriented behavior controls related objects and windows rather than users having to do so. Users can also sort objects in containers by a number of criteria, such as name (alphabetical), type, size, creation date, or last access date.

The use of contextual help, in addition to general help, provides a direct path to help information for the specific field or control users have selected. If no contextual help is available, users must open up a general help window and either look through the topic index or do a keyword search to find help for the specific item they are working with. This is very frustrating, as users might have found the help topic they were looking for at some previous time, but can't remember how they got there!

Object templates are also very powerful memory aids. Users don't have to remember what variable information is contained in an object, such as dates, invoice numbers, customer information, and so on. Users creating a new invoice by dragging from the invoice template will get a new invoice with an incremental invoice number generated automatically by the invoice template object. The use of templates relieves users of manually entering required information that can be automatically generated by the program or the computer. Templates will become more popular as designers and users realize the power and support they provide.

Menus as OOUI Memory Aids

One of the most important aspects of menus is that users don't have to remember all of the possible actions or choices available for objects. Objects in OS/2 and Windows 95 have pop-up menus that immediately show users what are the most frequently used actions for that object. To see all of the possible actions for a particular object in a window, users can select the object and view the choices available in the menu bar drop-downs.

The options in a window's menu bar also remind users of the interface paradigm they are working with. If the first menu bar choice is File and the first choices on its drop-down are New and Open, users are working with the application-oriented style. The object-oriented window menu bar has the class name of the object as the first choice, and Open as the first choice in the drop-down.

Visual Feedback as OOUI Memory Aids

Object-oriented interfaces are designed to encourage users to directly manipulate objects rather than use indirect methods such as command-lines and menus. Since it is not visually obvious what direct actions can be done with objects, it is very important that users get feedback about selections they have made and about direct actions they are trying to perform. This is done with visual emphasis techniques that have been carefully designed to provide immediate and dynamic feedback about the tasks being performed.

Selected emphasis indicates that a choice or object is selected. Selected emphasis is most often displayed by changing the background of the selected object's icon and text label, often to reverse video, where the text changes from white to black and the background changes from light to dark. One or many objects may be selected, and all selected objects in all windows should be displayed simultaneously. Also, the scope of selection is within a window. This is a memory aid because users can keep a set of objects selected within one window and switch to the desktop or other windows and select objects there without disturbing the selections in any other windows. Users can then return to any window and the previously selected objects are still selected. Selected emphasis is displayed only for the active window, but the selection state is saved for each area and is redisplayed whenever a window or area becomes active.

In-use emphasis is a visual cue indicating that a view of an object is open. This visual aid is available in OS/2 but not in Windows 95. Windows 95 uses the taskbar to show what windows are opened (in use), and does not show any emphasis on object icons when they are opened. I find it frustrating that I can't just look at my desktop and opened folders to see what icons are opened but may not be visible at the moment. I'm forced to go to the Windows 95 taskbar. OS/2 shows in-use emphasis by displaying diagonal stripes behind *each* appearance of an object's icon (see the OS/2 Clock icon in Figure 10.13). With the use of shadows of objects, this provides additional feedback. If an object, or any of its shadows, is opened, all of the icons representing that object, including all shadows, will show in-use emphasis. Now, that's visual feedback!

Unavailable-state emphasis is used in menus to indicate that a choice cannot be selected. This is done by dimming, or graying out, the choice that is unavailable. This feedback aids the memory, since it is a reminder of the possible choices and actions for selected objects. Users don't have to recall what actions can or can't be done with certain selections; all they have to do is look at the menu choices. All unavailable choices are dimmed and the system will beep if users try to select them. There are two important things to remember about unavailable emphasis. First, allow users to cursor to the choice so they can select help for that choice, even though it may not be currently available. Second, if a choice is *never* available to users, rather than displaying it with unavailable-state emphasis, simply do not display the choice.

KEY IDEA! *During direct-manipulation operations, there must be four types of feedback provided to users: source emphasis, target emphasis, a dragged image, and the mouse pointer.*

Source emphasis is a visual cue that indicates which object or objects are being manipulated. Selected emphasis is usually used to show this. Source emphasis is also shown for objects when users get a pop-up menu for the object(s).

Target emphasis is used to indicate when the hot spot of the mouse pointer is over an object that supports direct manipulation. The target object may be any object that supports direct manipulation. This includes icons, an open window of an object, or interface controls that accept or display information, such as an entry field. When a dragged object is over a receivable object, target emphasis is shown.

Windows 95 and OS/2 provide visual feedback during the direct-manipulation operation by attaching an image or outline of the object or group of objects to the pointer while the objects are dragged. This *dragged image* may be the icon(s) of the objects that are selected or an outline of the icon(s).

Finally, the *mouse pointer* itself is used to provide feedback to users while they are performing actions. The mouse pointer changes over areas of the screen and over objects as the mouse is moved, and reflects whether the action will result in a move, copy, or shadow/shortcut. The "do-not" pointer indicates that the target object is not a valid target for the direct-manipulation operation. An I-beam pointer indicates that the pointer is over an area where users can drop selected text.

The visual emphasis techniques I've discussed here are closely interrelated and can apply to any object or set of objects at the same time. The visual cues for these techniques have been carefully designed so they can appear with any other emphasis cues and still provide specific information.

KEY IDEA! *Visual cues are defined for standard operating system objects and common actions such as move, copy, and creating shadows or shortcuts. Product-specific objects and actions should use these cues for common actions and use additional visual emphasis techniques to provide meaningful, memory-aiding feedback cues concerning product-specific actions during direct-manipulation operations. Part of the intuitiveness of direct-manipulation interfaces is that users should know what objects they are working with, what operations they are performing on those objects, and what are the valid target destinations for their actions.*

The Semantics of OOUIs

An OOUI utilizes a GUI for its set of componentry but adds to it a significant semantic content on the meaning of objects and user gestures.

John Tibbetts (1995)

There is a key difference in the semantics, or meanings in the interface, between GUIs and OOUIs. In a graphical user interface, the icons on the screen often only represent computer applications and computer data files. There are some relationships among these objects, and users can associate some meaning with these icons and the actions they perform on them. For example, dragging a data file icon onto a program icon starts the program and loads the data file. However, these are more system-level actions and meanings rather than product-level actions.

In an object-oriented interface, the icons on the screen represent objects that have definite relationships with other objects. If these objects are designed to fit users' tasks, then users can understand the relationships among objects. Then they can build conceptual models regarding the interface. They can utilize the power of working directly with objects by performing actions directly on them rather than working through applications. For example, dragging a customer object and a car object to a worksheet object on an automobile salesperson's computer desktop brings all of the relevant customer and car information together for the salesperson to complete the worksheet and sell a car. In addition to the basic objects I've discussed, groups of objects and sequences of objects and actions can be brought together as processes that users do as part of their tasks.

The OOUI Way: Drag and Drop

Direct manipulation allows users to easily perform common actions directly on their objects. There are six general types of actions that users can perform directly on objects: copy, create, move, connect, change, and discard. These types of actions should be understood by all users and should apply to all objects in the interface, not only to system-defined objects. Designers must work carefully to ensure that these basic direct-manipulation techniques are implemented for their objects consistently with the ways users work with system objects and objects from other programs.

KEY IDEA! *The power of users' models and metaphors can be invoked with well-designed object-oriented interfaces. Building product-specific objects and defining meaningful and intuitive direct-manipulation operations among product objects is a critical element of the user interface design for the product. Operations such as data transfer, automated processes, and communications can be provided to users as simple drag-and-drop actions among objects.*

The basic building blocks of an object-oriented interface can be used to construct very powerful and sophisticated task-oriented interfaces in any environment. The interfaces you see today on most computers are designed for users who work with information to make their business decisions. Members of this audience are called knowledge workers. As computers proliferate in areas such as manufacturing, distribution, and other services, the interfaces should be different, because the users, their tasks, and their goals are all different. Object-oriented interfaces allow users to work with objects that are representative of the environment in which they work, rather than objects the computer understands.

How Users Interact with OOUIs

An important step in improving usability and functionality is enabling users to directly interact with every aspect of a product's user interface. Instead of sifting through a complex maze of commands and pull-down menus, object-oriented applications enable users to directly interact with and manipulate every element or "object" on the screen. This direct interaction empowers the user, dramatically enhances the usability of the application, and improves the user's productivity.

Philippe Kahn (1993)

To Keyboard or To Mouse, That Is the OOUI Question

As with GUIs, well-designed OOUIs provide users with multiple interaction techniques to complete their tasks. Users should be able to do all of their tasks either from the keyboard or by using a mouse, or by switching back and forth between the keyboard and mouse. Both Windows 95 and OS/2 provide both DOS command-line interfaces within a window or full screen. The OS/2 command-line interface crosses system boundaries; that is, users can type any DOS, Windows, or OS/2 command from the OS/2 command-line prompt.

Users who know how to navigate within the computer system and who know the commands they would like to use may find the command-line interface quicker than menus or direct manipulation. Some users switch back and forth between the command-line window and the desktop because they can do some tasks quicker using commands, or they may not yet have figured out how to do some tasks using the interface menus or by direct manipulation.

Menus are also accessible by both keyboard and mouse. Most standard menu bar drop-down choices and pop-up menu choices have predefined standard keyboard shortcut keys. These are fast-path keyboard techniques to select menu choices without having to navigate through menus to display the menu choice. The menus do not need to be displayed to use shortcut keys. For example, standard editing choices have predefined shortcut keys—unfortunately, the standards for Windows and OS/2 interfaces are different, but both sets of shortcut keys are implemented in most products. The Windows guidelines reserve these shortcut keys: Cut (Ctrl+X), Copy (Ctrl+C), and Paste (Ctrl+V). The OS/2 guidelines use these shortcut keys: Cut (Shift+Delete), Copy (Ctrl+Insert), and Paste (Shift+Insert).

Special interface operations may also be performed using either the keyboard or the mouse. These operations include directly editing the title text of an object, displaying pop-up menus, switching programs, displaying the window list, and accessing the taskbar. Users can even move quickly around the desktop using the keyboard. The cursor keys will move the selection cursor from one object icon to another and users can also type the first letter of an object to move the cursor directly to that object. If there are multiple objects with that first letter, pressing the key multiple times will move the user to each object whose title begins with that letter.

The OOUI Mouse: A Powerful Weapon

The mouse is used for directly manipulating objects, that is, if the operating system, the products, and the objects themselves support direct manipulation. Let's hope they do! The mouse is also heavily used to access all types of menus, including the menu bar, drop-downs, toolbars, palettes, and pop-up menus.

In Chapter 9, I discussed the differences that grew between IBM and Microsoft over the use of mouse buttons for selection and direct manipulation. Microsoft's Windows began by using mouse button 1 for both object selection and direct manipulation. IBM's CUA interface architecture and the OS/2 Workplace Shell chose a different strategy—to separate selection from direct manipulation. Mouse button 1 is for selection while mouse button 2 is used for direct manipulation. This allows users a wider range of interaction techniques for both selection and direct manipulation that are complementary and don't overload one button on the mouse. Windows 95 has moved in this direction with *default drag and drop* using mouse button 1 and *nondefault drag and drop* using mouse button 2.

The selection and direct-manipulation operations can be customized in the properties views of the mouse object so users can customize the mouse button mappings they like to use on their computer.

The process of selection allows users to indicate which items they want to work with. Selection can be accomplished by using a pointing device, such as a mouse, or the keyboard. The selection process is designed to model how users work with objects in the real world. To work directly with objects, users don't need to select the item first. By doing something directly with an object, it is implicitly selected. In the real world, you don't necessarily have to select something before you work with it. This means that users don't have to select an object to drag it, and dragging an object doesn't disturb the selected items in the same area as the dragged object. To work with a group of objects, they must be explicitly selected before an action can be applied to the entire group.

The scope of selection is the area within which users select items. This is defined at a number of levels: within a control, a group of controls, a window, and the desktop. For example, users choosing items from a list box are within the scope of that one control. Each open window has a scope of its own; that is, when users select objects in one window that selection will not disturb selections in any other windows. This also applies to the desktop, where selections on the workplace don't affect selections made in any open windows.

There are three types of selection: single, multiple, and extended. These are differentiated by the selection results. *Single selection* allows users to select only one item at a time in the scope of selection. *Multiple selection* allows users to select one or more items at a time within a given scope. *Extended selection* allows users to select one item and then extend the selection to other items in the same scope of selection. All of these selections can be made with either the keyboard or the mouse, using a number of techniques. These techniques are: point selection, random-point selection, and point-to-endpoint selection.

Who decides which type of selection is appropriate for a given control or object? Designers decide which type to implement, but their judgments should be based on the type of selection users want in that situation. Don't restrict users to single selection when they really want to do multiple selection. On the other hand, if there is only one valid choice allowed at one time in a certain situation, don't allow users to do either extended or multiple selection. If no choice is required, it is called zero-based selection. If at least one choice must always be selected, it is called one-based selection. Again, who should determine the minimum number of selections allowed? Users should determine it; designers should design for it and allow users to do it easily. The various combinations of selection types and techniques make selection decisions very important in interface design.

OOUI Drag-and-Drop Techniques

Direct manipulation is a way for users to work directly with objects using a pointing device such as a mouse. There are usually a few actions that can be directly applied to many objects. These actions apply to both system-level and product-specific objects. They may be common actions such as move, copy, print, and delete. Direct manipulation is also called *drag and drop,* since users can pick up and drag objects and drop them on other objects. This implies that there is at least one source object and a target object for direct-manipulation operations.

There are predefined default results for the drag-and-drop actions. These defaults are determined by the types of objects involved as the source and target of the drag-and-drop operation. CUA (IBM, 1992) specifies the following principles for direct-manipulation operations:

◆ When possible, the result of dragging and dropping an object should be the result that users would expect, given the source object and target object being manipulated.

◆ The result of direct manipulation should be comparatively "safe"— that is, users should not lose information unexpectedly.

◆ Users should be able to override a default result to obtain a different result.

Initially, users are afraid that once they begin a drag-and-drop action, they can't change their mind while they are dragging objects around the desktop. Users sometimes don't want to let go of the mouse button for fear they will do some action they don't want. Don't worry! Just press the Esc key on the keyboard and the current direct-manipulation action will be canceled.

The combination of selection and direct manipulation techniques allows users to work directly with objects in many ways to perform whatever operations they'd like to do at the moment. For example, to create shadows of a set of objects, simply select the objects in one of a number of ways and then perform the create-shadow direct-manipulation action with the mouse to create the shadows at the target destination.

Interacting with Objects and Views

Views allow users to work with multiple instances of objects at the same time. For example, users may wish to work with both the outline view and composed view of a document at the same time. Views also allow users to work differently with objects depending on their tasks. To restructure a document, users need only the outline view and don't have to use the composed view of the document.

Views allow users instant access to an object and its views. From an unopened object on the desktop, users can open any view of that object. From a view of an object, users can also open other views of the object. The same view may also be simultaneously opened in multiple windows. All views of an object are dynamically interrelated. For example, users may wish to open two composed views of a document in separate windows to work on different sections. The program and operating system must make sure that any changes to a view that affect other open views are displayed immediately wherever they apply. For example, changing the page format of a document in one composed view should also change the page format of the same document opened in another composed view. Changes in a view that are local, such as rearranging objects in an icon view of a container, don't affect other views of the same object.

The OOUI Editing Model

Users edit objects either by indirect- or direct-manipulation. Indirect manipulation techniques use the clipboard model via menus in similar ways as do Windows applications. The clipboard is a system object that holds entire objects or parts of objects and can hold any type of object. Users can copy, create, and move objects to and from the clipboard.

KEY IDEA! *One nice feature in OS/2 is the ability to use the clipboard across DOS, Windows, and OS/2 programs. Actually, users can choose either to make individual "private" clipboards for each session they are working in, or to share data across environments and programs by making the clipboard "public." That is, users can cut and paste data and objects to and from the OS/2 clipboard from any program, regardless of which environment the information was created in. This is a valuable tool in today's mixed application and data environment. It relieves users from having to remember the application and environment aspects of their work so they can concentrate on their tasks rather than on the computer system.*

The object-oriented nature of today's operating system and the more sophisticated direct-manipulation techniques available to users allow them to do much of their editing directly, rather than through the clipboard. The clipboard model will still be used by users migrating from a Windows GUI environment, by keyboard users, and by users editing information across DOS, Windows, and OS/2. Let users edit information and objects using any combination of indirect- and direct-manipulation techniques.

Migrating from GUIs to OOUIs

Unbundling Applications into Components with OLE and OpenDoc

Remember component software? Those little pieces of code that were supposed to be the building blocks for creating custom applications? . . . Suddenly, component software is back. And you know what? This time, the pieces just might come together.

Michael J. Miller (1996)

Software products are slowly migrating from the application-oriented world to an object-oriented model. Rather than providing large, self-contained applications, products are beginning to provide users with tightly integrated sets of objects that work together to form a product or task environment. Steve Cook (1992) sums it up well in his section of the *AIS 92 Proceedings,* entitled "The Death of Applications":

> The consequences of object technology on the way software is delivered to end users will be considerable. Applications as we currently know them will no longer be built. Instead, software packages will be of two kinds, which I will call components and frameworks. Users will configure combinations of these two kinds of software to create a working environment. This environment will be tailored for a particular individual's tasks much more than is possible with today's monolithic applications.

The key word here is *components,* both from the programming and user interface perspective.

Michael J. Miller (1996) defines component software well:

> The concept is simple: Take the best parts of today's huge, standalone programs and combine them to create applications tailored to our individual needs. For instance, you might take a good spell-checker and combine it with your favorite presentation program or with your Web browser.

In the past, and also in most of the current key products, there is considerable overlap in function among many applications, regardless of their specialized area. For example, today's word processors have sophisticated ways of working with text. Users also want some graphic capabilities while they are writing. Therefore, even though they are word processing programs, they also include some simple drawing features. On the other hand, designers of the major graphics and presentation programs understand that users include text with their graphics, so they provide text capabilities. Users end up paying for larger applications than they want or have room for on their systems. Consequently, they also end up with overlapping functions across applications. How many of the applications you use have some spell-checking, text, and graphic capabilities of their own? Doesn't it make sense to use a set of word processing objects, a set of graphic objects, and one spell-checking tool? Wouldn't it be great to have only one dictionary and spell-check object that you could use with all documents and objects, regardless of the program they were created with?

Lotus Development Corporation migrated their cc:Mail product to work with OS/2's Workplace Shell. Rather than a single application, as in previous versions, cc:Mail now provides users with an environment where they can act on mail messages by dragging and dropping icons. For example, users can reply to a message by dragging it to an out-box icon. cc:Mail objects can be deleted by dragging them to the OS/2 shredder. Users can also drag objects from other OS/2 Workplace Shell products over to a message object to mail them to other users.

Although the underlying structure of Apple's popular and user-friendly interface is still mostly application oriented, Apple is quickly moving in the object-oriented direction. Cohen, Raines, and Norr (1993) reviewed a new Apple open-document strategy: "The Apple-developed technology, called Amber, is designed to bring about a gradual shift from the application-centered approach that characterizes desktop computing toward a more document-centered approach." Documents created using this architecture will store and display any type of data and allow users to edit any data type directly from within the document. This is the composite document approach I've been describing for the object-oriented interface environment.

New technologies of major software companies are showing promise in providing the underlying object models and programming environments. IBM has developed SOM and DSOM (System Object Model and Distributed SOM). Microsoft has enhanced its OLE (object linking and embedding) technology. Finally, Apple, IBM, and others are working to support OpenDoc, a framework technology to embed objects within other objects. OpenDoc is an open-architectured compound document technology that allows applications to talk to each other dynamically, so that they can exchange life data, as opposed to OLE's bit-mapped representational links.

Objects in object-oriented programs are standardized parts that are designed to fit and work together in many different situations. IBM's System Object Model is the object technology underlying OS/2's object-oriented user interface, the Workplace Shell. SOM provides the operating system services that manage the creation and maintenance of program objects. By providing object management services at this level, rather than at the language level, OS/2 offers developers unique benefits, such as the ability to access object libraries across programs. From users' perspective, SOM can be used to provide them with real-world objects rather than applications at the interface level. SOM is being developed to run across hardware and software platforms.

Because there is an evolutionary step from the application-oriented world to the object-oriented interface environment, IBM CUA interface architects and OS/2 designers were very concerned about how users would react to the OS/2 Workplace Shell. In 1991, surveys were sent out to IBM customers and vendors, asking their opinions on a number of interface design issues. These issues covered a number of interface areas, including: pop-up menus; clipboard support; window and object menus; menu bars for system objects, folders, and work-areas; progress indicators; and keyboard support. Customer and vendor feedback was influential in the final design decisions regarding the OS/2 user interface. The voice of the user was being heard!

OOUIs and OO Programming: Similar, Yet Different

> In the last three years, nearly a thousand product announcements have included the magic phrase "object-oriented." The pace is still accelerating: In 1992 alone, PC Week Labs estimates that there will be more than half again this number. When a label is used this broadly, some precision is lost. What, precisely, are the components of an object-oriented technology, and why should end users care?
>
> Peter Coffee (1992)

Many people confuse object-oriented user interfaces (OOUIs) with *object-oriented programming* (OOP). They are very different, but related, areas that will become more related and less different as time evolves. There is no causal relationship between OOUIs and OOP—just because one of them is available or used doesn't necessarily mean the other is also there. *Object-orientation* applies at both the interface level and the programming level, but it doesn't mean the same thing, and its "users" are very different.

Object-oriented programming and the OOP acronym are now popular buzzwords in the computing environment. A *Business Week* special report (Schwartz, 1993) talked of new approaches to software development that are starting to get big results: "And just on the horizon are potentially huge gains from innovations such as object-oriented programming, a method for creating intuitive software out of prefabricated 'objects' that behave like objects in the real world." Not without an object-oriented *user interface,* they don't! My observations and experiences are that when some programmers obtain more sophisticated software technologies and tools, they then have new and exciting ways to build even worse user interfaces than before. *OOP skills don't necessarily make a programmer a skilled OOUI designer!*

The reader's imagination is further stimulated by another prophesy: "In the future, software will be even easier to create and use, thanks to object-oriented programming. At the Center for Advanced Technologies, individual programmers are achieving 100 percent leaps in productivity via such methods," says Jerrold M. Groshow, the lab's director. Note the reference that OOP will provide easier creation of software *and* software that is easier to use. As Porgy sang to Bess, "It ain't necessarily so!"

Remember, the programmer's world is very different from the user's world. *Programming objects do not necessarily correspond to user objects!* Object-oriented programming environments can enable OOUI development; however, OOUIs can be built using more traditional procedural languages and development tools. That is, an OOUI doesn't require OOP! At the same time, an object-oriented *programming environment* doesn't mean that an object-oriented *interface* must be or will be developed. An OOP environment doesn't necessarily provide an OOUI.

Don't fall into the trap of merging the areas of object-oriented interfaces and object-oriented programming. They are both new technologies, but their benefits are geared toward different audiences. OOP is similar to having new and better methods to build the guts of an automobile, but these methods aren't readily observable to the driver of the car. They provide a better working environment for the car designer and builders. OOUIs provide users with buttons, knobs, dials, and objects to work with. Users try to get from one place to another. They want and deserve the best of both worlds in their cars and in their software—a product that runs well under the hood, and an interface that hums, too!

KEY IDEA! *Good user interface design, even object-oriented interface design, should be somewhat independent of the underlying programming environment. The goal ought to be to build the best and most appropriate user interface for a product regardless of the hardware and software environment. However, in the real world of computing, user interfaces are often "the tail trying to wag the dog." A more realistic, user-centered goal would be to build the best user interface possible within the constraints of the hardware and software programming environment.*

What if users need and want a better user interface than can be built by your current programming environment, tools, and resources? Who wins in this situation? Unfortunately, the limitations of the programming environment and the development effort usually end up producing a less-than-optimal user interface. In the end, users lose.

The problem with object-oriented programming is that it is still a fairly new computing paradigm. Even skilled programmers in other procedural-oriented programming environments must learn new skills and techniques to become experienced in object-oriented analysis, design, and programming. It is also not easy for user interface designers to move to the object-oriented interface paradigm, partly due to a lack of nontechnical prototyping tools for building object-oriented interfaces.

Are OOUIs Ahead of Their Time?

> *Personal computing changed the way the people worked. Object computing will change the way the world works. It is the wave of the future, and it is here today.*
> Philippe Kahn (1993)

Most of the software available today, in the DOS and Windows environments, is definitely application oriented and is just now implementing graphical user interfaces. Object-oriented programming techniques are also just now being incorporated into popular development tools across all software operating system environments.

What's Next for OOUIs?

One of the phrases I used years ago when speaking about the evolution of user interfaces was "The 'C' in CUA doesn't stand for *cement*." You work with the latest user interface architectures, guidelines, enabling tools, and operating systems to develop new or improved product interfaces. Meanwhile, operating system vendors, tool vendors, and user interface architects are already developing newer versions of user interface technology that will gradually work their way into the operating systems and tools you use. It is an evolving cycle of technology and development.

Are object-oriented interfaces, as we know them today, the ultimate user interfaces of the future? Most everyone agrees that they are not, but object-oriented interfaces are still in their infancy. It is very difficult to find outstanding GUI or OOUI product interfaces. Users can look forward to many years of research, development, and end use as OOUIs evolve to help them be more productive. OOUIs should also help make computers less *technical* (and less scary) even as they become more and more *complex*. Then, one would hope, we'll be primed for another paradigm shift. Collins (1990) points out:

> New technologies, and new ways of understanding users, will produce systems that will make today's interfaces look slow and clumsy by comparison. But today's best interfaces are too seldom found. Users are too often saddled with interaction techniques based on obsolete technology. Inventing a better future for them is up to us.

References

Cohen, Raines and Henry Norr. 1993. Amber: Apple's answer to OLE. *MacWEEK* 7(20), (May 7): 1.

Collins, David. 1990. *What Is an Object-Oriented User Interface?* IBM Research Paper.

Cook, Steve. 1992. Beyond the desktop. *AIS 92 Conference Proceedings* (March 17–19), London, England, pp. 81–85.

IBM Corporation. 1992. *Object-Oriented Interface Design: IBM Common User Access Guidelines.* New York: QUE.

Miller, Michael. 1996. Rebuilding componentware. *PC Magazine* (June 25, 1996): 29.

Schwartz, Evan. 1993. The power of software. *Business Week* (June 14): 76.

PART THREE

THE USER INTERFACE DESIGN PROCESS

The process of building the application with the end user provides common ground, where the developer and the end user can reach an understanding as to how the application will appear and behave.

David Linthicum (1995)

Roadmap for Part 3: The User Interface Design Process

Chapter 12: An Iterative User Interface Design Process

This chapter covers an iterative user interface design process from start to finish. Detailed examples and a case study are offered for the reader. A design team approach is recommended. This process can be used for both GUI design and object-oriented interface design.

An Iterative User Interface Design Process

You can use an eraser on the drafting table or a sledge hammer on the construction site.

Frank Lloyd Wright

Follow a Design Team Approach

Design, even just the usability, let alone the aesthetics, requires a team of people with extremely different talents. You need somebody, for example, with good visual design abilities and skills, and someone who understands behavior. You need somebody who's a good prototyper and someone who knows how to test and observe behavior. All of these skills turn out to be very different and it's a very rare individual who has more than one or two of them. I've really come to appreciate the need for this kind of interdisciplinary design team. And the design team has to work closely with the marketing and engineering teams.

Donald Norman (1996)

Just as following design principles, guidelines, and standards doesn't guarantee a usable interface, there is no magic design and development process that can guarantee a successful product. The type of interface design process you follow should be tailored to your particular business, users, and development environment. A large company may have separate departments devoted to each area of the development process. Other organizations may rely on only one person or a few individuals. Regardless of the size of your organization, you should follow a *design team* approach. No one department or individual typically has all of the skills to do all of the required steps in the process.

For example, does your group have the skills to gather user requirements? Do you have usability testing expertise available? Do you have a graphics designer on staff? If you or your company don't have all the skills to complete the development process, there are many consultants and software design and development firms that can help with any and all aspects of your product design and development.

Baecker et al. (1995) point out:

> Interface design and development require software engineering and programming skills, of course, but can also benefit from the skills of graphic and industrial designers; human factors engineers and psychologists who understand human cognitive, perceptual, and motor skills; technical writers and training specialists' people knowledgeable in group and organizational dynamics; and those with expertise in input devices, display technologies, interaction techniques, dialogue design, and design methodologies. . . . The growing use of sound, voice, video, animation, and three-dimensional display draw upon still other specialties.

KEY IDEA! *An ideal product design team should possess the following skills: task analysis, programming, user interface design, instructional design, graphic design, technical writing, human factors, and usability testing. Users will buy into the design effort if they are represented on the design team. Some team members may have skills in more than one of these areas, but no one team member will have all of the skills necessary to design both the user interface and the product code. Business knowledge experts should also be part of the design team.*

Major software products follow the design team approach. Sullivan (1996) describes how Microsoft Windows 95 was designed: "The design team was truly interdisciplinary, with people trained in product design, graphic design, usability testing, and computer science." Instructional designers know how people learn while using computers. Graphics designers know how to design icons and use color and graphics. (Chapter 13 discusses some of their design techniques.)

User-Involved and Learner-Centered Design

In the past, software design and user interfaces were totally driven by the current technologies and the current systems on which the software was built. This is called *system-driven* or *technology-driven design* (see Figure 12.1). Users were not factored into the equation at all. Users were offered software function with whatever interface developers were able to provide. Computer power was limited and expensive, so there was barely enough power to provide program function and harness current technologies.

Since the early 1980s, the focus has been on *user-centered design* (Norman and Draper, 1986), where users are somewhat involved in the design process, but usually in a passive role, as the target of user task analyses and requirements gathering. Part of the human-computer interaction (HCI) community is moving beyond user-centered design to new methodologies called *user-involved design* and *learner-centered design*. Bannon (1991) describes user-involved design:

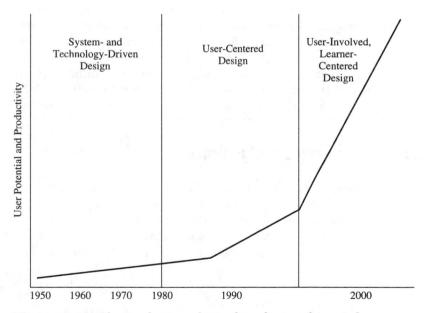

Figure 12.1   The evolution of interface design, from Soloway and Pryor (1996).

A more radical departure from current thinking within the mainstream HCI world is to look at users not simply as objects of study, but as active agents within the design process itself. This involvement of users in design is both a means for promoting democratization in the organizational change process and a way to ensure that the resulting computer system adequately meets the needs of the users.

Learner-centered design (LCD) focuses on enhancing the learning experience while performing tasks. Soloway and Pryor (1996) remark, "Ease of use, valuable as it certainly is, is too limited a vision. We need to raise our expectations for what computationally based technologies can support. We need to address the real issue of our times: nurturing the intellectual growth of children and adults, supporting them as they grapple with ideas, unleashing and training their imaginations, and developing all manner of expertise." This new design approach is discussed in great detail in the special section on learner-centered design in the April 1996 (Volume 39, Number 4) issue of *Communications of the ACM.*

KEY IDEA! *As you involve users in the design process, be careful not to rely only on user input to drive your user-centered or user-involved design. Business processes and new technologies will also drive system and interface design. Don't get so caught up with how users work now that you can't design for how they will work in the future! Users don't necessarily know about new directions your business is headed in and what technologies you plan to focus on. Integrate learner-centered approaches into designs driven by other forces.*

A Four-Phase Interface Design Process

The primary advantage of the spiral model is that its range of options accommodates the good features of existing software process models, while its risk-driven approach avoids many of their difficulties. In appropriate situations, the spiral model becomes equivalent to one of the existing process models. In other situations, it provides guidance on the best mix of existing approaches to a given project.

Barry Boehm (1988)

Developing the user interface may or may not be separate from the rest of the product development process. However, the focus is different from what it is in other areas of software development. The focus is on the interface elements and objects that users perceive and use, rather than program functionality. In many product development projects, user interface design and product programming can proceed in parallel, especially in early stages of product development. Later in the development cycle, user interface concerns and usability test feedback should drive program design.

In this chapter, I will define and walk through a process specifically geared toward designing and developing the appropriate user interface for your product. Figure 12.2 graphically shows the iterative design process. The four major phases in the process are:

Phase 1: *Gather* and *analyze* user information.

Phase 2: *Design* the user interface.

Phase 3: *Construct* the user interface.

Phase 4: *Validate* the user interface.

Although I use this process to design object-oriented user interfaces, it can be followed even if you are designing traditional application-oriented interfaces or GUIs. The process is also independent of the hardware and software platform, operating system, and tools you may be using for your particular product. Both the IBM and Microsoft user interface design guides promote an iterative interface design process. The CUA interface design guide (IBM, 1992) first described an iterative interface design process and used a car dealership sales product as a design case study. This book is a good reference if you are inter-

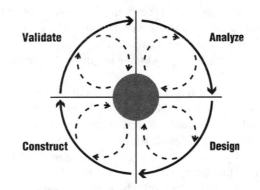

Figure 12.2 An iterative user interface design and development process.

ested in reading more about the object-oriented interface design process and want to see another design example.

The Windows 95 user interface style guide (Microsoft, 1995) also briefly discusses interface design methodology. The Windows guide describes three design phases—Design, Prototype, and Test—where gathering and analyzing user information are included in the design phase. There is no case study in the Windows design guide.

This chapter walks through the interface design process using a case study example. The major emphasis will be on the first two phases of the process, following the focus of this book.

KEY IDEA! *Start small if this is your first time through this type of an interface and product design and development process. Don't put too much pressure on your first attempts at iterative object-oriented interface design, especially if this is a major departure from your traditional product design process. Start with a pilot program rather than the "heart and soul" programs critical to your business. You may run into more political roadblocks within your company than technical obstacles when you introduce new processes and methodologies into a development organization.*

The Iterative Nature of Interface Design

Let's set development costs that occur in the analysis phase as a factor of 1. Changes made during design increase cost by a factor of 10. Changes made later in development increase that factor to 100.

                                    The Development Methodology Rule of 10

Any successful user interface design process must be iterative. *Webster's 1980 New Collegiate Dictionary* defines *iterative* as "relating to or being a computational procedure in which replication of a cycle of operations produces results which approximate the desired result more and more closely." In simple terms, this means that you really can't produce a well-designed interface without periodically going back and checking with your users. This includes both gathering their requirements and testing the interface with users themselves. Take the time to find out what users want and need. Be committed to providing the best user interface for them. User acceptance and product usability should be just as important as program functionality.

Traditional product design and development methodologies often follow a "waterfall" process. Their defined phases are similar to those I've described here—analyze, design, build, test—but the process is a *linear* rather than an *iterative* one. Any software development methodology you use today should promote the concept of iteration.

There are numerous ways to visually show what I mean by an iterative design process (see Figure 12.3 A through D). I have used a spiral starting in the center and widening out through the four phases to show that iterations early in the process can be quick and informal, becoming longer and more formal later (A). I have also used an inward spiral to show a gradual narrowing of focus and honing in on the appropriate user interface for the product (B). Both the CUA and Windows design guides show a circular process that keeps cycling through the different phases (C). Finally, I found it best to use a circle to highlight the process flowing through the four major phases, with spirals to show that at any time, in any phase, you may return to a central core of information, analyses, and techniques to further refine your product interface design (D).

KEY IDEA! *Designers often ask, "How do I know when an iterative design process is finished?" The answer is, "It depends." You may run short of time, money, or resources to further iterate the design. It is hoped that the criterion for completing an iterative product design is that the* validation *phase shows users' performance data and subjective ratings of the product meet or exceed the product's planned goals and objectives (see Chapter 7).*

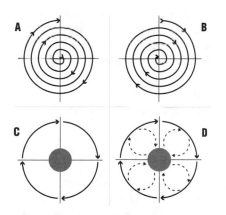

Figure 12.3 Different ways to depict the iterative process.

Continually incorporate iterative design revisions until you have met or succeeded the defined interface goals, or if you have reached a critical development deadline. Always keep users in mind when you reach critical design checkpoints. You must have a user interface designer involved who can be an advocate for the user community during the design process.

The Mandel Manor Hotels: An Interface Design Case Study

KEY IDEA! *A sample product is used in this chapter to illustrate design concepts and to show practical examples of user interface tips and techniques. This case study illustrates the steps of the interface design process. This product is fairly easy to describe and design in a book, yet it is representative of the type of software interfaces that you design and develop for your own business or products.*

Most of the projects I have worked on in the past few years have been in customer service industries, for example, banks, insurance companies, and telephone companies. The software programs designed are typically used in-house, where customer representatives collect and view information while interacting with a customer on the telephone or in person. This type of program is representative of many business software projects under development today.

As a software consultant and educator, I travel a great deal and constantly interact with hotel, airline, rental car, and travel agency representatives as I plan and conduct my activities around the world. I am a member of just about every frequent-flier and frequent-stayer program there is, so I know the *customer's viewpoint* of a reservation and customer service system very well. You may also be familiar with these systems from the traveler's viewpoint.

Welcome to a new chain of hotels called the Mandel Manor Hotels. As a new concept designed for the weary traveler, one of the goals is a program that would provide convenient ways for hotel customers to perform activities such as viewing hotel information, making reservations, and viewing their Mandel Manor Club "Honored Guest" program activity. Travel agents and Mandel Manor Hotels customer service representatives will also use this program to conduct activities related to their own particular job.

KEY IDEA! *A key design goal is to provide a similar interface for all users—customers, travel agents, and customer service representatives. With the proliferation of the Internet, this interface should run as a standalone PC program and as an Internet program accessed through the Web.*

Phase 1: Gather and Analyze User Information

Because system design is so intimately involved with how people work, designers need better approaches to gathering customer requirements. The current interest in participatory design, ethnographic techniques, and field research techniques grows out of the recognition that traditional interviewing and surveying techniques are not adequate for designing today's applications. These new approaches seek to improve requirements definition by creating new relationships between designers and customers.

Karen Holtzblatt and Hugh R. Beyer (1995)

We need to do a better job of thinking about technology from the point of view of all individuals—how they work, how they think, what they need to work and think more effectively.

Bill Gates (1990)

Here's where you must start—with your users. Before you can design and build any system, first define the problems that customers or users want solved and figure out how they do their jobs. Learn about your users' capabilities and the tasks they perform. Watch and learn from actual users of your programs. Notice the hardware and software constraints of their current computer systems and constantly remind yourself not to restrict your designs to what users currently can do with the system. Your solution must satisfy not only the current needs of users, but also their future needs.

There are key questions to ask during the user analysis phase. If you don't know the answers to these questions, don't assume that your design and development team or your marketing or sales group know the answers. The only way to find the answers is to observe users and ask them questions. A special section of *Communications of the ACM* (Holtzblatt and Beyer, 1995), entitled "Requirements Gathering: The Human Factor," devotes a number of articles to the emerging field of user analysis and requirements gathering. This is a good starting point if you are interested in learning more about this area.

Phase 1, gathering and analyzing activities, can be broken down into five steps:

1. Determine user profiles.
2. Perform user task analyses.
3. Gather user requirements.
4. Analyze user environments.
5. Match requirements to user tasks.

KEY IDEA! *There is an art to designing and asking questions, and to analyzing user feedback. Be careful what you ask users and how you analyze what they say. Borenstein (1991) says, "Listen to your users, but ignore what they say." Users tend to like whatever they are currently using, even though they will acknowledge that it could be better. It is difficult to get users to break out of their mindset concerning current systems and technology. Users are not necessarily aware of new technologies and business trends. The user analysis phase gathers information from and about users that will be factored in with parallel analyses of new technologies and business activities.*

Step 1: Determine User Profiles

User profiles answer the question, "*Who* are your users?" *User profiles* allow you to determine user demographics, skills, knowledge, background, and any other important information needed regarding *all* users of your planned system. How do you gather this information? Conduct user interviews and surveys, observe and videotape users, and also review other sources of information, such as industry reports, reviews, and press or marketing materials.

Step 2: Perform User Task Analyses

User task analyses determine *what* users want to do and *how* they accomplish their tasks. I will not cover a particular task analysis methodology here; rather I present the questions that must be answered by any methodology. In addition to procedure-based task analysis, there are cognitive-based task analysis methodologies that focus on decisions users make while performing their work.

Whatever formal and informal task analysis techniques you use should answer these *what* and *how* questions:

- What tasks do users perform?
- What tasks are most critical?
- What steps are taken to perform tasks?
- What are users' goals for performing tasks?
- What information is needed to complete tasks?
- What tools (computer and otherwise) are used to complete tasks?
- What output is generated from user tasks?
- How do users do their work (manual, computer, telephone, etc.)?

- How do users interact with others in their tasks?
- How do tasks flow in the business processes?
- How frequently do users perform tasks?
- How would a computer or other computer software help users with tasks?

Step 3: Gather User Requirements

Building a system for a 2,000-pound gorilla makes it clear that user requirements are the driving force behind any project.

Jerreld Hannis (1994)

User requirements gathering and analysis answer the question, "*What* do your users expect the product and interface to do for them?" Almost all software development projects collect some user requirements. In addition to determining the *functional requirements* for a software product, user requirements should help determine the appropriate *user interface design* and what the interface should look and feel like. Here are key questions to ask:

- What core technologies do users require?
- How much are users and managers willing to pay for a product?
- Who installs the products?
- Who supports the products once they are installed?

User requirements are typically gathered through focus groups, structured interviews, and user surveys. Some common user requirements for business programs are that a new product should:

- Reduce paperwork.
- Reduce user errors.
- Automate current manual processes.
- Improve transaction processing speed.

Step 4: Analyze User Environments

User environment analysis answers the question, "*Where* do your users perform their tasks?" You must determine *environmental* characteristics that may impact how users do their work. Collect information regarding:

- Physical work environment (light, noise, space, temperature, computers, telephones, people, etc.)
- User location and mobility (office, home, on-site, mobile, etc.)
- Human factors, ergonomics, and physical considerations (vision, hearing, sitting/standing, keyboard abilities, etc.)
- Users with special needs (accessibility, and physical, cognitive, speech, and other disabilities)
- Internationalization and other cultural considerations (translation, colors, icons, text, messages, etc.)

Some environments should have more of an impact on product design than others. If you are developing a product for an office worker, the office environment may have a small impact. However, if you are developing a product for a hospital operating room or for traders on the Stock Exchange, the environment is critical to the design of the interface and also to the testing of the product interface.

There are numerous sources for guidelines, tips, and techniques in these areas of software design. Some design considerations might need to be built into your product, but many special design aids are already available in software operating systems. For example, both OS/2 and Windows 95 offer ways to configure the screen, keyboard, mouse, and other input or output devices for users with special needs. Chapter 14 of the Microsoft (1995) guide, "Special Design Considerations," is a well-written reference in this area.

Step 5: Match Requirements to User Tasks

We do not now (and in fact may never) understand human activities in enough detail to merely list the attributes computer systems would have to incorporate in order to meet these requirements.

John M. Carroll (1995)

Matching requirements to user tasks is a reality check. Sometimes user requirements may not be realistic for the tasks they are trying to perform. In that case, you must manage users' perceptions and requirements so they won't expect more than what they will get. Also, check to see if you may be going beyond what users really require to get their job done. If users and customers need only text information, don't go overboard and give them full multimedia capability at a huge cost that is "nice to have," but beyond their needs and requirements.

By reviewing user tasks and requirements, you will see where certain interface elements are required by users to perform tasks. In the case study, in addition to text information, customers need to be able to view and print photographs of hotels and maps of hotel locations. This tells you to design an interface that supports more than just textual information. This matching process also tells you about product function that must be implemented to enable customer requirements.

For example, Mandel Manor Hotels customers demand up-to-date account information. This requires system databases to be frequently updated so customer and member information is current to within a few days of a customer request.

Results of Phase 1

Both customers (including Mandel Manor Club members) and customer service representatives are users of the software program. Results of phase 1 analyses are described in Table 12.1. This is a sample of analysis results, not a complete listing. For example, there are obviously more than five or six tasks that can be performed with the product. Results from each step should also have detailed backup information describing the source of the information, how the results were calculated, and how to access source data if needed.

Returning to the User Analysis Phase

The iterative method promotes returning to the user analysis stage to check whether your user profiles, tasks, environments, or requirements have changed during the design and development process. You must periodically return to phase 1 to update your user analyses. Otherwise, you might build a good product, but it won't meet current and future user needs. It would meet only their past needs.

Phase 2: Design the User Interface

On the order of 70 percent of product cost is spent on design of the user interface.

Bill Buxton (1991)

Designing the user interface for a software product usually requires a significant commitment of time and resources. The design phase progresses through a number of well-defined steps that should be followed *in sequence*. It is very tempting to start coding the final product now, rather than designing the interface. Follow the steps through the design process before you code the final design.

TABLE 12.1 Phase 1: User Analysis Results

Analysis Results	Customers/Program Members	Service Representatives
Step 1: User Profiles	◆ Female and male ◆ Adult ◆ Mostly USA, some International ◆ English-speaking skills ◆ Minimal computer skills ◆ No previous knowledge of program	◆ Female and male ◆ Adult ◆ Mostly USA, some International ◆ English-speaking skills ◆ Intermediate computer skills ◆ Previous training on program
Step 2: User Tasks	◆ View hotel information and rates ◆ Make/view/update reservations ◆ View/update certain account information ◆ Complete Club application ◆ Redeem hotel awards ◆ Print/save information and reservations	◆ View hotel information and rates ◆ Make/view/update reservations ◆ View/update all account information ◆ Complete Club application ◆ Redeem hotel awards ◆ Make account/reservations corrections and revisions ◆ Offer specials and discounts
Step 3: User Requirements	◆ Requires little or no training ◆ Requires little time ◆ Available 24 hours a day ◆ Able to view and print graphic and text information about hotels (pictures, maps, directions, etc.) ◆ Familiar "windows" interface style ◆ Successful task completion ◆ No other tools/programs required ◆ Up-to-date account and reservation information provided ◆ Tasks can be interrupted and canceled	◆ Requires minimal training ◆ Able to use program while customer is on telephone ◆ Similar interface style to customer's product ◆ Requires minimal technical support ◆ Up-to-date account and reservation information provide ◆ Acceptable system response time for customer on the telephone ◆ Tasks can be interrupted and canceled

Step 4:	◆ PC—Standalone program using local database
User Environments	◆ PC—Internet program using system database
	◆ Usable at home, office, or while traveling
	◆ Minimal computer system and telephone requirements
Step 5: Matching Requirements to User Tasks	◆ Hotel photos, maps, and other information must be available for viewing and printing to meet customer requirements
	◆ Customer profile and account information must be up to date to meet customer requirements

◆ Networked PCs used in a telephone-based customer service environment
◆ Multiple service representatives using system simultaneously
◆ Multiple service representatives accessing networked database simultaneously
◆ Standardized PC workstations and telephone systems

◆ Networked PC system must be capable of handling multiple customer service representative requests simultaneously with customers on the telephone
◆ Similar tasks must be performed with the same interface by service representatives and customers to ensure service representatives can support customer help requests

Phase 2, design, includes the following steps:

1. Define product usability goals and objectives.
2. Develop user scenarios and tasks.
3. Define interface objects and actions.
4. Determine object icons, views, and visual representations.
5. Design object and window menus.
6. Refine visual designs.

Step 1: Define Product Usability Goals and Objectives

Interface usability was discussed in detail in Chapter 7. Early in a product's design, you must determine just what you expect the product to do for users so those goals are clearly embedded in the minds of everyone working on the project. I was often amazed in some consulting projects that no one on the product development team could state or point to any documented product usability goals and objectives.

KEY IDEA! *How can you tell if a product works if you haven't even defined what is a usable system? It's like drawing a target around an arrow after it has been shot, rather than aiming an arrow at a target and seeing how close you got to it!*

Design goals are best expressed in terms of users' behavior and their performance terms, such as how long tasks take and how many errors are expected. Here are four areas in which goals and objectives are most appropriate (see Chapter 7 for more information):

◆ Usefulness
◆ Effectiveness
◆ Learnability
◆ Attitude

Table 12.2 lists some sample product goals and objectives for Mandel Manor Hotels system. These goals and objectives should drive the design of the product interface.

TABLE 12.2   Phase 2: Product Goals and Objectives

Product Goals and Objectives	Customers/Program Members	Service Representatives
Usefulness	Goal: ◆ Users will be able to use the program to perform their tasks Objective: ◆ 100% of the users will be able to use the system to perform a task after the first attempt	Goal: ◆ Users will be able to use the program to perform their tasks Objective: ◆ 100% of the users will be able to use the system to perform a task after training
Effectiveness	Goal: ◆ Users will be more productive using the program (compared to current manual processes) Objective: ◆ 100% of the users will complete their tasks within given time constraints	Goal: ◆ Users will be more productive using the program (compared to current manual processes) Objective: ◆ 100% of the users will complete their tasks within given time constraints
Learnability	Goal: ◆ Minimal user training will be needed Objective: ◆ Users will be able to use the product successfully after doing a tutorial	Goal: ◆ Minimal user training will be needed Objective: ◆ Users will be able to use the product successfully after completing 4 hours of training
Attitude	Goal: ◆ Users will be satisfied with the product Objective: ◆ Users will rate their satisfaction with the product at a high level	Goal: ◆ Users will be satisfied with the product Objective: ◆ Users will rate their satisfaction with the product at a high level

Step 2: Develop User Scenarios and Tasks

Computer systems and applications can, and should, be viewed as transformations of user tasks and their supporting social practices. In this sense, user interaction scenarios are a particularly pertinent medium for representing, analyzing, and planning how a computer system might impact its users' activities and experiences. They comprise a vocabulary for design and evaluation that is rich and yet evenly accessible to all the stakeholders in a development project.

John M. Carroll (1995)

It is difficult to define exactly what a scenario is, compared to a user task. A *scenario* is typically a high-level description of what the user does. I like to describe a scenario as a *sequence of user tasks* or events that make up a common transaction. "Buying lunch" is an example of a high-level scenario that would be composed of many smaller tasks such as going to a restaurant, ordering food, eating lunch, and paying for the meal. Tasks can be further decomposed into *subtasks,* if necessary.

KEY IDEA! *Remember, this is an iterative design process! The scenarios you develop now to drive the definition of the user interface will be the basis for testing the usability of the interface later. If scenarios don't drive the design of the appropriate interface, it is likely that later the interface will drive the scenarios. That is, you actually will develop scenarios that the* interface will allow, *rather than scenarios that* users want to perform.

In Step 2, develop as many user scenarios as possible. The more scenarios you develop, the less likely you will miss any key objects and actions needed in the user interface. If you have a range of users and skills, be sure to develop scenarios that cover the entire range of users and skills performing the range of tasks. Designing computer systems based on user scenarios has become an important part of user-centered system design. For a more theoretical discussion of scenarios, read John Carroll's (1995) book, *Scenario-Based Design: Envisioning Work and Technology in System Development.*

Table 12.3 presents some sample user scenarios and tasks for the Mandel Manor Hotels system.

Step 3: Define Interface Objects and Actions

This step is probably the most difficult (and most important) stage in the design process. If you can't figure out the appropriate set of objects, how can you expect users to understand, remember, or use the objects?

There are a number of activities in Step 3:

a. Derive objects, data, and actions from user scenarios and tasks.

b. Review and refine object and action lists with users.

c. Draw an object relationships diagram.

d. Complete an object direct-manipulation matrix.

TABLE 12.3 Phase 2: User Scenarios and Tasks

Customers/Program Members	Service Representatives
Scenario: Customer wishes to update telephone number in customer profile and see if latest hotel stay has been recorded. Customer also sends a comment card to the company.	Scenario: Customer telephones wishing to redeem account points for free hotel stay award and reserve a hotel room Customer wishes to receive a fax of the reservation and award.
Customer Tasks: ◆ Enters Mandel Manor Club account number and password ◆ Opens customer profile ◆ Updates telephone number ◆ Opens account summary ◆ Views latest recorded hotel stay ◆ Fills out comment card ◆ Sends comment card	Service Representative Tasks: ◆ Finds member's Mandel Manor Club account ◆ Validates member's password ◆ Opens account summary ◆ Redeems hotel award ◆ Views hotel requested by customer ◆ Reserves hotel stay for customer ◆ Sends fax of hotel award and reservation confirmation to customer
Scenario: Customer wishes to view hotels in Cancun, Mexico, print hotel information, and reserve a hotel stay for his family vacation.	Scenario: Customer telephones to correct an error in the room rate charged during a recent hotel stay and receive a credit card refund.
Customer Tasks: ◆ Enters Mandel Manor Club account number and password ◆ Looks for hotels in Cancun, Mexico ◆ Prints hotel photograph, map, and directions from airport ◆ Checks hotel availability ◆ Checks hotel rates ◆ Reserves two rooms for family vacation	Service Representative Tasks: ◆ Finds member's Mandel Manor Club account ◆ Validates member's password ◆ Finds hotel stay statement ◆ Verifies customer's rate correction ◆ Revises hotel stay statement ◆ Credits refund to member's credit card ◆ Sends fax of revised hotel stay statement and credit card refund receipt

First, define your initial set of user objects and actions based on the information collected in Phase 1 and from the scenarios you just developed in Step 2. It is easy to start listing objects and actions—just <u>underline</u> all of the <u>nouns</u> in your scenarios and tasks and circle (here *italicized*) all of the *verbs*. This gives you a first pass at your objects and data (<u>nouns</u>) and actions (*verbs*) that can be applied to those objects and data.

Table 12.4 illustrates the scenarios after you have identified <u>objects</u> and *actions* for the Mandel Manor Hotels system.

KEY IDEA! *Use a brainstorming approach as you first start to build your object and action lists. That is, use any materials you can find related to tasks and scenarios, write down as many objects and actions as possible, and don't worry about terminology or redundant items.*

Continue to brainstorm with your lists of objects and actions until you have a somewhat final list that eliminates duplication and contains other objects and actions that were not necessarily explicitly mentioned in the user scenarios.

Usually, any major object (for example, <u>hotel</u> or <u>reservation</u>) with (possibly) more than one instance requires a high-level container object to hold the entire collection of individual objects. In a car dealership system, for example, since there are multiple <u>car</u> objects, there probably should be a <u>car lot</u> object. These high-level container objects may end up as folders in the interface, or simply list controls. But for now, it is important not to forget that collections of similar objects typically are contained in a higher-level container object.

You will also need to define general device objects that users need to perform actions you have defined. For example, you may need <u>printer</u> and <u>fax</u> objects. You might also some kind of <u>trash</u> or wastebasket object.

As you refine your list of objects, start to think of what object type each object is. Remember our definition of the types of objects—data, container, and device. At this stage you may be fuzzy about objects types for some objects. As I discussed earlier, it may be difficult to figure out if some objects, such as the <u>customer</u> object, are data objects or container objects. Obviously there is a lot of data associated with a customer, but in the interface, users may see the customer as a container that holds *other* objects that are pieces of customer data, such as a <u>customer profile</u> or <u>customer account</u>. These issues tend to work themselves out through discussions with users as you move through this phase of interface design.

KEY IDEA! *You may think you have completed a* final *list of objects and actions after this step, but I guarantee you will return here multiple times (remember this iteration thing!) to revise and refine your lists of objects and actions.*

TABLE 12.4 Phase 2: Identifying Nouns and Verbs in Scenarios and Tasks

Customers/Program Members	Service Representatives
Scenario: Customer wishes to *update* telephone number in customer profile and see if latest hotel stay has been *recorded*. Customer also *sends* a comment card to the company.	Scenario: Customer *telephones* wishing to *redeem* account points for free hotel stay award and *reserve* a hotel room. Customer wishes to *receive* a fax of the reservation and award.
Customer Tasks: ◆ *Enters* Mandel Manor Club account number and password ◆ *Opens* customer profile ◆ *Updates* telephone number ◆ *Opens* account summary ◆ *Views* latest recorded hotel stay ◆ *Fills out* comment card ◆ *Sends* comment card	Service Representative Tasks: ◆ *Finds* member's Mandel Manor Club account ◆ *Validates* member's password ◆ *Opens* account summary ◆ *Redeems* hotel award ◆ *Views* hotel *requested* by customer ◆ *Reserves* hotel stay for customer ◆ *Sends* fax of hotel award and reservation confirmation to customer
Scenario: Customer wishes to *view* hotels in Cancun, Mexico, *print* hotel information, and *reserve* a hotel stay for his family vacation.	Scenario: Customer *telephones* to *correct* an error in the room rate *charged* during a recent hotel stay and *receive* a credit card refund.
Customer Tasks: ◆ *Enters* Mandel Manor Club account number and password ◆ *Looks for* hotels in Cancun, Mexico ◆ *Prints* hotel photograph, map, and directions from airport ◆ *Checks* hotel availability ◆ *Checks* hotel rates ◆ *Reserves* two rooms for family vacation	Service Representative Tasks: ◆ *Finds* member's Mandel Manor Club account ◆ *Validates* member's password ◆ *Finds* hotel stay statement ◆ *Verifies* customer's rate correction ◆ *Revises* hotel stay statement ◆ *Credits* refund to member's credit card ◆ *Sends* fax of revised hotel stay statement and credit card refund receipt

Table 12.5 shows the final list for the Mandel Manor Hotel example.

All objects on your list may not necessarily end up as separate interface objects in the final design. Some may become specific *views* of major objects. For example, a hotel will definitely be a key object in the final design. However, other things such as hotel information, photographs, maps, rates, and availabil-

TABLE 12.5 Phase 2: Objects, Object Types, and Actions Lists

Objects and Data	Object Type	Actions (Not Specific to Objects)
Customer list	container	
Customer	container/data	call
Mandel Manor Hotel list	container	cancel
Service representative	data	correct
Customer profile	data	credit
Account number	data	
Password	data	debit
Telephone number	data	
Account summary	data	fill out
Account points	data	find
Hotel stay	data	
Hotel stay statement	data	look up
Hotel reservation list	data	
Hotel reservation	data	open
Reservation confirmation	data	print
Hotel list	data	
Hotel	data	receive
Hotel information	data	record
Hotel rates	data	redeem
Hotel availability	data	request
Hotel photographs	data	reserve
Hotel map, directions	data	revise
Hotel stay award	data	
Hotel special	data	send
Comment card	data	update
Credit card	device	validate
Customer finder	device	verify view
Printer	device	
Fax machine	device	
Wastebasket	device	

ity may be data contained in the hotel object or separate views of a hotel object. Objects and views were defined in the previous two chapters. You will create their visual representations later in this phase.

Now that we have some idea of the objects users might expect, let's start to figure out how these objects relate to each other. One way to do this is to draw an *object relationships diagram* (see Figure 12.4).

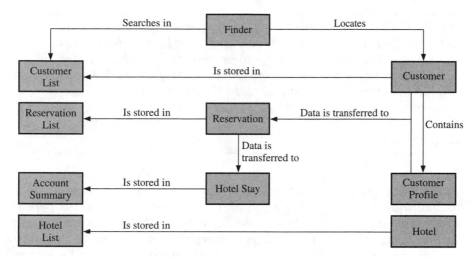

Figure 12.4   Phase 2: Object relationships diagram.

KEY IDEA! *A user interface object relationships diagram is different from traditional programming diagrams of object relationships.* User interface objects do not necessarily parallel programming or business objects.

One goal of user interface design is to hide as much of the complexity of the underlying business and programming models as possible. Users drag an object to a wastebasket—this may start a whole series of business transactions to delete or archive a database record—but all users care about is that the object was thrown away.

Look at the objects on the left side of the object relationship diagram. These high-level containers or lists represent underlying business and programming structures of the system. These relationships will show the database transactions your system will be processing on a regular basis. Bringing up a customer account on the screen may require accessing multiple databases under the covers, but users do not need to know what went on at the system level. Users see these objects only as tools for getting and storing information from the system—they don't need to know how they work. These are *system objects* rather than *interface objects.* Be careful how you represent them on the computer screen!

KEY IDEA! *Hide the functionality of "system" objects (such as customer lists, reservation lists, and hotel lists or databases) from users. They should only see these objects through a "finder" object or in lists of available items. From users' perspective, these are big containers back somewhere in the computer system that store all of the objects they work with. They don't want to know any more about these objects than is necessary to retrieve or store information.*

Next, continue Step 3 by thinking how (and, of course, if!) users would directly manipulate objects using a mouse or other input devices to perform their tasks. To do this, complete an *object direct-manipulation matrix* (Figure 12.5). Simply list all of your key objects down the left column of the matrix and across the top row. Then think about which objects might be dragged (*source objects*) and dropped on other objects (*target objects*). If it makes sense for an object to be dragged and dropped on another object, fill in that cell with the result of the direct manipulation. For example, an account summary could be dragged and dropped on a printer icon, thus printing a copy of the account summary. I have used only key objects in this chart to make it more readable.

KEY IDEA! *Notice that the matrix is not filled for most of the cells. Not all objects are candidates for drag-and-drop operations and you see that some objects are always used in certain ways as either source or target objects.*

Your devices (printer, fax, and wastebasket) will typically only be *target* objects for drag-and-drop operations, not *source* objects. As a target object, the actions performed when an object is dropped on it are listed in the column for that target object.

Also, look at the system objects (customer list, reservation list, and hotel list). Users work with objects presented in these lists, not the lists themselves. These list objects are not source objects for direct manipulation, so there should be no actions in their row of the matrix. For example, a customer in the customer list might be dragged onto a reservation to transfer the information about the customer and his hotel preferences to the reservation. Users might drag objects to these lists to complete a transaction such as a making a reservation or adding a customer to the system.

Source Object	Target Object										
	Customer	Customer List	Customer Profile	Service Rep.	Reservation	Reservation List	Hotel	Hotel List	Printer	Fax	Wastebasket
Customer		add customer to list		assign customer to service rep.	transfer data to reservation				print all customer info.	fax all customer info.	delete customer
Customer List											
Customer Profile					transfer data to reservation				print customer profile	fax customer profile	delete customer profile
Service Rep.									print service rep. info.	fax service rep. info.	
Reservation	attach reservation to customer			assign reservation to service rep.		store reservation in list			print reservation	fax reservation	delete reservation
Reservation List											
Hotel					transfer data to reservation			add hotel to list	print hotel info.	fax hotel info.	
Hotel List											
Printer											
Fax											
Wastebasket											

Figure 12.5   Phase 2, Step 3: Object direct-manipulation matrix.

KEY IDEA! *The work you've done in Step 3 is necessary to give you all of the background material on interface objects and actions. Now it is time to begin drawing representations of the objects you have identified. This is the fun part of design. All the work you have done up to this point begins to pay off here.*

In fact, it is a good idea to review your results so far from Phase 2 analysis with your users. Don't wait until you have completed the entire design phase before you go back to users for review and validation.

Step 4: Determine Object Icons, Views, and Visual Representations

Once objects have been defined, determine how to best represent them on the screen and how users will view these objects and the information they contain. When determining object views, consider the way users will interact with each object and its information.

Design Object Icons

A graphics designer should be an integral part of the interface design team and should be responsible for designing screen icons. User feedback and usability testing should also be incorporated to ensure icons are recognizable, understandable, and helpful in performing their tasks. Figure 12.6 shows the first pass at object icons—hand-drawn pictures of objects. Don't spend too much time early in the interface design on icons. Start with rough hand-drawn sketches and incrementally design and test icons through the entire design process. There are good books that cover icon design, notably William Horton's (1994) *The Icon Book: Visual Symbols for Computer Systems and Documentation.*

After hand drawing object icons, select icons from icon libraries or draw actual icon files for your demos and prototypes. Figure 12.7 shows a first attempt at computer icons for these objects.

KEY IDEA! *Developers don't view objects the same way as do users. Therefore, it makes sense that developers shouldn't design object icons. Let graphics designers work with users to design icons.*

Figure 12.6   Hand-drawn object icons.

Figure 12.7 Computer-drawn object icons.

Determine Object Views

Next, determine what types of views each object will have. The type of view will help you immediately determine window elements, menus, and layouts. Table 12.5 lists object types for all objects found in Step 3. Table 12.6 lists specific views needed for some of the key objects.

Design Visual Representations

> **KEY IDEA!** *Once you have created computer icons for objects, you can show how some objects—containers—will look when opened in a contents view, because they will basically contain some set of objects represented as icons.*

For instance, users of the Mandel Manor Hotels system first see the Desktop folder containing the objects they need to start most customer transactions—the Finder, Hotel List, and Special Promotions Folder. This folder is shown in Figure 12.8.

TABLE 12.6   Objects and Views

Objects	Object Type	Object Views
Customer	Container	Contents:
		Icons
		Details
Customer List	Container	Search Results Window
Customer Profile	Data	View/Update Information:
		Account number
		Password
		Name, address
		Telephone numbers
Account Summary	Container/Data	Hotel Stay List
		Account points
		Awards redeemed
Hotel	Data	Hotel Information:
		Summary
		Hotel rates
		Hotel availability
		Hotel photographs
		Hotel map, directions
Hotel List	Container	Contents:
		Icons
		Details
Reservation	Data	Create/View/Update Information:
		Name
		Hotel
		Arrival date
		Number of nights
		Room rate
Reservation List	Container	Contents:
		Icons
		Details
Finder	Data	Enter/Search for Information

Once a customer is found, either directly or by using the Finder search, the Customer folder is opened. A Customer folder would usually contain a Customer Profile, and Account Summary, and a Reservation List (see Figure 12.9).

Many of the other objects are data objects, and you must iteratively define and design the visual representations for each of these windows. Figure 12.10 shows a hand-drawn layout (actually drawn in Word using the graphics and text tools) of the Finder window.

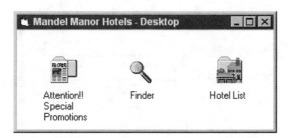

Figure 12.8 Mandel Manor Hotels desktop folder.

Step 5: Design Object and Window Menus

Once objects, their object type, and icons have been determined and designed, determine how users will interact with objects and windows using various types of menus. The following questions must be answered:

◆ What actions are appropriate for each object and view?

◆ What are the contents of object pop-up menus?

◆ Which windows need a menu bar?

Table 12.5 (Object and Actions list) and Figure 12.5 (Object Direct-Manipulation Matrix) from Step 3 are the starting points for Step 5. Now it's time to build on these charts and determine which actions specifically apply to objects when they are represented as icons and what actions are needed when objects are opened in view windows.

Figure 12.9 An opened Customer folder.

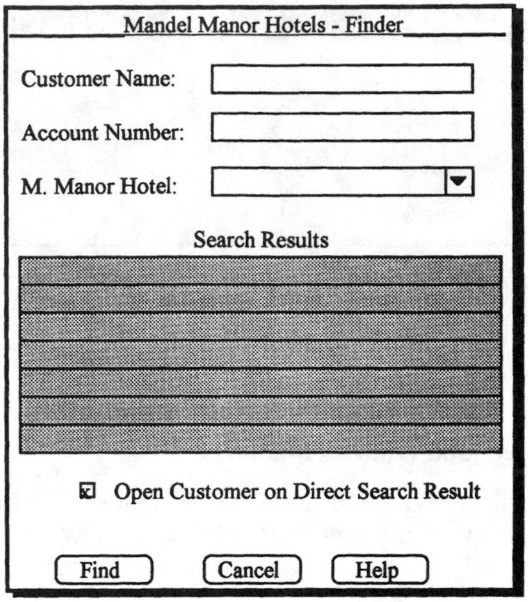

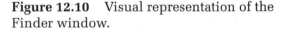

Figure 12.10   Visual representation of the Finder window.

First, determine what actions are appropriate for objects represented as icons on the screen. Figure 12.9 shows the Customer window opened, revealing three object icons. Both the Customer Profile and Account Summary are data objects and would have similar actions in a pop-up menu. Table 12.7 shows the menu choices in pop-up menus for these objects. The Reservation List is a container, and would have pop-up menu actions suitable for a container object.

Every window should be investigated to determine if a menu bar is needed. As software applications migrate toward objects and views, menu bars will give way to more direct interaction techniques like direct manipulation and pop-up menus. Single-windowed applications require complex menu bars to present all appropriate actions. As these applications are broken up into more object-oriented components, fewer actions are needed at the window level, and more actions can be done implicitly and with more dynamic pop-ups.

The Microsoft Windows guidelines offer no suggestions as to when menu bars are appropriate. The IBM (1992) guidelines state that a menu bar should be presented "when a window will provide more than six action choices or rout-

TABLE 12.7 Object Pop-Up Menus

Object	Pop-Up Menu Choices	Purpose
Customer Profile,	Open	Open into data view
Account Summary	Move	Move to another location
	Create New	Create a new object
	Cut	Cut object to clipboard
	Copy	Copy object to clipboard
	Delete	Delete object
	Print	Print on printer
	Send	Send to another person
	Fax	Fax to another person
Reservation List	Open	Open into contents view
	Contents . . .	List contents without opening window
	Move	Move to another location
	Create New	Create a new object
	Cut	Cut object to clipboard
	Copy	Copy object to clipboard
	Print	Print on printer
	Send	Send to another person
	Fax	Fax to another person

ing choices." The main difference between an application-oriented menu bar and an object-oriented menu bar is the first menu bar choice, File. An object-oriented menu bar lists the object as the first menu bar choice, and the drop-down contains choices that affect the underlying object presented in that window. Figure 12.11 shows the object-oriented menu bar for the Reservation object's window.

Step 6: Refine Visual Designs

When first designing window layouts, it is much easier to use pencil and paper. As designs become more stable, use a prototyping tool or development tool to create icons and window layouts. Figure 12.12 shows a redesign of the hand-drawn layout for the Finder window (Figure 12.10). Figure 12.13 shows a first design for the Account Summary object view done using a development tool.

Based on all of the menu designs in Step 6, you will probably go back and revise Figure 12.5, the Object Direct-Manipulation Matrix.

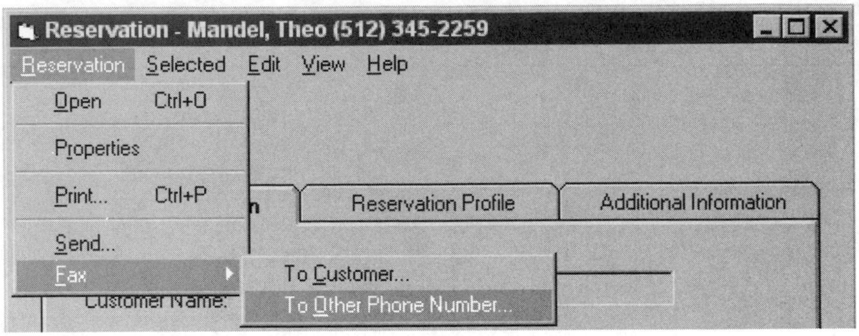

Figure 12.11 Object-oriented menu bar for Reservation object window.

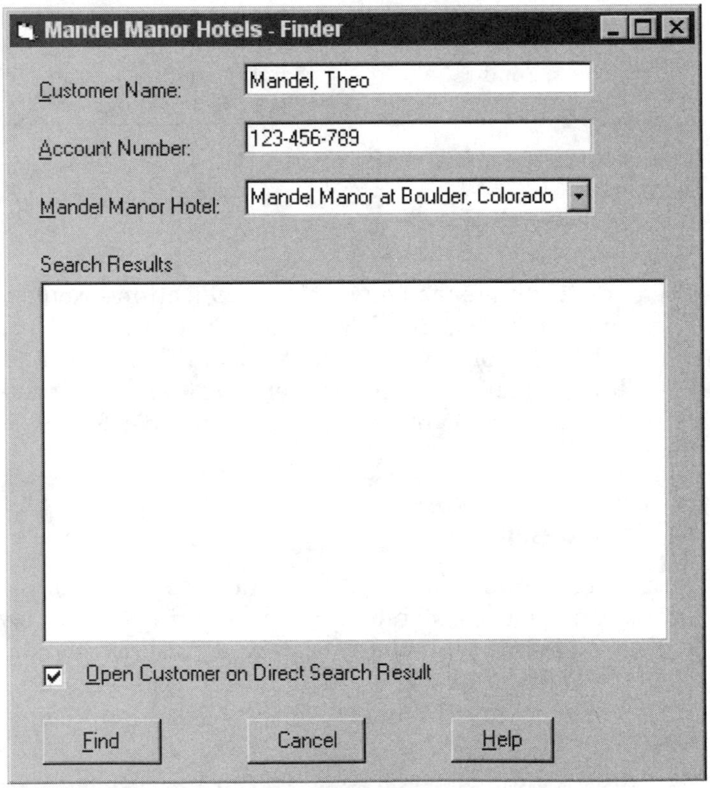

Figure 12.12 Redesign of the Finder window.

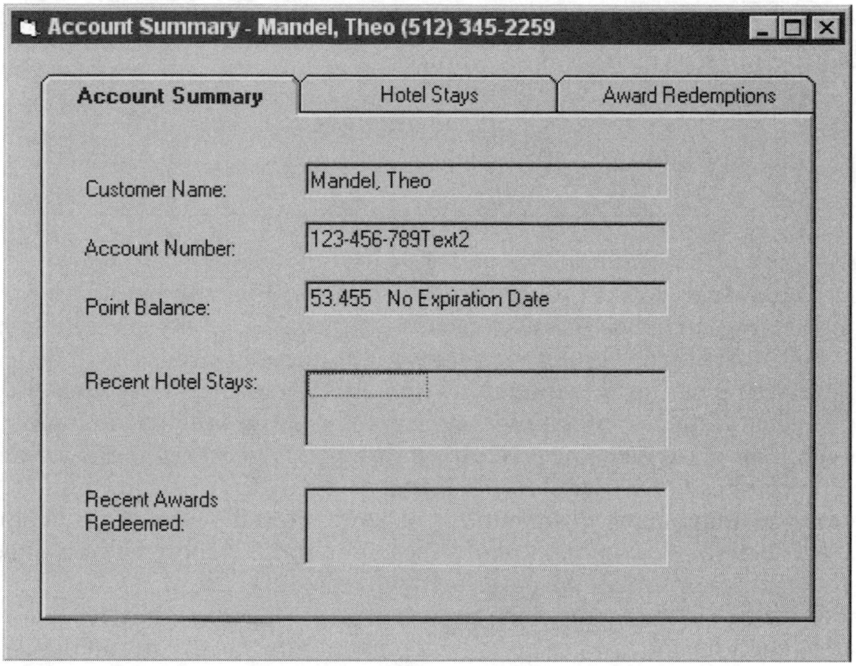

Figure 12.13   Initial online design of the Account Summary window.

Phase 3: Construct the User Interface

Prototyping as Interface Building

It is simply not possible to design a competitive user interface these days without powerful prototyping tools right from the start.

Edward Tufte (1994)

In your first pass through the iterative design process, you should *prototype,* rather than construct, the user interface. Prototyping is an extremely valuable way of building early designs and creating product demonstrations, and is necessary for early usability testing.

It is most important to remember that you must not be afraid to throw away a prototype. The purpose of prototyping is to *quickly* and *easily* visualize design alternatives and ideas, not to build code that must be used as a part of the product.

KEY IDEA! *Follow these three golden rules for using prototypes as part of the interface design process:*
- ◆ *Prototype early and iterate often.*
- ◆ *Prototype different design alternatives, not necessarily just one design.*
- ◆ *Be prepared to throw away prototype code.*

There are many ways to prototype interfaces, starting with pencil-and-paper methods using chalkboards, whiteboards, flipcharts, sticky pads, overhead foils, and storyboards. Prototypes may be animated, either by hand (with a person acting as the "computer" switching screens at user requests) or by using presentation graphics programs (such as Lotus Freelance Graphics or other tools) to show sequences of visual designs. A good reference for developing prototypes is *The Art of Rapid Prototyping,* by Isensee and Rudd (1996).

Prototypes may show *visualizations* of your interface—the high-level concepts—or they may show *functional* slices of a product, showing how specific tasks or transactions might be performed with the interface.

There are two ways to approach prototyping—use *prototyping tools* specifically designed for the task, or use *development tools* that are normally used to write product code. There are advantages and disadvantages to both types of tools. Prototyping tools are easier for nonprogrammers to use and can produce prototypes and demos very quickly. However, they are often very limited in their functionality and they usually use proprietary code that cannot be used in your final product development. Development tools are rich in functionality, but they are much more difficult for nonprogrammers to use.

KEY IDEA! *The code you build for a prototype using a software development tool can possibly be used in the final product, but be careful—this is a double-edged sword. If the prototype matches the final design, then some of the code may be salvageable, but if the prototype does not appropriately visualize the final design, the code should be thrown away. I have seen inappropriate or poorly designed prototypes become the core of the final product solely because decisions were made that the prototype code could not be thrown away— it had to be used! Remember, you must be willing to throw away prototype code. Don't use code from a poor design just because it is there!*

You should think about using a product prototype in place of (or in addition to) what is normally a lengthy written document, the *product functional specification* (PFS). If you have ever written a functional specification for a graphical user interface, you know it is very difficult to *write about* the presentation and interaction techniques involved in GUIs or OOUIs. It is much easier and much more effective to *show* a prototype, or demo, of the product interface style and behavior. Remember the old saying, "Don't tell me, show me!" You will find that a prototype can also serve as marketing and promotional aids to show managers, executives, and customers. A product demo is also a great giveaway item for business shows and promotional mailings.

KEY IDEA! *Even huge software projects follow the "prototype as specification" approach. The Windows 95 user interface design followed this approach. Sullivan (1996) noted, During the first few months of the project, the [written] spec had grown by leaps and bounds and reflected hundreds of person-hours of effort. However, due to the problems we found via user testing, the design documented in the spec was suddenly out of date. The team faced a major decision: spend weeks changing the spec to reflect the new ideas and lose valuable time for iterating or stop updating the spec and let the prototypes and code serve as a "living" spec. After some debate, the team decided to take the latter approach.*

Software prototyping is becoming a specialized area within software design and usability testing. Prototyping requires the skills and interests of both an interface designer and a software developer. Rudd and Isensee (1994) offer "The Official Prototyping Wallet Card" with twenty-two tips for a happier, healthier prototype (Table 12.8).

KEY IDEA! *Rather than developing real code as early as possible, use early design time to adequately prepare for development and create prototypes. By putting off development efforts until you have a better feel for the interface, you will actually avoid some of the rework you would do later if you had begun coding earlier. Just don't let an uninformed executive see your demo and declare, "That's not a demo, that's our product—ship it!"*

TABLE 12.8   The Official Prototyping Wallet Card, from Rudd and Isensee (1994)

1. Obtain upper-level development management support
2. Throw away your prototype
3. Make prototypes with high fidelity
4. Take every opportunity to show the prototype
5. Don't waste time prototyping add-ons
6. Start early
7. Make the prototype the functional specification
8. Disseminate to all technical leaders and developers
9. Develop idealistic instead of realistic prototypes
10. Use the best tools
11. Grab a piece of the action
12. The customer is king
13. Look outside the United States
14. Keep control of the prototype in your shop
15. Pay attention to aesthetics
16. Don't delegate the prototyping
17. Become multidisciplinary
18. Spread the word
19. Understand your corporate design guidelines
20. Research the key interface issues
21. Know the competition
22. Don't become a traditional (schedule-driven) developer

Phase 4: Validate the User Interface

One size fits all is usually ill-fitted to each person.

Mary Gorman (1996)

Usability testing is a key piece of the iterative development process. It's the way to get a product in the hands of many actual users to see if they can use it or break it! That's why I have devoted so much attention to this topic (Chapter 7). The goal of usability testing should be to measure user behavior, performance, and satisfaction. Many development processes address usability testing (if at all) near the end of the development cycle. However, this is much too late in the development cycle to make any changes based on usability test results. Even if changes are made, how can you tell if the revised product is usable unless it is tested again? Usability testing should be done early and often!

Schedule several stages of usability tests, beginning with early customer walkthroughs of initial designs. As pieces of the product and interface are built, get them in front of users and test again. When the product is nearing completion and all of the pieces are coming together, then conduct final system tests. You shouldn't see any surprises if you have tested iteratively and incorporated user results and feedback. Table 12.9 shows how various usability activities should be conducted during the different product development stages. These are generic product development stages that parallel the iterative design phases I've discussed.

Scenarios developed in Phase 2 now come back to life in the validation phase. Did you build a product that was guided by the user scenarios you developed? How do you know? You don't, unless you validate the product against predefined usability goals and objectives using the scenarios as the vehicle of measuring user performance.

TABLE 12.9   Usability Activities Throughout the Development Process

Product Development Stage	Usability Activities
Concept Definition	◆ User requirements gathering ◆ Conceptual design definition
Concept Validation	◆ Conceptual design evaluations (paper/pencil, prototypes)
Design	◆ Evaluations of rapid prototypes ◆ Track and fix usability problems
Development	◆ Iterative tests of early designs (individual modules, key tasks) ◆ Iterative tests of final designs (integrated product, all tasks) ◆ Track and fix usability problems
Pilot Deployment	◆ Field observations of pilot users ◆ Pilot user feedback ◆ Pilot user questionnaires ◆ Track and fix usability problems
Product Implementation	◆ Field observations of product users ◆ Product user feedback ◆ Product user questionnaires ◆ Track and fix usability problems
Operations and Maintenance	◆ Long-term usability comparisons (1-month, 3-month, 6-month intervals) ◆ Test updates and changes ◆ Pilot test new product designs

---

KEY IDEA! *Bring users into your own usability test lab or contract your testing to a company specializing in usability testing. One word of advice from experience—don't let developers test their own products! It just doesn't work. Go to usability experts or human factors professionals who are not biased in any way about the product. Get help from outside your company. Designers end up designing the same product over and over again unless they get a fresh view from outside their environment.*

Developers should definitely observe their product being tested so they can see how users really work with their products—just don't let them design or conduct the test themselves. Developers must also be on hand to provide technical support during usability testing.

You may want to install test systems at customer locations to let users give informal feedback as they use the system. IBM developed numerous information kiosk systems that were used in the 1984 Olympics and the 1991 World Games in Barcelona, Spain. They are also developing the computer systems to be used in the 1996 Olympics in Atlanta. These systems are thoroughly tested during the entire design and development process. A kiosk was installed in the lobby of an IBM building where the product was being developed. A notebook was attached so that people could record their comments as they used the kiosk. These comments were read by the designers and were used to redesign the product and add additional features to the kiosk. The important point is to get everyone to try the product, not just selected participants. Assemble a "committee of dummies" and let them test drive the user interface!

Usability activities don't stop after a product is shipped or it is put into production. The product design team should be eagerly awaiting usability feedback from pilot participants and actual users once the product is in their hands in the real-world environment. Microsoft even asks users to send them feedback and a wish list for future versions of their products. The About Microsoft Works dialog box (Figure 12.14) asks users to send comments directly to Microsoft. It asks, "Help us make future versions even better by sending us your ideas and suggestions."

Who's Driving the Design—The System or the Interface?

Unfortunately, there are too many instances where the impact and effectiveness of the difference and power of the object-oriented paradigm are weakened when the technology is introduced into a real-world business environment.

Paul Schwork (1994)

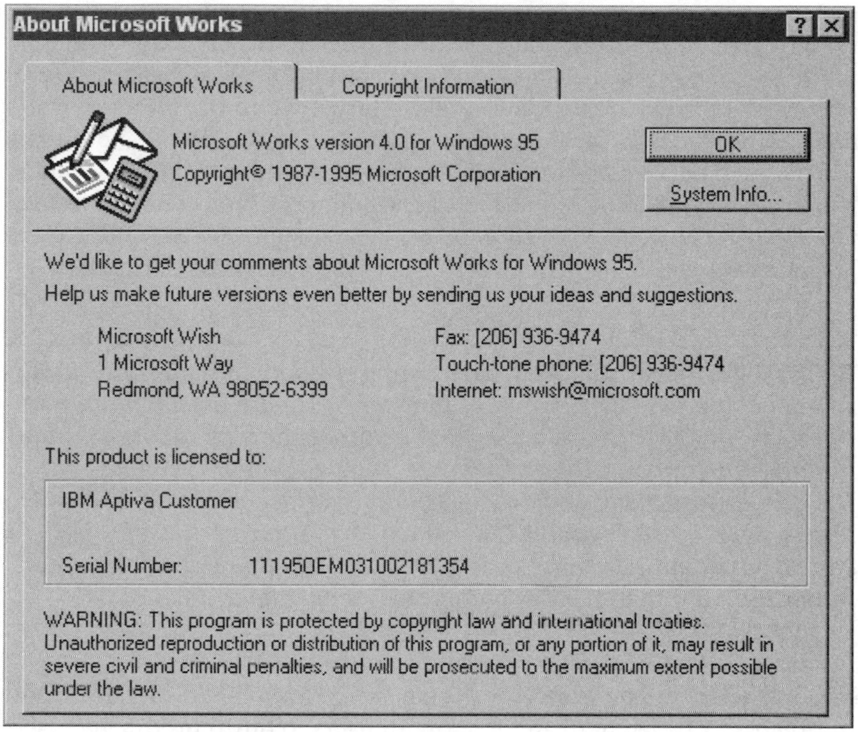

Figure 12.14 About Microsoft Works request for user feedback.

Obviously, designing and developing a software product may require integrating many subsystems, networks, databases, other programs, and so on. In many cases, the operating system, programming languages, and development tools are already in place or have previously been determined before the user interface is designed. This is reality—in most cases, we don't have the luxury of building a software product from scratch, with no ties to previous versions, other products, or a particular set of programming languages and tools.

Figure 12.15 shows two different approaches to interface design. Designing *from the system out* can predetermine and constrain what type of user interface can be designed and built. Paul Schwork (1994) discusses the problems with this approach: "The technology itself (the language selected, CASE tool chosen, etc.) often overshadows the *paradigm* (the frame of reference, way of seeing, process of understanding, method of mapping)." He points out the historical evolution of this approach:

Picking an object-oriented language or CASE tool first and then working backwards to find the business need that fits the given solution is no different from the way systems were developed and implemented when punch cards were still used. The solution was already there (usually COBOL, always a mainframe, probably CICS for the more sophisticated applications), and, in one way or another, the business need was force-fitted into the given solution. Moreover, the end users of the application, although stuck with the technological solution, were expected to be happy and appreciative. After all, the programmers worked nights and weekends to meet the project's end date.

KEY IDEA! *Unfortunately, preexisting system configurations and development environments often constrain the design of the interface. If you know your development tools don't support a certain interface metaphor or type of control, such as pen or touch screen, you will be less likely to try to design an interface using those elements, even if users want it. This leads to an interface design that can be easily supported by your system development environment, rather than an interface design that meets user needs.*

Let's look what happens if you design *from the user in.* If you follow the design process outlined here and work with users to build product goals, objectives, and user requirements (without undue influence from software develop-

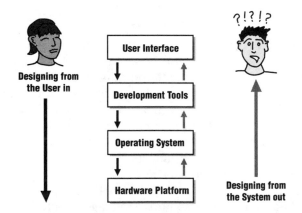

Figure 12.15   Designing from the user in versus from the system out.

ers), you are more likely to design interface metaphors, visual elements, and input/output techniques that match user requirements. *Then* see if it is possible to build the appropriate user interface using the current development environment. If it can be supported, great! If it can't, see *what can be done* to build the interface you've designed, rather than backing down from it. Can new widgets be built in-house? Can third-party controls or widgets be purchased to supplement the existing tool set? You might need to compare your current tools with other tools to see which can support the interface. I've seen even Fortune 1,000 companies switch operating system platforms to enable the development of interfaces for their future products.

The historical case study for designing a computer system from the interface in is that of Apple Computer when they built the first Macintosh computers. I always use this example as a classic success story for *first* doing the interface design, *then* building the box to support the design! Apple has always prided themselves on the user-friendliness of the Macintosh computer, and the order in which they designed the computer system is a big part of why these claims are grounded in truth. Peter Jones (1993) wrote:

> Apple reversed the usual order of machine design when it set to work on building computers. The interface came first, and the machine was engineered to support it. It began with the idea of making the computer easy to learn, and grew from the belief that people deal with the world in a variety of different ways. Physical actions are controlled by areas of our brain different from those we use for higher level thought. We focus our conscious attention on the task and our motor abilities on the tools. It seemed clear that a successful interface would be based on those ideas, and incorporate principles that put the user at the heart of the system.

KEY IDEA! *A user interface designer walks a fine line between the very different worlds of users and developers. If you put on your "systems" hat too often, you may design what you think users need, but you may be blind to what users really need and want. You should be the champion of the user community. I often find it easier to design interfaces as a consultant rather than as a company employee. As a consultant, I am not saddled with the political and historical baggage from previous development projects. I find it easier to think like users and identify with them. This makes it easier to then negotiate with developers about what should be designed, rather than what can be designed.*

Finally, remember that this entire design process is centered around users and what they do. A *user-centered* design approach is based on a set of guiding principles (Vredenburg and DiAngelo, 1995):

- An understanding of users is the driving force behind all design.
- Everything users see and touch is designed together.
- Innovative design results from intensive multidisciplinary teamwork.
- Competitive design requires a relentless focus on the competition.
- User-validated design drives code development.
- Product decisions are based on user feedback.
- User feedback is gathered often and with scientific rigor and speed.
- Feedback is sought from potential as well as current clients.
- User-centered design is standardized and deployed consistently.
- User-centered design is continuously being improved by its practitioners.

Epilogue: The Iterative Design Process—It Works!

- *More than a third of all large-scale software development projects are canceled.*
- *The average project runs 50 percent over its schedule.*
- *Three-quarters of all large-scale applications are "operational failures" that don't function as intended.*

Software Engineering Institute (1995)

One of the key success factors in software development today is time-to-market. How quickly can you figure out what computer users want? How quickly and appropriately can you design and build it? And, most importantly, how quickly and cheaply can you get the product in customers' hands and on their computers? Having a workable and efficient development process is the way to make this happen.

KEY IDEA! *The iterative design process may look like it takes more time because of multiple passes through the design phases. In fact, if done correctly,* it takes less time, *since quick early passes through the design phases can build designs and prototypes that take less time to implement and test in later iterations!*

I'm not the only one who believes in the importance of *rapid application development* (RAD) techniques. Christine Comaford (1992), a specialist in client/server application development, says, "RAD doesn't just happen because you buy a snazzy GUI application development tool. You need a staff trained in GUI and client/server technologies. Mix in the right tool, the right architecture and a common code repository—then you'll get applications out the door rapidly." Software products may be developed more quickly using RAD approaches. David Linthicum (1995) notes that "the time gained from using a RAD tool can be immense. Most Visual Age programmers report the ability to create up to 80 percent of an application visually, with the last 20 percent consisting of specialized functions."

There are many different software development processes to choose from. Just be sure you follow the basic elements, regardless of which process you choose. Here are Comaford's (1992) guidelines for rapid application development:

◆ Do intelligent prototypes.

◆ Stick to GUI design standards.

◆ Use only a few GUI designers.

◆ Apply modern metrics to project estimation.

◆ Write and distribute common code.

◆ Perform code and user interface reviews.

◆ Develop an enterprisewide data model.

Does the iterative interface design process work for all software products? I can't guarantee it, but the same process works for industrial-strength products, such as computer-aided design (CAD) applications. David Kieras, a psychologist at the University of Michigan, describes Phase 1 (gather and analyze user information) of a CAD design (Monkiewicz, 1992): "First you have to figure out what it is that people are actually doing. You can't just stay in the office and write some software."

Phase 2 (design) is outlined: "Interface designers must ask themselves whether a particular function can be accomplished more efficiently via graphical means or by menu selection." Also, Kieras notes, "The interface designers must at all times keep basic principles in mind, such as minimizing the number of steps required to perform basic functions, minimizing the overall time required to perform these functions, and accommodating all classes of users."

Finally, the article confirms the importance of Phase 3 (construct the interface) and Phase 4 (validate the interface): "Obviously, vendors must capture the user's view of the environment through an iterative process of testing, prototyping, and more testing." I couldn't have said it better myself!

TABLE 12.10   How to Get a Good User Interface, On One Foil, from Lewis (1995)

1. Find people who care about users and about how well things really work.
2. Set up unified responsibility for the user interface.
3. Figure out who's going to use the system to do what.
4. Choose representative tasks.
5. Set usability objectives.
6. Plagiarize.
7. Rough out a design.
8. Think about it.
9. Create a mockup or prototype.
10. Test it with users.
11. Iterate.
12. Build it.
13. Track it and change it.

Clayton Lewis (1995) covers many of these same topics in his article, *Task-Centered User Interface Design: An Overview.* He calls the article's table of contents "How to get a good user interface, on one foil." Using simple language and terms, he reinforces the phases I've described in this chapter. Table 12.10 lists Lewis's phases. He goes into each of these areas in depth. This article is available on the Internet at http://www.cis.ohio-state.edu/~perlman/uidesign.html.

KEY IDEA! *Building an effective interface and a successful product is a continual effort. Remember two things: "Know thy users," and "Iterate, iterate, iterate."*

References

Baecker, Ronald M., Jonathan Grudin, William A. S. Buxton, and Saul Greenberg. 1995. *Readings in Human-Computer Interaction: Toward the Year 2000.* San Francisco, CA: Morgan Kaufmann.

Bannon, Liam. 1991. From human factors to human actors: The role of psychology and human-computer interaction studies in system design. In Greenbaum, J., and M. Kyng (Eds.), *Design at Work.* Mahwah, NJ: Lawrence Erlbaum Associates.

Borenstein, Nathaniel. 1991. *Programming as if People Mattered.* Princeton, NJ: Princeton University Press.

Carroll, John M., Ed. 1995. *Scenario-Based Design: Envisioning Work and Technology in System Development.* New York: Wiley.

Comaford, Christine. 1992. Tips for truly rapid application development. *PC Week* (November 2): 60.

Holtzblatt, Karen and Hugh R. Beyer. 1995. Requirements gathering: The human factor. *Communications of the ACM* (May): 31–32.

Horton, William. 1994. *The Icon Book: Visual Symbols for Computer Systems and Documentation.* New York: Wiley.

IBM Corporation. 1992. *Object-Oriented Interface Design: IBM Common User Access Guidelines.* New York: QUE.

Isensee, Scott and Jim Rudd. 1996. *The Art of Rapid Prototyping.* New York: International Thomson.

Jones, Peter V. 1993. A GUI puts a friendly face on computing. *Business Quarterly* 57 (3): 110–113.

Lewis, Clayton. 1995. *Task-Centered User Interface Design: An Overview.* University of Colorado (available at http://www.cis.ohio-state.edu/~perlman/uidesign.html).

Linthicum, David. 1995. The end of programming. *BYTE* (August): 69–72.

Microsoft Corporation. 1995. *The Windows Interface Guidelines for Software Design.* Redmond, WA: Microsoft Press.

Monkiewicz, David. 1992. CAD's next-generation user interface. *Computer-Aided Engineering* (November): 50.

Norman, Donald and S.W. Draper. Eds. 1986. *User-Centered System Design: New Perspectives on Human-Computer Interaction.* Mahwah, NJ: Lawrence Erlbaum Associates.

Rudd, James and Scott Isensee. 1994. Twenty-two tips for a happier, healthier prototype. *ACM interactions* (January): 35–40.

Schwork, Paul. 1994. About the paradigm. *Object Magazine* (November–December): 60–61.

Soloway, Elliot and Amanda Pryor. 1996. The next generation in human-computer interaction. *Communications of the ACM* (April): 16–18.

Sullivan, Kent. 1996. The Windows user interface: A case study in usability engineering. *Proceedings of the ACM CHI'96.*

Vredenburg, K. and Michael DiAngelo. 1995. *IBM User-Centered Design: An Introduction and Overview.* IBM Corporation, Version 2, Draft.

PART FOUR

Advanced User Interface Techniques and Technologies

It's becoming clear that the relatively slow progress of GUIs over the past decade was only a transition period; PCs needed time to complete their move from DOS to graphical desktops. But that was just the first step. GUIs will continue to evolve because today's desktop metaphor isn't ideal for all kinds of users, and new demands are straining the ability of conventional GUIs to keep up. Tomorrow's graphical interfaces will reflect the growing diversity of users and the new tasks they need to accomplish.

Tom Halfhill (1996)

Roadmap for Part 4: Advanced User Interface Techniques and Technologies

Chapter 13: The Interface Designer's Toolkit

This chapter addresses the interface designer's toolkit containing numerous skills. Communicating with graphic excellence and integrity is addressed. Using color, audio, and animation are covered. You'll learn why terminology and international design are important. Key interface design issues are discussed, along with the top 10 usability problems with GUIs and OOUIs.

Chapter 14: Help, Advisors, Wizards, and Multimedia

Help and training are necessary components of successful software implementation. Topics covered include: Just-In-Time training, how to train for the "paradigm shift," and what is *electronic performance support* (EPS). Advisors and wizards are defined and examples are provided. Multimedia is defined and it is shown how multimedia can be used to enhance information presentation and user interaction.

Chapter 15: Social User Interfaces and Intelligent Agents

Are computers intelligent? Are agents and social user interfaces here to stay? This chapter starts with speech technology and goes on to define and show examples of agents and social user interfaces. Internet agents are also discussed.

Chapter 16: The New World of PC-Internet User Interfaces

The new world of the Internet and World Wide Web is addressed from the user interface viewpoint. Web design brings a new computing metaphor to the forefront. The new areas of ethics, morals, and addiction on the Internet are discussed. Future software products will combine PC-style interfaces with Web-browser interfaces. Web interface design skills are detailed. The key elements of Web interface design are covered and examples are discussed. You are provided with Web design guidelines and shown where to find design guidance on the Web. Usability on the Web is also discussed.

The book finishes by discussing the latest research and design in the world of newly evolving software and interfaces.

CHAPTER THIRTEEN

THE INTERFACE DESIGNER'S TOOLKIT

To design is to plan and organize, to order, to relate, and to control. In short, it embraces all means opposing disorder and accident. Therefore, it signifies a human need and qualifies man's thinking and doing.

Josef Albers (1975)

The Designer's Toolkit

This chapter addresses a number of topics critical to the art and science of user interface design. These topics include: communicating information, using color, audio, and animation, terminology and international design, determining interface controls, problems with direct manipulation, and window design and layout. I finish up with common usability problems with GUIs and OOUIs and some final advice for interface design. These topics are also covered in other publications, so I offer references for those who want to go even deeper. I have tried to cover the most important and practical aspects of software user interface design, and also some of the major pitfalls.

Communicating Information Visually

Engage within seconds, master within minutes.

Mary Gorman (1996)

The goal of any interface is to enable communication between two systems—in this case, humans and computers. The research and practical advice that have been developed over the years regarding software user interface design are grounded in the traditional ways we have learned to communicate with each other, using whatever media available—beginning with ancient ways of communicating on paper. The fields of visual and graphic design are based on the knowledge of both art and human visual perception. Edward Tufte has written two books (Tufte, 1983; 1990) that beautifully describe ways we can communicate information most appropriately.

KEY IDEA! *Gain an awareness of the importance and sophistication involved in portraying information graphically on paper and on computer screens.* Every line, every control, box, piece of text, color, and graphic *on the screen impacts users not only singly, but also in combination with everything else on the screen.*

For example, Figure 13.1 shows a series of screens containing various design elements. Screen A is a blank screen, so there are no visual elements present, right? Wrong—the background, or desktop, although it is empty, is a visual element itself, so there is one visual element in screen A. Screen B has a line in the middle of the screen. So there's one visual object in the screen? There are now *three* visual objects: (1) the space above the line, (2) the line itself, and (3) the space below the line. Get the idea now? Screen C has a box with a line in it (only two items, you would think), but the visual elements users perceive now jumps up to five: (1) the space outside the box, (2) the box itself, (3) the space in the box above the line, (4) the line itself, and (5) the space in the box below the line.

As you can see, with every graphic element you add to a screen, the visual effect on users is confounded far more than you might believe. Screen D is a partial screen capture showing one overused element—the group box—appearing four times in one small area on the screen. Extrapolating from the examples in screens A through C, you now begin to realize how cluttered most screens are and how complicated the visual processing is for information presented on computer screens. How many visual elements do you think there are in screen D? I'll leave this as an exercise for you. (Hint: There are over 35 visual elements, according to the way I've defined them here.)

When working with visual presentation of information, there are two areas to consider: graphic excellence and graphic integrity. Tufte (1983) wrote that *graphic excellence* "consists of complex ideas communicated with clarity, precision, and efficiency." *Graphical integrity* is using graphics to accurately portray data. It is very easy to purposely, or unintentionally, use data to mislead an audience. As an instructor of an undergraduate course on the principles of psy-

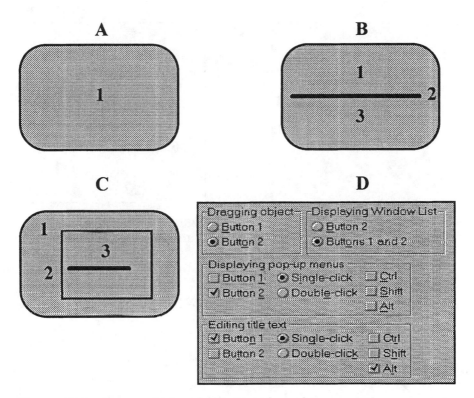

Figure 13.1 Screen design elements and graphic perception.

chological research, I taught a module that I called "The Art of Data Massage, or How to Lie with Statistics" (see Chapter 7).

Here's an example of visual perception and how it affects the way we organize what we see. In Figure 13.2, see how many three-number combinations you can find that add up to 15, and go as fast as you can. Time yourself—ready, set, go!

How many three-number combinations did you find? How long did it take you? This wasn't an easy task, was it? There doesn't seem to be an order to the numbers, so there is no orderly approach to finding the right combination of numbers.

Now take a look at Figure 13.3. All I've added to the puzzle are grid lines that place the numbers into visual locations that are very familiar to viewers. Now you can see that this is a simple tic-tac-toe puzzle. Each of the horizontal, vertical, and diagonal sets of numbers add up to 15. Now it is easy to see that there are a total of eight different combinations of three numbers that add up to 15 (three horizontal, three vertical, and two diagonal).

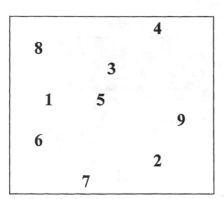

Figure 13.2   Visual perception—number puzzle.

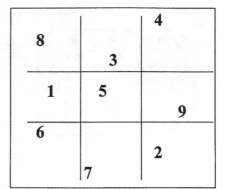

Figure 13.3   Visual perception—number puzzle with visual grid.

This example shows how important visual organization is. We automatically search for order in the information we view, so that we can *precompute* information and recognize familiar patterns and designs in the representations of information that bombard us constantly.

The Use and Misuse of Color

If one says "Red" (the name of a color) and there are 50 people listening, it can be expected that there will be 50 reds in their minds. And one can be sure that all these reds will be very different colors.

Josef Albers (1975)

Color is probably the most often misused element in user interface design. Color research and guidelines apply equally across all computer hardware and software systems. The use of color is a difficult area to cover. This book does not attempt to provide all the answers.

KEY IDEA! *As information-processing creatures, we try to attach meaning to what we see and perceive. Therefore, color in the user interface must be very carefully researched and designed. Color has often been misused as a decorative element. This limits its ability to portray meaningful information in the interface. Tufte (1992) reiterates one of the main principles in using color: "Above all, do no harm."*

People have various physiological, psychological, cultural, and emotional responses to colors. We say, "She got so mad, she saw red," and "He was green with envy." We even say, "You're yellow. You're a coward!" We associate colors with our emotional state. Artists, painters, and decorators know that warm colors (reds, oranges, and yellows) evoke feelings of action and excitement, while cool colors (blues, violets, purples, and grays) produce peaceful and calming feelings.

Here's an example of cultural differences in the use of color. The colors for traffic signals in the United States are green (go), yellow (caution), and red (stop). While this color scheme is very familiar to most drivers around the world, it is not universal. Even in countries where the same colors are used, there are often color variations and even additional methods for alerting drivers. Many countries use blinking to signal a change in the status of the traffic light.

While driving in Europe, I couldn't figure out why all of the other drivers waiting at the stop lights were getting a head start on me as the light turned green. I finally realized that the red light started blinking just before turning green to let you know to get ready to go. This attention-getting mechanism is possibly more dangerous than helpful, as most drivers jump the gun and go before the light even turns green. The meaning of the colors is somehow changed by the blinking effect. Green still (technically) means go. But in reality, out on the streets, it no longer means go, it means "You better get going fast, because everyone else has already gone!" Color used in a positive, attention-getting way for one purpose can cause problems in another area.

The use of color in a user interface can also cause problems for people with visual deficiencies, such as color blindness. Although *color blindness* really doesn't mean that people are blind to colors, this type of visual deficiency does affect about 8 percent of Caucasian males and less than 1 percent of females. I happen to be a member of that small color-blind male population. While I don't notice any problems with colors on my computer screen, I have serious trouble sorting my socks. I can't distinguish very well between dark colors, that is, black, dark brown, and dark blue. I also have trouble differentiating very subtle pastels such as light pink or yellow from white. However, with computer users ranging in age from very young to very old, there is a tremendously wide range of visual abilities and disabilities that have to be accounted for both in display hardware and screen software design.

Color: Should It Attract or Soothe Users?

Properly used, color can be a powerful tool to improve the usefulness of an information display system. The inappropriate use of color can seriously reduce the performance of such a system, however.

Gerald Murch (1984)

Color is often used in a *qualitative* way, to represent differences, but can also be used in a *quantitative* way, to show amounts (Murch, 1984). Take a closer look at the weather page of your local newspaper or the "Weather Across the USA" page of *USA Today*. Colors are used to show different temperature zones across the map. They range from light to dark to show the range of temperatures from cold to hot. Colors are extremely useful in adding additional meaning to the presentation of information. Colors are even useful in the plant world. When I was at Epcot Center in Orlando, Florida, the tour guide pointed out different colored sticky-papers that were used to attract and kill bugs that were eating the plants. The different colors attracted different types of bugs.

Since color is such an automatic attention-getting mechanism, lots of color in an interface will cause users to pay attention to the screen. This helps make a user interface seem somehow friendlier and easier to use. However, this "Las Vegas" effect can actually distract users from their tasks. On initial viewing, the Macintosh and Windows interfaces seem warm and friendly because they use lots of bright colors. On the other hand, the OS/2 interface has been criticized for its bland use of color. Bright colors attract customers and users, but when sitting in front of a computer screen for hours, users don't need colors that distract them from their work.

KEY IDEA! *Operating systems provide standard color palettes and color schemes. You should use these standard interface elements. They were created because colors are difficult to match and people often make poor choices when choosing colors and color combinations.*

In the Windows 3.X user interface, if users didn't like the default colors used in the interface, they could customize the color of interface elements *individually*. OS/2 and Windows 95 provide additional utilities that are extremely useful—color scheme palettes—where users are given *sets of coordinated color schemes* that have already been developed by graphics design experts.

OS/2 users can switch color palettes, modify the existing palettes, or create their own color schemes. This is an incredibly powerful utility, yet it is amazingly simple for people to use (see Figure 13.4). Windows 95 has also added color schemes to the desktop Display Properties dialog (Figure 13.5). OS/2 even has a font palette where users can immediately change the font style, size of text, icons, and window title names. This is very helpful for users with different visual abilities, working conditions, and types of computer displays.

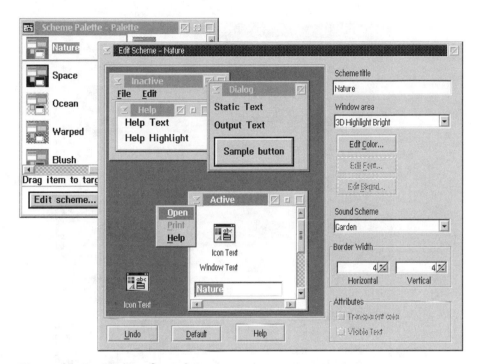

Figure 13.4   OS/2 color schemes.

The human perceptual system is attracted to colors. This basic characteristic is heavily counted on by the communications and advertising field. Which would you rather look at, an advertisement in black and white or in color? In his article, *The Power of Color,* Wayne (1991) states, "Research studies into printed forms of communication indicate color is 32 percent more effective in attracting attention, and 25 percent more effective in causing reader action." It's almost a subliminal effect, something we aren't aware of. Wayne continues, "Corporate print advertising is almost exclusively color, precisely because industry studies show full-color advertisements get up to 36 percent better response than their black-and-white counterparts."

KEY IDEA! *Because color has such a strong effect on human perception, use color appropriately. It is too often used to attract attention, rather than designed to be suitable for long periods of computer work.*

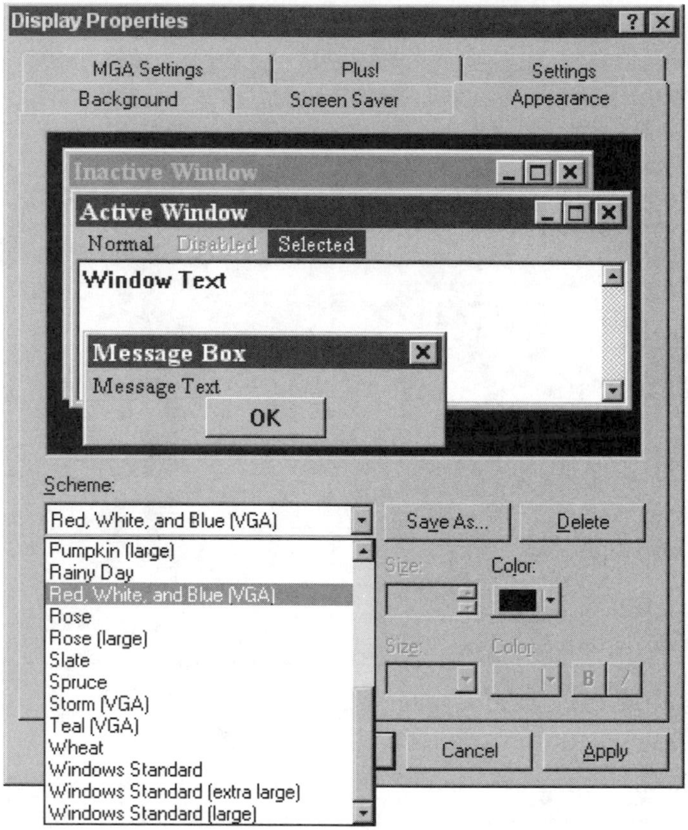

Figure 13.5   Windows color schemes.

Color Guidelines

Of all design elements, color most exemplifies the wholeness of design, the necessity to reason globally.

Edward Tufte (1992)

The knowledge of the human visual and perceptual system has led to the development of very important fundamental guidelines for the use of color, regardless of the media in which the information is presented. These guidelines apply to the use of color in printed materials and broadcast media, as well as on computer displays.

KEY IDEA! *Some of these guidelines for using color may seem out-dated (by their publication date). However, basic perceptual and cognitive characteristics of humans don't change over time. These guidelines remain constant; new computer hardware and software environments should improve your ability to follow them.*

Murch (1984) is a well-respected source of research on the psychological and physical aspects of color. Here are his twenty-five fundamental guidelines for the proper use of color on computer displays. I won't go into all of the details here, but these guidelines are based on years of research and our understanding of human color vision and perception. If you want to dig deeper, read the original article. As Murch states, "It is impossible to develop a complete set of guidelines for the effective use of color in all applications. We can, however, establish some broad principles based on the mechanisms of human color perception." Murch offered three sets of guidelines—physiological, perceptual, and cognitive (see Table 13.1).

Here is some additional guidance on designing with color. Aaron Marcus is a well-known interface designer and consultant in the computer industry with a background in information and graphic design. Marcus (1990) applies these principles to the use of color: organization, economy, emphasis, interactions, symbolism, and communication. His "Ten Commandments of Color" (Marcus, 1986) are a good list of guidelines, in addition to Murch's:

1. Use a maximum of from three to seven colors.

2. Use foveal (center) and peripheral colors appropriately. (Use red and green in the center of the visual field. Blue is good for slide and screen background and borders.)

3. Use colors that exhibit a minimum shift in color/size if the colors change in size in the imagery.

4. Do not use high-chroma, spectrally extreme colors simultaneously.

5. Use familiar, consistent color codings with appropriate references.

6. Use the same color for grouping related elements.

7. Use the same color code for training, testing, application, and publication.

8. Use high-value, high-saturation colors to draw attention.

9. If possible, use redundant coding of shape as well as color.

10. Use color to enhance black-and-white information.

TABLE 13.1   Guidelines for Color on Computer Displays, from Murch (1984)

Physiological Guidelines:

1. Avoid displaying highly saturated, spectrally extreme colors together.
2. Saturated blue should be avoided for text, thin lines, and small shapes.
3. Avoid adjacent colors that differ only in the amount of blue.
4. Older operators need higher brightness levels to distinguish colors.
5. Colors change in appearance as the ambient light level changes.
6. The magnitude of a detectable change in color varies across the spectrum.
7. It is difficult to focus upon edges created by color alone.
8. Avoid red and green in the periphery of large-scale displays.
9. Opponent colors go well together (red-green or yellow-blue).
10. For color-deficient observers, avoid single-color distinctions.

Perceptual Guidelines:

1. Not all colors are equally discernible.
2. Luminance does not equal brightness.
3. Different hues have inherently different saturation levels.
4. Lightness and brightness are distinguishable on a printed hardcopy, but not on a color display.
5. Not all colors are equally readable or legible.
6. Hues change with intensity and background color.
7. Avoid the need for color discrimination in small areas.

Cognitive Guidelines:

1. Do not overuse color.
2. Be aware of the nonlinear color manipulation in video and hardcopy.
3. Group related elements by using a common background color.
4. Similar colors connote similar meanings.
5. Brightness and saturation draw attention.
6. Link the degree of color change to event magnitude.
7. Order colors by their spectral position.
8. Warm and cold colors should indicate action levels.

Tests show that color can be effectively used to improve performance. One study (Widjaja, 1992) assessed program debugging performance by three groups of developers given three different color-coding schemes: (1) black-and-white, (2) color groupings that arranged loops and nested structures in five shades of green, and (3) color-flagging that highlighted potential error areas in orange. Their research suggested that the color-coding substantially improved error detections in C-language programs. Many studies similar to this one have shown the effectiveness of using color to highlight information.

Printing costs increase dramatically with each color that is added to any black-and-white material. Therefore, print designers use color very carefully to add value where needed and do so *only when the added value justifies the additional printing costs.*

KEY IDEA! *Utilize colors in the interface with the same care and frugality as if each color had to be cost-justified. Even if computer displays can show 256 colors, 1,024 colors, or even more, don't try to use as many colors as possible. The basic principle is:* Design the user interface first in black-and-white and then add color later, and use color only where needed.

If you are interested in reading more about the use of color, here's something new worth reading. The July/August 1996 issue of *ACM interactions* features an article by Shubin, Falck, and Johansen (1996) entitled, "Exploring Color in Interface Design." It even has cutout color swatches to play with as you follow the examples in the article.

Audio and Animation in the User Interface

Audio in the User Interface

> *The audio channel is an underutilized resource in human-computer interaction. . . . It becomes even more so when we come to the realization that in some (often critical) situations, all of us are visually impaired, perhaps because of the visual system being saturated, loss of light, or age. This is therefore an area that deserves and must receive more attention.*
>
> Baecker et al. (1995)

There is always a lot of discussion over the use of audio as feedback in the user interface. If it is done well, is unobtrusive, and can be turned down or off by users, that's great. But users are quick to look for the volume control if audio beeps, clicks, sounds, and voices start to bother them and interrupt their work. I'm talking here about simple forms of audio. In Chapter 15, I'll discuss how speech technology is being used to enhance current user interfaces and create new types as well.

KEY IDEA! *First figure out when it is appropriate to use auditory information rather than visual information (see Table 13.2). Then determine the appropriate type of auditory presentation for users in a given situation. Finally, audio must be customizable so users can either turn down the volume or turn the audio off altogether.*

As I discussed regarding color, guidelines regarding animation are also based on human perceptual and cognitive abilities and limitations, rather than on the software people use. Deatherage (1972) lists when to use either auditory or visual media to display information. Use these guidelines, summarized in Table 13.2, to help you decide *if* and *when* to use audio information. Even though these guidelines are over 20 years old, they still apply today.

Many work environments today are open; that is, workers do not have individual offices. When people work in areas where other people, telephones, and computers are all in close proximity, audio information will most likely not be effective. Workers in these situations often can't tell whose telephone is ringing or whose computer is beeping or talking to them.

Most computer software today uses at least some audio feedback, usually short beeps when an error is made or an invalid choice is tried. Even these seemingly inconspicuous beeps can be annoying and even embarrassing. In some cultures, workers lose face if they make errors, and they do not want colleagues to know if they make even the simplest error on the computer. In these cases, the last thing they want is their computer beeping at them. Most users in these countries immediately turn off computer sounds when they set up their systems.

Other software programs use prerecorded phrases to inform users of their actions. The CompuServe Information Manager program says, "Welcome to CompuServe," when users open the program. This audio greeting doesn't add

TABLE 13.2 Guidelines for Auditory or Visual Presentation, from Deatherage (1972)

Use Auditory Presentation if:	Use Visual Presentation if:
1. The message is simple.	1. The message is short.
2. The message is short.	2. The message is long.
3. The message will not be referred to later.	3. The message will be referred to later.
4. The message deals with events in time.	4. The message deals with location in space.
5. The message calls for immediate action.	5. The message does not call for immediate action.
6. The visual system of the person is overburdened.	6. The auditory system of the person is overburdened.
7. The receiving location is too bright or dark—adaptation integrity is necessary.	7. The receiving location is too noisy.
8. The person's job requires him or her to move about continually.	8. The person's job allows him or her to remain in one position.

much to the human-computer interaction and can become annoying. However, when users log on to CompuServe and there is electronic mail waiting, the program says, "You have new mail." This audio message does provide useful feedback for users who might otherwise forget to check if there is mail waiting for them. As you can see, there is sometimes only a slight difference between audio that is annoying feedback and audio that is welcome information.

Animation in the User Interface

Why do we believe that animation could help make interfaces more understandable? The reason is that animation is an effective means of portraying complex processes evolving over time.

Baecker, et al. (1991)

Animation, like audio, catches the interest of developers and users alike. Today, you can find hundreds or even thousands of icons on CD-ROM or online bulletin boards. When the mouse is moved over different areas of the screen, the mouse pointer changes to show the types of actions you can perform with that object or area of the screen. There are numerous types of mouse-pointer icons (arrow, move, size, wait, i-beam, do-not, and so on). Animated icons and mouse pointers are also available for these icon types. I've even seen an animation utility that makes the mouse-pointer arrow wag its tail as it moves across the screen.

KEY IDEA! Animation *is defined as a change in the visual appearance of a graphic element over time. As with audio, much of the value of animation is purely for entertainment, although animated cursors may make it easier to see the cursor on the screen, especially with smaller, low-resolution notebook computer screens. Animation can be used to enhance visual communication between computers and users. However, visual information is effective only if users can actually see and understand it.*

The Apple Macintosh was one of the first popular interface environments to utilize animation. Mac users can describe how the Macintosh trashcan bulges when they drop an object in it. Most of today's graphical user interfaces utilize at least a minimal set of animation techniques to show actions, progress, and status of user-initiated or system processes. Common operating system interface animations include zooming and shrinking windows as they open and close, using an hourglass or watch icon to show the progress of short processes, and using progress indicators to show progress of longer processes. Figure 13.6 shows the progress indicator animation in Windows 95. As items are moved or copied from one location to another, the dialog shows a piece of paper floating from one folder to another. A progress indicator bar is also provided below the animation to show completion progress. Also notice the textual feedback that is provided—the action (Move, in this example), the file name (EOSUN.ZIP), source location (OS2ZIPS), and target location (TEMP) are dynamically presented. Users are certain of what is happening when a well-designed dialog like this is presented on the screen.

Animation is also used in more complex applications. Patricia Sullivan (1991) noted, "When the National Science Foundation funded EXPRES, a project that developed methods for multimedia electronic document submission, interviews revealed that scientists wanted animation for the document so that they could demonstrate reactions inside the electronic text."

KEY IDEA! *With GUIs and OOUIs, users are usually faced with many more icons on the screen than they normally use. Icons, if well designed, provide information about what an object is and does. Animation can be used to highlight important icons, to show the status of a particular object, or even to explain the behavior of an object.*

A printer icon should be able to show users that the printer is out of paper and needs assistance. An in- or out-basket should give users an idea of the number of items in their mail and their urgency. In an early prototype of the OS/2 interface, we were able to display a count of the contents of each container on the screen, so users didn't have to open a folder to find out how many things

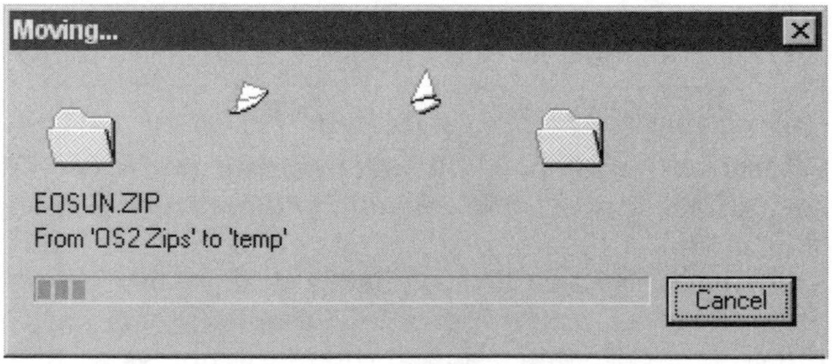

Figure 13.6 Animated progress indicator in Windows 95.

were in it. Although this isn't standard presentation behavior for any operating system's containers, you can possibly add this type of dynamic animation to the system's (or at least your own) class of container objects.

KEY IDEA! *There is very little guidance available on when to use animation in the user interface. The Microsoft guidelines have only about half a page on animation. The best general description I've seen of* when *and* why *to use animation is Baecker et al. (1991). They discuss ways to assist users through animation in their article,* Bringing Icons to Life.

Baecker et al. (1991) list ways animation should be used to specifically help the interface answer user questions (Table 13.3).

Interface Terminology and International Design

Eight issues ago (December 19, 1995), we asked why a French book about Microsoft Excel was called Excel: Fingers in the Nose. *Dozens of Franco-phones rushed to the rescue, and none was more articulate than our Swiss friend Adrian Breugger, who explained that "fingers in the nose" is the literal translation of the colloquial expression "les doigts dans le nez," which is meant to connote "easy," "with little effort," or "with one hand tied behind your back" (or up your nose).*

"Abort, Retry, Fail?," *PC Magazine* (1996)

TABLE 13.3   Questions Animation Can Answer, from Baecker et al. (1991)

User Interface Topic	Questions Animation Can Answer
1. Identification	1. What is this?
2. Transition	2. Where have I come from and gone to?
3. Orientation	3. Where am I?
4. Choice	4. What can I do now?
5. Demonstration	5. What can I do with this?
6. Explanation	6. How do I do this?
7. Feedback	7. What is happening?
8. History	8. What have I done?
9. Interpretation	9. Why did this happen?
10. Guidance	10. What should I do now?

Developers don't always speak the same language as users. That's one reason why they don't often communicate with each other—they don't have much in common! That's also why interface designers, information developers, and technical writers should determine interface terminology and be responsible for *every word* that appears on the interface.

Figure 13.7 shows two signs I've collected as examples of technobabble, where the message is simple but the words are not. The first sign is at the entrance to a golf course in Boulder, Colorado. You have to read it more than once to understand the meaning. The sign could just say, "Watch out for golf balls. Park here at your own risk." The second sign is in a restroom in a software development company office in Austin, Texas. It is a rather strange way to say, "Please hold down the handle to flush the toilet properly."

Earlier I described a system message that told users their password was too long and they should reenter at least a certain number of bytes of information. Terms like *abort, kill, terminate,* and many others do not belong on computer screens. A familiar message for Windows users is the dreaded GPF message— meaning *general protection fault.* Users don't know what it is, but they know it is bad news when it happens! Microsoft Bob tries to softens this rude situation with a more socially friendly message: "Something happened that I'm not quite sure how to deal with. Please restart your computer. If you still have trouble, running Bob Setup again might solve the problem." Isn't that a nice way to tell users that their computer is locked up and they must restart it?

As you can see, this is an area where most software interfaces need work. The problem is compounded by the international community of users. The examples above show poor use of the English language. Imagine what these messages would look like if they were translated into German, French, or Italian!

If you want to read more about the very interesting area of developing interfaces for international consumption, read Tony Fernandes' book, *Global Interface Design* (1995), and Jakob Nielsen's new book, *International User Interfaces* (del Galdo and Nielsen, 1996). Fernandes notes, "If usability and low training costs are really important, you can't get there by producing a solution for just one population in a multinational company. . . . Either pay at the beginning, when it's relatively inexpensive, or you will pay over and over again in higher training costs."

Warning!
Possible errant golf ball landing area. Park at your own risk.

Attention!
Effective flushing requires that the handle be held down for 5 seconds.

Figure 13.7   Examples of inappropriate terminology.

Not only are there cultural differences in language and terminology, but colors and visual organization can be interpreted very differently throughout the world. Objects and icons familiar to Americans may be totally unrecognizable to other populations. Fernandes uses Microsoft's Bob as an example of an interface that doesn't translate well in other countries. Bob's guides are characters based on animals. In other cultures, different animals can symbolize bad luck or have sacred connotations. Also, body parts and hand gestures should be avoided in international interfaces.

Be careful when organizing information in international interfaces. A favorite example is the monthly calendar. Most Americans don't realize that the U.S. calendar layout is not universal! Our calendar is usually arranged with the weekdays lined up horizontally across the top of the calendar and weeks in rows below. However, European calendars are laid out with days of the week arranged vertically in the left column with weeks arranged in columns. Figure 13.8 shows both the American and European calendars.

Other items such as telephone numbers, addresses, and postal codes are formatted quite differently across the world. Don't automatically format these types of fields when designing for an international audience.

Key Interface Design Issues

Which Controls to Use?

Never make assumptions about how your product will be used. People will always find new ways to use—and misuse, and abuse—your product.

Dinah McNutt (1995)

Sun	Mon	Tue	Wed	Thu	Fri	Sat
	1	2	3	4	5	6
7	8	9	10	11	12	13
14	15	16	17	18	19	20
21	22	23	24	25	26	27
28	29	30				

So		7	14	21	28
Mo	1	8	15	22	29
Di	2	9	16	23	30
Mi	3	10	17	24	
Do	4	11	18	25	
Fr	5	12	19	26	
Sa	6	13	20	27	

Figure 13.8   American and European calendar layouts.

Every detail and every control on the screen should serve some purpose in users' eyes. From the developer's perspective, each piece of data or input field on the screen can be presented in any number of ways. How do developers and designers figure out what controls, text, and labels should represent a particular piece of data or input field on the screen?

Look at Figure 13.9. I have shown nine different ways to design one simple input field that might be in any program, asking a question about the user's age: "Are you 21 or under, or over 21?" I'm sure there are even more ways to present the input field, but I just chose the controls I thought would be used most often. In the left column, the first field is a simple text box, where users are asked to type "Yes" or "No." Next is a set of option buttons with "Yes" and "No" labels. Third is a single-selection list box. Fourth, another set of option buttons uses different labels to capture the same information. The next column shows a check box, a drop-down list box, a "well" control (Microsoft term) or value set (IBM term), a spin button, and finally, a slider control.

KEY IDEA! *Which controls are best for gathering certain types of user input?* There is no one correct way to represent information in the interface! *Unfortunately, published industry guidelines and references give little guidance in this area. It really depends on the type of data that needs to be collected, how much data may be available, who users are, how other information is presented on the screen, and how users will most likely interact with the controls on the screen (keyboard, mouse, touchscreen, etc.).*

One key factor that must be addressed when choosing controls is *scalability*. A drop-down list box may work fine for a list of 5 items, but how will it work if the list contains 500 items? A vertical scroll bar works well for a 20-page document, but is it the best way to scroll a 200-page document? Dinah McNutt (1995) cautions, "Vendors should design software that works well for both the low-end and the high-end user. A menu with 10 items is quite manageable, but what if there are 1,000?"

Think about the amount of data that users could potentially work with when you choose to use a particular control. Look at cascading menus. If there are a limited number of choices per level and only a few levels, a cascading menu works very well. Used as a general-purpose interface element, as in the Windows 95 Start button menu, it can easily get out of control. Because I have many program groups, the Programs cascading menu fills the entire screen immediately, leaving me no way to actually traverse the menus to choose the item I want.

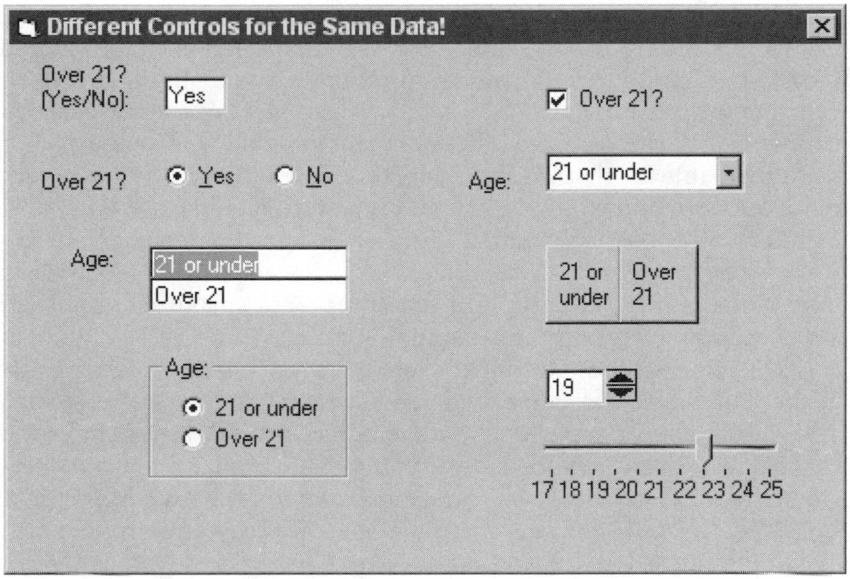

Figure 13.9   Different controls for the same data.

KEY IDEA! *Always investigate what will happen to your interface when more data than expected is pumped through it.*

Menu Bar and/or Toolbar? That Is the Question!

Menu bars, toolbars, and buttons can all be used to present the same user actions. In most cases, users are surprised when they don't see a familiar-looking menu bar in a window. Do users really need menu bars in all windows, or are toolbars an appropriate replacement (or addition to menu bars)? Can command buttons replace or supplement menu bars and toolbars? There isn't much research in this area, but I'll report what they say.

When IBM designed the OS/2 user interface, desktop folders did not have menu bars in the opened window. We tested whether this would be a problem for users. We developed a prototype where all windows had menu bars and all objects had pop-up menus. The background area of opened windows and the desktop background also had pop-up menus. Twenty-one evaluators were asked, if they could choose between using a pop-up menu and a menu bar menu, which one would they prefer to work with? Thirteen of them said they would prefer working with a pop-up menu, while seven said they would rather use the menu bar. One evaluator expressed no preference. However, they don't want to be limited to only using pop-up menus—18 out of 21 said they didn't want menu bars removed. While these results show a preference for pop-up menus, users want a choice. It was recommended that menu bars should be made available in the interface and that users should be provided with the option of using them or not, along with pop-up menus.

Ellis et al. (1994) researched users working with menu bars and toolbars. Using word processing tasks, groups of users were provided with menu bars only, toolbars only, or both. Test measures were speed of command selection and number of errors during selection. Subjective user satisfaction was also collected. Their results showed that users were much quicker at using the buttons on the toolbar for tasks that involved changing character styles, such as boldface, italics, and underlining. These actions required only a single mouse click to perform using the toolbar, while using the menu bar required users to select a menu bar choice, then select an action from the drop-down menu, and sometimes open a dialog box and manipulate check boxes and option buttons. Users given both menu bars and a toolbar did not perform as well as those using just the toolbar, even though they could have also used just the toolbar. Perhaps it was because they had to spend time thinking about which method to use, rather than having only one access method.

Most users said they liked the ability to perform frequent actions quickly using the toolbar, but they said the icon representations were not always easy to understand. As a result of this study, the researchers offered suggested guidelines for more effective design:

- Provide consistent icons across applications.
- Provide consistent button interaction.
- Group together buttons which summon related commands.
- Order buttons in a meaningful manner.
- Place buttons for speed.
- Allow for keyboard selection.
- Allow for user configurability.
- Avoid overly cluttering the display.
- Icons should be visually distinct.
- Use color, but be careful.
- Buttons should give visual cues to their activation.

KEY IDEA! *Research and guidelines reinforce professional experience in this area. Toolbars are a wonderful, yet strange interface beast. They are quicker to access—but are accessible only to mouse users! Familiar and common icons are easily recognized—but uncommon tasks often have unrecognizable icons. Menu bars and drop-downs are browsable—no action is performed until a drop-down selection is made—toolbars are clickable and it's done (tooltip help balloons now allow users to browse toolbars). Menu bars contain all actions and routings for the window; toolbars should only display common, frequently occurring actions.*

Whether to Drag-and-Drop, That Is the Question

As interfaces become more object-oriented, more graphic, and more visual, direct manipulation is becoming more prevalent. However, drag and drop has a problem—there is no visual indication that objects can or should be dragged and dropped on other objects. If users don't learn how and when to use drag-and-drop, the designed-in benefits won't be realized. Now, here's the tough part—*designers must build interface metaphors and offer intuitively obvious visual layouts that encourage and invite users to directly manipulate objects in the interface!* Otherwise, how will users figure out what objects can be manipulated? Jared Spool (1996) offers a four-step mindset that users must adopt to use drag-and-drop effectively:

1. What objects can I drag?
2. Where can I drop them?
3. What's it going to do when I let it go?
4. If I don't like it how do I undo it?

KEY IDEA! *The user interface needs to be so obvious as to what users should do that they don't have to think hard about or guess how to interact with what they see on the screen. Unfortunately, we haven't yet figured out how to indicate that an object can be dragged and dropped.*

Finally, in the rush to direct-manipulation interfaces, don't forget the *scalability* issue. Dragging one object or a few objects may be appropriate and easy, but what about working with hundreds of objects? How do users select the group of objects before they can even drag them? Should they have to drag and drop hundreds of objects, or is there a better way to do it? Don't force users to have to rely on direct manipulation when other techniques might be quicker and easier with large sets of data.

Window Layout and Design

The layout and design of elements within windows is both an art and a science. Color, font, size, which controls, size of controls, orientation of controls, layout symmetry, highlighting, and numerous other factors all influence the final design in even a simple window.

Figure 13.10 shows a simple registration wizard for a product I recently purchased. See how symmetrical the text fields are—the Name, Company, and Country fields are all the same length—allowing users to think they can type in a long string of characters. However, look at what happened in the Company field. I typed in my company name, *Interface Design and Development,* but the last two characters were not accepted. Based on the length of the text field, I was completely surprised when I was not allowed to type the complete name of my company. Visually, users are led to believe that they can fill the field with text characters, but from the developer's perspective, regardless of the length of the text field in the window, only a certain number of characters are accepted as input in the field. The visual layout looks clean and symmetrical, but it portrays an inaccurate picture of what users can do on the screen.

Top Ten Usability Problems with GUIs and OOUIs

Through research and practical experience, IBM usability professionals compiled a list of the ten most common usability problems found across most graphical and object-oriented interfaces. (This list should have some familiar themes if you have been involved at all in usability efforts on any computer software project.)

1. Ambiguous menus and icons
2. Single-direction languages
3. Input and direct-manipulation limits
4. Highlighting and selection limitations
5. Unclear step sequences

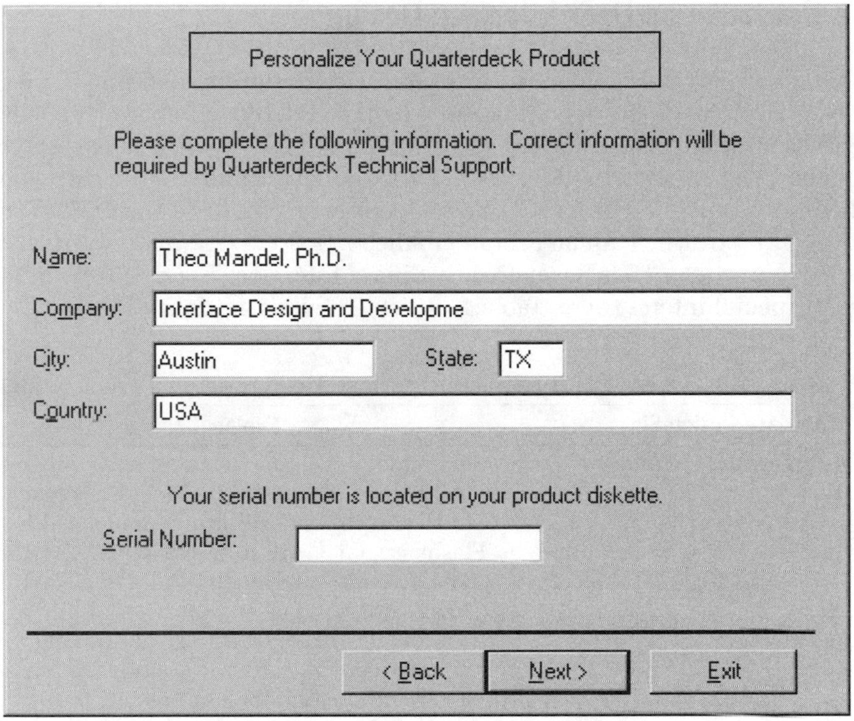

Figure 13.10   Visually confusing text fields.

6. More steps to manage the interface than to do tasks
7. Complex linkage between and within applications
8. Inadequate feedback and confirmation
9. Lack of system anticipation and intelligence
10. Inadequate error messages, help, tutorials, and documentation

As a software user and/or developer, you might recognize many of these problem areas from personal experience. No matter what operating system you use and what interface and product development tools you use, these are still the most problematic areas in software product user interfaces today. The interface principles and concepts, along with usability test results I've discussed, will help you design and build better product interfaces. If you're a product user rather than a designer or developer, let the product developers know your thoughts and feelings about their product's interface. Chances are, they could use the feedback from actual users of their product!

More Guidance on User Interface Design

Chapter 5 covered the "golden rules" of interface design by defining three areas of design principles. To conclude this chapter, I'd like to share some design guidelines from several interface design experts. Tandy Trower is director of Advanced User Interfaces at Microsoft. I worked with Tandy in the early days of the IBM-Microsoft effort on the CUA architecture for Windows and OS/2. Tandy's column (entitled "The Human Factor") in the *Microsoft Developer Network News* included one article, "The Seven Deadly Sins of Interface Design" (Trower, 1993), that is of special interest here. Table 13.4 lists Trower's guidelines.

TABLE 13.4   The Seven Deadly Sins of Interface Design, from Trower (1993)

Interface Design Sin	Explanation
1. Design for the technology rather than the user	Sometimes developers want to show off great technology. The user interface is designed after the technical underpinnings are locked in.
2. "Coolness"	Flashy graphics will not save a poor interface. There seems to be an obsession to make things "cool" or "sexy."
3. Logical vs. visual thinking	Software design requires logical thinking. Users interacting with software are typically more unstructured and don't appreciate the relationship between one piece of code and another.
4. User input as right or wrong	Don't assume input is accurate. Understand that users will make mistakes, so design the interface to be forgiving.
5. Overextend basics	Extend basic interface elements, such as standard dialogs. Don't compromise simple operations by extending them to include infrequent ones—"make simple things simple, complex things possible."
6. Fix it in the documentation	Consulting the documentation is usually the last thing users do, and typically by that time they are already frustrated. Don't try to fix a defect in the user interface through the documentation.
7. Fix it in the next release	This has the potential for unexpected, negative side effects because users often become accustomed to the quirks in an interface and may begin to be dependent on them. Because of our nature, it is often difficult to unlearn a task once we figure out how to do it, even if the new version is better.

Here are some general interface design and window layout guidelines from Wilchins (1995):

1. Asymmetry = active, symmetry = serene.
2. Never pursue moderation to excess.
3. Pursue consistency to excess.
4. Consistent interfaces mean better system implementation.
5. Take the time to line things (controls) up exactly.
6. If you're going to have objects out of alignment, do it dramatically.
7. People tend to gestalt screen objects like they were in the real, physical world.
8. Too much symmetry can make screens harder to read.
9. Items that break a pattern stand out.
10. Items of a similar size or color are perceived as belonging to a group.

Finally, here's some advice from the Macintosh side of interface design. Maggie Canon (1995) wrote in *MacUser* magazine:

1. Focus on content, content, content.
2. Keep your expectations realistic.
3. Learn to recognize what works and what doesn't.
4. Use the right tools for the job.
5. Know your own technical strengths and weaknesses.

To see some examples of good and bad designs, check out Michael Darnell's Home Page, *Bad Human Factors Designs* at http//www.baddesigns.com/. There you'll see a scrapbook of illustrated examples of real-world things that are hard to use because they do not follow human factors principles. Although these designs are not computer designs (they are similar to Don Norman's [1988] examples), they do give readers an appreciation for what people constantly face when "interfacing" with everyday things. Also check out *Visual Interface Design for Windows: Effective User Interfaces for Windows 95, Windows NT, and Windows 3.1*, a new book for Windows interface designers written by Virginia Howlett (1996), former director of Visual User Interface Design at Microsoft.

References

Baecker, Ronald, Ian Small, and Richard Mander. 1991. Bringing icons to life. *Proceedings of ACM CHI'91,* pp. 1–6.

Canon, Maggie. 1995. Golden rules: Implementing multimedia technology. *MacUser* 11(9): 21.

Deatherage, B.H. 1972. Auditory and other sensory forms of information presentation. In Van Cott, H., and R. Kinkade (Eds.), *Human Engineering Guide to Equipment.* Washington, DC: U.S. Government Printing Office.

del Galdo, Elisa and Jakob Nielsen. 1996. *International User Interfaces.* New York: Wiley.

Ellis, Jason, Chi Tran, Jake Ryoo, Ben Shneiderman. 1994. Buttons vs. menus: An exploratory study of pull-down menu selection as compared to button bars. Human-Computer Interaction Laboratory, Department of Computer Science, University of Maryland, CAR-TR-764.

Fernandes, Tony. 1995. *Global Interface Design.* Chestnut Hill, MA: Academic Press.

Howlett, Virginia. 1996. *Visual Interface Design for Windows: Effective User Interfaces for Windows 95, Windows NT, and Windows 3.1.* New York: Wiley.

Marcus, Aaron. 1986. Ten commandments of color. *Computer Graphics Today* 3(11): 394.

Marcus, Aaron. 1990. Principles of effective visual communication for graphical user interface design. *UnixWorld* (October): 135–138.

McNutt, Dinah. 1995. Way you see: What you want? *Byte* (November): 88–89.

Murch, Gerald M. 1984. Physiological principles for the effective use of color. *IEEE CG&A* (November): 49–54.

Norman, Donald A. 1988. *The Design of Everyday Things.* New York: Doubleday.

Shubin, Hal, Deborah Falck, and Ati Gropius Johansen. 1996. Exploring color in interface design. *ACM interactions* III(4).

Spool, Jared. 1996. Drag & drop has a learning problem. *Eye for Design* (January/February).

Sullivan, Patricia. 1991. Multimedia computer products and usability: Needed research. *Proceedings of the IPCC,* pp. 71–77.

Trower, Tandy. 1993. The seven deadly sins of interface design. *Microsoft Developer Network News* (July): 16.

Tufte, Edward. 1983. *The Visual Display of Quantitative Information.* Cheshire, CT: Graphics Press.

Tufte, Edward. 1990. *Envisioning Information.* Cheshire, CT: Graphics Press.

Tufte, Edward. 1992. The user interface: The point of competition. *Bulletin of the American Society for Information Science* (June/July): 15–17.

Wayne, Michael. 1991. The power of color. *Presentation Products Magazine* (January): 48.

Widjaja, T. 1992. Impact of color-coding in program debugging. *Human Factors Society Proceedings,* pp. 321–325.

Wilchins, Riki. 1995. Screen objects: The building blocks of user interfaces. *Data Based Advisor* 13(7): 66–70.

CHAPTER FOURTEEN

HELP, ADVISORS, WIZARDS, AND MULTIMEDIA

No matter how powerful the computer or how far-reaching the information network, it means little if the average office worker can't use it. Improved software is key to making information technology accessible and businesses more productive.

Evan Schwartz (1993)

Make it idiot-proof and someone will make a better idiot.

Anonymous

Help and Training: Why and When?

A revolution is taking place in education, one that deals with the philosophy of how one teaches, of the relationship between teacher and student, of the way in which a classroom is structured, and the nature of curriculum. At the heart is the idea that people learn best when engrossed in the topic, motivated to seek out new knowledge and skills because they need them in order to solve the problem at hand.

Donald Norman and James Spohrer (1996)

In 1995, more than two-thirds of help desks experienced 70 percent higher service volumes than in 1994.

Help Desk Institute (1996)

Software interface design is evolving from being user-centered to user-involved and learner-centered (see Chapter 12). At the heart of this movement is the understanding that users learn *while* they are performing. It is becoming very difficult to separate learning from performing and to design standalone learning and training for software products. Software products themselves should offer many ways for users to learn the product *while* they use it, rather than having to learn how it works *before* they can actually make use of it. Software and technology training is a billion-dollar industry worldwide, and many companies assume that it's easier and cheaper to export jobs and import skilled workers than it is to train their own employees. According to Dave Flach (1995), "If you work for such an organization and are trying to get a training budget in order to train yourself or your staff to learn the next technology, you could be in for a very long wait."

You may not realize it, but support and training make up a large portion of the costs of using and maintaining computers. Gartner Group shows that the five-year total cost of ownership for a PC grew from $19,500 in 1987 to more than $41,500 in 1996. Software products you buy or develop in the future (actually, beginning right now!) must provide learning aids such as visual feedback, online help, wizards, and tutorials. All of these aspects of a software system that support users performing their tasks fall under the umbrella of *electronic performance support,* or EPS. Well-designed and usable EPS can drastically cut training and support costs in any organization or company.

KEY IDEA! *Users ask many questions while they are learning and using software products. Where do users go to answer their questions? Some users see if online help will answer their questions, while others immediately seek out human support. Wherever users seek answers to their questions—whether it be online help, tutorial, colleague, help desk, or telephone support—they will not be satisfied unless they get timely and appropriate answers.*

Baecker et al. (1995) compiled a list of user questions (see Table 14.1). They drew their items from two articles worth reading—Sellen and Nicol (1990) and Baecker et al. (1991).

When to Train: Just-in-Time Training

Education on demand, in homes and on the job, will be a far bigger business than entertainment on demand.

R. Wayne Oler (1995)

TABLE 14.1 Questions Computer Users Ask, from Baecker et al. (1995)

Question Types	Example Questions
Informational	What kinds of things can I do with this program?
Descriptive	What is this? What does this do?
Procedural	How do I do this?
Interpretive	What is happening now? Why did that happen? What does this mean?
Navigational	Where am I? Where have I come from and gone to?
Choice	What can I do now?
Guidance	What should I do now?
History	What have I done?
Motivational	Why should I use this program? How will it benefit me?
Investigative	What else should I know? Did I miss anything?

Part of the overall training issue is *when* to train people. Many organizations send students to courses and training seminars well in advance of new technologies or programs they will use for their work. Unfortunately, little information is usually retained by the time people actually get to use what they had been trained on. Users often aren't given a chance to gradually ramp up their learning before new systems are put in front of them. More often than not, users face a threesome they can't cope with—(1) new hardware with new input devices (touchscreen, mouse, trackball, etc.), (2) new operating systems and interfaces, and (3) new general and task-specific products and interfaces. *Education on demand* addresses training workers *when they need the education,* rather than *before they need it.* "Organizations are linking learning to productivity, rather than training in advance of the act. This is what we call 'just-in-time learning,' " says Robert Johansen (1994).

Electronic performance support provides this type of training. The information is there at the request of users when they want it (and not before they need it), in the form they want it, and they can use it *while* they do their work and perform their tasks.

The Paradigm Shift—How to Train for It

> *If you tell me, I will listen.*
> *If you show me, I will see.*
> *If you let me experience, I will learn.*
>
> Lao Tzu (sixth century B.C.)

One major problem is the paradigm shift when migrating from mainframe systems or command-line–based user interfaces. Although GUIs and OOUIs seem very natural and easy-to-learn for those of us who design, develop, and use them, it is not the same for users who, having used older software for many years, suddenly find a new computer and new software sitting in front of them when they go to work one morning. People need an incentive to learn new skills—whether personal or job related. Some of these incentives are obvious—better jobs, job security, new careers, and so on. Lots of pressure is put on computer users when they are told they must master new skills or they will possibly lose their job!

As software systems are redesigned, people's job responsibilities and tasks may change. For example, in an insurance company, one type of claim processor may have been responsible for collecting personal information and basic claim information while others made the decision as to how much of the claim to reimburse and how to handle it. New software design and new corporate "empowerment" guidelines now allow all claims processors to perform all steps of the process themselves. Besides learning new computing skills, their job description has changed and they are now responsible for more decisions and more work than before. Are workers paid any more for this additional work and responsibility? No! Are they expected to maintain their previous levels of productivity in the new environment? Yes! You can see why user attitudes and expectations can drastically change in these situations. I've even seen workers cut the cable to their PC mouse to protest the change in their working conditions. Don't expect all workers to greet new software systems with open arms!

KEY IDEA! *When users face new hardware, new operating systems, and new software all at the same time in their workplace, we (designers, developers, and usability professionals) have a difficult time determining the source of usability problems. If users can't perform a particular task, is it because they can't use the mouse or they can't figure out how to navigate and use the new operating system, or is there a problem in the applications themselves? With the three confounded variables, you can't accurately determine the source of the problem!*

Although some costs may increase and productivity may decrease, users must be given the opportunity to *learn* and *use* PCs and new operating systems before they are asked to use new software products and be productive. Give users a chance to learn new *core skills* in a comfortable, unhurried learning environment. Set up training classrooms and labs, put PCs in break rooms, and offer employee paybacks and incentives if they purchase PCs for their home.

Let users play with their new computers and let them have fun while they learn!

KEY IDEA! *To get users over the paradigm shift, give them a fun and easy way to learn the basics of a graphical user interface—using the mouse to select, drag, and drop objects—and to use GUI menus. One program that has been quietly and sometimes secretly teaching novice users how to use a GUI since 1990 is Solitaire, the most-often-used (in my opinion) software program in the Windows environment. Although often criticized as a timewaster, Solitaire was given an industry award for its foresight in getting people to use the mouse as a pointing device.*

Many companies have banned computer games on PCs at work. These companies believe that time spent playing computer games is time wasted. However, this is not true when learning how to use a computer! Simple, common programs and tasks can greatly help users to learn PC skills. Schwartz (1993) illustrates the corporate view of Solitaire when it first came out: "Solitaire proved so distracting that Boeing Co. and other companies removed it from all their PCs." But then, people found out that it helped users through the early learning curve: "When useful applications for Windows arrived, workers had already mastered clicking and dragging on-screen objects—skills honed with Solitaire." PC educators and training specialists realize the importance of early and enjoyable training and there are now many educational and entertaining products to help users learn basic GUI and OOUI skills. Although many people play computer games for the enjoyment of the game, novice users can learn most of the necessary computing skills by playing games. Companies should rethink their ban of computer games when it comes to training and support. Users need help overcoming the paradigm shift!

Computer Anxiety

Many first-time and novice computer users are afraid of the computer. They may be afraid of what they might do to the computer or even of what the computer might do to them. One IBM study (Carroll and Mazur, 1986) addressing learning to use the Apple Lisa computer reported, "For example, learners often fear that they will damage the system. As one learner said, 'Will I damage this if I turn it off with the disk in? I have a terror of destroying things, so I'm still a bit tentative.' " This user already had four hours of experience with the system.

Other studies directly investigate the area of computer anxiety. The study of computer anxiety began in the early 1980s when personal computers began infiltrating the work areas of the United States. Although computers are now very common, especially in the office environment, the fear and hatred of computers is still prevalent. Many users have rational fears related to using computers, such as job displacement, repetitive stress injuries such as carpal tunnel syndrome, and even exposure to radiation from computer display screens. Other fears might be called irrational, such as feelings of impending doom or sure calamity because of contact with computers.

Many studies addressed the impact of computers in schools and universities. These studies have titles such as, "Initial Effects of Word Processing on Writing Quality and Writing Anxiety of Freshman Writers" (Teichman and Poris, 1989). This particular study concluded, "What is clear from our data is that word processing does not diminish writing quality among new users, despite the fact that the student must learn new skills and adjust to a new way of writing." They also noted that the one-semester study was probably not long enough to see if using computers could significantly improve students' essay writing. Computers have become a social and psychological area of study as the technology has invaded, and problematically enhanced, our lives.

Do Users Read Computer Documentation?

Insert quarter. Ball will serve automatically. Avoid missing ball for high score.
Instructions for use of Pong video game (1970s)

Computer hardware and software is almost always accompanied by documentation, in the form of installation-, learning-, and user-guides, reference materials, help, and problem determination information. Much of this product information is slowly being moved from hardcopy manuals to online information so users have the appropriate information immediately available while they do their work.

Most of the research in this area, and general experience with users during testing, tell us that people don't read computer documentation, even if it is necessary information for completing work or provides support or help. After years of usability tests, it is clear to me that there are three different types of users: those who won't read the documentation even if told to do so; those who read the documentation only when they can't figure out what to do on their own; and the rare case of those who will read information carefully before trying to do anything on the computer.

KEY IDEA! *Product documentation, including installation information, help, tutorials, messages, and any other support information for the product, should all be considered part of the user interface for the product. Don't forget to address these parts of the product when planning, designing, and conducting usability tests.*

Electronic Performance Support: What Is It?

Computers are increasingly mediating our moment-by-moment actions. The computer is an integral component in our work; we do our work through the computer. Thus, learning opportunities are omnipresent; instructional support can be interwoven naturally and beneficially into our daily activities.

Elliot Soloway and Amanda Pryor (1996)

Electronic performance support (EPS) is a set of "seamless and intuitive support mechanisms generating performance and learning through guidance, advice, and consistent access to information on demand" (Wood, 1995). This topic is addressed in *The Windows Interface Guidelines for Software Design* (Chapter 12, User Assistance). Microsoft states, "Online user assistance is an important part of a product's design and can be supported in a variety of ways, from automatic display of information based on context to commands that require explicit user selection. Its contents can be composed of contextual, procedural, explanatory, reference, or tutorial information. But user assistance should always be simple, efficient, and relevant so that a user can obtain it without becoming lost in the interface." EPS *interventions* (specific instances of support) include a variety of interface techniques and elements, ranging from simple help text to "wizards" or "advisors" that help users while they work.

Table 14.2 shows the range of learning styles that are supported by different types of EPS. Simple user assistance (such as tooltips, balloon help, messages, and help text) provides context-specific information for users to *read* so they can learn the product as they browse and explore.

The next level of learning is where users not only read text information, but can *see* (graphics, illustrations, etc.), and possibly *hear* (beeps, audio speech, etc.), information that supports their learning process and helps them do their tasks. GUIs and OOUIs have a rich visual environment where subtle (but important) visual and audible feedback lets users know *where* they are, *what* they are doing, and *how* to proceed from there.

The third level of learning activity allows users to *try something out* without actually performing the action. This is usually done through tutorials and sam-

TABLE 14.2　Types of Learning and Electronic Performance Support

Types of Learning	Type of Electronic Performance Support
Read Information ◆ Text-based ◆ Supports learning	◆ Messages ◆ Tooltips and bubble help ◆ Information line messages ◆ Help text
Read, See, and Hear ◆ Text, graphics, emphasis, animation, audio ◆ Supports learning	◆ Visual interface feedback ◆ Graphic emphasis ◆ Mouse cursors ◆ Mode indicators ◆ Animated icons and objects ◆ Help graphics and animation ◆ Screen animation (i.e., Lotus ScreenCam)
Read and Try ◆ Examples, procedures, samples ◆ Supports learning and performing	◆ Tutorials ◆ Advisors ◆ Samples
Do It! ◆ Perform steps or actions on actual work ◆ Supports learning and performing	◆ "Try it" ◆ Tutorial "Do it" ◆ Wizards ◆ Navigation and process maps

ple tasks where users can learn how a product works using similar data and doing similar tasks. Tutorials allow users to read and try techniques without using the actual product.

The highest level of learning occurs when users can actually perform real tasks while they are learning. More sophisticated tutorials not only allow users to practice simulated tasks within the tutorial, they allow users to jump into the product using the actual objects and real actions, while the tutorial is still there for further information and support.

KEY IDEA! *Wood (1995) points out that a proper EPS design "will integrate the worker, the work, and technology. It will teach and coach the system user with information at the point of need." A good EPS system and all user assistance techniques should provide information* when *users want it,* where *they want it, and* how *they want it! Remember, users are trying to learn while they are performing their tasks. EPS activities should support both learning and performance objectives.*

Electronic performance support has not been extremely successful to date. By their very nature, education and training exist because users can't do their job using only their software and online help systems. Although I am optimistic about new advances in EPS, we still don't know how best to support people while they do their work.

The New Breed of Tutorials: Advisors

Tutorials have been around for quite some time; they are a common form of online EPS help. Tutorials are typically standalone programs that walk users through the steps to complete a task, often using examples and sample code (see Table 14.2). Advisors are new types of tutorials that provide expert advice about how to complete a task in a linear format. It offers novice users a task-oriented route to complete a process. Advisors differ from *wizards,* which I'll describe next, by allowing users to view support information separately, yet simultaneously, while they manipulate the objects and data in the interface. Wizards control the flow and the task is performed by using the wizard, rather than using an advisor for support.

Advisors are a form of linear cue card. They typically can be accessed from a help menu on a menu bar drop-down, from a command button on a window, or from a pop-up menu. Advisors help users memorize common system and business processes by walking through processes step by step. Users must be able to perform the task themselves using the interface; the advisor does not actually perform the task with users.

Advisors can be used for general, operating-system-level tasks and objects, or for specific product-level support. Kurt Westerfeld, the developer of the popular OS/2 utility, Object Desktop, from Stardock Systems, Incorporated, has recently developed an exciting new *configurable* advisor for OS/2. The *Object Advisor* is a computer software invention that relates online help and computer-based training information directly to objects on a computer desktop. While online help has been provided for desktop objects in other products, such as IBM's OS/2 and Microsoft's Windows 95, this advisor presents online help for desktop objects as Web-based content, complete with full Internet link capability for relating desktop objects to internal and external computer resources. Figures 14.1 and 14.2 show the top and bottom sections of the advisor for the Stardock Extras folder object.

The configurable nature of the Stardock advisor is that information can be tailored for any object on the desktop, as determined by the content developer. Special tags, such as Properties, Help, Open, and Find, actually perform the action on the desktop object when selected. For example, clicking on Properties

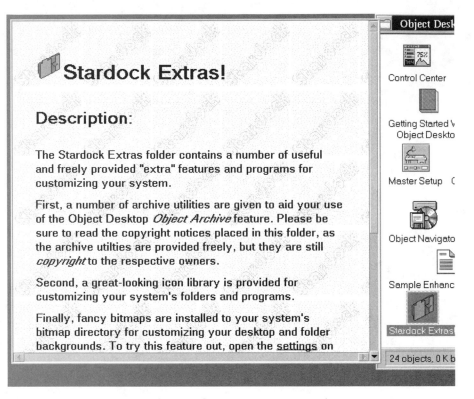

Figure 14.1   Object Desktop Advisor, part 1, in OS/2.

in the advisor will open a window with the properties view of the object addressed by the advisor on the desktop, not in the advisor! Other links, such as the Stardock Web Site, refer to an external Internet Web link that can be activated by selecting the text in the advisor. EPS developers can provide these additional features, rather than a standalone and separate information-only tutorial.

The content of the advisor is authored in industry-standard HyperText Markup Language (HTML), which is commonly used for Web-based information design. This means the same information and format can be created both for standard Internet access and for desktop access without any Internet connection. Updated information can easily be downloaded to replace existing advisor content. Figure 14.3 shows the Object Advisor—Definitions View window, where advisor content can be imported or created. The top panel of the window shows the content with HTML tags, while the bottom panel shows

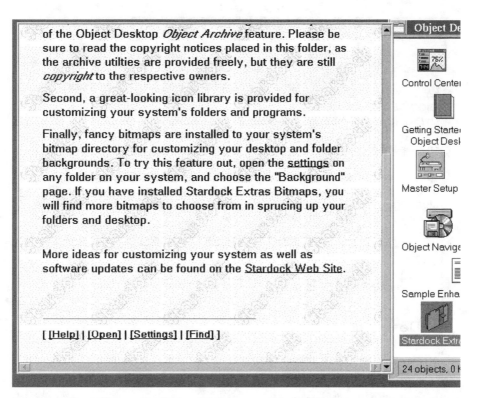

Figure 14.2 Object Desktop Advisor, part 2, in OS/2.

how the information will look in the advisor (WYSIWYG). I applaud those exciting advances in electronic performance support from innovators like Kurt Westerfeld. The goal is to make EPS and help content as easy to develop and as portable as possible.

User in Control or Program Guidance?

People often switch back and forth between different interaction styles without even thinking about what they are doing. I am a proponent of letting users be in control of the software rather than the program controlling user interaction and flow. In general, users want to be in control of their actions on the computer. There are other styles of computer interaction, however, that can be used as the main type of interface styles for a particular program or user. The three types of interface styles are:

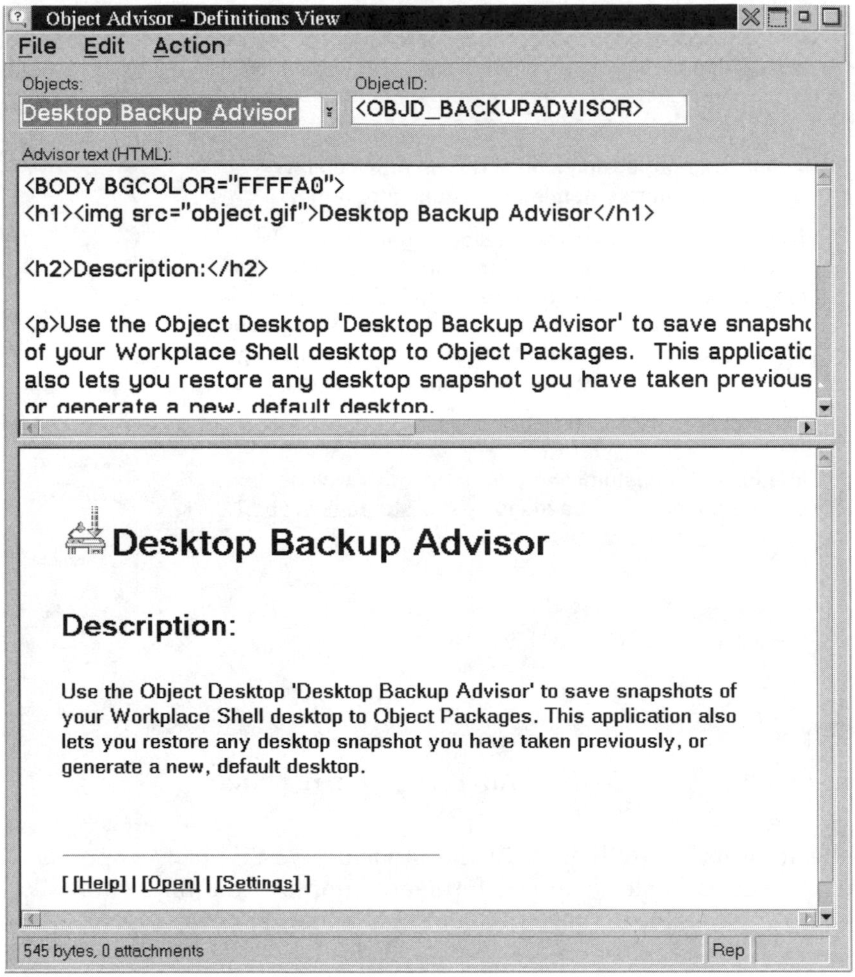

Figure 14.3   Object Desktop Advisor, Definitions View.

- ◆ User-driven
- ◆ Transaction-oriented
- ◆ Workflow

I have described *user-driven interfaces* throughout this book. The premise is that no preset sequence of actions or tasks is automatically assumed for users. *Transaction-oriented interfaces* are used where users perform repetitive processing tasks, usually through keyboard-only interaction. Users transferring data from paper forms basically need a simple interface where they can enter data with as few keystrokes as possible and proceed automatically to the next form to be entered.

Workflow interfaces allow novice and experienced users to follow a sequence of progressive steps to perform actions for well-defined tasks. Although somewhat system-driven, the workflow interface style is graphical, that is, it is window and mouse oriented rather than keyboard driven like the transaction-oriented interface. Workflow interfaces reduce the need to understand or navigate the system and reduce the time and effort to perform common tasks. Wizards are the main vehicle for creating workflow interfaces.

The Wonderful World of Wizards

Wizards can be used to perform common tasks such as installing programs and printers or more complex tasks such as filling out insurance claim forms or completing a job application. They can also be used to troubleshoot computer problems. Well then, just what is a wizard? A humorous definition, by Leonhard and Chen (1995), is "Oh, that's *easy*, a wizard is anything Microsoft damn well says it is." According to the Windows interface guidelines (Microsoft, 1995),

> a *wizard* is a special form of user assistance that automates a task through a dialog with the user. Wizards help the user accomplish tasks that can be complex and require experience. Wizards can automate almost any task, including creating new objects and formatting the presentation of a set of objects, such as a table or paragraph. They are especially useful for complex or infrequent tasks that the user may have difficulty learning or doing.

KEY IDEA! *Wizards take a few tasks that are done frequently and automate them. But the automation is often confusing, and different wizards work differently. Wizards are a new endeavor in user interfaces and we don't know how they will turn out. Just because wizards are new and are being used by operating systems and software programs doesn't mean that these aids will fulfill their promise. Design them and use them with care!*

Wizards can be developed for general operating system tasks (see Figure 14.4) and business-specific tasks. They are very powerful techniques for users to perform tasks quickly, accurately, and easily. A wizard's one downfall may be if users don't know the answer to a particular question required for the wizard to continue.

Windows is not the only platform on which wizards are being developed. Kurt Westerfeld (Stardock Systems, Inc.) has also developed one of the first commercial wizards that I know of, in a new product, Object Desktop Professional. The Object Desktop Backup Advisor (it really is a wizard, not an advisor, by my definitions) allows users to selectively configure the backup of their OS/2 desktop. Figure 14.5 shows one step in the wizard. Once users have successfully used a wizard on either Windows or OS/2, they should feel confident that they can use any other wizard on either platform. That's an example of cross-platform consistency!

Advanced research is being conducted to develop intelligent wizards that can dynamically display information based on user responses to previous questions. Microsoft's research group on Decision Theory has developed a Windows 95 Print Troubleshooter wizard that is available to anyone on the Internet. It is in the Microsoft Research section of Microsoft's Web site and can be found at http://131.107.1.182:80/pts/. The Welcome page tells users, "The Print Troubleshooter users *probabilities* and *costs* associated with different faults to gen-

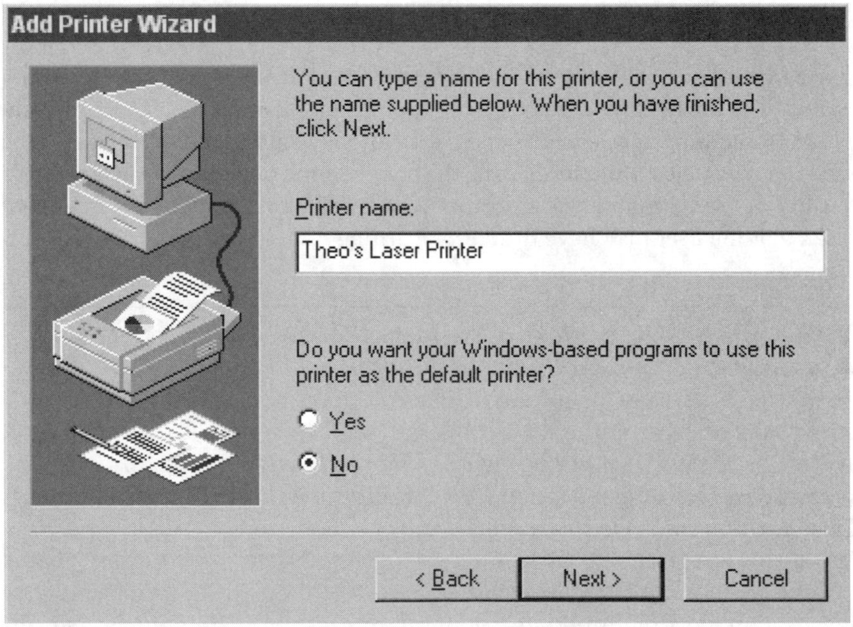

Figure 14.4   Add Printer wizard in Windows 95.

Figure 14.5 Object Desktop Professional backup wizard in OS/2.

erate a list of recommended troubleshooting steps. When you run the troubleshooter, the list of recommendations is regenerated after each question is answered, based on what the system knows about the problem you are having and the printing configuration." Figure 14.6 shows the first page of the wizard. Figure 14.7 shows the final page of the wizard, showing the answers to each page of questions along the way, and the final results. This wizard runs on the Internet, so it doesn't have the window elements and buttons you see in the Windows 95 Add Printer wizard in Figure 14.4. Also, remember that this is a research effort and is not meant to be a finished product. As you can see, the interface is rudimentary—the wizard is meant to focus on the underlying decision theory functional capability, and is not meant to be a user interface wizard design example.

Wizard Design Guidelines

Like any other area of the user interface, follow design principles, guidelines, and other good wizard implementations when designing wizards. Windows 95 itself and other utilities and programs offer many wizards (Microsoft Word, for example). Unfortunately, not all wizards look and work alike. Leonhard and Chen (1995) comment: "Take a look at some of Microsoft's wizards. They all

What type of problem are you having?

- ⦿ My document didn't print at all.
- ◯ Printing is unusually slow.
- ◯ I only got part of the page I expected.
- ◯ Graphics are distorted or incomplete.
- ◯ Fonts are missing or do not appear as they did on the screen.
- ◯ The printout is garbled or contains garbage.
- ◯ Some other problem.

[Continue]

Figure 14.6   Windows 95 Print Troubleshooter wizard on the Internet.

Status:

Problem	:	No Output		
Printing over Network:		⦿ No (Local printer)	◯ Yes (Network printer)	◯ Unknown
Print Environment	:	◯ DOS	⦿ Windows	◯ Unknown
Printer Driver Set Offline:		⦿ Online	◯ Unknown	
Printer On and Online:		⦿ Yes	◯ Unknown	
Print Buffer	:	⦿ Intact (not Corrupt)	◯ Unknown	
Local Disk Space	:	⦿ Greater than 2 Mb	◯ Unknown	
Local Printer Cable	:	⦿ Connected	◯ Unknown	
Printer Timeouts	:	⦿ Long Enough	◯ Unknown	
Correct Driver	:	⦿ Yes	◯ Unknown	
Printer Paper Supply:		⦿ Has Paper	◯ Unknown	
Correct Printer Selected:		⦿ Yes	◯ Unknown	
Correct Local Port	:	⦿ Yes	◯ Unknown	

Thank you for using the Enhanced Print Troubleshooter.

The Enhanced Print Troubleshooter is experimental software developed by the Decision Theory Group at Microsoft Research in collaboration with Microsoft Product Support Services.

Figure 14.7   Final page of the Windows 95 Print Troubleshooter wizard.

look and behave quite differently. It's almost as if the Windows people didn't talk to the Excel people, who didn't talk to the Word people. And forget about the NT group." Don't just choose a wizard at random and copy its design. The Windows design guide offers a small section on designing wizards. I've combined their guidelines with my own in Table 14.3. The guidelines are listed by design topic.

KEY IDEA! *Do not use wizards for information that is* just grouped together *rather than in a predetermined,* automated sequence. *That is, don't use wizards to replace* properties *dialogs. A property dialog should be used to present related sets of information that users may navigate among in any order.*

Figure 14.8 shows the Mouse Properties dialog with nine tabs of related information for viewing and changing properties for the PC mouse. Theoretically, each of these tabs could be presented as a step in a Mouse Properties wizard, but it would be totally inappropriate to ask users to step through nine panels to view and change properties that are not in any particular order and can be done independently of the other pages within the properties dialog.

Using Multimedia in Electronic Performance Support

Multimedia Defined

One goal of multimedia is to link and to present information in a manner more nearly like that we employ inside our own heads. That means pictures, sounds, words, and multidimensional links.

John Anderson (1989)

Actually, we all have been doing multimedia for many years, but we didn't have a fancy technical name for it. When your fourth-grade teacher played some music on the record player and asked you to write some words to go along with the music, you created some multimedia. Basically, multimedia is the combination of information of different types. *Webster's* defines it as *the use of several media as a means of conveying a message.* The types of information that can make up multimedia computing include text, graphics, sound, animation, and video.

TABLE 14.3 Wizard Interface Design Guidelines

Design Topic	Guidelines
When to use a wizard	◆ Use a wizard for well-structured, sequential tasks, such as collecting customer information where users follow a standard flow of interaction and input. ◆ Wherever appropriate, follow published guidelines such as Microsoft Windows Interface Guidelines.
Navigation within a wizard	◆ Provide forward and backward command buttons to navigate through a wizard page by page. Do not use tabs for navigation between pages. ◆ Use text alone, text and graphics, or graphics alone on command buttons. Use text and graphics (Next> and <Back) rather than text or graphics alone. ◆ If possible, allow users to navigate within a wizard without selecting any information (i.e., to browse a wizard). ◆ Avoid advancing pages automatically. Users may not be able to read all information before a page advances. Users should be in control of the process a wizard automates. ◆ Allow a way to cancel a wizard. ◆ Show context within a wizard using page numbers so users can tell where they are and how many pages are in a wizard (e.g., Page 2 of 5). Other terms may be used, such as Question 3 of 10. ◆ Offer techniques to make it possible for users to leave a wizard and return with the data intact.
Completing a wizard	◆ At the conclusion of a wizard, provide users with appropriate actions to choose from. ◆ Users should be able to see what will happen as a result of completing a wizard. ◆ Users should be able to navigate back through a wizard to review their work and make any desired changes before completing a wizard. ◆ Users should be able to complete a wizard and return to where they were when they invoked it.
User support and terminology	◆ Provide a help facility in a wizard. Help should explain the contents of pages and the purpose of the wizard, not just the controls within a wizard.

TABLE 14.3 *(Continued)*

Design Topic	Guidelines
	◆ Use a conversational, rather than instructional, writing style for the text you display in a wizard. ◆ Avoid using technical or programming terminology that may be confusing to novice users.
Wizard layout and design	◆ It is better to have a greater number of simple pages with fewer choices than a smaller number of complex pages with too many options or text. ◆ Highlight required fields using standard emphasis techniques. ◆ Include default values or properties for all controls where possible. ◆ Make graphic elements that are not interactive visually distinct from buttons and controls within a wizard that are interactive. ◆ Present additional information that is not critical to the flow of a wizard in secondary windows displayed by actions from within a wizard. This minimizes the amount of information presented in a wizard and shortens the basic path through a wizard. This follows the user interface design principle of *progressive disclosure*—only show information that is needed at the moment. ◆ Avoid a design that requires users to leave a wizard to complete a task. Users will lose their context if they have to leave a wizard to complete a task.

KEY IDEA! *Buxton (1990) rightly comments that discussions of multimedia as an emerging technology usually have a circular quality. The first discussion statement is "Multimedia is the future." The corresponding question is "What is multimedia?" So, the confused discussion carries on from there. Buxton suggests that we use more appropriate and focused terms when discussing multimedia.*

The following terms can better help define and distinguish how multimedia works with the various human sensory mechanisms:

◆ Multisensory: using multiple sensory modalities
◆ Multichannel: using multiple channels of the same or different modalities

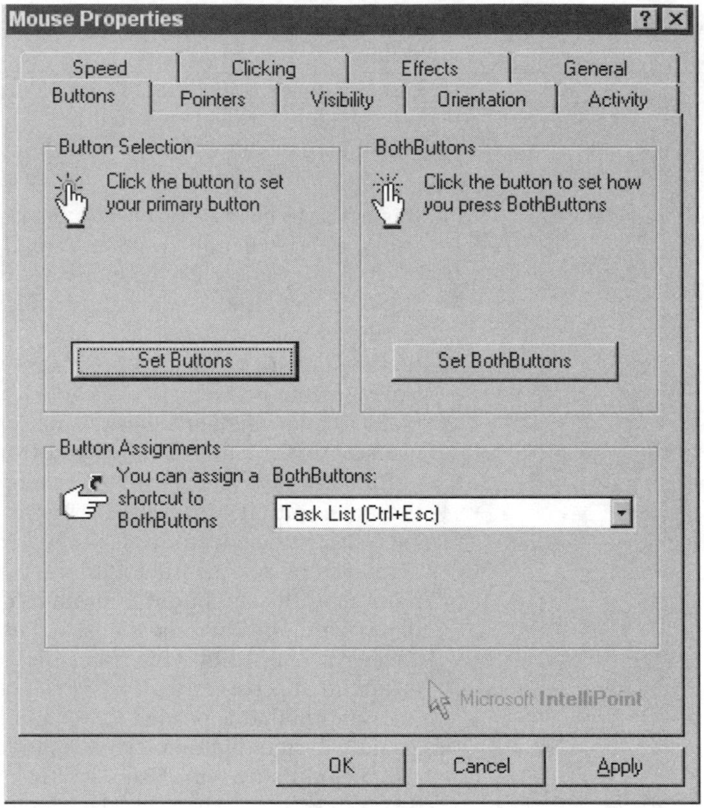

Figure 14.8   Mouse Properties dialog in Windows 95.

◆ Multitasking: recognizing that people can perform more than one
task at a time (such as everything we do while driving a car)

Buxton goes on to show how we aren't very accurate in our interface definitions. When we say "hands-on" computing, we really aren't allowing multitasking using the keyboard and mouse. Users can't really do two things at once
with their hands, such as scroll a document and select text at the same time.
Some high-end systems allow this type of interaction, but the mainstream PC
market has yet to incorporate these interaction concepts.

The combination of different types of information in meaningful ways can
serve to improve learning by involving more of the human senses and also by
making the computing experience much more interactive and enjoyable. The
human perceptual and cognitive systems are capable of simultaneously receiv-

ing input from various senses. The human brain is capable of creating multiply coded meanings that are stronger and more memorable than singly encoded information. Put simply, we understand something better when we can receive multisensory information. A common, yet somewhat unscientific phrase you may have heard is that we can remember 20 percent of what we hear, 40 percent of what we see and hear, and 75 percent of what we see, hear, and do. This gives you an indication of the power of interactive multimedia. The goal is to make the multimedia computing experience as close as possible to what goes on inside our own heads, hence redefining user-friendliness.

Why Hasn't Multimedia Caught Fire?

Why hasn't multimedia caught on so quickly with most users? When word processing and desktop publishing arrived on the PC platform, the set of skills needed to use the programs increased. The results that could be obtained with these new programs were enticing, but users needed some understanding of page layout, typography, color, and book design. Many novice users spent a lot of money and effort on computer hardware and software to do desktop publishing, only to find that it was beyond their capabilities.

Multimedia takes the complexity of the computing environment to a much higher level. With word processing, users needed to understand how to work with text. Now users will have to understand audio, graphics, animation, and video, and will have to have the programming and artistic skills to combine them all into an appropriate package for other users. Multimedia makes desktop publishing look like child's play.

Multimedia is still in its early stages. Today's multimedia products are created mostly by a few talented professionals using extremely advanced multimedia technology. These products are meant to be viewed by a select audience with multimedia-capable computers. This is the *few-to-many* type of multimedia environment. The main goal is for multimedia presentations and products to become easy enough to develop so that we have a *many-to-many* multimedia computing environment. This ultimately means that anyone should be able to create a multimedia presentation that anyone else can view. That's when we really will have a groundswell of multimedia activity.

More is not necessarily better for users! Now, with the explosion of multimedia, it is easy to create even worse user interfaces using the various types of information.

The multitude of graphical user interfaces has paved the way for multimedia technology to work its way onto the desktop. The object-oriented user interface is a perfect environment in which to gracefully merge multimedia into the current interface where users can easily work with data and objects composed of different types of information.

KEY IDEA! *The hope is that multimedia will make computing easier and more user-friendly, so that the computer will be as friendly as a television set. Unfortunately, computer multimedia is more like the unfriendly VCR attached to the friendly TV. The most important feature of any technology, including multimedia, that contributes to ease of use is the user interface. Because of the very nature of multimedia, with its combinations of many complex types of data, it is vital to have a well-designed interface.*

Multimedia is the arena for the blending of computer technology with the entertainment and television industries. Hollywood has been the target of several new ventures involving computer companies. IBM has joined with three major Hollywood effects experts to form a company called Digital Domain. The company will be a visual effects and digital production studio based in Los Angeles. The following quote shows how important user interfaces are in the new world of multimedia. "The principals emphasized that they will provide new and friendlier interfaces so directors of traditional films can tap the new digital tools, integrating the effects with live-action footage" (Silverstone, 1993). That's an ambitious goal, given the complexity of the world of multimedia and filmmaking, and the current state of computer user interfaces.

Will Multimedia Help Users Work Better?

With a ground swell of hardware and software finally reaching market, corporate users are finding that multimedia is slowly evolving from its cutting-edge niche into the mainstream.

Erica Schroeder (1992)

It is easy to list the obvious benefits of multimedia for users. Users have access to more information simultaneously to stimulate their learning processes. The information presented to them should also be the most appropriate form of information for what they are doing at that moment. Remember Bill Gates's phrase, "information at your fingertips"? Multimedia gets us part way toward this goal.

For example, say you are learning how to repair the engine in your car and you have a software product that teaches you how to do this. When you first work with the program, the information might be in the form of text, graphics, and video. However, later when you might be lying under the car, doing a particular task, you can't see the computer display, so it would be nice to have audio instruction to lead you through the steps as you work under the car. Going even further, wouldn't it be useful to have the computer program understand voice commands, so you could say, "Stop. Back up. Repeat Step 3," if you wanted to hear part of the instructions again?

KEY IDEA! *The same difficult questions for graphical user interfaces must also be asked for multimedia: Do the increased hardware, software, support, and training costs and resources provide any worthwhile increase in user productivity?*

A survey conducted by WorkGroup Technologies, Incorporated, reported in *PC Week* (Schroeder, 1992), asked the basic question, "Does multimedia improve productivity?" People were asked to state their level of agreement with the statement, "Multimedia improves productivity." Their answers from 208 respondents responsible for coordinating 59,000 PCs were:

- 12%—Agree
- 38%—Somewhat Agree
- 26%—Somewhat Disagree
- 16%—Disagree
- 8%—No Answer

Respondents were also asked, "Do you plan to install multimedia PCs in the next 12 months?" Thirty percent responded "Yes" while 70 percent responded "No." Surveys like this show that most corporations and users aren't quite ready to make the necessary hardware and software commitments to move to the multimedia platforms. Why? Because multimedia is not quite a mature enough technology to fully impact productivity across the range of products on the desktop. Specific work areas and specific tasks can be shown to be made easier by using well-designed multimedia, but it is too early to give positive answers to general questions like those asked in these surveys.

The Key to Success: Choose the Right Media

The medium is the message.

Marshall McLuhan (1964)

KEY IDEA! *There are many benefits to multimedia. Multimedia widens the range of information presentation and interaction techniques and media available to developers. This can lead to the development of wonderful new software programs for users. However, don't use multimedia as a shotgun approach to presenting information. That is, don't just give users information in all the possible different types of media just because you have the ability to do so. This is another example of the Las Vegas effect.*

When working with multimedia, it is vital to know how people will use the product. The critical factor in developing successful multimedia products is to ensure that the information is delivered using the correct media. Only one type of information, such as text, might be needed for a particular task; some combination of media might be called for in other cases. Task analyses must be conducted to determine what the best media are for the type of information, for the tasks users are performing, and for the way users want to work at that time. For example, if you find that users don't want and don't need animation and video in their work environment, your product should use text, graphics, and audio and shouldn't force users to buy animation and video-capable computers to use your software.

A more difficult question to answer is how do people learn most effectively? Using the car repair education example, is it more efficient for someone to watch an expert fix a car engine rather than read step-by-step instructions accompanied by graphic illustrations? This is not an easy question to answer and the answers will vary among tasks, users, and situations. People have different cognitive styles, or ways of processing information, and optimally any multimedia instruction should be customizable by users to match their personal learning preferences. Some people would rather watch someone else perform a task, while others might prefer to read the step-by-step instructions.

The Costs of Multimedia

There are many costs associated with multimedia computing. Multimedia hardware may include larger systems; faster processors; additional graphics; audio and video capture and playback cards; high-resolution displays; alternative input devices, such as touch screens, pen, and voice; and other multimedia peripherals such as cameras, videocassette players, laserdisc players, speakers, and so forth. Many multimedia computer systems are advertised as *plug-and-play* systems that are multimedia-capable right out of the box. I've found that many systems are actually "plug and play . . . and add memory and play . . . and add cards and play . . . and add. . . ."

One of the most critical aspects of multimedia that must be thoroughly understood is the amount of storage required to work with multimedia data. Here are some general facts about multimedia storage requirements (Pedersen, 1993):

◆ 640 Kilobytes—10 fax-quality images

◆ 1 Megabyte—500 pages of text

◆ 2.4 Megabytes—Five minutes of uncompressed voice-quality audio

◆ 52.8 Megabytes—Premium-quality audio on CD

◆ 75 Megabytes—10 color or detailed images

◆ 147 Megabytes—Uncompressed animation-quality digitized video (per minute)

◆ 2 Gigabytes—Two hours of television-quality video

One of the most important boosts to multimedia computing was the introduction of CD-ROM as an alternative storage device. Multimedia CD-ROM drives were first introduced in 1984. The Optical Publishing Association (OPA) estimated that 5 million CD-ROM computer drives were sold in 1993, and today it is difficult to purchase a PC without a CD-ROM drive. With all of the wonderful advantages of multimedia technology, we had to wait for the advances in hardware storage devices before multimedia became practical. Multimedia is beginning to become practical and affordable, and that will only improve over time.

Multimedia and GUIs

The No. 1 use for multimedia is training, and the No. 2 use will be multimedia mail using audio. Online multimedia help is also going to be very important—the demand for that will be really explosive.

Chris Vanover (1992)

The overall goal for multimedia used on computers is to enhance the communication between users and the computer. Multimedia products and interfaces are used for training, education, presentations, sales and marketing, arts and entertainment, reading, reference material, and research. Today's user interfaces allow multimedia to fulfill its potential.

Adding sound to business presentations, memos, and documents is one of the fastest growing applications for multimedia. Estimates of sales of add-on PC audio boards show a threefold growth from 2 to 4 million units in 1992 to 6 to 9 million units in 1996.

In the advertising industry, multimedia has opened a whole new area for presenting information and "getting the message across." Companies are now sending electronic brochures and financial reports to customers and stockholders. Electronic bulletin boards are now targets for companies trying to advertise their products. How do you advertise on an electronic bulletin board? It's done with multimedia, of course.

Multimedia has also opened the doors to easy access of information in other areas. There are multimedia medical and health books that can show text, illustrations, audio clips, and video of any medical or health topic. Electronic maps and travel guides are handy for travelers who want to plan their trips from their computers before they ever leave their homes.

GUIs are providing multimedia software capabilities in their operating systems. Early in 1993, Apple released version 1.6 of their QuickTime multimedia architecture software for the System 7 operating system on the Macintosh line of computers. They have also moved QuickTime onto the Microsoft Windows platform with their QuickTime for Windows. QuickTime allows the ability to edit multimedia data, such as video, sound, and animation, with the same cut, copy, and paste techniques used for other data in the user interface.

KEY IDEA! *GUIs provide a visual environment for multimedia development and presentation, but their basic limitations hamper the user of multimedia in a number of ways.*

Multimedia development in the GUI environment is hampered by these problems:

◆ GUIs are application-oriented, rather than object-oriented, so you must first run an application to do anything with multimedia data.

◆ Current operating systems don't allow complete simultaneous processing, so users can't receive the full advantage of multiple sensory presentations from multiple sources on the computer.

◆ GUIs don't typically provide robust direct manipulation techniques, which would help when working with multimedia data.

Multimedia and OOUIs: A Perfect Match

Human-centric interfaces allow multiple senses to be engaged simultaneously, making users more productive and applications more interesting.

Amy Wohl (1996)

With object-oriented interfaces, things should look like they work and work like they look. Multimedia carries this concept even further. With multimedia, things should look, move, and sound like they work, and they should work like they look, move, and sound!

Multimedia is a natural extension to OOUIs, as OOUIs provide features that are key to multimedia development and end use. To summarize these key ideas, OOUIs:

◆ Present and interact with multiple objects at the same time.

◆ Present multiple views of objects at the same time.

◆ Allow direct manipulation of data and objects, rather than via applications.

◆ Shield object media and technology complexities from users.

I'd like to discuss how users interact with multimedia on computers. The first aspects are the issues of multimedia as data and as objects. Another aspect is the use of multimedia as part of the user interface to better enhance communication between users and their computers. These aspects are by no means exclusive, and in fact they are all very important.

Multimedia as Data

For years, selling multimedia CD-ROM titles has been jokingly described as a "zero-billion dollar industry." Struggling developers have seen their Herculean efforts greeted with nothing but a trickle of orders. But the gallows humor enjoyed by CD-ROM publishers may soon be a thing of the past. New marketing figures indicate there may finally be a "there" there: CD-ROM sales are skyrocketing.

Tony Reveaux (1993)

The storage requirements for even small amounts of multimedia data can cause headaches. This situation even has its own name—the *mediated* problem. Large amounts of data and large data files are not limited to the realm of multimedia, but the problem arises immediately and looms large when you are in the multimedia arena.

Not only is the size of multimedia a problem, but the types of data—either text, graphics, animation, audio, or video—have different data formats and different input/output access rates. Audio and video are time-based data, which means they depend on the accurate representation of time to derive their meaning. A Mozart violin concerto does not have the same meaning if it is played at half-speed. So, too, does a video clip lose its meaning when the frame rate is varying constantly and it is not synchronized with its audio information.

Multimedia Objects and Views

The object-oriented user interface is perfectly suited for multimedia. Older, application-oriented interfaces forced users to use many different applications to work with different data types. Integration of these data types into one document or presentation was difficult, if not impossible. Object-oriented interfaces focus on the objects required to accomplish tasks. If done correctly, it doesn't matter what types of objects users work with; they should share all of the common aspects of all objects in the interface.

KEY IDEA! *Most multimedia objects fall in the general category of data objects (see Chapter 10). Text, graphics, image, audio, animation, and video are all multimedia data objects. Users may mix and match any type of data objects within a composite object, such as a document or presentation. Even multimedia objects may be composite objects.*

At the most basic level, a song contains other objects, such as musical notes. At a more sophisticated level, a symphony is a multimedia composite object. One view of the object is the actual audio soundtrack for the symphony. Another view might be the musical score for the symphony. A biography of the composer might be another view of interest to listeners. The background of the symphony's composition could also be viewed. These views may also be dynamically interrelated. As the soundtrack is played, the exact position in the musical score is highlighted for users to follow.

Each object type has associated with it a number of views, just as the system objects have the standard views (see Chapter 10). Properties views are a part of all object types. Most media objects will also have some type of player or viewer associated with them, as we see today with users associating text objects with their favorite word processing program. Using these player views, users can manipulate the media objects in some way. An audio object will have a player view that will play any type of audio data, whether it is a MIDI (musical instrument digital interface) data file, waveform audio, digitized audio, or pre-recorded audio. Other views should also be available for more sophisticated manipulation of the object's data, such as advanced audio, animation, or video editing.

KEY IDEA! *As with other objects in an object-oriented user interface, users don't have to know about the underlying structure of their work objects. This is very important for multimedia objects. Users should not have to be concerned with the actual format of the data or the location of the object. The location of the object and data may be somewhere on the computer's hard disk, floppy disk, CD-ROM, laserdisc, or any other type of input medium, such as a live microphone, TV signal, or videocassette system. Users don't care about the location of multimedia data and shouldn't have to know about it.*

The computer hardware associated with multimedia can also be represented as device objects in the user interface and, as such, would have standard views, such as properties and contents. For example, a CD-ROM drive will be displayed like any other drive in Windows and OS/2. If the CD disk contains data, a contents view is presented when the object is opened. The operating system should also detect the presence of other types of data and present the appropriate view. For example, if the CD contains audio data, then an audio player would be presented so that users can access any track of audio on the disc. Allowing users some control to customize their CD-audio listening, they can skip tracks on the CD. This information is saved and automatically remembered when a particular CD is played again.

KEY IDEA! *Interactions with an object as a whole should not depend on the type of media contained in it. This is what the object-oriented interface brings to multimedia. Objects are objects, regardless of the type of data they contain. Creating, copying, moving, connecting, and deleting objects on the desktop should be done with exactly the same techniques for all types of objects and data. That is part of the design goal of not forcing users to know more about the computer system and the information they are working with than they need to know.*

The extensive use of direct manipulation in OOUIs also lends itself to working with multimedia objects. All interface interaction techniques must strive to hide the complexities of the underlying media. Technically, user data manipulation, such as editing and cut/copy/paste actions, may be very complex under the PC covers for multimedia data. All direct-manipulation techniques should work with different types of objects in similar ways so users don't have to learn new interaction techniques for each type of data or object.

Multimedia as Part of the User Interface

A human being learns and retains best when looking at a map, hearing a sound, watching a moving picture, or choosing a path. Multimedia offers exactly this capability.

Andrew Himes (1989)

Let's look at multimedia as part of the user interface. The goal is to use multimedia to enhance computer-user interaction in two ways: presentation and interaction. Multimedia should not be limited only to new types of data for users. Multimedia has already been used to enhance communication between users and computers for many years, if only in very simple and unimpressive ways. Every time computers beep when users press a key that doesn't do anything at the time, that's multimedia! It's an example of the interface using one form of information, an audio sound, to provide feedback to users that what they are trying to do doesn't work.

The goal of multimedia should be to enhance the user interface and enhance usability. It should not be to add sound and animation whose only purpose is to contribute to the Las Vegas effect. Gratuitous animation, graphics, video, and sound can further complicate the already confusing interface most users deal with on their computers.

Multimedia should be looked at as additional ways of using the interface design principles to enhance the quality of interaction with the computer. Each of the principles—place users in control, reduce memory load, and make the interface consistent—can be strengthened by using multimedia wisely and appropriately.

Enhancing Presentation

Object designers can use multimedia to enhance the power of the object-oriented interface. They should look to see where multimedia can be used as alternative representations of data and more meaningful views of objects. For example, a car dealership program could have many ways of presenting the available options for a car. Still photographs or a video segment could show the exterior and interior colors available, as well as the different seat upholstery options. An audio clip could highlight the sound systems available. A textual list of the available options probably won't excite customers to purchase the products as much as some form of multimedia presentations of colors, patterns, and sounds. These things have to be seen and sensed, rather than read about on a description or label.

Information presentation does not have to be limited to only one medium or even some combination of two media, like text and graphics. Think of objects that users work with as generic objects (mail) rather than as a certain type of data (text). Mail might be the written words, the spoken voice, or a video of the author of the mail. Multimedia has incredible potential to enhance common objects like help, tutorials, and other instructional presentation vehicles.

Enhancing User Interaction

Some of the most popular PC software utilities are screen savers, icons, animation, and sound add-ons. Almost all of these products are designed to make the computing experience more enjoyable and they don't pretend to be productivity enhancers. These products use multimedia in the interface to entertain users and alleviate stress in the workplace. In addition to these characteristics, multimedia can be used to provide additional meaning and information in the user interface. Most people talk and listen more naturally than they read and write.

Why can't a spreadsheet speak the numbers to users from a monthly expense report? This can reduce eye fatigue from reading on the computer screen all day. Why can't a word processor tell users that there are too many run-on sentences in a document? It should also highlight the longest sentences to make it easy to find and correct them. And finally, why can't a mailbox object blink when there is an urgent note that should be read right away?

Will Multimedia Fulfill Its Promise?

KEY IDEA! *Cognitive psychologists don't fully understand the amazing workings of the human brain, even for simple tasks such as reading text. To justify the benefits of multimedia, we assume that the brain processes information more thoroughly when all of the sensory systems are simultaneously stimulated. That may be true if all of the different information is interrelated and communicates meaning to users. However, if information is poorly designed and inappropriate, it can lose all the meaning it may be attempting to convey.*

Investigate how multimedia technology can enhance both the presentation and interaction aspects of product interfaces. Then, as multimedia techniques are integrated into the interface, pay even more attention to users and the basic principles of interface design. Nielsen (1990) summed it up well:

> Modern interaction techniques only increase the need for the designer to pay attention to the usability principles since these techniques increase the degree of freedom in the interface design by an order of magnitude. There are only so many ways to ruin a design with 12 function keys and 24 lines of 80 characters, but a 19-inch bitmapped display with stereophonic sound can be an abyss of confusion for the user.

Multimedia is a very complex computing environment and even more care must be taken in designing multimedia interfaces. People use computers to work with information in ways they couldn't necessarily manage by other means. Users have three basic goals—they try to *find* information, *use* information, and *remember* information. Multimedia can be used to enhance all of these areas. Design goals must be to ensure that users have the most appropriate information available in the most appropriate medium at the most appropriate time. If this is done, then multimedia will fulfill its ultimate potential.

References

Baecker, Ronald M., Jonathan Grudin, William A. S. Buxton, and Saul Greenberg. 1995. Designing to fit human capabilities. In Baecker et al. (Eds.), *Readings in Human-Computer Interaction: Toward the Year 2000.* San Francisco, CA: Morgan Kaufmann, pp. 667–680.

Baecker, Ronald, Ian Small, and Richard Mander. 1991. Bringing icons to life. *Proceedings of ACM CHI'91,* pp. 1–6.

Buxton, Bill. 1990. Smoke and mirrors. *BYTE* (July): 205–210.

Carroll, John and Sandra Mazur. 1986. LisaLearning. *COMPUTER Magazine* (November): 35–49.

Flach, Dave. 1995. Training realities in the '90s. *Open Computing* (November): 9.

Johansen, Robert. 1994. *Upsizing the Individual in the Downsized Organization.* White Plains, NY: Addison-Wesley.

Leonhard, Woody and Vincent Chen. 1995. Word wizards made (relatively) easy. *PC Computing* (July): 194–196.

Microsoft Corporation. 1995. *The Windows Interface Guidelines for Software Design.* Redmond, WA: Microsoft Press.

Nielsen, Jakob. 1990. Traditional dialogue design applied to modern user interfaces. *Communications of the ACM* 33(10): 109–118.

Pedersen, Elinor. 1993. In the multimedia driver seat. *Midrange Systems* (February 23): 26–27.

Schroeder, Erica. 1992. Multimedia nears the mainstream. *PC Week* (December 7): 64.

Schwartz, Evan. 1993. The power of software. *Business Week* (June 14): 76.

Sellen, Abigail, and Anne Nicol. 1990. Building user-centered on-line help. In Laurel, B. (Ed.), *The Art of Human-Computer Interface Design.* White Plains, NY: Addison-Wesley, pp. 143–153.

Silverstone, Stuart. 1993. IBM stakes out a digital domain in Hollywood. *New Media* (May): 19–20.

Teichman, Milton and Marilyn Poris. 1989. Initial effects of word processing on writing quality and writing anxiety of freshman writers. *Computers and the Humanities* 23: 93–103.

Wood, Del. 1995. Electronic performance support: "Look, Mom! No training." Unpublished IBM manuscript, September 13, 1995.

CHAPTER FIFTEEN

Social User Interfaces and Intelligent Agents

The future of computing will be 100% driven by delegating to, rather than manipulating, computers.

Nicholas Negroponte (1995)

The current dominant interaction metaphor of direct manipulation requires the user to initiate all tasks explicitly and to monitor all events. This metaphor will have to change if untrained users are to make effective use of the computer and networks of tomorrow.

Pattie Maes (1994)

Are Computers Intelligent?

The question thus arises as to whether or not we would credit such a machine with intelligence. I would say that we must. What I would very much like to do is to educate a computer, partly by direct training, partly by letting it find out things for itself. We don't know how to do this yet, but I believe that it will be achieved in the very near future—and I feel sure that by the year 2000, it will be considered perfectly correct to speak of an intelligent machine or to say that a computer is thinking.

Alan Turing (1953)

The computer science field known as *artificial intelligence* (AI) addresses the issue of intelligent machines. Typical computer users don't usually think of their computers as possessing intelligence, but the nature of computing and interfacing with computers is changing dramatically. Depending on your definition of "intelligence," today's computers usually involve some level of intelligent processing, and tomorrow's computer programs will surely look and behave in more "human" ways.

A major event happened at the ACM Computing Week '96 in Philadelphia, Pennsylvania in February 1996. Garry Kasparov, the World Chess Champion, played a six-game, $500,000 match against Deep Blue, IBM's chess computer. Although the computer won the first game, Kasparov went on to win the match 4–2. This chess match sparked renewed debate on the issue of computer intelligence. Even Kasparov stated that, for the first time (he has played chess against computers before), he noticed some real signs of artificial intelligence in the computer. He saw some natural, human-like play from the computer, even though the computer's power is based on raw calculation rather than on a human mixture of intuition, instinct, experience, and calculation. These events will become more common in the future and will continue to keep the debate over computer intelligence alive for many years.

Although some believe that the field of artificial intelligence hasn't lived up to its expectations, others believe that AI is alive and well. A 1995 Department of Commerce survey (reported in Port, 1995) showed that more than 70 percent of America's top 500 companies are using some form of AI software. The survey showed sales of AI software were over $900 million worldwide in 1993 and probably topped $1 billion in 1994. However, AI still seems to be the victim of poor press and doesn't get the credit it's due. David Shpilberg of Ernst & Young says, "Whenever something works, it ceases to be called AI. It becomes some other discipline instead, such as database marketing or voice recognition."

KEY IDEA! *Edward Feigenbaum (1996), a pioneer in the field of computer science and artificial intelligence, describes the evolution of software development as progressive increments in translating what people want to do into how the computer works. He describes software as tools that translate human needs, desires, goals, language, and knowledge into computer instructions. Early software, such as Assembly language or FORTRAN code, forced users to translate their own goals and needs into terms the computer could understand. The latest efforts in intelligent agents, expert systems, and artificial intelligence, allow users to express their wishes in their own terms and language, rather than in terms of the computer's language.*

Every time you provide users with fastpath techniques such as mnemonics, accelerator keys, and macros, you offer a way for the computer to automate a series of steps that users would normally have to process manually. With today's popularity of the Internet and the World Wide Web, many products offer the ability to search and scan through volumes of dynamic information behind the scenes and then present results to users on demand. Are these programs intelligent agents or simply sophisticated macros or search engines? How do you know?

Why Do We Need New User Interfaces?

So why do we need these software agents in the digital world or in cyberspace? I'm convinced that we need them because the digital world is too overwhelming for people to deal with, no matter how good the interfaces we design. There is just too much information. Too many different things are going on, too many new services are being offered, etc. etc. etc. I believe we need some intelligent processes to help us with all of these computer-based tasks. Once we have this notion of autonomous processes that live in computer networks, we can also implement a whole range of new functionalities or functions. We won't just be helping people with existing tasks—we'll also be able to do some new things.

Pattie Maes (1994)

The "desktop" user interface metaphor isn't the optimal human-computer interface and it doesn't make computers as easy to use as they should be. It is a step in that direction, but not much more. Many people still don't feel comfortable using computers. Learning how to work with computers is still too much like learning a foreign language. Users have to do too much work to learn the computer's language and culture, because the computer doesn't understand them. Many people are also overwhelmed by the Internet, or haven't yet figured out the power of search and navigation tools that are now available. Because the Internet is something different from a standard PC application on the desktop, some users may experience a paradigm shift similar to the one users often experience when migrating from mainframe or DOS interfaces to today's graphical- and object-oriented user interfaces.

Part of the problem in human-computer interaction is that much of the computing experience is still a mystery and a source of confusion for users. Jennifer Glos (1996), in a presentation at the MIT Media Lab, points out some of the problems with the computer systems we use today:

- System and application features are hidden.
- The user interface is overwhelming and visually confusing.
- The user interface is passive.

- Pieces needed to do a task are scattered throughout the application and the system.
- Terminology is confusing and too technical.

As Pattie Maes points out in the opening quote for this section, one main reason for improving the human-computer interface is the sheer volume of information that is now available to users willing to look for it. We are not yet in a paperless society, but the Internet allows us to access an unlimited amount of information without necessarily having to store things locally and print them out.

KEY IDEA! *As we read about social user interfaces and agents, a whole new area of concern becomes apparent. As we move toward more humanistic interaction between humans and computers, these interactions must follow traditional social, cultural, and linguistic rules and procedures. Ethical issues in human-computer interaction for interactive computing, groupware computing, electronic mail etiquette, and social interfaces and agents must now be addressed.*

How should agents behave on the Internet? How should a *guide* in a social user interface behave? What if an agent were given the authority to purchase products for you on the Internet using your credit card? This could lead to substantial financial problems. What security measures should be taken when information is exchanged between agents? These issues will need to be addressed as technology and the social implications become apparent.

Enabling New Interaction and Interfaces—Speech Technology

Within a decade, industry watchers say, the spoken user interface will fundamentally alter the way we interact with machines, just as the graphical user interface did a decade ago. Speech recognition has already become commonplace on high-end workstation-class machines used in telephone information systems, training for air-traffic controllers and data entry in research labs. And it's beginning to migrate to the desktop.

Chris Chinnock (1995)

Speech is remarkable for the variety of rules it follows and even remarkable for the rules it violates.

George White (1990)

KEY IDEA! *New interface technologies, based on years of research, are now being introduced to the marketplace that go beyond simply using prerecorded audio clips to incorporate a wide range of speech recognition and language processing. The first wave of speech technology in consumer products may be a little shaky, but the use of speech in the interface can lead to fundamental changes in the types of interfaces that can be developed, rather than simply enhancing today's style of user interfaces.*

Bill Gates is excited about voice technology, especially in the area of his current interest—the Internet and the World Wide Web. At the 1996 Microsoft Developer's Conference, Gates predicted that, "In ten years, 95 percent of Web access will be voice-driven."

Audio has been introduced as interface feedback over the years to enhance users' sensory experience. Sensory and auditory feedback begins at a low level, for example, with the sound each keystroke makes as users type on the keyboard. Software programs use audio for confirmation and feedback on user actions. For example, when users open CompuServe's Information Manager, they hear a pleasant voice saying, "Welcome to CompuServe." Users also get audio feedback when they check their electronic mail and when they leave CompuServe. The use of prerecorded audio in software programs is a double-edged sword—it can be a pleasant secondary form of interface feedback, or it can be irritating and bothersome to some users, especially over time.

People get very excited when they see and use voice- and speech-enabled computers. They feel like Captain Kirk and Dr. Spock talking to the computer in *Star Trek,* and HAL, the talking computer in the movie *2001, A Space Odyssey.* As we move into *voice-enabled* computing, a whole new range of user interface and usability issues surface. If a new technology isn't fun or easy to use, it can significantly diminish the widespread appeal for most computer users.

Recently, I heard that a voice-controlled VCR was coming to market. The concept sounded very interesting and I thought it might catch on quickly. Then I read that the system came with a 70-page manual that customers had to work through, step-by-step, to learn how to use the system. If users survived that experience, *then* maybe the system might be fun or easy to use! I heard that users were outraged at the difficulty of training the system to understand their voice commands. Now I know why I haven't seen any of these systems on the store shelves or in people's homes! The tradeoff of ease of learning for eventual ease of use is often too great for users ever to get past the learning phase with new products that use not-quite-mature technologies. Developers of speech technology products are keenly aware of the usability issues associated with speech. Says Jan Winston (Watson, 1995), "We're moving aggressively to improve the ease-of-use and usability of speech products, since that's been one of the major contributors to their growth."

Early implementations of speech technology gave us text-to-speech capabilities, where a computer could read stored text to users. This technology allowed vision-impaired users to work with computer screens and files. It also allowed users to work at other tasks on the computer or away from the computer while the computer read text to them.

Today's speech products offer speech recognition for two main purposes—voice command/control and voice dictation. Captain Kirk of the Starship Enterprise used both types of speech when conversing with the ship's computer: "Computer, give me a damage report for the B Deck" (voice command/control) and "Captain's Log—Stardate 3067. The Enterprise is on route to meet with a Romulan ship at the edge of the galaxy" (voice dictation).

Voice command/control requires the computer to analyze human speech, recognize the speech as verbal commands, and respond with the appropriate action or response. Voice dictation does not require quite the same kind of analysis as voice control, since the system needs to analyze human speech and store it in written form, but does not necessarily have to respond to voice commands.

KEY IDEA! *There can be significant productivity and cost savings associated with voice dictation technology. Dr. Mitchell Goldstein, an assistant clinical professor in the Neonatology Department of Queen of the Valley Hospital in California, quickly realized usability and cost benefits of voice dictation software. Goldstein observed (Watson, 1995): "Given the cost of six months of dictation services, we saw that we could save upward of $120,000 to $130,000 a year if we switched over to dictation-based software. Those kinds of numbers are hard to ignore."*

In the same article, Karen Jackson, a New York–based information technology consultant, stated: "Nobody wants to be the first one to use speech, but once they recognize the competitive potential and find an application, no one wants to tell anybody else about it." In truth, none of Jackson's clients would contribute to the article "for fear of publicizing what they consider to be a considerable competitive advantage" (Watson, 1995).

Speech systems can be classified along two variables. The first variable is whether they are *speaker dependent* or *speaker independent.* Speaker-dependent systems are designed for situations where only one person will be interacting with the system. The user trains the system to recognize his or her voice usually by reading a prepared text or lists of key words. Speaker-independent systems must be able to interact with many users. The second variable is whether the system can recognize *continuous speech,* where users can speak at a natural pace, or *isolated-word speech,* where users must pause slightly between words.

Speech recognition is the ability to recognize real-time, continuous, speaker-independent speech. *Natural language processing* enables users to express their requests in ways they find most natural.

IBM's newest version of the OS/2 Warp operating system folds in the Voice Type Control software developed by IBM's speech researchers. Code-named Merlin, OS/2 Warp version 4 is called "the first human-centric-enabled operating system." The voice-enabled system does not require any special hardware or voice training, so it will work on any PC with a 16-bit OS/2-supported sound card. Figure 15.1 shows a voice dictation window and one of the windows

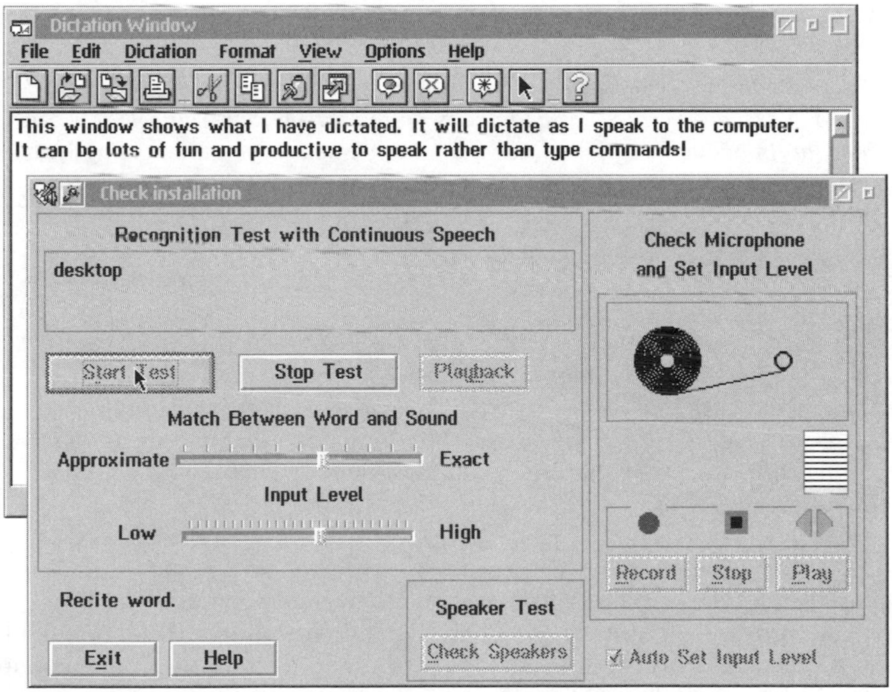

Figure 15.1 Voice-enabled software in OS/2 Warp version 4.

helping users set up their speech recognition system. Users can use voice to navigate around the OS/2 Workplace Shell, select controls, and use speech dictation with any program that supports the system clipboard. This means users can use their calendar, address book, to-do list, write memos, send faxes—in fact, do all of their common tasks—without using the keyboard or the mouse! This will be the first integrated speech input technology in a PC operating system for the general public to try. It will be very interesting to see users respond to this new style of interface interaction.

KEY IDEA! *Things are getting easier for software developers to include voice technology in their products. In addition to integrating voice technology into the operating system, IBM and Voice Pilot Technologies, Inc. are developing a series of advanced speech-based object components and extensions, called SpokenDoc, to add to the industry OpenDoc object technology environment.*

What Is a Social User Interface?

A social interface is designed to follow the social and natural rules of the real world. That means there are characters on the screen that would follow the rules of interaction and politeness that another person you are dealing with would follow. It also means that objects follow the rules of the natural world— have gravity, have location, and when they leave one place they reappear in the same place.

Clifford Nass (1995)

Although the rest of Microsoft is touting Windows 95 as the latest, greatest computer interface, Bill Gates believes the GUI is on the way out. The graphical user interface is too difficult for the "casual use" mainstream applications of the future. Instead, we'll all be using the so-called social interface, in which the machine uses computer-based characters to watch us work and suggest improvements.

Jesse Berst (1995)

A *social user interface* is one where the interaction between users and the computer takes advantage of users' social skills and natural language to make the interaction more a human-to-human than human-to-computer conversation. They are generally geared toward users who have very little experience with computers and don't want to have to understand how computers and software work to do their tasks.

KEY IDEA! *Intelligent agents are a separate but related concept. Social user interfaces usually include some type of software agents or assistants. One of the overall goals of social user interfaces and agents is to hide the complexity of the underlying computer or information system for users. Don Norman (Ubois, 1996) says, "I think you shouldn't even know that there is an operating system."*

Psychologists at Stanford University have conducted some interesting research on the social aspects of human-computer interaction. Clifford Nass and Byron Reeves have shown that interactions between humans and computers are fundamentally of a social nature. Nass et al. (1994) reported:

> The present research provides a wide range of experimental evidence that a limited set of characteristics associated with humans provides sufficient cues to encourage users to exhibit behaviors and make attributions toward computers that are nonsensical when applied to computers but appropriate when directed at other humans. Thus we demonstrate that users can be induced to elicit a wide range of social behaviors, even though users know that the machines do not actually possess feelings, "selves," genders, or human emotions.

Based on their research, Nass et al. (1994) defined some basic principles of social responses in human-computer interaction:

1. An individual's interactions with any information-processing or communication technology are fundamentally social. First, people use social rules to guide their behavior, so their interactions with a computer are a lot like human interactions. Second, people bring social expectations to bear when evaluating the behavior of communication technologies.

2. People are strongly biased toward a social orientation. When confronted with any stimulus, people begin by assuming the stimulus is a social entity. For example, when people view a blurry picture, their first impression is that it is a face.

3. People are biased toward a natural rather than symbolic orientation. When people see something on a screen, their first impulse is to view it as a present, actual object rather than a symbol that represents something that is not present.

4. Social responses are induced by primitive cues. When people associate characteristics of technology with human characteristics, social responses increase. For example, hearing sounds or voices rather

than simply reading text more strongly encourages people to use social rules.

Implications for Social User Interfaces

Nass et al. (1994) conducted five studies on the social interaction between users and computers. Based on their results, they derived five *theoretical* implications of their experiments:

1. Social norms are applied to computers.
2. Notions of "self" and "other" are applied to computers.
3. Voices are social actors. Notions of "self" and "other" are applied to voices.
4. Computers are gendered social actors. Gender is an extremely powerful cue.
5. Computer users respond socially to the computer itself. Computer users do not see the computer as a medium for social interaction with the programmer.

Their research also detailed some *design* implications of their research. Their five studies showed these implications that should be taken into account when designing social user interfaces (see Table 15.1).

TABLE 15.1   Design Implications for Social User Interfaces, from Nass et al. (1994)

Study	Design Implications
Study 1	◆ Usability testing should not be same-machine based.
Study 2	◆ Modesty is a complex phenomenon.
	◆ Integration is highly consequential.
	◆ Uniformity of interface is double edged.
	◆ Social cues need not be heavy handed.
Study 3	◆ Choice of voices is highly consequential.
	◆ Agent integration/differentiation is easily created.
	◆ Agent integration/differentiation is powerful.
	◆ Social actors can be easily portrayed on multiple computers. Cross-computer continuity of social actors is easily obtained.
Study 4	◆ Gender of voices is highly consequential.
Study 5	◆ Computers need not refer to themselves as "I" to generate social responses.

KEY IDEA! *Social user interfaces may seem strange to those who view computers as a complex tool and interact with them in a nonsocial way, rather than the way we interact with people. However, for the millions of users who don't know much about their computers (and don't want to), if it helps to view the human-computer interaction as a social one, then all the better! As other sensory technologies, specifically speech, pen-input, animation, and video, mature to the point where we can realistically mimic human communication, we should strive to build interfaces that make the computer all but invisible.*

Social User Interfaces—The First Wave

I don't think Apple or Microsoft believe the current Windows or Mac environment is the one that will succeed, long term, in the home . . . it is still too hard to use. It needs to evolve to bring in the people who are still afraid or have been turned off by computers.

Karen Fries, Microsoft (1995)

Karen Fries of Microsoft met Clifford Nass and Byron Reeves of Stanford University, and that led to the design and development of Microsoft's Bob, the first social user interface shell for the Windows operating system. When I tested the beta program, it was called UTOPIA Home, where UTOPIA stood for *U*nified *T*ask-*O*riented *P*ersonal *I*nteraction and *A*ctive interface. The name was changed to Bob for the retail product. Why "Bob"? Microsoft's promotional brochure answers that question:

> Microsoft selected the name Bob because it emphasizes the personality of the product. The name Bob makes the computer more approachable, familiar, and friendly. Bob was chosen because it is such an unassuming name. Bobs are familiar, Bobs are common. Everybody knows a Bob. Therefore, a product named Bob is easy for everyone to identify with and use.

The central components of Bob's social user interface are the *personal guides.* The guides are a simplistic form of software agent. Users choose a guide from one of 14 characters, each of which has a different personality. Some are friendly and helpful, while others are less likely to offer help. Users choose a guide they feel comfortable with and who provides the amount of help they wish to receive. The guide prioritizes program options and choices relevant to where users are and what is being done. Figure 15.2 shows how users choose a

Figure 15.2   Microsoft Bob's animated personal guides.

personal guide when using Bob. The current guide even breathes a sigh of relief if a user changes guides and then decides to remain with the current one.

Microsoft's Bob generated a lot of press, both favorable and unfavorable, as the first attempt at a commercial product with a social user interface. Like any first attempt at a new technology or computing metaphor, its commercial success or failure is actually less important than the introduction of a new type of human-computer interaction. In fact, Microsoft Bob was only released in the United States. Microsoft won't reveal sales figures for Bob, but it is not generally available now.

Experienced computer users have found the interface style and use of guides simplistic and distracting, while novice users may find them friendly and simple to use. Ben Shneiderman, in a electronic mail response to discussions of Bob, noted his reaction to Bob's guides: "The first time you see such characters it is cute, the second time silly, and then the third time it may be annoyingly distracting."

KEY IDEA! *Schneiderman's criticism of social user interfaces reflects a general concern of user interface experts. Historically, attempts to personalize computer software have been dismal failures. Social interaction between humans and computers is a complex area and we don't know much about it yet. You need to go slow here. Just because we* can *create more personal interaction doesn't mean that we* should.

Figure 15.3   Microsoft Bob, a social user interface.

Bob tries real hard to make users feel comfortable when interacting with the computer (see Figure 15.3). When installing Bob, you are asked many personal questions, including your birthdate. Bob uses this information so your guide can throw you a birthday party, complete with balloons. You can even pop the balloons by pointing at them and clicking the right mouse button. Not exactly a necessary or important function for a software interface, but it is one of the little things a social user interface can do to make the computing experience less intimidating and more personal.

Bob even goes so far as to make the documentation as user-friendly as possible. The only documentation shipped with the product is a small 30-page brochure that almost looks like *TV Guide.* It is called *The Bob Magazine, premiere issue.* Inside the cover, users are told, "Welcome to the Microsoft Bob Magazine! This is your 'manual' for Bob. *This is the only reference you'll need—no more thick manuals!*" Instead of computer-oriented chapter titles, sections of the magazine are "Are you new to computers?" or "A day in your life with Bob." Following the home metaphor, instead of a *troubleshooting* chapter the last section is called "Home repair."

KEY IDEA! *The user interface encompasses the whole experience users have when using the computer. This includes all documentation associated with a product. A typical function-oriented product reference manual would not be appropriate for Bob, given the social user interface Microsoft carefully crafted on the screen.*

Other examples of social interfaces that serve as operating system *shells* or application *launchers* are General Magic's Magic Cap PDA (personal digital assistant), Packard Bell's Navigator, and Computer Associates' Simply Village. These interfaces, like Microsoft Bob, rely on real-world metaphors to guide users through familiar places such as cities, homes, and offices. However, these interfaces are most often merely thin layers over existing operating system interfaces—they do not fundamentally change the way users work with computers. They also don't fundamentally improve the usability of computer systems.

An Enjoyable Social Interface—Software Pets!

Dogz, a program from PF.Magic, Inc. (see Figure 15.4), shows how a social user interface can be fun and enjoyable, especially if the sole purpose is entertain-

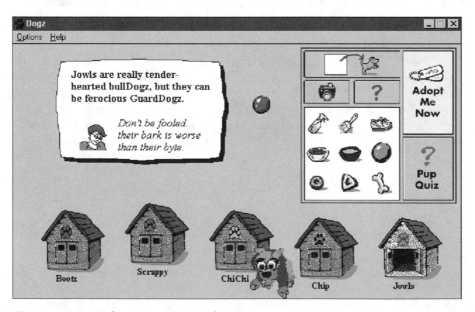

Figure 15.4   Adopt your Dogz playmate.

ment. Users answer a few questions on a questionnaire and then choose one of five dogs as a pet. You can do all the things you would do with a real dog: Call it, pet it, give it treats, teach it tricks, play ball, and even take photographs! Your dog is animated—it will run all over the screen (or stay in its playpen), react while you pet it, and make sounds, even whimpering when you pick it up and put it back in its doghouse. PF.Magic's latest program is (guess what!) called Catz (Figure 15.5), since we all know the world is divided into two types of people—dog people and cat people!

Dogz and Catz use "complex artificial intelligence technology" to offer multiple character interaction (a mouse). Your pet's personality is shaped by the amount and type of attention and interaction you have with the pet. I was amazed at the sophisticated level of interaction and animation in the program. I love the toys and interaction users can have with their onscreen pets. Dogz and Catz pets actually age and mature, they have moods, and they fall asleep when they are tired of running around. This is a fun program for adults and kids, and it shows how realistic and natural a social user interface can be. This is just the beginning—you will see more sophisticated and powerful social user

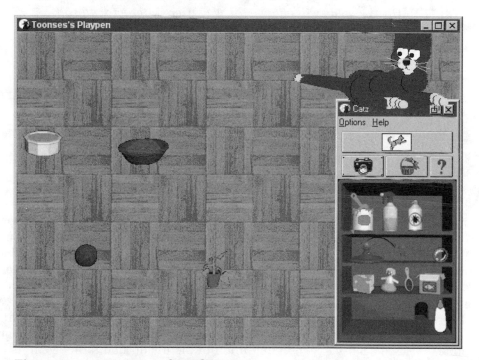

Figure 15.5   Toonses in her playpen.

interfaces and agents in the future. They will be used for entertainment and for work.

What Is an Agent?

Workers involved in agent research have offered a variety of definitions, each hoping to explicate his or her use of the word "agent." These definitions range from the simple to the lengthy and demanding. We suspect that each of them grew directly out of the set of examples of agents that the definer had in mind.
Stan Franklin and Art Graesser (1996)

Whether you call them agents or not doesn't matter. Rather than worry about the definition, we should talk about the new kinds of services, ask what their virtues are—or for that matter, what their problems are.
Donald Norman (1996)

KEY IDEA! *Agents will change the way users interact with soft-ware. Today's interfaces are* direct manipulation *interfaces, where users manipulate representations of data and information to do their work. Agents take over the burden of working with all of the information and data users might want to look through. When users delegate authority to agents to manage their work, this style of inter-action is called* delegated manipulation. *Agents can greatly ease information overload by automating such tasks as prioritizing elec-tronic mail, managing a department's calendar, electronic shopping, and searching through daily news sources for information of particu-lar interest.*

Here's a scenario. You are browsing the Internet. You need some help buying music CDs, and you want to find the best restaurant in New York based on your location, favorite foods, and expense account. There are places to go on the Internet that can help you with your shopping and dining interests. Chances are these programs are using agents that are somewhat intelligent software that can help you reach your decision.

There is much debate over what qualifies a piece of software as an agent. According to Jim White, inventor of General Magic's Telescript language for mobile software agents, "A good definition of the unadorned term 'agent' is a piece of software to which a person can delegate some degree of responsibility.

That's consistent with the original definition of agent, which comes from artificial intelligence. Our particular definition has to do with programs that not only have been delegated responsibility but that can move and carry around that responsibility." (Ubois, 1996). Amy Wohl (1995) describes agents simplistically: "An agent is simply a program that acts on your behalf to provide a desired result, just as a human agent acts on your behalf to extend your resources and capabilities."

Pattie Maes (1994), an expert on software agents at MIT's Media Lab and founder of Agents, Incorporated, describes the home of the future:

> By now, I'm sure most of you are convinced that the home of the future will have a physical or real component as well as digital, virtual components. But a point that hasn't been stressed very much is that this virtual half of our home will be inhabited by agents or creatures. So the virtual half of our home won't just be a passive data landscape waiting to be explored by us. There will be active entities there that can sense the environment—the digital world—and perform actions in the digital world and interact with us. We call these entities software agents. A software agent has a very broad definition. It's a process that lives in the world of computers and computer networks and can operate autonomously to fulfill one or more tasks.

Agents may be visible or invisible. Visible agents may be "talking heads" or "actors" (sometimes called *avatars*) that are often visible on the screen as a system output device. At Comdex in November 1993, IBM demonstrated Charlie, a 3-D actor that provided feedback from a PowerPC system. Such early actors were intentionally made visually simple to save processing cycles and to present a less intimidating image to users. Since some users may find actors a distraction, there should be a way to turn them off.

What Makes an Agent Intelligent?

Many current products state that they utilize an interface agent. In many cases, this may be true, but you might question the level of intelligence a particular agent might have. Microsoft's Bob interface is definitely a social user interface, but are the personal guides really intelligent, in the sense we define here? I'd like to present some guidelines based on relevant research regarding what makes agents intelligent. It's up to you to decide whether and how to use agents in your computing efforts. You can also decide if you are willing to do the work to build interface agents into your products.

For an agent to be intelligent, it must have access to a variety of knowledge sources. In her article, "Ingredients of Intelligent User Interfaces," Rissland

(1984) lists the required sources of knowledge and gives examples for three domains—a lawyer, technical writer, and secretary. Rissland's knowledge sources are:

1. Knowledge of the user
2. Knowledge of the user's tasks
3. Knowledge of the tools (available and being used)
4. Knowledge of the domain (of the user's task)
5. Knowledge of interaction modalities
6. Knowledge of how to interact
7. Evaluation knowledge

Agents won't necessarily always be staring users in the face on the screen. Much of their work goes on behind the screen, so they shouldn't necessarily be visible unless they have something to say to users. Whether an interface agent is visible or invisible, it must provide certain benefits to users. Wilson (1995) describes the possible attributes of an intelligent software agent. An agent:

1. Demonstrates beliefs, desires, intents
2. Is artificially intelligent in some knowledge domain
3. Learns from its environment
4. Adapts to a user's skill level, personality, or technique
5. Cooperates or interacts with other agents
6. Automates tasks according to a flexible set of rules
7. Acts autonomously

Ball et al. (1996) add some other requirements for a successful assistant-like interface. An assistive agent:

1. Supports interactive give and take
2. Recognizes the costs of interaction and delay
3. Manages interruptions effectively
4. Acknowledges the social and emotional aspects of interaction

Even Don Norman (1994), the guru of real-world design, conducted early research on intelligent agents. Norman also lists factors that designers must consider when building agents:

1. Ensure that people feel in control of their computational systems.

2. Pay attention to the nature of human-agent interaction.

3. Employ built-in safeguards to eliminate or minimize runaway computation and the effects of agent errors.

4. Provide a user with accurate expectations.

5. Cater to privacy concerns.

6. Hide complexity while simultaneously revealing underlying operations.

KEY IDEA! *Much research has been done on the necessary considerations for designing agents. Software developers need to know the important aspects of graphical- and object-oriented user interfaces (objects, metaphors, layout, color, widgets, etc.) that designers and cognitive psychologists (among others) bring to the table. Developers also need to have behavioral and social psychology skills in order to build "socially acceptable" user interfaces and agents!*

Agents come in different styles and have a wide range of purposes and tasks they can perform. It is important to establish some sort of taxonomy, or classification scheme, by which we can better address agents. Jim White (Ubois, 1996) describes three interesting categories of agent applications—watching, searching, and orchestration. Maes (1994) defines four levels of distinguishing abilities of agents:

1. *The usefulness of tasks agents perform.* Some agents may entertain you rather than perform user tasks. Some agents perform tasks for a whole community or network, rather than for a particular user.

2. *The roles agents perform.* Different agents do different things. They can be navigators through information spaces. They can be personal reminders or schedulers. They can watch users and memorize their actions. Agents can watch your stock portfolio and alert you if the stock prices start to drop drastically.

3. *The nature of the agent's intelligence.* Today's agents don't have that much intelligence. Tomorrow's agents will have more common-sense knowledge about users, their tasks, and the real world.

4. *The ability of an agent to learn.* Certain agents can program themselves, for example, by watching users perform tasks over and over

again. The agent can then offer to automate the task for users in a similar way.

Categories of Intelligent Software

If you read software advertising material, there are intelligent software agents running rampant through the software industry. Based on the level of intelligence discussed here, it is possible (and very important when discussing agents) to categorize different types of software components based on a number of factors. For example, a wizard is very different from an interactive agent.

Wilson (1995) describes the different categories of intelligent software. The first category is wizards (Chapter 14). I classify wizards as Help and EPS since they are hard-coded and do not usually include any artificial intelligence. Rather, they are task-specific guided workflows for users to follow to perform particular computing tasks. The major categories for intelligent software are described in Table 15.2.

IBM published an *Intelligent Agent Strategy* (IBM, 1996) that is available on the Internet (http://activist.gpl.imb.com:81/WhitePaper/ptc2.htm#Ref1). Their definition of agents involves three dimensions—*agency, intelligence,* and *mobility:*

◆ *Agency* is the degree of autonomy and authority vested in the agent, and can be measured at least qualitatively by the nature of the interaction between the agent and other entities in the system.

◆ *Intelligence* is the degree of reasoning and learned behavior: the agent's ability to accept the user's statements of goals and carry out the task delegated to it.

◆ *Mobility* is defined as the degree to which agents themselves travel through the network. Some agents may be *static,* either residing on the client machine (to manage a user interface, for instance) or instantiated at the server. Mobile scripts may be composed on one machine and shipped to another for execution in a suitable secure environment; in this case the program travels before execution, so no state data need be attached. Finally, agents may be *mobile with state,* transported from machine to machine in the middle of execution, and carrying accumulated state data with them. Such agents may be viewed as mobile objects, which travel to *agencies* at which they can present their credentials and obtain access to services and data managed by the agencies.

TABLE 15.2   Categories of Intelligent Software, from Wilson (1995)

Intelligent Software Category	Description
User Interface Agents	◆ Covertly monitor and use the user event stream to trigger advice about the human-computer interaction in progress.
(Coaches, angels, guides, advisory agents, avatars, actors)	◆ Depend on the system or application to notify them of suitable events so they can "understand" interactions taking place.
	◆ Use pop-up windows, balloons, cue cards, animation, speech, etc. to communicate.
	◆ Offer advice such as:
	◆ What is about to happen or which options are available.
	◆ Tips for doing things better.
	◆ How to correctly perform an action.
Personal Assistant Agents (Softbots)	Conversational agents:
	◆ Accept and respond to natural language.
	◆ Mimic the behavior of a human assistant.
	◆ Are highly interactive (like a pet)—they hear a command, go perform the work, and return, waiting for another command.
	Automation agents:
	◆ Are independent agents—they perform tasks delegated by users.
	◆ Users describe the task and the conditions under which the task should be performed.
	Application agents:
	◆ Perform application-specific functions, for example, filter electronic mail, search databases, and schedule meetings.
Autonomous Agents	◆ Generally separate processes that perform work with little or no user interaction.
	◆ Their interface is usually provided by an application or a system interface agent.
	◆ Fixed agents connect to and search for data across information services and databases.
	◆ Itinerant agents can physically carry information and their executable programs from machine to machine. They can perform specific tasks in each machine they visit, using local data and programs.

KEY IDEA! *There are now almost more attempts at defining intelligent software agents than there are efforts to create them! This trend will reverse as agents become familiar both to users and developers. Object-oriented programming, object-oriented interfaces, electronic performance support, social interfaces, and agents are a combination of technologies that together will dramatically change the way we use computers. They're coming, but it will be a slow evolution.*

Agents—The First Wave

We are now starting to produce a very interesting array of programs—in which you can spell out your personal preferences and the program will sort of support you through life—help you use your computer system or help you find information that you desire, or remind you of things that you might have forgotten, or find tickets or find items for sale. This is a very interesting development.

Donald Norman (1996)

Agents on the Internet

Most of the interesting software agents now are roaming the Internet. Quarterdeck Corporation has developed WebCompass, a "search-and-discover robot based on an intelligent agent that travels to multiple search-engine sites on the Web, gathering as much raw data as possible relating to your search topic (which can be keyword-based or conceptually defined)" (Griswold, 1996). This is just one of numerous types of agents running around on the Internet. *Robots* are automated programs, and *spiders* are a type of robot that continually crawls the Web, jumping from one page to another in order to gather statistics about the Web itself or build centralized databases indexing the Web's contents. WebCompass is one such spider. There are even robots called *cancelbots* (short for "cancel robots") that automatically detect and classify mass postings (*spammings*) of the same message and delete these messages based on the number of postings.

The Open Software Foundation (OSF) Research Institute has been working to ensure that the World Wide Web infrastructure is "agent-ready and agent-aware" (Griswold, 1996). OSF has even developed a test utility to see how agents should be developed and used (available from the OSF Web site at http://www.osf.org).

There has already been a surge into the realm of three-dimensional agents on the Internet. *New Media* magazine (Elia, 1996) describes a new product, the Oz

Virtual Browser, that lets users choose from "some remarkable humanoid multi-user avatars and experience real-time text chat and 3-D sound. You can modify avatars with a built-in editor and imbue them with realistic motions and facial expressions. The browser client includes an intelligent 3-D help angel that responds to natural-language questions with text-to-speech answers."

Social User Interfaces and Agents—The Future

The future will fundamentally change the way people do business and interact. There will be no penalty anymore for being remote. It won't matter where you work.

Samuel May (1995)

Computer interfaces, which 10 years ago were recall-based and now are recognition-based, will evolve by 2003 into dialogue-based cognitive user interfaces based on more natural human communications to serve a wider range of users.

Gartner Group, Inc. (1995)

Intelligent software agents are a popular topic on the Internet. If you are interested, there are many resources and lists of products and research. One good summary of Web links on agents is put together by Sverker Janson and can be found at http://www.sics.se/ps/abc/survey.html. The MIT Media Lab (where Pattie Maes, one of the experts on agents, can be found) is also a very good place to start looking for agent resources. Also, the Autonomous Agents Group can be found at http://agents.www.media.mit.edu:80/groups/agents.

Microsoft's Advanced User Interface Research Group is working on a project called Persona, an attempt to create a *lifelike computer character* (LCC) that converses with users in natural spoken language. One example is Peedy the parrot, a three-dimensional expressive conversational assistant that helps users select audio CDs and songs from a collection of CDs. *Peedy* stands for *Pe*rsonal *Di*gital Parrot One. Advanced research like this involves work in an interrelated number of complex areas of computer science, as shown in Figure 15.6. These areas include:

◆ Speech recognition
◆ Natural language analysis
◆ Interface agents
◆ Decision theory

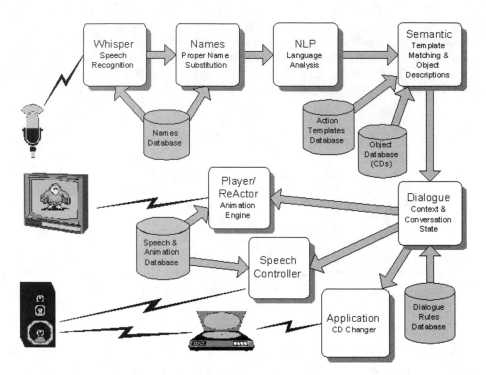

Figure 15.6   System diagram of the Persona Conversational Assistant, from Ball (1996).

- ◆ Reactive 3-D animation
- ◆ Video and audio output

Peedy has been given animal (and human) characteristics. He sleeps (and snores!), shows emotion, and has a sense of humor. Figure 15.7 shows Peedy bringing his wing up to his ear and responding verbally "Huh?" when he misunderstands a command. Peedy also has the ability to understand the history of the interaction, so he does not continue to say "Huh?" if there are repeated speech recognition failures. Depending on previous interactions, Peedy can change his reaction to a given input (for instance, he can say "What's that?" instead of "Huh?"). His selection of a response also depends on how frequently or how recently the utterance has been spoken. Finally, interaction with users can adjust the model of Peedy's emotional state, and this emotional state can then affect the choice of a spoken utterance or animation in a particular situation. It really is amazing how quickly you become used to Peedy—your inter-

Figure 15.7 Peody the Parrot indicating a mis-recognition, from Ball (1996).

action with him becomes very humanlike and therefore the conversation feels quite natural and comfortable.

Microsoft plans to incorporate this research into future versions of Bob, says David Thatcher, group product manager for Bob. Look for Peedy to take dictation for a letter, find a fax number, and fax the letter. Peedy might even search the Internet or the Microsoft Network for information requested by users.

References

Ball, Gene, Dan Ling, David Kurlander, John Miller, David Pugh, Tim Skelly, Andy Stankosky, David Thiel, Maarten Van Dantzich and Trace Wax 1996. Lifelike computer characters: The Persona project at Microsoft Research. In

Bradshaw, Jeffrey (Ed.), *Software Agents* Cambridge, MA: MIT Press (available from the Microsoft Research Home Page at http://www.research.microsoft.com/research.ui/).

Elia, Eric. 1996. VRML 2.0 tools aim at 3-D multi-user interactivity. *New Media* (June 24): 13.

Feigenbaum, Edward A. 1996. How the "What" becomes the "How." *Communications of the ACM* 30(5): 97–104.

Franklin, Stan and Art Graesser. 1996. *Is it an Agent, or Just a Program?: A Taxonomy for Autonomous Agents.* University of Memphis (available at http://www.msci.memphis.edu/~franklin/AgentProg.html).

Glos, Jennifer. 1996. *Microsoft Bob and Social User Interfaces.* MIT Media Lab presentation (available at http://gn.www.media.mit.edu/groups/gn/meetings/bob.html).

Griswold, Steve D. 1996. Unleashing agents. *Internet World* (May): 55–57.

IBM Corp. 1996. *Intelligent Agent Strategy* (available at http://activist.gpl.imb.com:81/WhitePaper/ptc2.htm#Ref1).

Maes, Pattie. 1994. Interacting with virtual pets and other software agents. *Proceedings of the Doors 2 Conference* (available at http://mmwww.xs4all.nl/Doors/Doors2/Maes/Maes-Doors2-E.html).

Nass, Clifford, Jonathan Steuer, and Ellen Tauber. 1994. Computers are social actors. *Proceedings of ACM CHI'94,* Boston, MA.

Norman, Donald. 1994. How people might interact with agents. *Communications of the ACM* 37(7): 69–71.

Open Software Foundation. 1996. *Human Computer Interaction—Intelligent Browsing Agents* (available at http://www.osf.org/ri/QuadCharts/HCI.QuadChart.frame.html).

Port, Otis. 1995. Computers that think are almost here. *Business Week* (July 17): 68–73.

Rissland, Edwina L. 1984. Ingredients of intelligent user interfaces. *International Journal of Man-Machine Studies* (21): 377–388.

Ubois, Jeff. 1996. Agents of change. *Internet World* (May): 61–76.

Watson, Todd. 1995. Machine talk: Speech recognition software comes of age. *Software Quarterly* 2(4): 35–42.

Wilson, Les. 1995. Intelligent agents: A primer. *IBM Personal Systems* (September/October): 47–49.

Wohl, Amy. 1995. Not-so-secret agents. *Beyond Computing* (December): 12–13.

CHAPTER SIXTEEN

THE NEW WORLD OF PC-INTERNET USER INTERFACES

In the 1960s, people wanted to communicate with computers. In the 1970s, we learned to work with them, but eventually learned the programs were not what we needed. In the 1980s, computers did what we needed them to do, but they took too long and cost too much. In the 1990s, price has dropped and programs meet our needs. Now we have to learn the advantages of Ethernet, how to access the Internet, and what bandwidth our system requires to run multimedia.

Michael Ayers (1994)

The Internet is kind of like a gold rush where there really is gold. . . . In fact, it will mean that our industry will change the way people do business, the way they learn, and even the way they entertain.

Bill Gates (1995)

The Internet and World Wide Web

The World-Wide Web (W3) was developed to be a pool of human knowledge, which would allow collaborators in remote sites to share their ideas and all aspects of a common project. . . . The idea of the Web was prompted by positive experience of a small 'home-brew' personal hypertext system used for keeping track of personal information on a distributed project.

Tim Berners-Lee (1994)

The Internet and the World Wide Web (also called W3, WWW, or just the Web) has become the latest playground for software developers. Look at computer magazines and bookshelves. The Internet, home pages, Web design, Java, Netscape—these are the new hot topics in computing technology and tools today. This new wave of computing is bringing with it a whole new style of user interfaces. Users *search, browse,* and *view* text and graphic information for business, knowledge, and entertainment, while the information content is stored in computers all over the world.

What's the difference between the Internet and the World Wide Web? Here are some basic definitions. Horton et al. (1996) write: "The Internet is a sizable community of cooperation that circles the globe, spans the political spectrum, and scampers up and down the ladder of economics. It's a collective society, really, in the largest sense of the word—a wiry ball of agreements between the administrators and users of a bunch of independent computers hooked up to (or dialing in to) shared or linked computer resources."

On the other hand, "The World Wide Web is the collective name for all the computer files in the world that are (a) accessible through the Internet; (b) electronically linked together, usually by 'tags' expressed in HyperText Markup Language (HTML); and (c) viewed, experienced, or retrieved through a 'browser' program running on your computer." The WWW is the graphical and most popular portion of the Internet, but the Internet also includes FTP (File Transfer Protocol) servers, Gopher servers, Internet Relay Chat servers, and more.

The previous hot topic was client/server computing, which has now evolved into intranet computing. An *intranet* is basically a cordoned-off area of the Internet behind security *firewalls* that is for the private use of a company. These internal Internet corporate networks replace or supplement local-area and wide-area networks. In October 1995, Zona Research reported that intranets linked more than 15 million workers. Sales of intranet software hit $142 million in 1995, and were projected to reach $488 million in 1996 and $1.2 billion in 1997. In fact, the intranet market will soon outgrow the Internet. Greg Cline, director of network integration and management research at the Business Research Group, estimates that soon 80 percent of Web sites will be intranets.

KEY IDEA! *Users now work in an even more mixed computing environment. Until now, we worried about corporate users working with mainframe-emulation windows, character-based applications, and GUI programs on their desktops at the same time. We try to smooth over the inconsistencies and differences in interface presentation and interaction across these generations of interface styles. Here comes a new computing interface metaphor—the Web browser. The desktop is now even more overloaded with different interface styles. No wonder users suffer from metaphor overload!*

The excitement over the Internet and the Web reminds me of a presentation I saw a few years ago. Alan Kay, Apple Fellow and former Xerox PARC researcher, demonstrated how hypertext can greatly enhance the power of computing. His simple example was quite dramatic and it still stays with me today. Kay put two dots on a blank piece of flip-chart paper (see Figure 16.1, Step A). This represents today's world where physical distances exist between objects, information, and places. Then he simply creased the paper in the middle (Step B) and folded it so that the two dots touch (Step C). This showed that adding a new dimension to what we use today can remove physical distances between things. This is what the Internet and WWW add to the computing environment—a new dimension that erases the physical distance between points of information in computers around the word. This simple example shows the benefits of a complex new dimension in computing technology.

This chapter discusses some of the key issues with the evolution and metamorphosis of PC computing and Web browsing into PC-Internet computing. These are exciting times for software developers, but as you rush headlong onto the information superhighway, don't forget the history, principles, and basics of good user interface design.

KEY IDEA! *It is even harder than ever before to create interfaces that work for users. User interface guidelines were created largely in a pre-Internet world that was much simpler than the computing world we are now experiencing.*

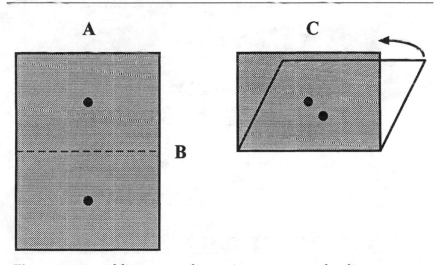

Figure 16.1   Adding a new dimension to remove the distance between objects.

Introduction to the Web Interface

Not all readers are familiar with the Web interface. Figure 16.2 shows a typical Web page—the Yahoo! Web Search page—running in the Netscape browser on Windows 95. I'll describe each of the interface elements you see here.

First, the Netscape application is running in a standard Windows 95 window. You see the standard window elements across the top of the window frame—the system menu, the title bar (with the application name, Netscape, and the name of the current Web page, [Yahoo!]), and the standard window buttons (Minimize, Maximize, and Close). The window also contains standard vertical and horizontal scroll bars, and a status/information area at the bottom of the window.

Below the title bar you see a menu bar with some choices that are very familiar—File, Edit, View, Options, and Help. These drop-down menus contain standard application actions and routings. The other menu bar choices are application specific—Go, Bookmarks, and Directory. These menu bar items and their drop-down menus contain choices relevant to the browser style interface.

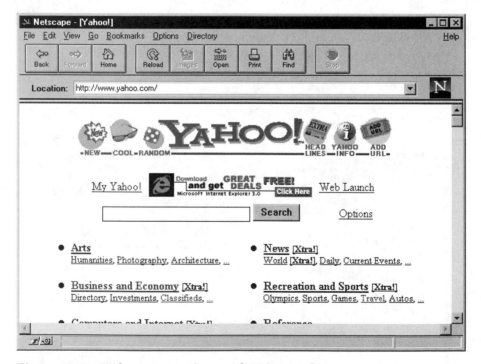

Figure 16.2   Web page interface with Netscape browser.

Users navigate from page to page using different navigation techniques. The Go menu choices are Back, Forward, Home, and View History. . . . These actions allow users to go anywhere they have been in their current session, either one step at a time (Back and Forward), going directly to the home page (Home), or by displaying a list of all of the locations to choose from (View History . . .).

Bookmarks are pointers to specific Web sites and pages that users can store so they don't have to type them every time. For example, a bookmark for the Yahoo! Search page will always take users to the Web page shown here. The Bookmarks menu allows users to add bookmarks to their own list and view their list of bookmarks in a separate window list. This drop-down menu also lists users' bookmarks.

The Directory menu drop-down lists common Web locations, such as the Netscape home page, and other designated locations like What's New, What's Cool, and Newsgroups.

Below the menu bar is another standard window interface element, the toolbar. In this case, it contains frequently used actions for mouse users to select quickly. All of these toolbar actions are available from the menu bar.

Below the toolbar is the location area. This lists the URL (Uniform Resource Locator) for the current page. URLs are the path to the file containing the content of what users see. As one of many ways to navigate to a particular Web page, users can type the URL in this drop-down combination box and press Enter, or they can select a URL from the drop-down list.

These are the standard window elements of the Netscape browser application. Different browsers, such as Microsoft's Internet Explorer, have slightly different interface elements, but they allow users to perform the same basic browser actions and routings.

The contents of the main area of the window change as users navigate from location to location on the Web. I chose the Yahoo! Search page as an example because it contains the Web interface elements that make up most pages.

The Web can be navigated by single-clicking on buttons, text, or graphics that perform an action or take users to another URL. Users can tell what areas of the screen are selectable because the mouse pointer changes when they move the mouse over a selectable area. The top of the Yahoo! page shows both graphic and text images that are navigational *hotspots.* Selectable areas are the graphics and text labeled NEW, COOL, RANDOM, HEADLINES, YAHOO INFO, and ADD URL.

Most selectable text areas on Web pages are shown in a different color (usually blue) and are underlined. Examples in Figure 16.2 of selectable text areas are: <u>My Yahoo!</u>, <u>Web Launch</u>, <u>Options</u>, and all of the bulleted list text items that are underlined (<u>Arts</u>, <u>News</u>, etc.). Each underlined text item is a separate selectable item.

Finally, Web interfaces may contain interface elements common to PC application interfaces. To search for particular key words or phrases using the Yahoo! search engine, users click on the entry field in the middle of the window and type in the search items. For example, if you want to find all Web links related to me, you might type "Theo Mandel" in the field. Pressing the Search button starts the search. The program will then display a page showing a list of all references found.

Searching on the Internet is a learning experience. There are many ways to more specifically focus the search with parameters and also by using the <u>Options</u> item. For example, the above search is a little misleading. It will find all links to the words "Theo" *or* "Mandel," which is not really what we wanted. This search came up with 10,571 items, most of which have nothing to do with me, Theo Mandel. To conduct a search to find only those links to me, you should type "Theo+Mandel." This search will find all references that have both "Theo" *and* "Mandel," resulting in a search results list with 17 items, all relating to me. The <u>Options</u> item allows other search parameters to be manipulated.

There are certainly other interface elements that I have not discussed here. The best way to learn about Web interfaces is to start up a browser application, dial in, and start exploring!

New Computer Interface Metaphors

The human mind does not work that way [i.e., linearly]. It operates by association. With one item in its grasp, it snaps instantly to the next that is suggested by the association of thoughts, in accordance with some intricate web of trails carried by the cells of the brain. It has other characteristics, of course; trails that are not frequently followed are prone to fade, items are not fully permanent, memory is transitory. Yet the speed of action, the intricacy of trails, the detail of mental pictures, is awe-inspiring beyond all else in nature.

Vannevar Bush (1945)

Most PC operating system and application interfaces today follow the common office desktop metaphor. The Internet breaks away from the desktop metaphor where users keep things in all-purpose or specific *containers,* such as folders, cabinets, and workspaces. Instead, the Internet follows the metaphor of viewing and navigating through a *browser.* This type of interface allows users to see "onto the limitless resources of the global network" (Baecker et al., 1995). Rather than manipulating data and information on a virtual desktop, users *search, browse,* and *view* using an intricate web of information links. There is no need to store materials on a local machine, because the original, or even updated, information can easily be accessed with a few button clicks or a bookmark. Baecker et al. (1995) describe the change in metaphor and interaction style: "This shift in perception leads to a shift in behavior that has ramifications. I no longer keep copies of information because I believe I can return to view it again. What if the actual owner does remove it? I will complain, as will others, and slowly those who make information available will start recognizing an imperative to keep it online."

The concept of *hypertext* links and worldwide access to information was originally formed by Ted Nelson in 1965. Although his dream project—Xanadu—was never completed, Nelson is a legendary (and somewhat bizarre) figure, often talked of as one of computing history's visionaries who never produced anything resembling his dream. *Wired* magazine (Wolf, 1995) documents the "amazing epic tragedy" of Ted Nelson and Xanadu in an articled entitled "The Curse of Xanadu." Nelson is now in Japan, hired by Japanese software firms eager to gain a foothold in the computer software market. Ted Nelson's published works (mainly Nelson, 1987) are worth reading, if only for a historical perspective on hypertext.

Television is another model that some interfaces on the Web are emulating. Internet companies are fighting TV for advertising dollars. But TV is not a good role model for Web design. Brueckner (1996) describes the different good points of each media type (Table 16.1). TV follows a *passive model,* where users can't control much of what is happening. The Web follows an *active model*, where users make a choice to visit a Web site, and the site assumes users came there for a reason. The Web site tries to anticipate user questions and provide materials that answer those questions. This type of interface seeks a dialogue with users. Unfortunately, many sites entice users with the lure of promised content, only to show them numerous advertising "banners" promoting their own and other companies' products.

KEY IDEA! *Brueckner (1996) offers a combination of these two models, called the* assisted-interest *model. The goal is interactivity between users and site content. This model relies on carefully selecting site content based on what you know the target audience finds interesting. This content may pertain to a particular topic or product, but it goes beyond just content to provide further information of value to users who come to the site.* One difference from PC interfaces is that Web interface content must be interesting and refreshed often enough to keep people coming back to the Web site.

TABLE 16.1   Good Points of Television and the Web, from Brueckner (1996)

Television Is Good at Providing:	The Web Is Good at Providing:
◆ Moving pictures	◆ Information
◆ Sound	◆ Communication
◆ Passive entertainment	◆ Active (self-directed) entertainment
◆ Commercial breaks	◆ Personal choice

Following this theme, Brenda Laurel's (1991) book, *Computers as Theater,* put forth new ideas about human-computer interaction. Alexandra Fisher (1996) writes, "She [Laurel] advocates user interfaces that directly engage users in a designed experience." This framework can be used on the Web, where, "A Web site can be seen as a performance, seeking to create an exciting experience for a live audience. Users revisit Web sites *over* time, so the site should be viewed as an ongoing performance." Successful Web sites create a sense of involvement with users by evolving over time.

These new user interface metaphors are the result of the intertwining of business PC software, video and PC games, and information found on the Internet. Table 16.2 shows some of the key characteristics of these three types of user interface styles.

KEY IDEA! *Two key elements of the Internet affect software developers. First, computers are now accessible by more people with varying computing skills throughout the world. This impacts developers as they assess users and their tasks. Second, the information explosion is here. The Internet allows users access to information they never knew existed and never knew they could access. Finding information, navigating within information, and using information are key user tasks. You must ensure your design methods incorporate new users and new tasks allowed by the expansion into the Internet.*

Merging PC and Web Interfaces

The idea of a common user interface as used on the Mac and Windows is dead. Nobody cares anymore. It was an interesting experiment killed by both Hyper-Card from Apple (which reversed the rigidity of the common user interface concept) and modern CD-ROMs, each with a unique interface designed to be fun and functional.

John C. Dvorak (1995)

TABLE 16.2 User Interface Characteristics of Games, PC Business Programs, and Web Programs

User Interface Characteristic	Games, Theater	PC Business Programs	Web Programs
User goal:	Entertainment, education	Productivity	Information search, viewing, productivity, entertainment, education
Mystery:	Yes	No	Somewhat
Fashionable:	Yes	No	Yes
Entertainment:	Yes	No	Yes/No
Consistency across products:	No	Yes	Yes/No
Standard user interface elements:	No	Yes	Yes/No

> *I find it hard to imagine that browsing your hard disk is better than using the sophisticated, hierarchical display/viewer technology that began with the Norton Desktop. But when you have a hammer, everything begins to look like a nail.*
>
> Bill Machrone (1996)

While I don't agree with John Dvorak's belief that the common user interface on the PC is dead, the influence of the Web is having dynamic effects on PC software design. Bill Machrone's comments are less radical, and represent the more traditional PC interface stylo. It's an interesting question—should all software products become "browser" enabled? How (or why) would familiar software products like Quicken or Excel benefit from a browser interface? After reading this chapter, you should be able to answer questions like these.

Users of the Web expect dynamic and linked information while they work. However, when they go back to standard PC applications and presentations, they are disappointed. Tom Farre (1996), executive editor of *VarBusiness* magazine, wrote:

> The Web, with its hyperlinked text and graphics, is changing the way we expect digital data to be presented. And that's big. I realized this the other day as I suffered through the usual graphs and bulleted points of a PowerPoint presentation. When the presenter came to something interesting, I wanted to click on it so I could see more detail, download the full white paper, or send for a piece of demo software—just like on the Web. A mere taste of this rich medium has whetted our appetites for more.

> **KEY IDEA!** *The Internet has broken down the barrier between local and remote storage of information. Interface designers try to hide the complexity and location of underlying information. This is now magnified by the Internet—users don't know and don't care where information is stored. They just want consistent ways to find and view information, regardless of where it is.*

Even the major PC operating systems have changed their interfaces to accommodate the new wave of Internet computing. The idea is to provide a common interface for presentation, navigation, and interaction with data, both local and remote. The assumption is that a browser metaphor is better for this task than traditional GUI file system "explorers" and "file managers" that were designed for cataloging and navigating small, local information archives. Hopefully, the browser metaphor is not force-fit where it is not appropriate. This we will learn only from experience in the coming years.

Both Microsoft and IBM updated their PC operating systems to embrace the new world of the Web. Microsoft updated Windows 95 by changing the Explorer metaphor to a browser metaphor for viewing local files and directories of users' PCs and for browsing the Internet. Users can move from directory to directory the same way they navigate from page to page on the Web (see Figure 16.3). The goal is for users' desktops to seem no more than a part of the Internet. Familiar browser Back and Forward buttons can also be used to navigate from directory to directory. "Favorite places" links enable users to jump directly to other files, directories, programs, or even to Web sites on the Internet. IBM also updated OS/2 with Internet capabilities on the object-oriented desktop. Users can drag and drop Internet resources on the OS/2 desktop, and native Java support is also provided.

> **KEY IDEA!** *Even before operating systems incorporate new Internet capabilities, utilities such as Starfish Internet Utilities, Smart Bookmarks 2.0, and PowerDesk 1.1 offer drag-and-drop Web access to specific sites and other utilities to monitor Web usage and other statistics. Utility programs are usually the first implementers of new technologies and new interface styles, since they can bring their products to market sooner than complete new versions or updates of operating system software.*

Figure 16.3 Windows 95 "browser" style Explorer.

Even CD-ROMs, which have changed interface styles on the PC, are incorporating online information technology. CD-ROM encyclopedias provide a huge advantage over traditional printed materials. New products such as the Grolier Interactive Encyclopedia combine the multimedia benefits of storing information on CD-ROM with dynamic links, product and information updates, and support provided by various online services, including the World Wide Web. Glaser (1996) notes, "Hybrid developers hope to combine the CD's brisk local access to multimedia files with online links that provide immediacy, community, and ties to a vast range of related information. The benefits of hybrids include improving customer support with online registration, technical support and bug fixes; building new revenue streams via online marketing and direct sales; and expanding the CD-ROM medium with updated information, multi-player games, and online chat." Software products and companies are also offering technical support and help desk support over the Internet. Software Artistry, Inc. developed a product, SA Expert Web, a help desk offering that links users to IS support data over the Internet. Users can browse a company's help desk information to answer frequently asked questions (FAQs) and get translations of error-code messages.

KEY IDEA! *The Internet-only browsing interface style is gradually merging with more traditional PC interfaces to provide users with newer "business product" style interfaces that are more appropriate for the task, rather than appropriate for the location of the underlying data and information. User tasks have also changed from traditional PC business and entertainment tasks to entertainment, browsing, gathering information, and new types of business tasks made possible by dynamically accessing remote data rather than being restricted to local or static data.*

Dynamic Data Behind the User Interface

To have a new metaphor, you really need new issues. The desktop metaphor was invented because one, you were a standalone device, and two, you had to manage your own storage. That's a very big thing in a desktop world. And that may go away. You may not have to manage your own storage. You may not store much before too long. . . . The minute that I don't have to manage my own storage, and the minute I live primarily in a connected versus a standalone world, there are new options for metaphors.

Steve Jobs (1996)

The information space shouldn't have arbitrary boundaries between local information and information that's found elsewhere in the world.

Bruce Horn (1996)

Web users are accustomed to seeing dynamically updated data. This is very different from standalone PC computing or other media, like television. For example, during the 1996 Wimbledon Tennis Championships, there were so many rain delays that interrupted TV coverage that I couldn't stand waiting for the latest match scores on television. So while the rain delays caused TV coverage to show the previous day's matches, I used my computer to visit some of the many sports sites on the Web. There, I could see all of the match scores for the day, since London is 7 hours ahead of Austin, Texas. I was getting the data live from London, rather than delayed from the TV coverage. In fact, I had to travel on the final Sunday of Wimbledon, so I watched as much of the men's final match as I could, then I went to a Web site where I could view and print out all of the results and news stories on the finals to take with me on the airplane.

As technological computing and communications advances have made the distinction between local and remote data almost indistinguishable, the face of computing is changing. In the past, if I wanted to track a UPS, Airborne Express, or Federal Express package I had shipped, I had to call a toll-free number where I could speak with a customer representative. That person would type my airbill number into their computer and he or she could tell me where my package was at that time. *The reason I had to telephone them was because that's where the data was!* The data was *in their computer at their location.* There was no other way for me to access this information than to call and have someone there look it up.

Now, when shipping business materials and book manuscripts via FedEx service around the country, I track the shipment *on my computer* using software from Federal Express to track the status of my shipment at any point in time. Figure 16.4 shows the tracking log for a FedEx 2 Day shipment from Austin, Texas to Boulder, Colorado. The log shows the package left the FedEx location in Austin on May 14 at 7:59 P.M., went to Memphis to the FedEx sorting facility, and was delivered in Boulder on May 16 at 11:36 A.M.

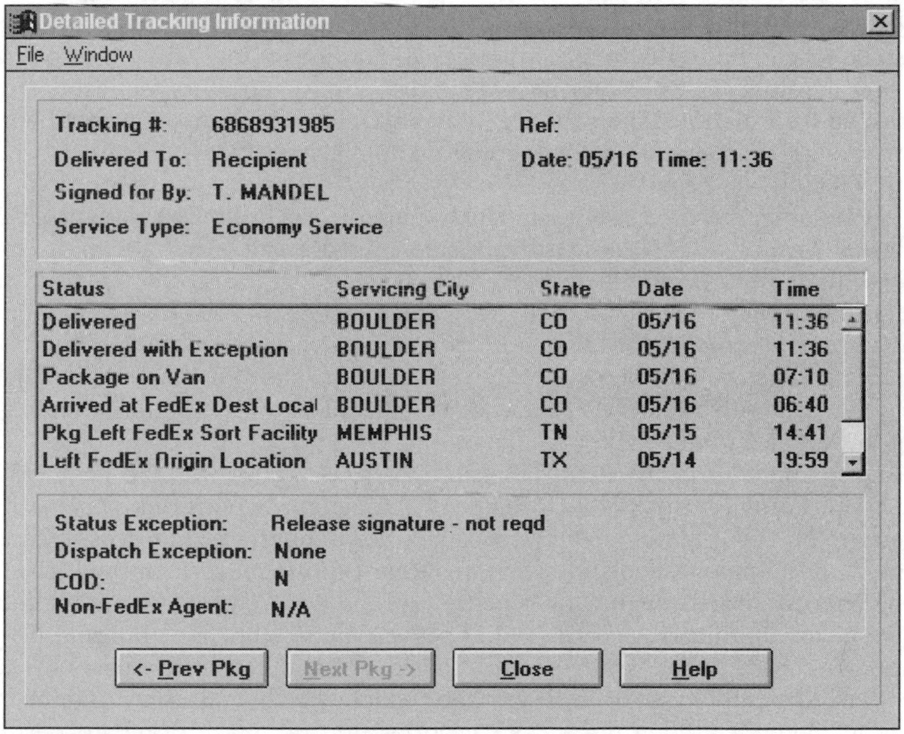

Figure 16.4   Tracking log for a Federal Express shipment.

The data you see here comes from the same Federal Express computer as before, in the same location, wherever it is located. However, instead of using the telephone to call someone who then accesses the data *locally,* I now access the *remote data directly,* from a software program, using a computer modem rather than manually using the telephone. The key is that I don't have to think about where the data is and how to access it; I just select the Detailed Tracking Information action and the rest is handled by the software program. This is not an Internet or Web application, it is simply a PC program accessing remote data to provide information that users request. The program also prints shipping labels on any printer, and after filling out some details, computes the shipping price for the package. All FedEx special services are also available with a few mouse clicks. *PC Computing* gave this program a five-star Excellent rating. The program is free for FedEx accountholders. Other shipping companies offer similar software tracking products.

Federal Express also has a Web version for users to track shipments using the Internet. Figure 16.5 shows the results of a search on the same airbill number as above. The Web version does not have as much information regarding the shipment, nor does it have the functionality of the PC software program. Users must also be logged on to the Internet to access this information, while the software program quickly dials its own access number only when users request detailed tracking information. The software program does not require Internet access. This example shows that Web programs do not yet have as many features as traditional software program!

A Web program that has attracted lots of attention is PointCast Network, a PC-Internet service. PointCast is a free, personalized service that allows users to create their own customized digital "newspaper" containing only news and information they request, and only when they request it. This has been referred to as *narrowcasting,* rather than a *broadcasting* news service. Since there is so much information out there to be viewed, narrowcasting serves to deliver a targeted, unique selection of news to each member of an audience, rather than giving the entire audience all of the news.

Figure 16.6 shows the PointCast user interface. Again, like the FedEx Ship program, PointCast looks like a regular PC program. It performs personalized searches on the Internet for news, weather, horoscopes, stock quotes, business news, entertainment, and sports updates from various sources on the Web. The program uses users' existing Internet browser and service provider, rather than a separate communication access. PointCast was named the "Best Internet Application" for 1996 by C|Net. The interface is not elegant, but offers users ways to navigate through the set of collected information. The left column contains buttons to navigate among the news categories (top of column) and to perform actions such as Update and Personalize at the bottom of the column. The middle window pane at the top lists the news items for the selected category. The

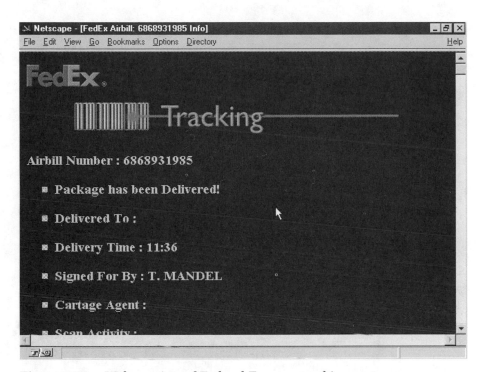

Figure 16.5 Web version of Federal Express tracking system.

top right window is an advertising window that animates and changes advertiser information every few minutes. If users click on the advertising pane, they are immediately taken to the Web site for that advertisement. The large window pane shows the content of the selected news article. This pane expands to cover the upper windows for larger viewing with a single mouse-click.

A nice feature is a built-in screen saver that scrolls all of the news information dynamically across the screen after a selected period of inactivity. Selecting a news item while the screen saver is running opens PointCast to that news item.

This combination of PC program and information-gathering tool will become more popular and sophisticated as users become more aware of the scope of information available to them and the ability of intelligent search strategies to seek and gather information targeted to their individual tastes and needs. PointCast is one of the first programs of this type and is receiving lots of positive comments and some criticism also. The constant flow of advertisements has been criticized, and also the time it takes to download updated news. A *ComputerWorld* article recently told of horror stories at some companies where the many workers using PointCast nearly ran the internal network down to a halt as they were constantly updating their news items.

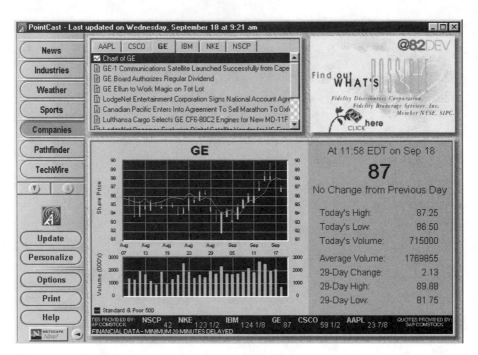

Figure 16.6   PointCast network user interface.

The Magic Help Button

Software programs should utilize communications technology to enhance users' experience with the program and to give them the most relevant and up-to-date information. In addition to offering standard Help topics on the Help menu bar drop-down, why not offer an action such as Frequently Asked Questions . . . that takes users to a page on the Web listing a current series of FAQs for the product? Other Help routings could also link users to online services provided by the product's developers.

KEY IDEA! *Interfaces must keep up with user expectations and needs. After browsing the Web, users want the same content, interaction, and timely information from their PC software. PC interfaces should not simply change to browser interfaces, they should incorporate those elements of the browser-style interface that are appropriate. They should also allow dynamic access to worldwide information from within PC programs. The key is to match technology to user needs and tasks, not to jump to new technology without regard for user needs!*

Ethics, Morals, and Addiction on the World Wide Web

The Web is the ultimate manifestation of Attention Deficit Disorder—Click. Zoom. Gone. There's no coma like Web coma.

Paul Somerson (1996)

To some extent, addiction is an inevitable phase in the life of a new Internet user. We get excited about all of the nifty things that we can find and do. We spend a few too many long days and nights trying to see it all. Eventually, for most of us, reality prevails because there aren't a lot of 37-hour days.

Glee Harrah Cady (1996)

With any new technology, there are always users who go overboard and don't come up for air. Articles in newspapers and magazines describe the latest computer disease—addiction to the Internet. There's even a name for this new disease—Internet Dysfunctional Disorder (IDD). A *ComputerWorld* In Depth article (Dern, 1996) discusses the issue of Web addiction. Larry Chase, president of Chase Online Marketing Strategies, says, "It seems like everybody I know is a Web addict. They stay on and continue to surf after the mission has been accomplished. The worst cases are in denial and call it work so they can then complain about how overworked they are." College campuses are full of students that spend every waking moment surfing the Internet. Somerson (1996) describes five categories of Web addicts:

1. *Click-Candy.* Users can't stop following Web links. It's like "Let's Make a Deal," where opportunity lies behind Door #1, Door #2, or Door #3. If a Web page doesn't have what they want, users keep clicking and go to another link. If they find a good page, then they follow all links from that page.

2. *Search Me.* Users keep tweaking search parameters in their favorite search engine to narrow down search results. If they don't like the results, they switch to another search engine. They don't reach their goal until they have conducted the ultimately perfect search.

3. *Interglut.* Users are hypnotized by any product that advertises it is "Internet-ready." Even hardware products claim they are primed for the Internet because they are part of the chain of PC hardware that makes up the telephone connection between the PC and the Internet services.

4. *Vote No.* The Internet community is constantly under investigation by congressional technophobes trying to regulate illegal and immoral material.

5. *Hates Gates.* There are people who love the Internet simply because it is something that Bill Gates hasn't yet figured out how to control. There is talk of the "network PC" that will sell for under $500 and will kill the PC as we know it. We're still waiting, but we're not holding our breath!

Another critical issue is what users can say and do on the Internet, and what they can do with material they find on the Internet. In her article, "What You Can and Can't Get Away With Online," Roberta Furger (1996), writes: "Even the lawyers can't agree on what's legal. For now, assume that if it's illegal off-line, it's illegal online." There are two key things to remember as both users and developers on the Internet and WWW: (1) You are just as liable for what you say and do online as you are off-line; (2) A "harmless" copying of a magazine article online can become a serious case of copyright infringement. Libel, freedom of speech, and copyright issues are now being discussed and debated regarding the Internet. In the Furger article, Mark Grossman recommends five tips for keeping Internet users out of trouble:

1. Do not use somebody else's work on your Web page or in your e-mail without their permission.
2. Be careful about making statements that can harm a person's or company's reputation.
3. Do not post adult-oriented materials on the Internet or on any online service.
4. Assume that online agreements are enforceable.
5. Use digital signatures in your business if you are arranging substantial deals online.

To humorously (yet accurately) highlight that the Web is a place where users feel free to do what they like, avoiding any "legal" repercussions, one site has a large link simply labeled, "Don't Click Here." Of course, most users click on it. Where does this link take users? Right to the page with all the advertising. Gotcha!

KEY IDEA! *As Internet developers, realize that your thoughts, information, and designs are open to anyone who accesses your Web site. Web site layouts designs, text, and graphics can easily be downloaded by any users and potentially used for their own purposes. Although your original work, such as your home page, is protected by copyright law, people assume everything is free since the Internet feels like such a public place.*

Web Interface Design Skills

Web developers must be Renaissance creators, marrying skills and knowledge as disparate as graphic design, information and interface design, writing, editing, and programming. They aren't zooming down a proverbial information highway, they are creating an island where business, art, and people come together to create a community.

Eric Elia (1996)

Got just 20 minutes? Build your own web page. We show you how!!

PC Computing cover (1996)

These two quotes show the vast difference between reality and perception regarding Web design. After reading this book, you'll have a deeper appreciation for the art and science of user interface design, as described in the first quote. However, as we rush to implement new technology, everyone believes they can do the work themselves, as proclaimed in the second quote. This perception continues to haunt the area of user interface design. The August 1996 issue of *PC Computing* tells readers, "Eat your competitors for lunch! Boost your bottom line! We have everything you need to build the perfect Web site—quickly and easily." Too many companies get sucked in by this do-it-yourself hype, and they believe Web site development is as easy as tying your shoes. On the other hand, it is often assumed that PC software development teams have the skills to do Web design and development. This chapter discusses what makes Web design different from most of the programs developed for desktop PCs.

KEY IDEA! *Most companies with Web sites will agree that, for now at least, a Web site costs more to design, develop, and maintain than the amount of money the Web site currently brings in to the company. A study by Forrester Research found that the cost of creating and running a site for one year ranged from $300,000 to design and maintain a corporate promotional site, to $1.3 million for an online publication, to nearly $3.4 million for a site offering catalog shopping.*

The computing magazines tell stories of young "Web weavers"—sixteen-year-old entrepreneurs who have set up their own companies to design Web sites. It takes only a family PC and a few hundred dollars' worth of software to create Web sites. While these young business people grew up with video games and computers, they don't usually have the skills to do user interface design. Many Web site designers are not professionals but hobbyists who can read a book and master hypertext markup language (HTML), the Web's basic writing tool. Easy-to-use Web authoring tools such as Microsoft's FrontPage make it easier for both experienced and inexperienced designers to develop Web sites and pages.

Snyder (1996) notes, "Creating a Web site requires assembling a team with four unique talents and setting design and management issues up front." Snyder's four talents include:

1. First, you need the overall architect and designer—the team leader. This person should have the grand vision for the site.

2. Next, your team will need a programming member. This person understands HTML and whatever programming interfaces are used to give life to your site.

3. The third member of your team is a graphic designer and user interface designer. Whether they're your corporate logo or navigation buttons, graphics and interface elements are always going to be part of the big picture. You need someone who not only has artistic talent, but also knows the tools that computer-based designers now use.

4. The fourth team member is the user. A designer can lay out the storyboards, a programmer can build the HTML, and an interface designer can create eye-catching logos and controls, but without the content and guidance from users, the site is just someone else's ideas of your business. No one knows what users do and what users need, and that insight is crucial to guiding the team.

Jakob Nielsen, SunSoft Distinguished Engineer and well-known author and researcher, discusses the differences between Web design and traditional UI design in his monthly column, *The Alert Box,* on Sun's Web site (see http://www.sun.com/951001/columns/alertbox/). Nielsen (1995) wrote, "You need to hire someone to design your Web site. What should you look for before signing on the dotted line? Let's look at a few different types of consultants":

1. *HTML hackers* are great at building single pages but often have no clue about interface design. The real challenge is to design the complete *site* and not just individual, disconnected pages that don't have a navigational structure.

2. *User interface professionals,* on the other hand, know how to design pages that are easy-to-use and, if they have some hypertext experience, they can also design a usable structure and navigation features.

As a UI specialist myself, I [Nielsen] must admit that the traditional emphasis in this field has been on making systems easy-to-learn and efficient-to-use. Not nearly as much effort has been devoted to "seductive interfaces" (to use a term coined by Tim Skelly). On the Web, ease-of-learning is certainly still important, since users will leave a site immediately if they cannot figure out what it does or how to navigate it. But attractiveness is increasingly important.

3. *Advertising agencies* are happy to charge from $20,000 to $150,000 to design a Web site that looks like a series of beautiful magazine ads but doesn't necessarily take full advantage of the interactive medium. An increasing number of agencies are starting new media groups with the aim of getting your Web business. Unfortunately, the very term "new media" is sometimes a clue that the department is staffed by *old media* types who are just now learning about electronic publishing. However, online information is not all that new, given its rich history.

Nielsen concludes, "Okay, so no one is perfectly suited to designing your Web site. What should you do? I recommend a team approach. Include people with implementation knowledge as well as user interface backgrounds, and at least one advertising or non-software communications specialist."

KEY IDEA! *Realize that Web interface design takes a team effort (like PC-based interfaces) that encompasses a number of key skills. A* PC Computing *article (Lindquist and Will-Harris, 1996) concludes, "Sometimes it just doesn't pay to do things yourself. Creating a professional-quality Web site requires more time, technical skill, and artistic talent than many businesses have to spare. If that's your situation it's time to turn to a Web designer or consultant." Let's hope that is the rule, rather than the exception!*

Key Elements of Web Interface Design

For a while there, interface designers were talking about 'modeless' computing and efficiency. Today, it seems that most of those gains have been sacrificed on the altar of entertainment. Software designers are straining so hard to come up with new user interface metaphors that they tax our patience even as their products clamor for our attention.

Bill Machrone (1996)

Know Thy Medium, For It Is the Message

Tomorrow's GUIs will be friendlier in more concrete ways than just smiley faces and cute icons: They'll be cleaner and less cluttered, present error messages in a consistent tone and style, and, most important, be a tool to access any information we desire, whether it's on our local hard drive or halfway around the world on a Web server. To accomplish this, designers are mixing and matching the best characteristics of current GUIs and Web browsers to develop interfaces with a completely new look.

Alan Joch (1996)

I recently received a brochure in the mail for a design seminar from CareerTrack entitled, "How to Design Eye-Catching Brochures, Newsletters, Ads, and Reports." I was about to throw it away when the course objectives caught my eye. They looked remarkably similar to user interface design objectives, and also Web design objectives—"How to achieve the 'look and feel' that works best," "How readers react to what they see," and "How to manage the design process." So I opened up the flyer and read on. The course content includes:

- ◆ Know your reader
- ◆ Know your message
- ◆ Know your mission
- ◆ The best use of art and captions
- ◆ Using heads and subheads
- ◆ Sidebars and call-outs—how they can help readers
- ◆ Hot to make your type "talk"
- ◆ Putting it all together—creating pages that please the eye and deliver the message

KEY IDEA! *If you were given this brochure to look at without reading the seminar title, you might well think the course is on Web page design. This shows that Web design is an extension of communication using more traditional media such as printed materials and today's software interfaces. In fact, the seminar even addresses this, as the rest of the seminar title is ". . . (and everything else you want people to read)."*

Web design is an evolutionary step in software user interface design. Unfortunately, *revolutionary* activities often overtake *evolutionary* design. Software developers migrating to the Web need to ask a significant number of questions before they put a "browser" style interface on their product so it looks up to date. Richard Miller (1996), project manager of the InterMedia Lab at Bell Communications Research, authored a Web article, "Web Interface Design: Learning from our Past." This article is required reading for developers and designers migrating from legacy systems and PC software to Web design. Miller offers these helpful comments:

1. Do not port legacy systems—rethink, redesign, test, and implement using the most appropriate and robust design paradigm available on the Web. Balance the use of graphics with a proper design and consideration for users' limited bandwidth.

2. Do not expect that as a developer and HTML programmer, you will be capable of creating effective user interface design. The best of the Web combines useful content, competent Web mastery, an experienced interface designers, and coordinated graphic design.

3. Ask users for input—try to work with them to create sensible icons and designs. Redesign and test with users.

4. Create modular graphics and text to allow for flexibility and adaptive interfaces.

5. If you are creating Web systems people need to use day in and day out, consider the functional questions first and spend time designing useful icons.

6. The Web is not so radical that traditional concepts of design should be ignored, but knowing how to design for the Web is different than for other media.

7. Spending time doing usability testing and/or a user-centered design session can save a project significant resources in the long run.

Navigating Web Interfaces

Navigation is key to the whole Web experience. If users don't know how to navigate from one place to another on the Web, they will never figure out where they are, where they've been, or where they're going. Baecker et al. (1995) discuss the key navigation aids on the Web. Without them, users will loose the context of where they are and what they are doing. Web sites should provide the following navigation aids:

◆ Active table of contents
◆ Backtracking and history lists

- ◆ Bookmarks
- ◆ Maps or web viewers
- ◆ Timestamps

Conklin (1987) summarizes the perceived advantages that hypertext links, an integral part of navigating the Web, offer users. He also identifies two potential disadvantages for users and designers—disorientation (lack of context) and cognitive overhead (having to keep track of creating, naming, and remembering hypertext links). Here are the advantages (Table 16.3):

TABLE 16.3   Perceived Advantages of Hypertext, from Conklin (1987)

Hypertext Advantage	Description
Ease of tracing references	Machine support for link tracing means that all references are equally easy to follow forward to their referent, or backward to the reference.
Ease of creating new references	Users can grow their own networks, or simply annotate someone else's document with a comment (without changing the referenced document).
Information structuring	Both hierarchical and nonhierarchical organizations can be imposed on unstructured information; even multiple hierarchies can organize the same material.
Global views	Browsers provide table-of-contents style views, supporting easier restructuring of large and complex documents; global and local (node or page) views can be mixed effectively.
Customized documents	Text segments can be threaded together in many ways, allowing the same document to serve multiple functions.
Modularity of information	Since the same text segment can be referenced from several places, ideas can be expressed with less overlap and duplication.
Consistency of information	References are embedded in their text, and if the text is moved, even to another document, the link information still provides direct access to the reference.
Task stacking	The user is supported in having several paths of inquiry active and displayed on the screen at the same time, such that any given path can be unwound to the original task.
Collaboration	Several authors can collaborate, with the document and comments about the document being tightly interwoven.

The Las Vegas Effect, or, Let's Use a Really *Big* Box of Crayons!

The browser metaphor is not the Last Great User Interface. In fact, it's pretty bad. It's bereft of most of the useful controls that we've come to know and love. It's overburdened with big, graceless buttons and that stupid animation in the upper-right corner, which tells you nothing more than 'working. . . .' The browser metaphor is the computer equivalent of platform shoes—great for people who want to be taller, but essentially ugly and uncomfortable.

Bill Machrone (1996)

The Web represents the ultimate digital soap box. Practically anyone can put almost any kind of information out there for everyone to visit. This freedom of speech provides an incredible amount of *content,* but the *presentation* of information and *navigation* within and among sets of information in most cases is not yet implemented in very usable or consistent ways. Remember, there is a difference between good content and good presentation.

The Web is currently experiencing the same design problems that occurred when developers first started building GUIs. I've described the Las Vegas effect, where colors are used because they are available, not because they are needed. The mentality is, "I've got this big box of crayons, why shouldn't I use them all?"

A problem with many Web sites I've visited is the use of background colors, graphics, and/or textures that overpower the content, causing poor legibility and readability of the page's content. Often it is impossible to tell what's part of the graphic background of the page and what is the content. Users shouldn't have to guess what are selectable areas in a page. Figure 16.7 shows a home page from the Web. Look at how many different fonts, type styles, and type sizes there are on the page. What are the selectable areas on this page? Some of the text is underlined, indicating that they are hyperlinks, but there are many other selectable areas. When visiting this page, I had no idea what to select, and if something were selectable, where it would take me when selected. There is no background-foreground relationship here for users to make sense of what they see.

Finally, a limitation in current Web design is the lack of standard interface widgets and the immature graphic representation of widgets. On one hand, Web pages can look like graphic posters (as in Figure 16.7), where no standard interface controls are used. On the other hand, often in the same Web site, pages requesting user input look like the page in Figure 16.8. You can't tell that this interface didn't come from a ten-year-old PC application!

The E-mail text box is much longer than needed for an e-mail address. The contents of the Country? list box are not displayed in any recognizable order, except that the United States is first. Do you have any idea what the next coun-

Figure 16.7   "Las Vegas" Web page design. What's selectable? What isn't?

try is in the list after Afghanistan? Not unless you're a mind reader! The Birthday? field uses drop-down lists for the month, which is fine, but also uses the control for each digit of the day and date! I have never seen it done like this before, and I hope I don't see it ever again. Also notice that the first two digits of the year are hardcoded as 19. What happens if a user happens to be born before 1900? I guess this application will not be used after the century changes when users have birthdays in the year 2000. Developers in 1997 should be well aware of the computer problems that will occur when the clocks turn midnight on New Year's Eve in 1999. The Gender? question uses radio buttons, which is standard, but notice that the radio buttons, and all of the controls on the page, are graphically two-dimensional and look very crude compared to today's three-dimensional interface controls.

> **K**EY IDEA! *As Web programming and design tools mature, sophisticated three-dimensional and shadowed interface elements users see on the PC will become available for Web designers. Remember, users should not even know whether the information they interact with on the screen is part of a local standalone program, a remote communications interface, or a Web page.*

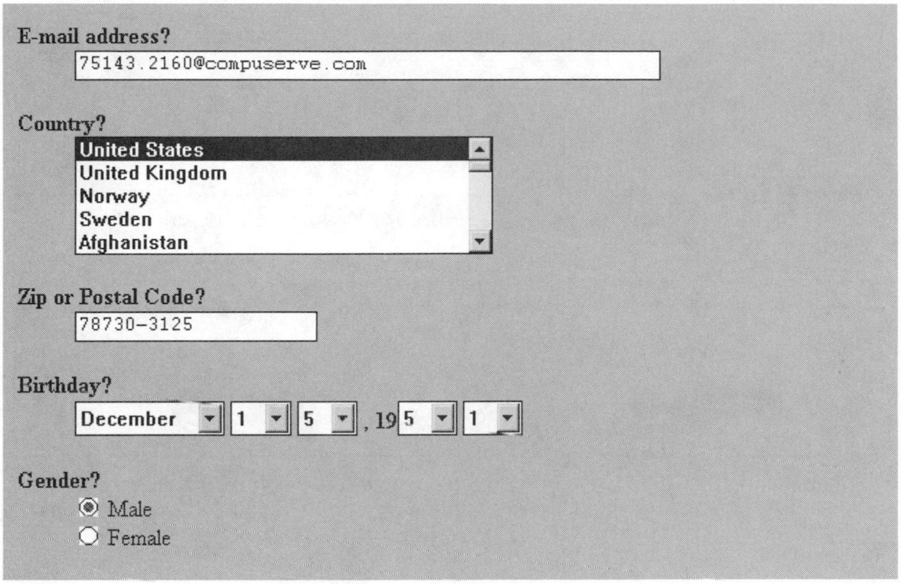

Figure 16.8 Interface controls on Web pages.

Let's take a further look at the push button (or command button), a common interface control. In most PC interfaces, designers make buttons look like buttons, so users have no doubt about what they are and what they do. Web designs and interaction elements confuse this issue, since images, image maps, text, and buttons are all potentially selectable areas of the screen.

Recently, Sun redesigned their Web site. As part of this process, they conducted usability studies of existing and redesigned page designs. One known usability problem was that the top button bar was seen as mere decoration by users (Figure 16.9, top). Changing the button bar on the new design (Figure 16.9, bottom) contributed to a 416 percent increase in Web usage over a two-month period. Nielsen (1996) concluded, "Considering that the use of the server in general increased by 'only' 48% in the same period, there can be no doubt that usability engineering worked and resulted in a significantly improved button design." That's a pretty good productivity increase for basically making buttons look like buttons!

Time and Dynamic Data on the Web

> *In designing Sun's home page, we decided we needed to change it drastically every month to keep the users' interest. Stability can be boring!*
>
> Jakob Nielsen (1996)

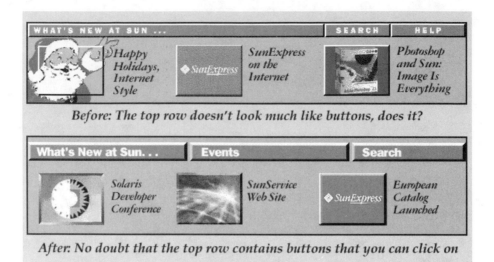

Figure 16.9   Button redesign on Sun's Web site.

The Web is often used to present time-sensitive information or information that is updated periodically—for example, stock market prices, weather reports, and news items. Interfaces for time-related information should be designed differently from static interfaces, such as print or static documents. Business on the Web revolves around repeat customers. You want users to come back to your site often for new information. Users will return to Web pages that are alive and dynamic; static pages become stale and do not invite return visits.

Since a design goal is to entice users to be repeat customers, here are some guidelines for designing Web sites with time-sensitive information:

1. Don't date information unless it is updated frequently. Users will immediately leave a site if they see that the information is not current.

2. Tell users how often information will be updated. Update information automatically. Let users decide how often to refresh information, if possible.

3. If users can update information themselves, let them.

4. Offer a What's New area, with highlights of the most current information.

5. Determine whether Web site visitor counters are appropriate for your pages. Although some users enjoy seeing them, a counter can also point out how *few* times the page has been visited.

6. Use expiration dating. When information has a defined expiration date (daily, weekly, monthly), send the information to an archive that is available to users.

The Good, the Bad, and the Ugly

I don't really have any unique ways of describing what the Internet actually is. It is what it is. It's a hundred gazillion pages of Net stuff, and every page is different.

Jim White, General Magic (1996)

An entire book could be written just looking at good and bad interface design on the Web. This chapter highlights the key elements of Web design so that you can distinguish between good and poor Web interface designs. Nielsen (1996), in an illustrated article on the Web (http://www.sun.com/sun-on-net/uidesign/), documents Sun's redesign of their Web home page. They went through at least 15 different designs, and show 9 variations of the home page beginning with the original page and ending with the final design. Click on the picture of a design variation and you will learn more about that particular design variation. These designs are worth looking at to emphasize the iterative nature of interface design, even when designing for the Web.

There are a number of Web sites that specialize in offering their opinions on the best and the worst Web designs. A compilation of good Web designs can be found at http://www.highfive.com. A well-known site devoted to showcasing the worst sites on the Web is at http://www.suck.com.

Web Interface Design Guidelines

Order and simplicity are the first steps toward the mastery of a subject—the actual enemy is the unknown.

Thomas Mann

This chapter, and this section in particular, should not be read in isolation. Before designing Web interfaces, familiarize yourself with the background material in Part 1, specifically the chapters on human psychology, golden rules of interface design, interface usability, and interface standards and guidelines. You should also read Chapter 10 before doing Web design.

KEY IDEA! *Although part of the excitement of the Internet is the freedom and creativity seen on the Web, following design principles and guidelines will not dampen the spirit of the Web—rather, it allows users to learn the obvious and necessary look and feel of the interface quickly, enabling them to focus on the essence and experience of the sensory content and design of the information.*

Where to Look for Web Design Guidance

More and more software interface designers are turning their attention on Web design. There are specific design issues particular to the Web. Where do you find this information? I have found the best Web interface guidance on the Web itself. Many companies' sites offer a wide variety of assistance in Web design. For example, Apple's *Web Design Guide* is organized into the following categories:

1. Plan your site.
2. Provide the basics.
3. Communicate effectively.
4. Help users find their way.
5. Tell users what to expect.
6. Design for efficiency.
7. Accommodate differences.
8. Make it look nice.
9. Encourage dialog.
10. Think globally.
11. Maintain your site.
12. HTML tips.

Table 16.4 lists key places to look for Web design guidance. Although the location and content of these sites may change over time, this list gives you starting points for your search for Web interface design guidance. Look for links to new resources as you view these and other sites.

There are also many books on Web design; however, most of them focus more on the tools and language used to create Web pages than on the design of the interface. One good book is Horton et al. (1996), *The Web Page Design Cookbook: All the Ingredients You Need to Create 5-Star Web Pages.* Horton is a well-

TABLE 16.4   Web Interface Design Resources

Web Interface Design Resource	Web Site Location
Apple Web Design Guide	http://www.cybertech.apple.com/hi/web_design/web_design.html
IBM Human-Computer Interaction: UI University	http://www.ibm.com/ibm/hci/designer/uides/webdesign.html
Sun Microsystems: Guide to Web Style Jakob Nielsen, *Alert Box*	http://www.sun.com/styleguide/ http://www.sun.com/columns/alertbox/
Web Style Guide for Indiana University, Bloomington campus	http://www.indiana.edu/~wwwdocs/guidelines.htm.
Web Style Manual, Yale Center for Advanced Instructional Media	http://info.med.yale.edu/caim/StyleManual_Top.HTML http://www.cis.yale.edu/webguide/
Assoc. for Educational Communications and Technology (AECT) Web Design Workshop '96	http://www.indiana.edu/~iirg/ARTICLES/AECT96/index.html
HCI Resources: WWW-related issues	http://www.ida.liu.se/~miker/hci/www.html
Web Wonk: Tips for Writers and Designers	http://www.dsiegel.com/tips/
Yahoo! Search Engine:	http://www.yahoo.com/Computers/World_Wide_Web/Page_Design_and_Layout/
Computers and Internet: World Wide Web: Page Design and Layout	

known expert on information and visual design. The book also includes a CD-ROM with hundreds of Web templates for pages and elements of pages.

Guidelines for Web Interface Design

People won't spend lots of time looking for something and they don't have a long attention span when they do find what they were looking for. Jakob Nielsen (1996) describes three major findings based on extensive usability testing of Web interfaces. These findings give us the high-level design concepts that must be kept in mind when designing interfaces for the Web.

1. *People have very little patience for poorly designed Web sites.* As one user put it, "The more well-organized a page is, the more faith I will have in the information." Other users said, "Either the information is there or it is not; don't waste my time with stuff you are not going to give me."

2. *Users don't want to scroll information.* Information that is not on the top of the screen when a page comes up is only read by very interested users. In usability tests, users stated that a design that made everything fit on a single page was an indication that the designers had taken care to do a good job, whereas other pages that contained several screens' worth of lists or unstructured material were an indication of sloppy work that made them question the quality of the information contained on those sites.

3. *Users don't want to read.* Reading speeds are more than 25 percent slower from computer screens than from paper, but that does not mean that you should write 25 percent less than you would in a paper document. You should write 50 percent less! Users recklessly skip over any text they deem to be fluff (e.g., welcome messages or introductory paragraphs) and scan for highlighted terms (e.g., hypertext links).

Table 16.5 lists design guidelines for Web interface design. Follow all appropriate user interface guidelines described in this book and elsewhere; in addition, follow these Web-specific guidelines. These guidelines are gathered through my own experience and that of others, including Nielsen (1996), Heller and Rivers (1996), and Langa (1996).

Usability on the Internet

For the most part, Internet Web pages and applications have been designed like PC applications were ten years ago, with little knowledge or regard for screen design, layout, colors, fonts, and user interaction. One well-documented exception to this type of Web design is Indiana University's home page project. Let's look at this as a Web design usability case study (available at http://education.indiana.edu/ist/faculty/iuwebrep.html). In 1995, they undertook a major effort to redesign the Indiana University at Bloomington home page (Boling, 1995). A Home Page Evaluation and Remodeling Team was formed, and a *user-centered design* approach was followed: "The methodology largely consists of conducting usability tests of design prototypes with the target audience to identify and remedy problems in an iterative manner" (Frick et al., 1995).

TABLE 16.5 User Interface Guidelines for Web Design

Design Goal	Design Guidelines
Determine user demographics and experience	◆ New visitor to your Web page? ◆ Previous visitor returning to Web page? ◆ Any previous Web experience?
Define user tasks	◆ Find information ◆ Learn about a product ◆ Order a product ◆ Track an order ◆ Contact a customer representative ◆ Contact a company employee ◆ Seek technical support ◆ Give feedback ◆ Download product demos ◆ Download drivers and updates
Help users navigate and search	◆ Offer clear and intuitive organization of site information (Table of Contents, Index, What's New?) ◆ Offer an understandable and obvious visual navigation scheme (buttons, text, image maps) ◆ Offer ways to search for topics, keywords, names, etc. within a site ◆ Tie topics, keywords, and names into Web search engines ◆ Provide navigation aids on every page (make it possible for users to jump right to any page from a Web search engine ◆ Let users know where a navigation link will take them ◆ Label all linked graphics ◆ Do not leave orphan links, where users must back up. Always provide at least a way to get back to the home page ◆ Keep links updated—check to see if all links are still valid ◆ Use standard text link colors and highlighting
Help users perform task quickly	◆ Reduce search time ◆ Reduce time to load pages and images ◆ Reduce scrolling within a page ◆ Limit number of choices at a level ◆ Group important choices together ◆ Organize information and pages to anticipate frequent tasks ◆ Provide an overview of the site ◆ Use familiar and recognizable navigation controls ◆ Don't use bleeding-edge technology gratuitously (use VRML only if you have information that maps naturally to three-dimensional space) ◆ Keep content simple—address only one topic per page

TABLE 16.5   *(Continued)*

Design Goal	Design Guidelines
	◆ Get to the content quickly—place important content at the top of the web hierarchy and at the top of a web page
	◆ Make pages easy to read. Use simple, unobtrusive backgrounds that don't compete with text and buttons
	◆ Use lots of white space
	◆ Use standard palettes and fonts—don't use special colors or fonts
	◆ Use text fonts that are big enough
	◆ Use text types that have enough contrast with the background
	◆ Provide printable versions of Web pages
Establish user interface consistency	◆ Establish a corporate identity using graphics, images, colors, fonts, and layout
	◆ Use the corporate identity consistently throughout the Web interface
	◆ Establish a page layout grid and follow it on all pages
	◆ Use consistent headings and terminology
	◆ Use link and navigation names and terminology consistently throughout the interface
	◆ Display background information (URL, copyrights, e-mail addresses, etc.)
	◆ Be consistent in your navigation scheme
	◆ Design the interface to be accessible and usable from multiple browsers and platforms
	◆ Don't hardcode interface elements that users or browsers should be able to control and change (text, colors, etc.)

Usability activities were conducted to define the target audience (a needs analysis). Task analyses determined the type and frequency of user questions, from questions that were asked more than 1,000 times per week to questions asked with unknown or unreported frequencies. Frequently asked questions were sorted into six broad categories, under which questions could be placed. These categories were:

1. Attending Indiana University at Bloomington—the Basics
2. Academic Programs and Research
3. People at Indiana University at Bloomington

4. Recreation, Entertainment and Tickets
5. Services Used Often
6. General Information

These topic areas were used to design the first prototype of the new home page and provide the organization for the information structure. An early usability paper test was conducted comparing the existing Web home page with the first prototype of the new Web home page. Test results were used to redesign the Web home page and a second round of paper testing was conducted. Finally, a third version of the home page was tested online against the existing home page. The third version was recommended as a result of usability testing. Usability test tasks and measures were as follows:

1. Tasks—Users were asked to find answers to frequently asked questions.
2. Navigation among pages, as well as when users backtracked and tried another route.
3. Problems users had in determining the path they wanted to follow.
4. Time to load pages on the screen.
5. Time to read and search screens.

You will see more and more usability tests conducted on Internet information, Web pages, and Web sites as they become part of mainstream computing. Users expect a certain level of consistency and usefulness from business programs on the PC, and they will expect and demand the same level of usability from the Internet.

A new article, "A Heuristic Evaluation of a World Wide Web Prototype" (Levi and Conrad, 1996), follows the history of the design and usability testing of a prototype for the new Web site of the U.S. government's Bureau of Labor Statistics. One interesting aspect of the study was that two groups evaluated the prototype—a group of user interface experts and a group of developers who worked on the prototype. The results were interesting—there were relatively few differences between the two evaluator groups. Each group identified numerous problems with the prototype. The user interface expert group was clearly more attuned to broad usability issues, such as consistency and visual clutter. This group didn't know the internals of the prototype, so they were unable to identify content-related problems, such as missing links and inconsistent granularity. However, they were able to focus more on one area the developers were less sensitive to—navigation within the prototype. This article is well worth reading if you are designing Web interfaces.

KEY IDEA! *From the user interface and usability perspective, Web design is about ten years behind the times. Like many programmers in the past, Web designers don't necessarily think about conducting usability testing on their Web pages and sites. Information on the Web is no different from PC programs—there are goals and objectives, users, tasks, a design process, and development tools. Usability activities are just as important, if not more so, for Web pages that can be visited by anyone in the world with computer access to the Web site.*

International Web Design and Usability

By its very nature, the Web is an international interface. Chapter 13 discussed some aspects of international interface design. These international design issues are covered in two good books: Fernandes (1995) and del Galdo and Nielsen (1996).

Where Are PC and Web Interfaces Going?

> *The Web does not yet meet its design goal as being a pool of knowledge that is as easy to update as to read. That level of immediacy of knowledge sharing waits for easy-to-use hypertext editors to be generally available on most platforms. Most information has in fact passed through publishers or system managers of one sort or another. However, the incredible diversity of information available gives great credit to the creativity and ingenuity of information providers, and points to a very exciting future.*
>
> Tim Berners-Lee (1994)

The migration toward dynamic information access and the integration of PC-based software and Internet software will continue at a dramatic rate. Each interface style will change to incorporate appropriate aspects of the other technology. PC software will fold in more of the Internet-enabled browser interface aspects, while Web programs will grow from the small set of interface elements that are currently allowed to utilize the full set of interface elements available in PC software programs.

As PC software slowly migrates from GUIs to object-oriented user interfaces, objects are also invading the Web. Steve Jobs' NeXt Software offers WebObjects, a cross-platform middleware technology that allows dynamic Web programs to be created without the complexity of today's Internet client/server development efforts. For example, the Online Airline Guide (OAG) was transformed from a mainframe-based application to a Web site in about a week.

Look for a smoother blend of entertainment, theater, business, and information gathering and viewing interfaces between PC software and the Web. Build the right interface for the task, not just the most fashionable interface of the moment!

Epilogue

> As technological artifacts, computers must product correct results; they must be reliable, run efficiently, and be easy—or at least possible—to maintain. But as artifacts of general culture, computer systems must meet many further requirements: They must be accessible to nontechnologists (easy to learn/easy to use); they must smoothly augment human activities, meet people's expectations, and enhance the quality of life by guiding their users to satisfying work experiences, stimulating educational opportunities, and relaxation during leisure time."

John M. Carroll (1995)

As we move into innovative areas of computing and user interfaces, new ideas come from many areas. However, not all good ideas become new paradigms. Lieberman (1996) writes:

> A new paradigm is not just something that's a good idea. There are plenty of merely good ideas, but a new paradigm must go beyond simple innovation. A new paradigm is often introduced to solve a particular problem, but it must do more than that. It must fundamentally change the way we look at problems we have seen in the past. It must give us a new framework for thinking about problems in the future. It changes our priorities and values, changes our ideas about what to pay attention to and what to consider important.

A recent issue of the *Communications of the ACM* (August, 1996, 39(8)) discusses some of the issues of future interfaces. Ted Selker's (1996) article, "New Paradigms for Using Computers," discusses evolving user interfaces and new forms of computers. Selker notes:

Since our eyes are the major input to our brains, it is no wonder that new paradigms for using computers often involve making better computer images and animated interfaces. As good displays and enough memory to drive them have become available, people have found themselves immersed in graphically-rendered interfaces.... Productivity gains for general user interface actions are coming as we begin to articulate the value of the striking 3D spatial landmarks and other qualities that characterize efficient navigation in physical space.

Gentner and Nielsen (1996) explore alternative new interfaces in their article, "The Anti-Mac Interface." I strongly recommend that you read it. The authors do not criticize the current Mac and PC user interfaces; rather they describe new alternatives that change the way designers and users work with computers. They go through the basic, traditional Mac and PC interface principles and offer new approaches that have evolved beyond them. (see Table 16.6).

The design principles of the anti-Mac interface are:

♦ The central role of language

♦ A richer internal representation of objects

♦ A more expressive interface

♦ Expert users

♦ Shared control

TABLE 16.6 Traditional PC and Mac Interface Design Principles and the New Approach, from Gentner and Nielsen (1996)

Mac Principles	Anti-Mac Principles
Metaphors	Reality
Direct Manipulation	Delegation
See and Point	Describe and Command
Consistency	Diversity
WYSIWYG	Represent Meaning
User Control	Shared Control
Feedback and Dialog	System Handles Details
Forgiveness	Model User Actions
Aesthetic Integrity	Graphic Variety
Modelessness	Richer Cues

I won't describe these principles here, but I want to point out that we are now starting to evolve beyond the traditional GUI style of computing. The key is to understand where users lie along the continuum from inexperienced and novice to expert and computer-savvy. For example, throughout this book, I have described the key design principles of consistency. That is still a valid design principle, but as Gentner and Nielsen (1996) point out, "We're still children in the computer age, and children like stability. But as we grow more capable and better able to cope with a changing world, we become more comfortable with changes and even seek novelty for its own sake."

KEY IDEA! *We are seeing the beginnings of changes to interface design principles with the Web browser interface. But we're still in the infancy stages where users are stimulated by the novelty of the Web interface but not necessarily comfortable with the lack of consistency in interface presentation and interaction. Tune in to what users need; give them something that expands their horizons, yet allows them to be comfortable in what they do. That's why interface design is sometimes the leading edge, and often the "bleeding-edge," of software development.*

Nolan Bushnell (1996), former video game developer and futurist, describes how games have influenced computer design. He offers a classification scheme for computer software that focuses on the user environment and the way people react with software. Table 16.7 lists the classification schemes and Bushnell's descriptions.

TABLE 16.7   Software Classification Scheme, from Bushnell (1996)

Type of Software	Description
Deskware	The current dominant type of software. It is meant to be viewed approximately from 18 inches away and is manipulated with a keyboard and pointing device. It is expected that one can read large amounts of text if necessary and modify text as well as manipulate small objects on the screen. It presupposes a one-on-one relationship of human to computer.

TABLE 16.7   (*Continued*)

Type of Software	Description
Couchware	This is what is put on the television set in the family room and will become more important as the television becomes a two-way communication device. The control for couchware is always supposed to be hand-held in free space and can be wired or remote. Couchware cannot presuppose a great deal of reading or text manipulation and small object control is out of the question.
Kitchenware	This piece of software is in fact the nerve center of the family. It is viewed from 18 inches but it is presumed the user is standing and the display screen is mounted on the wall. The user interface is in all cases a touch screen. This software has to actually be used by family members as young as four years old, even if a chair must be used to reach the device.
Bedroomware and Bathroomware	They are very close in function and form factor to kitchenware, with the function being scheduling and communications. The home-control features are all accessible and for bathroomware games are also very important. There are those that presuppose the bedroom has a TV and that modified couchware is the operative mode. Location mobility is a necessary feature of all these and a remote control that has any kind of pointing feature must work with this mobility.
Autoware	Autoware must be based on assumptions about its use for the driver or passenger. Many believe there should be no visual software for automobile drivers.
Storeware	Storeware is the stuff of the electronic checkout counters and product information material. Some of its unique features are language flexibility and extremely high graphic content. Touch-screen input and ruggedized construction of other controls are also presumed.
Bankware	We have all seen the terrible job that the automatic teller machines have done in making the process of bank transactions about following instructions to press keys. Clearly new software is needed.
Gameware	The coin-operated video game's user interface was in some ways the first user interface used by ordinary people. We learned many things that are true today more than ever in all forms of software: 1. People hate to and will not read instructions. 2. If people cannot get up the learning curve in 15 seconds they will not spend the second quarter. 3. If you must give instructions, make them short, direct, and in as large a font as possible.

KEY IDEA! *I want to end this book with these categories to expand your definitions of computer software and to reinforce the idea that computers will not just be sitting on users' desks in the workplace.*

When it is written, the history of computers will, I believe, be quite simple. In the beginning was the computer. Then it disappeared. Of course, it didn't go away completely. It just dissolved. Either it became part of the physical background, forming part of ordinary objects such as tables, chairs, walls, and desks. Or it became part of the social background, providing just another part of the context of work.

John Seely Brown (1996)

References

Baecker, Ronald M., Jonathan Grudin, William A. S. Buxton, and Saul Greenberg. 1995. Cyberspace. In Baecker et al. (Eds.), *Readings in Human-Computer Interaction: Toward the Year 2000.* San Francisco, CA: Morgan Kaufmann, pp. 897–906.

Boling, Elizabeth. Usability testing for Web sites. 1995. *Seventh Annual Hypermedia '95 Conference,* Bloomington, IN.

Brueckner, Robert. 1996. Taking on TV: TV is a bad role model for the Web. *Internet World* (July): 59–60.

Bush, Vannevar. 1945. As we may think. *Atlantic Monthly* (July).

Bushnell, Nolan. 1996. Relationships between fun and the computer business. *Communications of the ACM* 39(8): 31–37.

Conklin, J. 1987. Hypertext: An introduction and survey. *IEEE Computer* 2(9): 17–41.

del Galdo, Elisa and Jakob Nielsen. 1996. *International User Interfaces.* New York: Wiley.

Dern, Daniel. 1996. Just one more click . . . *Computer World* (July 8): 93–96.

Farre, Tom. 1996. Editor's letter: Internet steak and sizzle. *VaRBusiness* (May 1): 13.

Fernandes, Tony. 1995. *Global Interface Design.* Chestnut Hill, MA: Academic Press.

Fisher, Alexandra. 1996. Web as theater. *Internet World* (June): 36–38.

Frick, Theodore, Michael Corry, Lisa Hansen, and Barbara Maynes. 1995. *Design-Research for the Indiana University Bloomington World Wide Web: The "Limestone Pages."* Indiana University School of Education (http://education.indiana.edu/ist/faculty/iuwebrep.html).

Furger, Roberta. 1996. What you can and can't get away with online. *PC World* (August): 185–188.

Gentner, Don and Jakob Nielsen. 1996. The anti-Mac interface. *Communications of the ACM* 39(8): 70–82.

Glaser, Mark. 1996. The look of links: CD-ROM/online hybrids. *NewMedia* (May 13): 31–32.

Heller, Hagan and David Rivers. 1996. So you wanna design for the Web. *ACM interactions* (March): 19–23.

Horton, William, Lee Taylor, Arthur Ignacio, and Nancy Hoft. 1996. *The Web Page Design Cookbook: All the Ingredients You Need to Create 5-Star Web Pages.* New York: Wiley.

Langa, Fred. 1996. Seven deadly Web sins. *Windows Magazine* (June): 11–14.

Laurel, Brenda. 1991. *Computers as Theater.* White Plains, NY: Addison-Wesley.

Levi, Michael and Frederick Conrad. 1996. A heuristic evaluation of a World Wide Web. prototype. *ACM interactions* III(4).

Lieberman, Henry. 1996. Intelligent graphics. *Communications of the ACM* 39(8): 38–48.

Lindquist, Christopher and Daniel Will-Harris. 1996. Ultimate Web publishing guide. *PC Computing* (August): 112–122.

Machrone, Bill. 1996. Avatarred and feathered. *PC Magazine* (April 9): 83.

Microsoft Corporation. 1995. *The Windows Interface Guidelines for Software Design.* Redmond, WA: Microsoft Press.

Miller, Richard. 1996. Web interface design: Learning from our past. *Bell Communications Research* (available at http://athos.rutgers.edu/~shklar/www4/rmiller/rhmpapr.html).

Nelson, Theodor Holm. 1987. *Literary Machines: The Report On, and Of, Project Xanadu Concerning World Processing, Electronic Publishing, Hypertext, Thinkertoys, Tomorrow's Intellectual Revolution, and Certain Other Topics Including Knowledge, Education and Freedom.* Sausalito, CA: Mindful Press.

Nielsen, Jakob. 1995. Who should you hire to design your Web site? *The Alert Box,* Sun Microsystems (October 1995) (available at http://www.sun.com/951001/columns/alertbox/).

Nielsen, Jakob. 1996. Interface design for Sun's WWW site. *Sun on the Net: User Interface Design,* Sun Microsystems (available at http://www.sun.com/sun-on-net/uidesign/).

Selker, Ted. 1996. New paradigms for using computers. *Communications of the ACM* 39 (8): 60–69.

Snyder, Joel. 1996. Web lessons learned. *Internet World* (June): 96–97.

Somerson, Paul. 1996. Web coma. *PC Computing* (July): 57.

Wolf, Gary. 1995. The curse of Xanadu. *Wired* (June).

INDEX